THE MODERN HOUSEWIFE,
OR
MÉNAGÈRE

THE MODERN HOUSEWIFE,
OR
MÉNAGÈRE

ALEXIS SOYER

ISBN: 978-93-89614-53-4

Published: 1850

LECTOR HOUSE LLP
E-MAIL: lectorpublishing@gmail.com

THE MODERN HOUSEWIFE
OR,
MÉNAGÈRE

**COMPRISING NEARLY ONE THOUSAND RECEIPTS,
FOR THE ECONOMIC AND JUDICIOUS PREPARATION OF
EVERY MEAL OF THE DAY,
WITH THOSE OF THE NURSERY AND SICK ROOM,
AND MINUTE DIRECTIONS FOR FAMILY
MANAGEMENT IN ALL ITS BRANCHES.**

ILLUSTRATED WITH ENGRAVINGS.

BY

ALEXIS SOYER,

AUTHOR OF "THE GASTRONOMIC REGENERATOR."

**EDITED BY
AN AMERICAN HOUSEKEEPER.**

1850.

PREFACE BY THE EDITOR.

IN adapting M. Soyer's admirable receipt book to the use of American families, I have not presumed to amend, or attempted to improve upon the text of so accomplished a master of the art, which may with entire propriety be called the "preservative of all arts." All that I have ventured to do has been to make a verbal correction here and there, necessary to render the meaning of the author more plain; to erase certain directions for cooking different kinds of game and fish unknown in the new world; and to omit the purely local information, and scraps of history, which only increased the cost and bulk of the book, without, in any way, adding to its value.

Except in one instance, nothing has been added; for the object in republishing the MENAGÈRE, was to furnish a new and valuable work on the preparation of food, which should contain important receipts hitherto unknown. Every country must have its indigenous dishes, and it is to be presumed that every American housekeeper likely to profit by M. Soyer's receipts, will need no instruction in the art of preparing the many excellent dishes peculiar to the United States.

It is a vulgar error to suppose that French cookery is more costly and highly flavored than English; an examination of the MENAGÈRE will abundantly prove that the reverse is the fact, and that M. Soyer's system, which has rendered him famous in Europe, is not only simple and economical, but the best adapted to insuring the enjoyment of health, the elevation of the mental faculties, and converting the daily necessity of eating into a source of daily enjoyment. M. Soyer's great work, The Gastronomic Regenerator, was prepared for the highest classes of English society, and public festivals; but the MENAGÈRE is adapted to the wants and habits of the middle classes, and, as presented in the present edition, calculated for the use of the great bulk of American families.

M. Soyer is the good genius of the kitchen; although he is the renowned *chef* of one of the most sumptuous of the London Club Houses, and the pet of aristocratic feeders, he has labored continually to elevate the mind, and better the condition of the poor by instructing them in the art of obtaining the greatest amount of nourishment and enjoyment from their food. The dietetic maxims and culinary receipts of M. Soyer are not less needed in the United States than in England; but for different reasons. Happily, our countrymen do not suffer for lack of raw materials, so much as for lack of cooks; and, in the Modern Housewife of M. Soyer, our housekeepers will find a reliable guide and an invaluable friend.

New York, December, 1849.

CONTENTS

INTRODUCTION.

IN the following gossipping conversation between Mrs. B— — and Mrs. L— —, and in the two letters which follow, M. Soyer explains the motive of the work; and, in a natural manner introduces the subject. — Ed.

DIALOGUE BETWEEN MRS. B—— AND MRS. L——, HER FRIEND AND VISITOR.

Mrs. L. I have now, my dear Mrs. B., been nearly a fortnight at your delightful Villa, and I must say, with all truth, that I never fared better in my life, yet I am considered somewhat of an epicure, as is likewise my husband; but, of course, our means being rather limited, we are obliged to live accordingly.

Mrs. B. Well, so must we; and I assure you that, during the first few years of our marriage, our pecuniary resources were but small, but even then I managed my kitchen and housekeeping at so moderate an expense compared with some of our neighbors, who lived more expensively, but not so well as we did, that, when any of them dined with us, they flattered me with the appellation of the "Model Housekeeper," and admired the comforts of our table, but would leave with the impression that I must be the most extravagant of wives. Now, believe me, I have always prided myself, whether having to provide for a ceremonious party or dining by ourselves, to have everything properly done and served, that, if any friends should come in by accident or on business, they were generally well pleased with our humble hospitality, and that without extravagance, as my husband is well convinced; for when we dine with any acquaintance of ours he is very eager to persuade them to adopt my system of management; for though he is no great judge of what is called the highest style of cookery, yet he does not like to live badly at any time; as he very justly says, it matters not how simple the food, — a chop, steak, or a plain boiled or roast joint, but let it be of good quality and properly cooked, and every one who partakes of it will enjoy it.

Mrs. L. Nothing more true!

Mrs. B. But since you talk of limited income and economy, let me relate to you a conversation which occurred a few years ago between Mr. B. and a friend of his, who declared to him that his income would never allow him to live in such luxury, which he called a comfortable extravagance.

"Extravagance!" exclaimed Mr. B., "if you have a few minutes to spare, I will convince you of the contrary, and prove to you that such an expression is very unjust, if applied to my wife's management. Now, to begin; what sum should you suppose would cover our annual housekeeping expenditure, living as we do, in a style of which you so much approve, but consider so extravagant? there are ten of us in family, viz., myself and wife, three children, two female servants, and three young men employed in my business, and including our usual Christmas party, which, of course you know, (having participated in the last two), besides two separate birthday parties of twenty each, and three juvenile petits-soupers and dances for the children upon their natal anniversaries, also a friend dropping in occasionally, which is never less than once or twice a-week." — "Well, I do not know," answered our friend; "but having nearly the same number to provide for, and in a more humble way, my expenses for housekeeping are never less than £—— per annum." — "Less than what?" exclaimed Mr. B.; "why, my dear friend, you must be mistaken;" at the same time ringing the bell." I wish I were, with all my heart," was the reply, as the servant entered the room; "Jane," said Mr. B., "ask your mistress to step this way for a few minutes; I wish to look at her housekeeping book." But being busy at the time in the kitchen, I sent up a key for him to get it, which happened to be a wrong one, but, upon discovering the mistake, sent up the right one with an apology for not coming myself, as I was superintending the cooking of some veal broth, which the doctor had ordered for our poor little Henry, who was ill at the time. "Well," said his friend, "there is a wife for you; I must confess mine can hardly find the way to the kitchen stairs." "Now!" said my husband, opening my desk, and, taking up my book, he showed him the last year's expenditure, which was £——. "No! no! that is impossible," replied the other. "But," said Mr B., "there it is in black and white." "Why, good heavens!" exclaimed he, "without giving so many parties, and also two less in family, my expenditure is certainly greater." To which Mr. B. replied, "So I should imagine from the style in which I saw your table provided the few days when we were on a visit to your house; therefore I am not in the least astonished. Here, however, is the account for the closing year just made up to the 28th December, 1848. Let us see what it amounts to, probably to £50 or £60 more." "So, so," replied the other, "that is an increase;" — "Let it be so," said Mr. B.; "but you must remember that we are twelve months older, and as our business increases, so do we increase our comforts; and this year Mrs. B., with the children, had a pretty little house at Ramsgate for two months, which will account for the greater part of it."

Mrs. L. But, my dear Mrs. B., I am as much astonished as your friend could possibly have been. I should, however, have liked you to explain the matter; but here comes your husband, who will probably initiate me in your culinary secrets.

Good morning, my dear Mr. B. I have been talking to Mrs. B. about her system of housekeeping, who was relating to me a conversation you had with a gentleman, who was surprised with its economy. I am also surprised, and should like to take a few leaves out of your most excellent book, if you will allow me.

Mr. B. Certainly, my dear madam; in my wife, without flattering her too much, you see almost an accomplished woman (in hearing such praise, Mrs. B. retired, saying, "How foolish you talk, Richard"); she speaks two or three different languages tolerably well, and, as an amateur, is rather proficient in music, but her parents, very wisely considering household knowledge to be of the greater importance, made her first acquainted with the keys of the store-room before those of the piano; that is the only secret, dear madam; and this is the explanation that I gave to my friend, who thought it a good jest and one of truth. I told him to do the same by his two daughters, which would not only make them more happy through life, but transmit that happiness to their posterity, by setting an example worthy of being followed. I always say, give me a domesticated wife, and with my industry I would not change my position for a kingdom; "Very true, very true," was my friend's answer, and we then parted.

I have never seen him since nor his wife, who was probably offended at the economical propositions of her husband; for nothing, you are well aware, is more common than for people to be offended when told the truth respecting themselves; or perhaps she was too advanced in years to think of changing her ideas of housekeeping.

I see, my dear Mrs. L., the Brougham is waiting at the gate to convey you to the railway; allow me to see you safe to the station; you will not have many minutes to spare, for the train will shortly be up.

About an hour after the above conversation, Mrs. L. was seen entering her cottage at Oatlands, fully resolved to follow as closely as possible the economic management of Mrs. B.; but a little reflection soon made her perceive that she possessed only the theory, and was sadly deficient in the practice: she then determined to beg of her friend a few receipts in writing, and immediately dispatched the following letter:—

LETTER NO. I.

From Mrs. L—- to Mrs. B——.

Oatlands Cottage; Jan. 1st, 1849.

MY DEAR HORTENSE,—Upon my arrival at home, I am happy to say that I found all quite well, and delighted to see me, after (to them) so long an absence as a fortnight, which my husband was gallant enough to say appeared months; but to myself the time appeared to pass very swiftly; for, indeed, every day I felt so much more interested in watching closely how well you managed your household affairs, that, believe me, you have quite spoiled me, especially with your recherché style of cookery, which even now I cannot make out how you could do it at such moderate expense: and, apropos of cooking, Mr. L., expecting me home to dinner, had, I have no doubt, a long interview and discussion with Cook respecting the bill of fare. "Well, sir," I will suppose she said, "what can be better than a fine fat goose, stuffed with sage and ingyons; we have a very fine 'un hanging in the larder." (You must observe, dear, that my cook is plain in every way.) "A very excellent notion that, Cook; nothing can be better than a good goose;" was no doubt, my husband's answer, who, although very fond of a good dinner, cannot endure the trouble of ordering it.

Well, then, here I am in my little drawing-room (the window slightly open), enjoying the fresh country air, which seems to have been amalgamated with a strong aroma from the aforesaid goose, especially the sage and onions; and I am almost certain that the inseparable applesauce is burnt or upset on the stove, from the brown smoke now ascending from the grating over the kitchen window. This style is now to me quite unbearable, and I mean to have quite a reform in my little establishment, and first of all to bring up my daughter in the way recommended by Mr. B. to his friend, to make her more domesticated than I am myself, as I begin to perceive that a knowledge of household affairs is as much required as intellectual education; and, for my part, I have come to the determination of adopting your system of management as closely as possible; but first, you must know, that, without your scientific advice, it will be totally impossible; therefore I beg to propose (if you can afford the time) that you will, by writing, give me the description how you lay out your breakfast-table, with the addition of a few receipts for the making of rolls and the other breakfast bread, which I so much enjoyed while with you; even how to make toast, and more especially how you make coffee, chocolate, cocoa (tea, of course, I know). And should this meet your approbation, I mean to make a little journal, which may some day or other be useful to our families and friends.

Until I hear from you I shall be waiting with anxiety for your decision upon this important and domestic subject.

Yours very sincerely,
ELOISE.

LETTER NO. II.

From Mrs. B — —, in reply.

Bifrons Villa; Jan. 3d, 1849.

MY DEAR ELOISE, — In answer to yours, I agree, with the greatest pleasure, to contribute towards your domesticated idea, which, I must say, is very original, and may, as you observe, prove useful; but why should we confine our culinary journal to breakfast only? why not go through the different meals of the day? that is, after breakfast, the luncheon; then the nursery-dinner at One; and here it strikes me that, in that series, we might introduce some receipts, to be called Comforts for Invalids; even our servants' dinners and teas; then the early dinner at two or three for people in business, the parlor-dinner at six, the coffee after dinner, and even suppers for a small ball or evening party; but all on a moderate scale, leaving the aristocratic style entirely to its proper sphere.

To show my approbation of your idea, I enclose herewith the first receipt, *How to make Toast*.

BREAKFASTS.

WHEN we first commenced housekeeping, we were six in family, five of whom breakfasted together, the three young men in the shop, Mr. B— —, and myself. The cloth was laid by the servant girl at half-past seven precisely; at ten minutes to eight I used to make tea, and at eight o'clock we were seated at breakfast, which was composed merely of bread and butter at discretion, fresh water cresses when plentiful, or sometimes boiled eggs, and for variation, once a week, coffee, and if in the winter, we had toast, which I never suffered any servant to prepare more than five minutes before we were seated, for, if standing any time, the dry toast becomes tough, and the buttered very greasy, and consequently unpalatable, as well as indigestible. Twenty minutes only was the time allowed for breakfast, after which the table was cleared, the cloth carefully folded and put by for the next morning, for we kept a separate one for dinner, and imposed the fine of a half-penny upon any one who should spill their tea or coffee over the cloth by carelessness. Such was always my plan when in business; for you must know as well as myself, it is not only the expense of the washing, but the continual wear and tear of the linen, which make such frequent washings so ruinous, but my cloth used always to look clean, and I am confident that not less than five pounds a-year were saved on that very trifling matter, and you know we thought as much then of five pounds as we perhaps now do of twenty.

Before partaking of a breakfast, you must provide the materials (which I always select of the best quality), and require to know how to prepare them. I shall, therefore, give you a series of every description of articles which may properly be partaken of at the breakfast-table.

FIRST SERIES OF RECEIPTS.

PERHAPS some housekeepers may laugh at the presumption of M. Soyer in attempting to give a formal receipt for so trifling a matter as making a piece of toast. But, in Cookery, there are no trifles. Every preparation of food, however simple, requires thought, care, and experience. Among the unpleasantnesses of our breakfast-tables, there are none more common than poor toast. — Ed.

1. *Toast.* — Procure a nice square loaf of bread that has been baked one or two days previously (for new bread cannot be cut, and would eat very heavy), then with a sharp knife cut off the bottom crust very evenly, and then as many slices as you require, about a quarter of an inch in thickness (I generally use a carving-knife for cutting bread for toast, being longer in the blade, it is more handy, and less liable to waste the bread); contrive to have rather a clear fire; place a slice of the bread upon a toasting-fork, about an inch from one of the sides, hold it a minute before the fire, then turn it, hold it before the fire another minute, by which time the bread will be thoroughly hot, then begin to move it gradually to and fro until the whole surface has assumed a yellowish-brown color, when again turn it, toasting the other side in the same manner; then lay it upon a hot plate, have some fresh or salt butter (which must not be too hard, as pressing it upon the toast would make it heavy), spread a piece, rather less than an ounce, over, and cut into four or six pieces; should you require six such slices for a numerous family, about a quarter of a pound of butter would suffice for the whole; but cut each slice into pieces as soon as buttered, and pile them lightly upon the plate or dish you intend to serve it. This way you will find a great improvement upon the old system, as often in cutting through four or five slices with a bad knife, you squeeze all the butter out of the upper one, and discover the under one, at the peril of its life, swimming in an ocean of butter at the bottom of the dish.

N.B. The warming of the bread gradually through, on both sides, is a very great improvement upon the quality of the toast; it may give a trifle more trouble, but still it is quicker done, and much lighter.

All kinds of toast require to be done the same way, but if to be served under a bird, eggs, or kidneys, it requires to be toasted drier.

Being in every way an economist, I have generally saved the remnants of the loaf that have become too dry to be eaten as bread, and by just dipping them in warm water, toasting them gradually, and buttering them, I have generally found that they have been eaten in preference, but their being stale is a secret of my own, which, if divulged, would prevent their ever being eaten after.

2. *Dry Toast.* — Ought not to be toasted until quite ready to serve; when done,

place it in a toast-rack, or standing upon its edges, one piece resting against another; any kind of toast that has been made half an hour is not worth eating.

3. *To toast Muffins* (for Receipt, see No. 6.)—Just open, half an inch deep, the sides of the muffins, exactly in the centre, with a knife, then put your toasting-fork in the middle of the bottom, hold it a little distance from the fire, until partly warmed through, when turn it and put it again to the fire until it becomes lightly toasted, when again turn it to toast the other side; when done, pull it open, spread a thin layer of butter on each side, close them together; lay them upon a plate, then with a sharp knife divide them across the middle, and serve very hot. If more than one muffin is required, cut them all separately, and pile them lightly one upon another, on the plate; when well prepared, they are, in my opinion, a very great luxury, obtainable at a trifling expense.

4. *To toast Crumpets.*—Crumpets stand lower in the general estimation of the public, probably from not being so *distingué*, and having the misfortune to be cheaper than their sister muffins; but, for all that, the poor ought never to be forgotten, and a crumpet toasted as follows is not to be despised. Choose your crumpets fresh if possible, though they are not bad after having been made three or four days; toast them by warming both sides first, like muffins, then give them a nice light brown color on each side, lay them in a plate, and spread some rather soft butter lightly upon each side; cut in halves with a sharp knife, and serve; half a pat of butter to each crumpet is quite sufficient. If you have several to serve, lay them separately upon a large hot dish; some people lay them one upon the other, which is a very bad plan, as it causes the under ones to eat like a piece of dough, and such food cannot be wholesome. Crumpets require to be toasted rather quick.

5. *To make Rolls and other Breakfast Bread.*—Put four pounds of flour into an earthen pan, make a hole in the centre, in which put three parts of a pint of warm water, to which you add a gill of white brewer's yeast, free from bitter, mix a little flour to form a leaven, which set in a warm place to rise (it must be allowed to remain until the leaven has risen and begun to fall), then add a little salt and a pint of warm milk, form the whole into a flexible dough, which keep in a warm place for another hour; it is then ready, and may be moulded into the form of rolls, twists, little crusty loaves, or any shapes most pleasing for the breakfast-table.

6. *To make Muffins.*—Mix a quart of warm water in which you have dissolved a quarter of a pound of German yeast, with sufficient flour to form a stiffish batter, which let remain in a warm place four hours, then stir the mixture down, and break it into pieces weighing a quarter of a pound each, which mould round with your hands, and put into wooden trays containing a round bed of flour for each; let them remain in a warm place two hours to prove, when have your muffin-stove hot; have a round piece of iron; place on the fire to get hot; set the muffins upon it, and when nicely risen, turn them gently over, baking them upon the stove until sufficiently set, when they are done; they will take about ten minutes baking if the stove is at the proper heat, which is known by throwing a little flour on it and becoming brown. Muffins may also be made of brewer's yeast, but then they would require longer proving, and great care must be taken that the yeast be not bitter.

7. *To make Crumpets.*—Mix a gill of brewer's yeast, free from bitter, with two quarts of water, just lukewarm, to which add sufficient flour to make a thinnish batter, and let it stand six hours in a warm place, when stir it well with a wooden spoon, and let it remain four hours longer; have the muffin-stove hot, upon which lay a number of tin hoops, the size of crumpets, pour a small ladleful of the batter into each hoop, and when the top is covered with small bladders, turn them quickly over (hoops and all) with a large palate knife, and in about five minutes afterwards they will be sufficiently baked.

8. *Rusks.*—Put three pounds of flour upon a dresser, make a hole in the middle, into which put two ounces of German yeast, dissolved in a pint of warm water, mix a little of the flour in, and leave it half an hour in a warm place to rise, then add two ounces of powdered sugar, and a quarter of a pound of butter, dissolved in half a pint of warm water; mix the whole into a dough, and let it remain in a warm place until well risen, when work it down with the hands, divide it in three pieces, each of which form into a long roll about two inches in thickness, place them upon a buttered baking-sheet, four inches apart, and put them in a warm place to prove, occasionally moistening the tops with milk; bake them in a moderate oven; when cold, cut them in slices the thickness of a penny piece, which lay upon a clean baking-sheet, and put into a warm oven, when well browned upon one side, turn them over, put them again into the oven until the other side is browned, when they are done and ready for use.

9. *Tops and Bottoms.*—Make a dough exactly as described in the last, but using only half the butter; have a deep-edged baking-sheet well buttered, and when the dough is ready, turn it on to a dresser, well floured; divide into small pieces the size of walnuts, which mould into round balls, and place close together upon the baking-sheet; put them in a warm place to prove, and bake well in a moderate oven; when cold, divide and cut each one in halves (making a top and bottom) which brown in the oven as directed for rusks.

10. *Buns.*—Put three pounds of flour in an earthen pan, make a hole in the middle, in which put two ounces of German yeast, dissolved in three parts of a pint of warm water, and stir in a little of the flour, forming a thinnish batter, let it remain in a warm place nearly an hour, until well fermented, when add half a pound of sugar, a few currants, and half a pound of butter, dissolved in nearly a pint of warm milk, mix the whole well together, making a soft but dry dough; let it remain in a warm place until it rises very light, when turn it out of the pan on to a board; work it well with the hands, shaking flour over lightly, then mould it into small round balls, double the size of walnuts, which place upon a buttered baking-sheet, four inches apart; moisten the tops with milk; put them in a warm place to prove, not, however, permitting them to crack, and bake them in a hot oven.

11. —*Brioche Rolls.*—Put four pounds of flour upon a dresser, one pound of which put on one side, make a hole in the middle into which pour nearly three parts of a pint of warm water, in which you have dissolved an ounce of German yeast; mix it into a stiff but delicate paste, which roll up into a ball: cut an incision across it, and lay it in a basin well floured, in a warm place, until becoming very light, then make a large hole in the centre of the three pounds of flour, into which

put half an ounce of salt, two pounds of fresh butter, half a gill of water, and sixteen eggs, mix it into a rather softish flexible paste, which press out flat, lay the leaven upon it, folding it over and working with the hands until well amalgamated, flour a clean cloth, fold the paste in it and let remain all night. In the morning mould them into small rolls; put them upon a baking-sheet, and bake in a moderate oven. Unless your breakfast party is very large, half the above quantity would be sufficient; but these rolls being quite a luxury, I only make them upon very especial occasions.

12. *How to choose Eggs.* — New-laid eggs should not be used until they have been laid about eight or ten hours, for that part which constitutes the white is not properly set before that time, and does not until then obtain their delicate flavor; that which is termed milk in eggs being, according to my opinion, very insipid; but that entirely depends upon fancy.

Nothing being more offensive than eggs in a state of decomposition, it is very important that every person should know how to detect them (especially in the winter), if, by shaking them, they sound hollow, you may be certain they are not new-laid, and not fit to be boiled for breakfast: but, if broken, they may prove fit for any other culinary purpose, except for soufflés, for which eggs must be very fresh. The safest way to try them is to hold them to the light, forming a focus with your hand; should the shell be covered with small dark spots, they are very doubtful, and should be broken separately in a cup, and each egg smelt previous to using; if, however, in looking at them, you see no transparency in the shells, you may be sure they are rotten and only fit to be thrown away; the most precise way is, to look at them by the light of a candle; if quite fresh, there are no spots upon the shells, and they have a brilliant light yellow tint; in the spring of the year, it would be scarcely excusable to use any eggs that are not quite fresh.

13. *Eggs for Breakfast, — plain boiled.* — Put about a pint of water to boil in any kind of small stewpan (or saucepan) over the fire; when boiling, put in two or three fresh eggs, gently, with a spoon, being particular not to crack them or allow them to boil too fast, or the interior of the eggs would partly escape before they were set, giving them an unsightly appearance, and entirely prevent their cooking regularly: three minutes is sufficient to cook a full-sized egg, but if below the average size, two minutes and a half will suffice.

14. *Eggs au Beurre: a new method.* — Let the eggs boil six minutes instead of three, then take them out, dip them for two seconds in cold water, crack and peel off the shells, and lay them in a hot plate (they will remain quite whole if properly done), cut each egg in halves lengthwise, spread a little fresh butter and sprinkle a little salt over the interior, and eat them very hot.

Eggs done in this manner are delicate and digestible.

15. *To boil Eggs hard.* — Never boil eggs for salads, sauces, or any other purposes, more than ten minutes, and when done place them in a basin of cold water for five minutes to cool: take off their shells, and use them when required.

Nothing is more indigestible than an egg too hard-boiled.

16. *Poached Eggs.*—Put a pint of water in a stewpan, with four teaspoonfuls of vinegar and half a teaspoonful of salt, place it over the fire, and when boiling, break your eggs into it as near the surface of the water as possible, let them boil gently about three minutes; have rather a thin piece of toast, as described (No. 1), upon a dish, take the eggs out carefully with a small slice, lay the slice with the eggs upon a cloth for a second to drain the water from them, set them carefully upon the toast, and serve very hot. If the eggs are fresh they will look most inviting, but the way of breaking and boiling them must be most carefully attended to, and care should be taken not to boil too many together; if the yolks separate from the white it may be presumed that the egg is not fresh, but it may be eatable, for the same thing may happen through awkwardness in poaching.

Again, the toast upon which they are served may be buttered either with plain or maître d'hôtel butter, or two small pats of butter may be melted, without boiling it, and poured over, or a little melted butter sauce, or the same with the addition of a little maître d'hôtel butter poured over when just upon the point of boiling, or a little anchovy butter instead of the other; thus you may be able to indulge in nice little luxuries at a trifling expense.

17. *Toast and Eggs.*—Break three eggs into a small stewpan, add a saltspoonful of salt, a quarter of that quantity of pepper, and two ounces of fresh butter (the fresher the better), set the stewpan over a moderate fire, and stir the eggs round with a wooden spoon, being careful to keep every particle in motion, until the whole has become a smooth and delicate thickish substance; have ready a convenient-sized crisp piece of toast, pour the eggs upon it, and serve immediately.

18. *Eggs sur le Plat.*—Lightly butter a small oval dish, upon which break two, three, or more eggs without breaking the yolks, season lightly with a little white pepper and salt, put a few small pieces of butter here and there upon them, and then set the dish in a small oven, where let it remain until the whites become set, but by no means hard, and serve hot; if the oven is moderately hot, they will take about ten minutes; if no oven, put the dish before the fire, turning it round now and then until the eggs are set regular. This is a most excellent dish.

19. *Omelettes* may also be served for breakfast with great advantage, being very relishing, especially the omelettes *aux fines herbes*, *au lard*, and *aux champignons*, but as they are considered to belong to the dinner, they will be given in that series of receipts.

20. *Herring Toast Sandwich.*—Choose a bloater for this purpose not too dry, which split in two, cutting it down the back; lay them upon a plate and pour a pint of boiling water over; let them soak five minutes, when lay them upon a cloth to dry; then broil them very gradually upon a gridiron; when well done, which will be in about four or five minutes, have ready two thin slices of toast, made very crisp, butter them lightly, then take away all the bones from the herrings, lay the fleshy parts equally upon one piece of toast and cover with the other: serve very hot.

21. *Toast and Eggs with Herring.*—Prepare your toast and eggs as directed (No. 17), but previous to pouring the eggs over, lay the flesh of a herring as directed in

the last, and pour the eggs over that. Herrings upon toast, with a layer of mashed potatoes over, is also very good.

Dried haddock may also be served the same, as also may sardines, but they being ready-cooked, are laid over cold without splitting them; they are very delicious; if wanted hot, set them a few minutes before the fire.

22. *Fish for Breakfast, — Bloated Herrings.* — They require to be freshly salted, for if dry they are quite rank and unpalatable; scrape them lightly with a knife, and wipe them well with a cloth; pass the point of a knife down the back from head to tail, making an incision about a quarter of an inch in depth; place them upon the gridiron over a sharp fire; they will take about six minutes to cook, of course turning them occasionally; when done, put them upon a hot dish, open the backs, and place half a small pat of butter in each; again close them: cooked this way they are delicious, especially if they are real bloaters. Another way is to cut them quite open and broil them flat upon the gridiron, and serve quite plain; this way they are done much more quickly. Or, if nice and fresh, oil half a sheet of white paper for every fish, in which fold them and broil fifteen minutes over a slow fire, turning them over three or four times, and serve in the papers. Should you have any that have become dry, soak them about twenty minutes in lukewarm water, and proceed as first directed. (Same process will do for red herrings.)

23. *Dried Haddock.* — A very excellent thing for breakfast, but they never ought to be cooked whole, for one side being thinner than the other is of course dried up before the other is much more than half done, especially the larger ones; the better plan is to cut them in halves lengthwise, put them upon the gridiron over a moderate fire, keeping them frequently turned, and taking the thinnest half off first; the thickest will require about ten minutes to cook it thoroughly; when done, spread a pat of fresh butter over, and serve upon a very hot dish.

Haddocks may also be skinned and broiled in oiled paper, but of course would take rather more time in cooking.

24. *Whitings.* — Of all the modes of preparing and dressing whitings for breakfast I cannot but admire and prize the system pursued by the Scotch, which renders them the most light, wholesome, and delicious food that could possibly be served for breakfast: their method is, to obtain the fish as fresh as possible, clean and skin them, take out the eyes, cover the fish over with salt, immediately after which take them out and shake off the superfluous salt, pass a string through the eye-holes, and hang them up to dry in a passage or some place where there is a current of air; the next morning take them off, just roll them lightly in a little flour, broil them gently over a slow fire, and serve very hot, with a small piece of fresh butter rubbed over each, or serve quite dry if preferable.

25. *Slips or Small Soles.* — When cleaned, season them with a little pepper and salt, dip lightly into flour, and broil them slowly over a moderate fire about ten minutes, or according to the size; when done, place them upon a hot dish, pour two tablespoonfuls of cream over and serve immediately. They may of course be served dry, but pouring the cream over is a new and very good idea. Nothing but small white fish could be tolerated for breakfast.

26. *Sprats* when nicely cooked are very commendable. Dip them lightly into flour, and place them upon a gridiron over a slow fire; when about half done, turn them; when done (which would be in about five minutes from the time you put them on), serve dry in a very hot dish.

27. *Meat for Breakfast, —Sheep's Kidneys.*—Procure as many as you may require for your party, about one each is generally sufficient; be sure that they are fresh, which any person can ascertain by smelling, if not able to judge by their appearance; cut them open very evenly lengthwise, down to the root, but not to separate them; then have some small iron or wooden skewers, upon which thread the kidneys quite flat, by running the skewer twice through each kidney, that is, under the white part; season them rather highly with pepper and salt, and place them upon a gridiron (the inside downwards), over a sharp fire; in three minutes turn them over, and in about six they will be sufficiently done; then take them off the skewers, place them in a very hot dish, and serve immediately. In opening them be careful to cut them in the centre, for should one half be thicker than the other, one would be dried before the other was sufficiently cooked.

28. *Kidneys on Toast.*—Prepare the kidneys precisely as in the last, but when done have ready a piece of hot toast, which butter lightly; lay the kidneys upon it; have ready a small piece of butter, to which you have added a little pepper, salt, and the juice of half a lemon; place a small piece in the centre of each kidney, and when melted serve.

29. *Kidney bread-crumbed, à la Maître d'Hôtel.*—Prepare the kidneys as before, and when upon the skewer, have ready upon a plate an egg well beat up with a fork; season the kidneys with a little salt and pepper, dip them into the egg, then lightly cover them with bread-crumbs, put them upon the gridiron, which place over a moderate fire, broil them about ten minutes, turning them when half done, have ready a little maître d'hôtel butter, put about half an ounce in each kidney, and serve immediately upon a very hot dish; by the time it gets upon the table the butter will be melted, and they eat very relishing; dressed this way they may also be served upon toast.

30. *Sautéd Kidneys.*—Should you not have a fire fit for broiling, put an ounce of butter into a sauté-pan (which of course must be very clean), cut the kidney in halves lengthwise; and when the butter is melted, lay them in, the flat side downwards, having previously well seasoned them with pepper and salt; set the pan on a moderate fire three minutes, then turn them, place them again upon the fire until done; when have ready a piece of dry toast, which place upon a hot dish, pour the kidneys with the butter and gravy over and serve very hot, care must be taken in sautéing that the butter does not become burnt.

Another way is to sprinkle about a teaspoonful of chopped eschalots, or onions, over them whilst being sautéd; this materially changes the flavor, and meets the approbation of many.

For the cooking of mutton chops, steaks, cutlets, broiled fowl, broiled bones, or remnants of poultry or game, I must refer you to where they are given as receipts for the dinner-table.

31. *Bacon and Ham, how to choose both fit for broiling.*—Ham for broiling ought not to be too old or too dry, it would perhaps eat rank: nothing requires more care than broiling. Either get a slice of ham weighing a quarter of a pound or two ounces, which lay on your gridiron; put them over the fire; it will take perhaps five minutes, if the fire is good, and more, of course, if slow, but in that short space of time turn them three or four times, and it is done. Proceed the same if you want to serve it with poached eggs, but be careful that the eggs be ready at the same time as the bacon or ham, or both would eat badly. If you happen to have a whole ham by you for that purpose only, begin to cut the slices in a slanting direction and the same thickness, and proceed to the end of the ham with the remainder; it will prove more profitable to broil with greens, peas, broad beans, &c., &c.

To sauté it, put a little butter or good fat in the pan; set it on the fire with your slice in it, sauté very gently, turning very often, and serve it on very thin toast.

32. *Ham and Eggs.*—While your ham is doing, break two fresh eggs in the pan, season slightly with salt and pepper, set it before the fire till the eggs are delicately done, and slip them whole carefully into your dish, without breaking the yolk.

33. *Bacon.*—The streaky part of a thick flank of bacon is to be preferred; cut nice slices not above a quarter of an inch thick, take off the rind, put to broil on the gridiron over a clear fire, turn it three or four times in the space of five minutes; this will be all the cooking required: serve it very hot. Though this is the best part, the whole of the bacon is still good, especially if not rank, which can be easily detected by its yellowish color: if too dry or salt, after it has been cut in slices, dip it into a little vinegar and water three or four times, and sauté as usual, it will make it softer and less salt: serve as usual. If any remain after a dinner of boiled bacon, it is also very good broiled or fried for next day's breakfast.

34. *Sausages.*—Sausages are very frequently esteemed for breakfast. By all means, never use them, except you are confident that they are fresh. The skin must be transparent, that the meat should be seen through; they keep good two or three days in a cold place in summer, nearly a week in winter (with care). For the receipt how to make them in the homely way, see future letter.

35. *Sausages, how to cook them.*—Prick them with a pin all round about twenty times, put them on the gridiron over a gentle fire, turn three or four times, by doing which you will have them a very nice yellow color; dish them, and serve them very hot.

36. *Sautéd Sausages.*—If your fire smokes, it is preferable to sauté them; put some butter in the pan, with four sausages; after you have pricked them as before-mentioned, sauté gently, a few minutes will do them, turn them often; in many instances a thin slice of bread sautéd in the fat they have produced is a great improvement; save the fat, as it is always useful in a kitchen. In case you are in a hurry to do them, throw them into hot water for one minute previously to their being broiled or sautéd; they will then be the sooner cooked, and even eat rather more relishing to a delicate stomach, having extracted the oil from the skin; they may also be fried in the frying-pan.

37. *Black Puddings, broiled.*—Make about six or eight incisions through the skin

with a knife, in a slanting way, on each side of the pudding; put it on the gridiron for about eight minutes, on rather a brisk fire, turn it four times in that space of time, and serve it broiling hot.

I should recommend those who are fond of black puddings to partake of no other beverage than tea or coffee, as cocoa or chocolate would be a clog to the stomach. In France they partake of white wine for breakfast, which accounts for the great consumption of black pudding. Now really this is a very favorite dish with epicures, but I never should recommend it to a delicate stomach.

ON COFFEE.—Coffee, which has now come so generally into use, originally came from Arabia, where it has been known from time immemorial, but was brought into use in England in the year 1653; as it is not generally known how it was introduced, I will give you the account of it from "Houghton's Collection," 1698. "It appears that a Mr. Daniel Edwards, an English Merchant of Smyrna, brought with him to this country a Greek of the name of Pasqua, in 1652, who made his coffee; this Mr. Edwards married one Alderman Hodges's daughter, who lived in Walbrook, and set up Pasqua for a coffee-man in a shed in the churchyard in St. Michael, Cornhill, which is now a scrivener's brave-house, when, having great custom, the ale-sellers petitioned the Lord Mayor against him, as being no free-man. This made Alderman Hodges join his coachman, Bowman, who was free, as Pasqua's partner; but Pasqua, for some misdemeanor, was forced to run the country, and Bowman, by his trade and a contribution of 1000 sixpences, turned the shed to a house. Bowman's apprentices were first, John Painter, then Humphrey, from whose wife I had this account." Having examined the renter churchwarden's book of St. Michael, Cornhill, I find that the house or shed Bowman built is now part of the Jamaica Coffee-House; it was rebuilt by Bowman, after the fire, in 1667.

It is a very remarkable fact that but few persons in England know how to make good coffee, although so well supplied with the first quality of that delicious berry; but, by way of contrast, I must say that the middle classes of France are quite as ignorant of the method of making tea.

I remember, upon one occasion, whilst staying at Havre with Mr. B., where we were upon a visit at the house of one of his agents, who invited a few of his friends to meet us at a tea-party *à l'Anglaise*, as they used to call it, about an hour previous to tea, and previous to the arrival of the guests, I was walking upon the lawn before the house, when my attention was attracted by a cloud of steam issuing from the kitchen-window, smelling most powerfully of tea: my curiosity led me to the kitchen, where I found the cook busily engaged making cocoa and most delicious coffee, but preparing the tea in a ridiculous fashion, the leaves of which were in an awful state of agitation, attempting as it were to escape from an earthen pot at the side of the fire, in which the delicious soup we had for dinner was made a few hours previously. (*See* Pot-au-Feu.)

"My dear girl," said I (in French), "what process do you call that of making tea? it never ought to be boiled."

"I beg your pardon, Madame," says she, "master and mistress like it well done, and it will be another short half-hour before it is properly cooked (ce sera alors copieux)."

"You are decidedly wrong," said I, "and I shall be most happy to show you the way we make it in England."

"Yes, I know what you mean, Madame," replied she; "I used to make it that way before, but no one liked it, that is, to boil it one hour in a copper-pan over a charcoal fire." Upon which I retired, making a most comical grimace, to refrain from laughing at her still more ridiculous fashion.

You must, however, observe that this occurred nearly twelve years ago, and I have no doubt but a reform has taken place since then by the continual traffic of the English through that part of the country. I must say, with respect to ourselves, we do not make quite such a blunder respecting coffee, but still our middle classes very seldom enjoy the aroma of that delicious beverage, which should be made as follows:

Choose the coffee of a very nice brown color, but not black (which would denote that it was burnt, and impart a bitter flavor); grind it at home if possible, as you may then depend upon the quality; if ground in any quantity, keep it in a jar hermetically sealed. To make a pint, put two ounces into a stewpan, or small iron or tin saucepan, which set dry upon a moderate fire, stirring the coffee round with a wooden spoon continually until it is quite hot through, but not in the least burnt; should the fire be very fierce, warm it by degrees, taking it off every now and then until hot (which would not be more than two minutes), when pour over a pint of boiling water, cover close, and let it stand by the side of the fire (but not to boil) for five minutes, when strain it through a cloth or a piece of thick gauze, rinse out the stewpan, pour the coffee (which will be quite clear) back into it, place it upon the fire, and, when nearly boiling, serve with hot milk if for breakfast, but with a drop of cold milk or cream if for dinner.

To prove the simplicity of this mode of making coffee, I shall here give a repetition of the receipt as it actually is:

38. Put two ounces of ground coffee into a stewpan, which set upon the fire, stirring the powder round with a spoon until quite hot, when pour over a pint of boiling water; cover over closely for five minutes, when pass it through a cloth, warm again, and serve.[1]

------

[1] This entirely new system of making coffee has never yet been introduced to the public, and was found out by the author of this work through the following circumstance: Whilst travelling by night in a railway train, and arriving in due time at the station, where positively no less than five minutes are allowed to restore exhausted nature, after a long and tedious journey, and then, by using a certain portion of manual strength, to push through the crowd to get at what is called the refreshment room, after waiting for nearly two minutes for my turn to be served with some of the boiling liquid which they called coffee, being as bad as any human being could possibly make it, having probably waited patiently by the side of a winter's fire until the last train made its appearance, it tasted anything but palatable; but having a long journey before me, and requiring something to eat and drink, I was obliged to put up with it; but before I could even partake of half, or finish masticating some stale toast or over-buttered muffin, the unsociable bell violently rung to acquaint the passengers that their appetites were perfectly satisfied, though that incredulous organ would

The foregoing proportions would make coffee good enough for any person, but more or less coffee could be used, if required; the cloth through which it is passed should be immediately washed and put by for the next occasion. A hundred cups of coffee could be made as here directed in half an hour, by procuring a pan sufficiently large, and using the proper proportions of coffee and water, passing it afterwards through a large cloth or jelly-bag.

39. *Coffee, French fashion.*—To a pint of coffee, made as before directed, add a pint of boiling milk, warm both together until nearly boiling, and serve. The French never use it any other way for breakfast.

40. *White Coffee, a new style.*—Put·two ounces of unground coffee, slightly roasted, into a clean stewpan, which set upon a moderate fire, slowly warming the coffee through, shaking the stewpan round every half-minute; when very hot, which you will perceive by the smoke arising from it, pour over half a pint of boiling water, cover the stewpan well, and let it infuse by the side of the fire for fifteen minutes, then add half a pint of boiling-hot milk, pass the coffee through a small fine sieve into the coffee-pot or jug, and serve with white sugar-candy or crystallized sugar; it is, as you will perceive, a great novelty, and an agreeable change; but if by neglect you let the coffee get black, or the least burnt, do not attempt to make use of it; it should only be sufficiently charred to break easily in a mortar if required.

---

not let us believe it; and every one being perfectly aware that railway trains, like time, wait for no one, the hurry of which event, though unpleasant, made me escape the swallowing the thick part which was deposited at the bottom of the cup; rushing out of the refreshment room, I jumped into the wrong carriage, the fidgetty train having changed its place, and the time being too short to rectify the mistake, I was obliged to make fresh acquaintance with my new compagnons de voyage, who happened to be as much dissatisfied with the steaming-hot refreshment as myself, who had patronized the steaming Mocha. I was at last much pleased to find a wise man among my new travelling friends, who said, "I never travel at night without being provided with a *spirited* companion;" and pulling out of his carpet-bag a small bottle and gutta-percha goblet of new invention, we partook of a drop of the best *eau de vie* I had ever tasted, which produced on me the pleasant sensation of being relieved of a very annoying pain. Grateful for his kindness, and always desirous to improve the domestic comfort, I told him, in making myself known, that, as soon as I arrived at the Reform Club, I would try several experiments to simplify the present method of making coffee; and should I be successful in my researches, I would forward him the receipt on my arrival in London. I tried to find my first travelling friends, who, more unfortunate than myself, got in their proper place, and, consequently, did not meet with the "spirited" friend I did, vowing they would never take any more coffee at night, especially in a railway train. Having forwarded the receipt to my friend, he, after having tried it, wrote me the following note:

"MY DEAR SIR,—I have made an experiment of your new receipt for coffee, which you have kindly forwarded to me, and beg to acquaint you that I never recollect having lasted better. Yours, &c.

W. C."

I do strongly advise my readers to give it a trial, and recommend all providers of refreshment at railway stations not to make the coffee boiling hot, but to keep the cafetière in a bain-marie, which would avoid all the above inconvenience, both as regards quality and heat.

41. *Coffee, made with a filter.*—To make a quart; first put a pint of boiling water through the filter to warm it, which again pour away, then put a quarter of a pound of ground coffee upon the filter, upon which put the presser lightly, and the grating, pour over half a pint of boiling water, let it drain three or four minutes, then pour over a pint and a half more boiling water; when well passed through, pour it into a clean stewpan, which set at the corner of the fire until a light scum arises, but not boiling; pour it again through the filter, and when well drained through, pour into the coffee-pot, and serve with hot milk, or a little cream, separately.

42. *Another way, more economical.*—Proceed as in the last, but draining the coffee through once only, and serve, after which pour another quart of boiling water over the coffee-grounds, which, when drained through, reserve, and boil up for the next coffee you make, using it instead of water, and an ounce less coffee.

TEA is, without doubt, one of the most useful herbs ever introduced into England, which was in the year of the fire of London, 1666: it has replaced an unwholesome and heavy drink (ale) which used to be partaken of previously, and has created habits of sobriety. It is indigenous to China, Japan, and Siam, and consists of many varieties, the proper mixing of which constitutes the great art of a tea-dealer. It is exceedingly useful in many cases of sickness, and particularly after having partaken of any liquor to excess, or after extraordinary fatigue. When new, it is a narcotic; but when old it has a different effect,[2] and in its native country is never partaken of until a year old, and not then, unless exceedingly desiccated. I cannot recommend you any one in particular, as that depends on taste; but this I advise, that when you have a kind to your liking, to keep to it.

And now, my dear friend, without wishing in the least to offend you, or attempting to aggravate your good nature, I must beg to contradict your assertion made at the commencement of our undertaking, where you say, respecting tea, of course I know how to make it; you made it whilst staying at our house occasionally, and Mr. B. found there was a great difference between it and mine. But to tell you the truth respecting tea, I have a little secret of my own, being a discovery which I made a short time ago by accident. Whilst in the act of making tea, I had just put the dry tea in the pot, when I heard a fearful scream up-stairs in the drawing-room; rushing there, I found my little girl had had a severe fall in reaching something from the chimney-piece, the stool upon which she stood having upset: twenty minutes at least had elapsed before I returned to my tea (which, being alone, I was in no particular hurry for), when I found that the servant, thinking there was water in the pot, and fearing the tea would be spoiled, put it into the oven, which was rather hot; when she brought it to me, I was rather annoyed, when all at once it struck me that the leaves being hot through, the tea would not require so long to draw; I then filled the teapot with boiling water, and in a minute afterwards had a most delicious cup of tea, since which I have adopted the system

---

[2] Some few years since, having a great deal of writing to do within a certain time, and which could not be done without employing the night as well as the day, I partook of weak green tea, with a little brandy, sugar, and lemon-juice in it, as a beverage, and, with light food, I was enabled to do with but eighteen hours' sleep from 8 o'clock on Monday morning to 5 o'clock on the following Sunday morning.

upon all occasions, and am now having made a small spirit-lamp to warm the pot and leaves, as the oven is not always hot: it may, however, be made hot in front of the fire, but not too close of course. I gave the receipt to one of our neighbors, who actually laughed at the idea, but never tried it, saying, "We cannot teach anything to our grandmothers, and that what did for them would do for us." Now what could you say to such people? why nothing, but let them alone, as I shall do for the future. But you, my dear, I know have better sense; proceed as I have directed, and you will find it a great improvement. Put your tea in the pot a quarter of an hour before ready for it, warming both tea and pot, fill with boiling water, and leave it from three to five minutes to draw, when it is quite ready.

CACAO was first known in Europe after the discovery of America, and it retains its Indian name; of course, it was first used in Spain, and did not come into use in England until much later; and we find that there was imported into England, in the year 1694, about 13,000 lbs. weight of it; at the present day there was, in 1848, 410,000 lbs. It is a long fruit, about five to eight inches, and three or four thick, which contains about thirty nuts: the tree grows to only a few feet in height.

In the course of my experiments, I have found that the shell is almost as nutritious as the kernel, with less oily particles in it, which, to many, are unpleasant.

43. *Chocolate.*—Scrape two ounces of the cake, which put into a stew or saucepan, with a gill of water, upon the fire, keeping it stirred with a wooden spoon until rather thick, when work it quickly with the spoon, stirring in half a pint of boiling milk by degrees; serve very hot, with sugar separate.

44. *Chocolate made in the Italian method.*—Procure a regular chocolate-pot with a muller, the handle of which comes through the lid, one might be procured at any brazier's, put in two ounces of chocolate (scraped), over which by degrees pour a pint of boiling milk, put on the lid, with the muller inside, which keep well moving, setting the pot upon the fire, and when very hot and frothy, serve.

45. *Cocoa.*—Put a teaspoonful and a half of canistered cocoa into a cup, which fill by degrees with boiling milk, stir it until dissolved, when it is ready to serve; sugar separately.

LETTER NO. III.

Oatlands Cottage, Jan. 20, 1849.

DEAR HORTENSE,—I have inclosed the whole of the receipts which you have sent me for the breakfasts, properly classified, having omitted the cold meats (as you desired me) from this series, thinking, as you do, they are more suited for the luncheon. To save useless repetition, I have placed the receipts in numbers, by which references can be easily made, and any dish appearing in the dinner or luncheon series, but available for breakfast, can be directly found.

But one thing I remember when at your house was, that when the remains of a joint were rather large, you used to put it upon a side table, and let any one help themselves from it there; your idea being, I believe, that very few persons liked to have a large dish of meat before their eyes almost immediately after rising from their beds, or at the first meal of the morning. Respecting the way your table was laid out, to the best of my recollection, it was as follows:—First the large table-cloth, over which was laid a small napkin before each person, with cups and saucers for tea or coffee, at choice, small plates for rolls, and a size larger for meat, sausages, eggs, &c., a small knife and fork for each; the butter in a pretty freezing butter-glass, just covered with clear spring water, and garnished with a few sprigs of parsley or watercresses; the cream in a small china cream-jug, and a larger jug containing hot milk for coffee; orange marmalade in its original pot, honeycomb, watercresses, and once a few nice young radishes, which were excellent, although a little out of season; one day also dry toast was served, another day buttered, the next muffins, then crumpets, white and brown bread, and small rolls, thus making a continual change, but all so small and inviting. I shall always, when I have company, as you had then, arrange everything in the same manner, especially now that I have your receipts down. But when you are alone, you tell me, you never make any such display, which of course would be ridiculous; still even then you vary, by having either tea, coffee, or chocolate, which change I like as well as you. I eat meat but occasionally, but Mr. L— — generally likes a little broiled bacon, or boiled egg, things in themselves very simple and pleasant to have upon the table. Yours, in haste,

ELOISE.

EARLY LUNCHEONS.

LETTER NO. IV.

MY DEAR FRIEND,—I feel perfectly satisfied with the manner in which you have classified my receipts respecting the breakfasts, and must say I felt very much interested in looking over them; I am confident they would prove interesting and instructive to any young housekeeper; I hope, therefore, you will preserve the originals, as I do not keep any copies, fearing they would confuse me by making reference to them; so that, if at any future time I should make a repetition in other series, you would be able to correct me, for I am as willing as yourself that we should complete our work by going through every series comprising meals of the day.

The next meal, then, to breakfast, in the ordinary course of events, is the luncheon. Although it is a meal we never touch ourselves, I am aware many small families make it a regular one, so our little journal would not be complete without some few remarks, which I intend making as short and concise as possible. When we were in business, our luncheons were comprised of any cold meats which were cooked for previous dinners; if a joint of cold roast or boiled meat, it requires to be nicely trimmed before making its appearance at table, but reserving the trimmings for hash, if of roast meat, or bubble-and-squeak, if salt beef, which is an excellent method of disposing of the remainder of a joint to advantage; if the joint happened to be cold veal, I used to send for a plate of ham to serve with it, unless there was a piece of bacon also left; if mutton, I used to dish up the leg with a pretty little paper frill upon the knuckle, also trimming the joint lightly, for you must be aware that, after four or five have dined from a leg of mutton, its appearance becomes quite spoiled, and looks blackish when cold. Pork I also serve the same; when parsley was cheap, I always laid a few branches round it, which used, as my visitors said, to make the meat look very refreshing and inviting. Our only addition was sometimes the remainder of game, which at that time used frequently to be presented to us—pheasants, partridges, or grouse; as it would then have been very extravagant to have purchased them, especially when they were so expensive. As an accompaniment to the meat, I always kept two different sorts of mixed pickles, good bread, butter, cheese, and a glass of excellent table ale; or, if our guest was some bosom friend or good customer, a bottle of sherry (not decantered), never any port, thinking that more fit for the dinner-table. Such was my plan in the first five years after my marriage: everything upon our table was of the first quality, and every one used to admire the neatness with which the table was laid out.

My method now, when luncheon is required (as we do not dine until half-past five o'clock, Mr. B. being engaged until four in the city), I have the cloth laid at twelve, and lunch at half-past; and that time being just after the nursery dinner, we generally have some sort of pudding or tart, made at the same time with theirs. For cold meat, I always serve that up which has been left from a previous dinner, if any, or any remains of poultry, game, ham, or tongue. When, however, we have six or eight friends from the country at Christmas, I feel proud to show them my style of doing things well and economically, for they are very intelligent people, and can appreciate good living, though at home they really live too plain for their incomes; but they say, "We do not understand how it is that you make a nice little dish almost out of nothing." For should I have the remnants of any poultry or game not very inviting to the sight, I generally cut it up and show my cook how to hash it in a variety of ways; and I always remark, that they never partake of any cold meat whilst any of the hash remains. For the methods of making various hashes of fowl, game, hare, rabbit, beef, mutton, as also curries, minced veal and poached eggs, cold pies of game, poultry, mutton, beefsteak, or pigeon, as also plain mutton cutlets, steaks, and broiled bones, the whole of which may be served for luncheon, I must refer you to the series of receipts belonging to the dinner; any of these articles are placed in order upon the table, with the pickle-stand, two different cruet-sauces, orange marmalade, potatoes, butter, cheese, sherry and port wines. This style of luncheon will no doubt surprise you, but I can assure you it scarcely increases my expenditure, having the same number to provide for daily, so that the luncheon is generally made up from the remains of dinner, and the remains of luncheon will dine our three servants at half-past one. In the summer, I introduce a few dishes of fruit, and less meat; and when there are several ladies, I often introduce some English-made wine, which once I used to make myself, but which I can now buy cheaper.

THE NURSERY DINNER.

LETTER NO. V.

DEAR FRIEND,—Now here I must call your especial attention to the way many people treat this department of domestic comfort, which is often very slight and irregular. Now, for my part, I have made quite a study of it, and could prove that health is always dependent on the state of the digestive organs; and that, if you should improperly treat young stomachs, by over or under supplying their wants, or using them to ill-cooked food, you not only destroy the functionary coating of the stomach, but also impede the development of the intellect. It is, then, as much a science to manage the food of children, as to cater for the palate of the gourmet, and I shall always consider that good food is to the body what education is to the mind.

My plan of managing the nursery meals is as follows:—At eight o'clock in the morning, which was my usual time, I used myself to prepare that glutinous food upon which our ancestors and race were first reared, rather unclassically denominated pap. My method was very simple:

46. —Put two ounces of rusk, or tops and bottoms, in a small saucepan, with just sufficient water to moisten them; set the saucepan upon the fire until its contents are thoroughly warmed through; pour a little of the water away, if too thin, pressing the rusk with a spoon; then add a teaspoonful of brown sugar, and beat the whole with a spoon until quite a pulp; it is then ready for use.

I have seen some poor people in the country make it with a stale piece of bread, previously well dried and lightly toasted before the fire, and you could scarcely tell the difference from rusks; and you must observe, that people in a country village cannot always supply themselves with everything in the way of luxury; but look at the greater part of those country urchins,—are they not a real picture of health? for, after all, nothing is more advantageous to a delicate child than country air and country food. When Mr. B. and myself were staying at Boulogne for a few weeks, I was astonished to hear that everybody used to put their children out to nurse. I was so surprised, that I made every inquiry, and found it literally true, that even respectable tradespeople sent their children a mile or two in the country, some to the houses of very poor people: I cannot say that I approve of such a style of bringing up infants, but even there they seem as healthy and as joyful as possible. I also found there something to be learned, and that was, how to make French pap, which I think very nutritious, but which I considered at the time rather heavy for our climate; but having afterwards made a trial of it upon our little Henry, I found him doing so extremely well, that I continued feeding him upon it for nearly eight months, until he was old enough to eat other food. The following is the receipt:

47. —Put a tablespoonful of flour into a pap saucepan, to which add by degrees two gills of milk, mixing it into a very smooth batter with a wooden spoon; place the saucepan upon the fire, let it boil ten minutes, keeping it stirred the whole time, or it is liable to burn or become brown, then add about half an ounce of sugar and a little salt, put it into a basin, and it is ready for use. A little butter is also very good in it.

You will observe, that it is more difficult and troublesome to make than our pap; but when used to it, you will expend no more time over it; and, as the French people say, cooking is all pleasure and no trouble. But what convinces me that it is more palatable and nutritious is, that I have seen a very robust man make a hearty dinner of two plates of it by introducing bread in it. I have no doubt that our own hasty pudding was taken from it, for the use of children of three or four years old, being thought too heavy for infants. These long details may appear rather insignificant and tedious to you, but I leave them to your good judgment, begging of you to curtail my remarks should you think proper; but, although you may consider that every person is acquainted with these domestic habits, you would find upon inquiry that very many persons neglect them almost entirely. Having written thus much upon the food of infants, we must next consider the proper diet for children of twelve months old, commencing with bread and milk.

48. —For which, cut about two ounces of any white bread into small thin slices, which put into a small basin or a large breakfast cup, in a little saucepan (only used for that purpose) have half a pint of milk, which, when upon the point of boiling, pour over the bread; cover the cup over five minutes, and it is ready for use.

I much prefer this method to that of boiling the bread and milk together. In first commencing to feed a child upon the above, I always added a little sugar, which I withdrew by degrees, as I do not like to accustom children to too much sweets, as it inclines them when a little older to be always wanting or eating sweet stuff, which often spoils the best set of teeth; and here let me remark, that the finest fortune you can give to your children is health, and as loving mothers, whilst we have them under our control, it is our duty to study their little comforts, and direct their first steps in life in the road of happiness.

49. *Porridge.*—When children are delicate, porridge is often preferable to bread and milk. Put two tablespoonfuls of Scotch grits or oatmeal in the milk saucepan, which moisten with half a pint of milk; let it boil ten minutes, keeping well stirred, add a small piece of butter and a little sugar, and it is ready for use.

When my children were about eighteen months or two years old, I used to give them a little tender meat, such as boiled mutton, and broth, but in very small quantities, keeping still for the general food the bread and milk and porridge; but now they are old enough to eat anything wholesome (one being nine and the other ten years of age), their meals are composed thus:

50. —Bread and milk for breakfast at eight; the dinner at one, which was com-

posed as follows throughout the week: roast mutton and apple pudding, roast beef and currant pudding, baked apples; boiled mutton with turnips, after which rice or vermicelli pudding; occasionally a little salt beef, with suet dumplings, plain and with currants in them, or pease pudding; or if unwell, a little veal or chicken-broth, or beef-tea (the receipts for which will be found in the series entitled Comforts for Invalids).

When in business, the first three years we could not afford to keep a nursery, in fact, we had no room to spare; the children then used to dine with us at one, but at a side-table with their nurse.

51. —They then had a little plain meat, cut small in their plates, with potatoes, pieces of bread, and gravy, after which, three times a week, plain rice, bread, or other plain pudding, or rhubarb or apple tart; and, at five o'clock, their bread and milk again, previous to going to bed.

But if for people who could afford it, I should recommend the following diet-table, for nurserymaid and all:

52. —First, about two pounds of mutton well-cooked, but with the real gravy of the meat in it, which will require about one hour before a moderate fire, dredge it ten minutes before being done; when taken up and in the dish, sprinkle a little salt over the meat, and pour over three or four spoonfuls of hot water to make a little light gravy.

Many persons will, I am aware, quite disapprove of this system of washing the meat: they would serve it as if it were for full-grown people, but you well know what would do for children as well as I—plain, simple, and wholesome food; I always carried out this system, and I now make my cook do the same.

53. —Then the next day I would give them a small piece of mutton, plain boiled, with turnips, and apple tart; or a few slices of roast beef, or a small piece roasted on purpose, after which a very plain currant pudding; or, occasionally, a little pickled pork, with pease pudding, or roast pork, with baked apples, and now and then a little salt beef, but very well boiled, with suet dumplings, and occasionally, for change, either bread, vermicelli, or tapioca puddings; in case of illness, and with the approbation of the doctor, veal, mutton, or chicken-broth, sago, gruel, panada, &c., for which refer to the receipts for invalids.

Now the more I write the more I am convinced that, for the method of preparing certain articles for the children's dinners, we must refer to the kitchen department of receipts and receipts for invalids, especially as regards broth, meat, puddings, &c., or otherwise we should have so many repetitions; so that it would be better, upon the completion of the journal, to make references, either by numbers of receipt or page; it will be more intelligible, and less confused.

Many people would, perhaps, imagine that there is too much variety of food for children; but it is quite the contrary, for change of food is to the stomach what change of air is to the general health, but, of course, with children, those changes must be effected with judgment, and their food administered in smaller quantities; but you must observe when children are well brought up with regard to their meals, they possess extraordinary organs of digestion, the proof of which is that they require feeding oftener than a full-grown person, and never appear to be tired of eating, thus, of course, they do not require such quantities at a time. Having here terminated my remarks upon the Nursery, I shall leave this scene of romp and confusion, to walk on tip-toe to the sick-room door, and carefully enter, without noise, into this mournful abode of human suffering and captivity, in hopes that, by watching over their diet, my small efforts may improve their comforts, which, by being properly managed, may assist in their restoration to health. I shall, therefore, proceed to give some receipts, entitled Comforts for Invalids.

Nothing is to me more painful than to see any food ill-prepared for sick people, where the sense of taste is partially gone; everything ordered by the doctors as food, should be cooked in the greatest perfection, especially as everything they require is so very simple and easily done, that it is unpardonable to do it badly, although I am sorry to say that it is too often the case, even in many of our first hospitals and other public establishments, where they have provisions in abundance, and of the first quality.

Perhaps you may fancy I am too severe upon that delicate subject, but I can assure you that I have for years been in the habit of visiting some of these institutions for the sick, and can therefore speak with confidence. I have grieved often to see it, and have wished that they would follow a system I would lay down, but there are some people who would not change their style, however bad, for a better one, for the world.

Now I must here claim all your intelligence, for pointing out those receipts the accomplishing of which is most plain, and will insure success to those who may try to do them, and cause them to persuade others to follow their example. I therefore inclose the following. Yours, &c.

HORTENSE.

COMFORTS FOR INVALIDS.

54. *Meat for Invalids.*—The best meat as food for invalids is, in fact, that which is principally used, mutton and beef, lamb, if not too young (sweetbreads, I consider, ought oftener to be introduced), and calves' feet or head, scalded and boiled until tender, are very nutritious; chickens, pigeons, partridges, are also very inviting. All the above-mentioned articles are easy of digestion, excepting perhaps the beef, which may require to be gently stewed until tender, if for a delicate stomach just ordered to take meat after a serious fit of illness.

55. *Plain Mutton Broth for Invalids.*—Get one pound of scrag of mutton, break the bone with a chopper, without separating the meat, then put it into a stewpan with three pints of water and a salt-spoonful of salt; boil gently two hours, carefully removing all the scum and fat, which is easily done by allowing it to simmer slowly by the side of the fire; it will be by that time reduced to about one quart, and is then ready to serve. This broth must not be expected to drink very palatable, being deprived of vegetables and seasoning, being in fact more like a beverage than a soup: at the commencement of convalescence more strength may be given if ordered by the doctor, by reducing the original quantity to one pint. This broth is often administered by a spoonful only at a time.

56. *Seasoned Mutton Broth.*—Put the same quantity of mutton and water into your stewpan, add double the quantity of salt, and a quarter ditto brown sugar, quarter of a middle-sized onion, very little celery, and one ounce of turnip; set it upon the fire, and when beginning to boil draw it to the side; let it simmer gently two hours; skim off all the scum and fat, and pass it through a sieve, and use it when required. When finished, there ought to remain about a quart of broth; but if by neglect it has boiled too fast, add more water, and set to boil for a quarter of an hour longer. If the patient is getting better, his medical man will probably order him to eat a little of the meat, or even turnips, in which case serve them on a plate separately; should the meat not be required by the patient, it is very excellent for a healthy person, with a few spoonfuls of onions or caper sauce, or even plain. If pearl-barley is required to be taken with the broth, put a tablespoonful of it in with the water when you first put it upon the fire, the whole will then be done together; if the barley is to be eaten by the patient, take out the meat and vegetables, and skim off every spot of grease; but if the barley is not required, pass the broth, as before, through a sieve.

57. *Mutton Broth (with variations). With Vermicelli.*—Having made your broth, and passed it through a sieve, as before, put the meat and vegetables upon a plate, and the broth back into the same stewpan; when boiling, if about a quart, add one

or two tablespoonfuls of vermicelli, depending upon the strength of the patient's stomach; ten minutes' boiling will be sufficient to cook vermicelli.

58. *With Rice.*—One spoonful of best rice in the stewpan, with mutton and water the same as the barley, as it is better for the rice to be in pulp than underdone.

59. *With Semoulina.*—Semoulina is very delicate and glutinous, and I am quite confident that the faculty would approve of it after a trial or two; it is good in any kind of broth or milk for invalids, of very easy digestion, and having also the advantage of being tolerably cheap and quickly cooked; proceed as directed for vermicelli.

60. *With Arrow-root.*—After having passed your broth, place it again into the stewpan to boil; when boiling, put two teaspoonfuls of arrow-root into a cup, which mix smoothly with a gill of cold broth, or half ditto of water; then pour it into your boiling broth, which keep stirring with a spoon; let it simmer ten minutes, and it is ready for use.

61. *Veal Broth (French method).*—The following is much recommended by French physicians:—Put one pound of veal from knuckle, with but very little of the bone, into a stewpan with three pints of water and a salt-spoonful of salt, place it over the fire to boil; when boiling, take off all the scum; then add a small cabbage-lettuce and a few sprigs of chervil, if handy; let simmer slowly for two hours, it will then be reduced to about a quart; pass it through a sieve, letting the meat drain, and it is ready to serve.

62. *Another way, more palatable.*—Take the same quantity of veal as before, which cut into small dice (as you should cut all meat if possible), put it into the stewpan, with a small pat of butter, half an onion, about the same quantity of carrot and turnip, a little celery, and a teaspoonful of salt; set the stewpan upon the fire, keeping the contents stirred, for about ten minutes, until the bottom of the stewpan is covered with a whitish glaze, then add three pints of hot water; let the whole simmer one hour at the corner of the fire, skim well, pass it through a sieve, and use when required. This broth is most palatable and very digestible, but of course only to be given to the convalescent; it may be served with vermicelli, rice, arrow-root, and semoulina, as directed for mutton broth.

63. *Another very Refreshing and Strengthening Veal Broth.*—Put two pounds of knuckle of veal into a stewpan, with a calf's foot split, and the bone taken out and chopped up, add three quarts of water, a good-sized onion, one leek, a piece of parsnip, and two salt-spoonfuls of salt (if allowed by the doctor, if not, the salt must be omitted), set it upon the fire, and when beginning to boil, skim, and let it simmer at the corner of the fire four hours; twenty minutes before passing, again skim off all the fat, and add ten large leaves of sorrel, or twenty small, one cabbage-lettuce, and a handful of chervil, and when done pass it through a sieve, when it is ready for use. This broth is very cooling and nutritious when taken cold, as it is then quite a jelly; vermicelli, rice, &c., may be added when served hot, and the veal and calf's foot is very excellent, eaten with parsley-and-butter or sharp sauce; but should the patient require any, it must be quite plain, with a little of the broth and only the gelatinous part of the foot.

The above also makes an excellent dinner soup, and if put in a cool place, would keep a week in winter and three days in summer.

64. *Soyer's new way of making Beef Tea.*—Cut a pound of solid beef into very small dice, which put into a stewpan, with a small pat of butter, a clove, two button onions, and a salt-spoonful of salt, stir the meat round over the fire for a few minutes, until it produces a thin gravy, then add a quart of water, and let it simmer at the corner of the fire for half an hour, skimming off every particle of fat, when done pass through a sieve. I have always had a great objection to passing broth through a cloth, as it frequently quite spoils its flavor.

The same, if wanted plain, is done by merely omitting the vegetables, salt, and clove; the butter cannot be objectionable, as it is taken out in skimming, pearl-barley, vermicelli, rice, &c., may be served in it if required.

65. *Real Essence of Beef.*—Take one pound of solid beef from the rump, a steak would be the best, cut it into thin slices, which lay upon a thin trencher, and scrape quite fine with a large and sharp knife (as quickly as possible, or the juice of the meat would partially soak into the wood, your meat thus losing much of its strengthening quality), when like sausage-meat put it into a stewpan or saucepan, and stir over the fire five or ten minutes, until thoroughly warmed through, then add a pint of water, cover the stewpan as tightly as possible, and let it remain close to the fire or in a warm oven for twenty minutes, then pass it through a sieve, pressing the meat with a spoon to extract all the essence.

I beg to observe that here you have the real juice of the meat; but if wanted stronger, put only half instead of one pint of water; seasoning may be introduced, that is, a little salt, sugar, and cloves, but no vegetables, as they would not have time to cook, thus leaving a raw, bad flavor.

66. *Pure Osmazome, or Essence of Meat.*—Take two pounds of the flesh of any animal or bird (the older the better for obtaining the true flavor), as free from sinew as possible, and mince it well; place it in a Florence oil-flask, and cork it; put this in a saucepan filled with cold water, leaving the neck uncovered; place it on the side of the fire until the water arrives at 160° Fahr., at which temperature it must remain for twenty minutes; then remove it, and strain the contents through a tammie, pressing the meat gently with a spoon; should it require to be kept for some time, put the liquor in a basin or cup, which place in the saucepan; subject it to a boiling heat until it is reduced to a consistency like treacle, removing the scum; this, when cold, will become solid, and will keep for any number of years. Osmazome is known under various names in different cookery books, as "fumet, essence," &c., but which are obtained in a different way, which causes the gelatine to be produced with the osmazome; but, by the above plan, it is left in the meat, and the osmazome, with a small quantity of the albumen, is extracted, and the albumen is afterwards removed as the scum.

67. *Chicken Broth.*—Put half a raw chicken into a stewpan, with a quart of water, a little leek and celery, with a salt-spoonful of salt, and a few sprigs of parsley (if allowed), set the stewpan upon the fire; when boiling, skim well, and let simmer upon the corner for one hour; pass it through a sieve, and it is ready for use.

The chicken would eat very nice with a little maître d'hôtel sauce, or any other from that series would do for the parlor, that is, when the patient is not allowed to eat it.

For a change, chicken-broth in the following way is very nutritious; that is, after having passed the broth through a sieve, pour it back again into the stewpan, which place over the fire; moisten a teaspoonful of flour in a cup with a little cold broth or water, and when quite smooth pour it into the broth whilst boiling, stirring quickly, let simmer a quarter of an hour, and it is ready. Mutton or veal-broth may also be varied the same.

68. *Eel Broth, very strengthening.*—Take a small eel, which skin as described, and wash well, then cut into slices, which put into a small saucepan, just covered with water, add a little salt, a few sprigs of parsley, two button onions, and a clove; let it simmer very gently until the eels are tender, when skim off all the fat, pass the broth through a very fine sieve into a cup: it is then ready to serve when required, but a spoonful only should be taken at a time.

A patient is sometimes allowed to take part of the fish, which being so much boiled, constitutes a lighter food than eels are in general; a little melted butter and parsley might be served with them.

69. *Lait de Poule, French remedy for colds.*—May be made from any of the foregoing broths, and for colds is excellent. Break a fresh egg, separate the white from the yolk, put the yolk in a basin, with a quarter of a gill of good cream or milk, which mix well with a spoon, have half a pint of broth boiling, which pour gradually over the egg and cream, mixing it (as you pour the broth) with a wooden spoon; it is then ready, and ought to be taken when going to bed, if only for a cold.

70. *Sweet Lait de Poule.*—This is also reckoned very good for a cold. Put two yolks of eggs into a cup, with two teaspoonfuls of pounded sugar, a few drops of orange-flower water, or the eighth part of the rind of a fresh lemon grated, beat them well together for ten minutes, then pour boiling water gradually over, keeping it stirred, until the cup is nearly full. Drink this very hot when in bed; I can strongly recommend it from experience.

71. *Riz au Lait, or Rice Milk*, is a very favorite food, or soup; in France many persons make their suppers from it, even when in a state of perfect health. Proceed as follows: wash a tablespoonful of good rice in water, which drain and put into a stewpan, with a pint of milk, upon the fire, and when boiling, place it at the corner to simmer, until the rice is quite tender, but for invalids, must be in a pulp; sweeten with a little sugar, and it is quite ready.

72. *Rice Milk seasoned.*—Proceed exactly as in the last, but when the rice is quite tender add an ounce of butter, two teaspoonfuls of sugar, and a little salt, stir well together, and it is then ready; this must neither be too thick nor too thin, but about the thickness of well-made gruel; in France they always add a few drops of orange-flower water, but that depends upon taste. These two last are very nutritious, especially after a long illness.

73. *Vermicelli au Lait.*—Boil a pint of milk, and when boiling add sufficient ver-

micelli to make it about the thickness of the last article; it may be served quite plain if required, or seasoned as for the riz au lait, but omitting the orange-flower water.

74. *Semoulina au Lait.*—Boil a pint of milk, and when boiling add a tablespoonful of semoulina, stirring it gently, to prevent its becoming lumpy; let it simmer twenty minutes, and serve either plain or seasoned, as for the riz au lait.

75. *Tapioca au Lait.*—Proceed exactly as in the last, but it will require rather longer to simmer before the tapioca is tender; and, by way of change, add a little grated lemon-peel, or a glass of white wine, if allowed by the doctor, or season as for the last.

76. *Arrow-root.*—Put two teaspoonfuls of arrow-root, which mix gradually with enough water or milk, stirring it with a spoon, let it boil a few minutes, and if made with milk, add only a little butter, sugar, and salt, or serve plain; but if made with water, add the eighth part of the rind of a fresh lemon to boil with it; when done add a glass of port or sherry, sugar, a little salt, and a small piece of butter, unless prohibited.

77. *Gruel.*—Put two tablespoonfuls of oatmeal or prepared groats into a stew-pan, and by degrees add a pint of water, mixing smoothly with a wooden spoon, place it upon the fire, keeping it well stirred, until it has boiled a couple of minutes, when pour it into a basin, add half a salt-spoonful of salt, two teaspoonfuls of brown sugar, and two ounces of butter, the latter especially, if for a cold in the chest, even more than that quantity, if the stomach is strong enough to bear it.

Gruel when properly made ought to adhere rather thickly to the back of the spoon, but not to be pasty; it ought, likewise, to be eaten directly it is made, or it becomes thick and unpleasant to eat; if required plain, omit all the seasoning; it might also be made of milk.

78. *Gruel from Scotch Groats.*—Proceed as above, but adding rather more water, and boiling a few minutes longer; many people prefer eating it with the rough groats in it, but if objectionable, place a small clean sieve over the basin you intend serving it in, pass the gruel through, and season as in the last. Some people add spirits or wine; but that I should never recommend any one to do, unless by the doctor's orders, and that would be but very seldom, especially as regards spirits.

79. *Sago Gruel.*—Put two tablespoonfuls of sago into a small saucepan, which moisten gradually with a pint of cold water, set it over a slow fire, keeping it stirred until becoming rather thickish and clear, similar to a jelly, then add a little grated nutmeg and sugar according to taste, and serve; half a pat of butter might also be added with the sugar, or it might be made with new milk, and a little salt added, and a glass of wine in either case makes it more palatable.

80. *Arrow-root, Transparent Jelly.*—Put a good teaspoonful of arrow-root into a basin, which mix smoothly with two spoonfuls of water, then add enough boiling water to make it about the consistency of starch, stirring all the time, pour it into a stewpan, and stir over the fire until it has boiled two minutes; add a little cream, a small glass of wine, and a little sugar, and serve.

81. *French Panada, for aged people, invalids, and children.*—Break a stale penny

roll into a saucepan, in which pour just sufficient water to cover the bread, stir well over the fire, allowing it to boil five minutes, then add half a teaspoonful of salt, and two ounces of fresh butter, mix them, and take from the fire; have one yolk of egg well beaten, with two tablespoonfuls of milk (if handy) or water, which pour into the panada, stirring very quickly for half a minute, it is then ready to pour into a basin and serve. Any common bread would do for panada, but would not eat so light as when made from a roll.

I knew a very aged lady in France who accustomed herself to eat a basin of panada every night, a few minutes previous to going to bed, for a period of eighteen years, which will prove that, although very substantial in appearance, it must be very easily digested.

Panada ought to be rather thicker than gruel, and may likewise be made of milk, but water is preferable, especially when for bilious people.

82. *Barley Water.*—Put half a gallon of water into a very clean saucepan, with two ounces of clean (but unwashed) pearl barley, when boiling, carefully skim it with a tablespoon, and add half the rind of a small lemon, let it boil until the barley is quite tender; sweeten with half an ounce of white sugar, strain it through a fine hair sieve, and use when required. The juice of half a lemon in some cases may also be introduced.

83. *Rice Water.*—Put a quart of water to boil in a saucepan, with a handful of clean rice (but not washed), place it upon the fire, and let boil gently until the rice is quite in a pulp, then pass it through a hair sieve into a jug, pressing as much of the rice through as possible, and when getting cold, sweeten moderately with honey, which will make it very palatable; it should be drunk lukewarm.

84. *A New Drink.*—Put half a gallon of water upon the fire, and when boiling, have ready four pippin apples (quite ripe), cut each apple into eight slices, without peeling them, throw them into the water, which keep boiling until the apples are quite soft, pass the water through a sieve, pressing the apples gently against the side of the sieve, but not rubbing them through, add enough honey to make it a little sweetish, and drink lukewarm.

Two apples thrown into the rice-water and boiled the same would be a great improvement. People in good health would much enjoy such drink, during the summer especially; as also would poor people in the country, where apples are plentiful. Any kind of apples would suit, and brown sugar instead of honey, or even no sugar at all.

85. *Cooling Drink.*—Bake four or six apples, without peeling them; when done and quite hot, put them into a jug, and pour over three pints of boiling water; cover the jug over with paper, and when cold it is ready for use; a spoonful of honey or brown sugar added makes it very palatable.

86. *Almond Water.*—Put five ounces of sweet and two of bitter almonds into a saucepan, with a pint of hot water, set them upon the fire, and, when boiling, strain them upon a sieve, take off their skins, and set them in spring water to cool, then dry them upon a cloth, pound them in a mortar until very fine, adding a few

drops of water occasionally, to prevent their becoming oily, set a pint of syrup to boil, when throw in the mashed almonds; boil together a minute, then set it at the corner to simmer for a quarter of an hour; it is then ready to pass through a fine sieve for use. When required, add any quantity of cold water you please to make it palatable, according to taste or direction.

87. *Barley Lemonade.* —Put a quarter of a pound of sugar into a small stewpan, with half a pint of water, which boil about ten minutes, or until forming a thickish syrup; then add the rind of a fresh lemon and the pulp of two; let it boil two minutes longer, when add two quarts of barley-water, from which you have omitted the sugar and lemon; boil five minutes longer, pass it through a hair sieve into a jug, which cover with paper, making a hole in the centre to let the heat through; when cold, it is ready for use; if put cold into a bottle and well corked down, it would keep good several days.

Barley Orangeade is made the same, substituting the rind and juice of oranges; the juice of a lemon, in addition, is an improvement, when taken as a refreshing beverage.

88. *A Refreshing Beverage.* —Slice two oranges and one lemon, which put into a jug, with two ounces of sugarcandy, over which pour one quart of boiling water; stir it occasionally until cold, when drink it a little at a time, as often as ordered by the medical attendant. This drink is also very excellent for persons in health, especially in warm weather.

89. *Raspberry Vinegar Beverage.* —Put two tablespoonfuls of raspberry vinegar into a cup, over which pour half a pint of boiling water; when cold, use it as you may be instructed or when necessary; any kind of fruit syrup would answer the same purpose, and be equally as good, that is, currants, cherries, strawberries, mulberries, &c.

90. *A very Strengthening Drink.* —Put a teacupful of pearl-barley into a saucepan, with three pints of cold water, the rind of a lemon and a small piece of cinnamon; boil the whole very gently until the barley becomes tender, when strain it through a fine sieve, and sweeten with a spoonful of treacle: if treacle should be objectionable, honey or sugar will do.

91. *Fresh Fruit Water.* —Fresh fruits, when in season, are very preferable to syrups, which are but seldom well made, except at some of the first confectioners or Italian warehouses.

Pick a bottle of fresh raspberries or strawberries, whichever you may require, rub them through a sieve into a basin, which mix well with half a pint of syrup, the juice of a lemon, and a quart of spring water; pass it through a fine hair sieve, and put it by in a jug for use; both the syrup and water may either be increased or diminished according to taste.

Red or white currant waters are made precisely the same, only omitting the lemon, the currants themselves being sufficiently sharp.

92. *Cherry Draught.* —Choose a pound of good fleshy cherries, from which take the stalk and stones, have a pint of syrup boiling, into which throw them, to boil

as fast as possible for ten minutes, then take them from the fire, and add a good wine-glassful of Madeira or sherry, and a quart of boiling water; put it into a jug, with a cup over; when cold, pass it through a sieve, and it is ready for use: the wine may be omitted if not required. A drink of the same description may likewise be made from mulberries, but then a little lemon-juice must be added.

93. *Arrow-root Water.*—Put half a gallon of water to boil with two apples, the same as in No. 84, with the addition of a stick of cinnamon; let the whole boil half an hour, then mix two large spoonfuls of arrow-root with half a pint of cold water, very smoothly, and pour it into the boiling water: let the whole boil ten minutes, and pass it through a sieve; when cold, it will drink light and thickish.

94. *French Herb Broth.*—This is a very favorite beverage in France, as well with people in a state of health as with invalids, especially in the spring, when the herbs are young and green. Put a quart of water to boil, but have previously prepared about forty leaves of sorrel, a cabbage-lettuce, and ten sprigs of chervil, the whole well washed; when the water is boiling, throw in the above, with the addition of a teaspoonful of salt and half an ounce of fresh butter; cover your saucepan close, and let them simmer a few minutes, then pass it through a sieve or colander. This is to be drunk cold, especially in the spring of the year, after the change from winter. I generally drink about a quart per day for a week, at that time; but if for sick people, it must be made less strong of herbs, and taken a little warm. To prove that it is wholesome, we have only to refer to the instinct which teaches dogs to eat grass at that season of the year. I do not pretend to say that it would suit persons in every malady, because the doctors are to decide upon the food and beverage of their patients, and study its changes as well as change their medicines.

95. *Dry Plum Beverage.*—Put a quart of water in a saucepan upon the fire, and, when boiling, throw in twelve fresh dry French plums, and let them boil twenty minutes, then pour them in a basin with the liquor to cool; when cold, take out the plums, which put into a basin; add two tablespoonfuls of brown sugar and a very small quantity of port wine. They are excellent to eat, and the liquor to drink.

96. *Figs and Apple Beverage.*—Have two quarts of water boiling, into which throw six fresh dry figs, previously opened, and two apples, previously cut into six or eight pieces each; let the whole boil together twenty minutes, then pour them together into a basin to cool, then pass through a sieve; drain the figs, which will be also good to eat.

97. *Stewed Plums.*—Put twelve French plums in a stewpan, with a spoonful of brown sugar, a gill of water, a little cinnamon, and some thin rind of a lemon; let them stew twenty minutes, then pour them in a basin until cold, take them from their syrup and eat them dry. They are sometimes stewed in wine and water, either port, sherry, or claret.

98. *Baked Apples* are very much used by invalids: have a common yellow dish, such as you frequently see in farmhouses, into which put about twelve apples (previously well wiped) and about a gill of water, and put them in a hot oven for half an hour, or rather more should the apples be large; when well done, take them out to get cold upon the dish, and eat them cold, either with powdered lump or

moist sugar.

99. *Cooling Lemonade.*—Put a quart of water in a stewpan to boil, into which put two moist dried figs, each split in two; let it boil a quarter of an hour, then have ready the peel of a lemon, taken off rather thickly, and the half of the lemon cut in thin slices; throw them into the stewpan and boil two minutes longer; then pour it into a jug, which cover closely with paper until cold, then pass it through a sieve: add a teaspoonful of honey, and it is ready for use.

100. *Imperial, a cooling Drink for the Spring.*—Two ounces of cream of tartar, two lemons, juice and peel, four ounces of sugar; place in a stone jug, and pour about six quarts of boiling water; allow it to get cold, and bottle for use; or, instead of sugar, add three tablespoonfuls of raspberry vinegar, and six ounces of honey. This is excellent aerated-like soda water. Essence of ratafia, or any other, may be added, with about half a pint of pure spirit at proof, for those accustomed to spirits.

101. *Orangeade.*—Proceed as for lemonade, but using the whole of the orange, a little of the peel included, sweetening with sugar candy, and adding a teaspoonful of arrow-root mixed with a little cold water, which pour into the boiling liquid at the same time you put in the orange. The arrow-root makes it very delicate.

102. *Toast and Water.*—The ease and simplicity of making this popular drink is probably the cause of its not being well made one time in ten, that is, in private families; the bread is too much or too little done, or there is too much or not half enough water, or more or less bread; I venture to say that if any person would take the trouble to go from house to house, where there are patients, and taste toast and water at each, they would not find two of the same flavor, and perhaps not any of it properly made. To make it to perfection, proceed as follows: cut a piece of crusty bread, about a quarter of a pound in weight, place it upon a toasting-fork, and hold it about six inches from the fire; turn it often, and keep moving it gently until of a light yellow color, then place it nearer the fire, and when of a good brown chocolate color, put it into a jug, and pour three pints of boiling water over; cover the jug until cold, then strain it into a clean jug, and it is ready for use: never leave the toast in it, for in summer it would cause fermentation in a short time. I would almost venture that such toast and water as I have described would keep good a considerable time in bottles.

The idea that bread must be burnt black to make toast and water is quite a popular delusion, for nothing nourishing could come from it: if your house was burnt to ashes, it would be valueless; and the same with burnt bread, which merely makes the water black, but the nutriment of the bread, intended to relieve the chest, has evaporated in smoke by being burnt.

PUDDINGS FOR INVALIDS.

103. *Apple and Rice.*—Boil half an ounce of Carolina rice in a gill of milk until very tender, then add a very small piece of butter, sugar, a little cinnamon, and a grain of salt; then peel, core, and slice a middling-sized apple, which put into a stewpan, with a small piece of butter, a little sugar, and a drop of water, and stew it until tender; when done, put the apple in a small tart-dish, mix an egg with the rice, which pour over the apple, and bake ten minutes in a moderate oven; it may also be made quite plain, if preferred.

104. *Custard Pudding.*—Boil one pint of milk, with a small piece of lemon-peel and half a bay-leaf, for three minutes; then pour these on to three eggs, mix it with one ounce of sugar well together, and pour it into a buttered mould: steam it twenty-five minutes in a stewpan with some water (see No. 112), turn out on a plate and serve.

105. *Rice Puddings.*—Wash well two ounces of rice in some water, strain, then put it into a pint and a half of boiling milk, with a small piece of lemon-peel, cinnamon, and half a bay-leaf, tied together; let it boil gently, stirring it occasionally, until quite tender; then put to it one ounce of butter, a little grated nutmeg, a tablespoonful of sugar, and two eggs; pour it into a buttered tart-dish, and bake it half an hour.

106. *Macaroni Pudding.*—Blanch two ounces of Naples macaroni in some water for eight or ten minutes; strain it, add it to one pint of boiling milk, in which you have previously boiled a piece of lemon-peel, cinnamon, and one ounce of butter; when the macaroni is quite tender, add two eggs and sugar enough to sweeten it: steam it one hour in a stewpan, in a buttered tart-dish.

107. *Vermicelli Pudding.*—Boil one pint of milk, with a piece of lemon-peel, half a bay-leaf, and a piece of cinnamon, then add one ounce of vermicelli; when reduced to half, add two eggs, and a little sugar; pour these in a buttered mould, and steam it half an hour.

108. *Tapioca Pudding.*—Boil one pint of milk, with a piece of lemon-peel and a little cinnamon; then add two ounces of tapioca; reduce to half; add two eggs, and one ounce of butter; pour these in a buttered mould, and steam half an hour.

109. *Bread Pudding.*—Boil one pint of milk, with a piece of cinnamon and lemon-peel; pour it on two ounces of bread-crumbs; then add two eggs, half an ounce of currants, and a little sugar: steam it in a buttered mould for one hour.

110. *Cabinet Pudding.*—Boil one pint of milk, with a piece of lemon-peel, pour it on one ounce of sponge biscuit, let it soak half an hour, then add three eggs, half

an ounce of currants, and very little sugar: steam it in a buttered mould, lined with raisins, one hour.

111. *Bread and Butter Pudding.* —Butter a tart-dish well and sprinkle some currants all round it, then lay in a few slices of bread and butter; boil one pint of milk, pour it on two eggs well whipped, and then on the bread and butter; bake it in a hot oven for half an hour.

112. *A Small Bread Pudding.* —Cut an ounce of the crumb of bread into thin slices, with the least piece of butter spread over each, which place in a small tart-dish; then break an egg into a cup with a teaspoonful of sugar and a little powdered cinnamon, beat well; then add about six tablespoonfuls of boiled milk, mix well together, pour over the bread, and bake in a slow oven, or steam it, if preferred, by standing the dish in a stewpan containing about half a pint of water, that is, the water should be about half way up to the rim of the dish; set the stewpan (covered close) upon the fire, and let it slowly boil about ten minutes or longer, until the pudding is properly set, then take the cover from the stewpan, which let remain a few minutes longer upon the fire; then take out the pudding, wipe the dish, and serve.

Fish for Invalids. —Slips, soles, flounders, whitings, and smelts are the lightest of any fish, and upon that account more to be recommended to invalids in a state of convalescence.

113. *Whiting, plain boiled.* —Put two quarts of water into a small fish kettle, with about an ounce of salt; when boiling, put in the whiting, draw the kettle to the corner of the fire to keep it just simmering, and no more; a whiting of the ordinary size would take about ten minutes; when done, which you can tell by trying with the point of a knife whether it leaves the bone easily, take it up carefully, and dish it upon a clean napkin, with a few sprigs of parsley round; although the parsley is of course useless as far as the stomach is concerned, nothing can be more pleasing to an invalid than to see his meals carefully cooked and invitingly served.

At any time I prefer a whiting with the skin on, whether boiled, grilled, or fried; a little butter just melted, with a pinch of salt, and the least drop of lemon-juice added, is very excellent to eat as sauce with them. Should you purchase your fish in the country, it will of course require cleaning, by opening the belly and pulling out the gills and interior; but never wash these fish, merely wipe them with a cloth.

114. *Broiled Whiting.* —Having cleaned your whiting, and wiped it gently dry with a cloth, flour it all over lightly, rub the gridiron over with a little oil, lay the whiting upon it, and put it over a clear fire, but not too close, turn it carefully three or four times, and when it feels firm to the touch of the finger, it is done; if a large one, it will take about twenty minutes; sprinkle a little salt over, if required, and serve with plain melted butter, with a few drops of essence of anchovies in it.

115. *Sautéd Whitings.* —Put some fat or butter in a frying-pan, which place over a clear but moderate fire; have your whiting floured as in the last, and when the fat or butter is melted, lay it in the pan; let it sauté slowly until it is done, which try as in either of the last two; when done, drain it upon a cloth, sprinkle a little salt

over, and serve.

If fried, enveloped in bread-crumbs, dip the fish lightly into flour, then egg it all over with a paste-brush, and dip in some very fine bread-crumbs, and fry it rather longer, but do not let the fat get black, or it will give the fish a black, heavy appearance, and quite spoil the flavor. Fish fried in oil would have a much better appearance than when fried in fat, but probably would be objectionable to a weak stomach. They ought to be completely covered with the fat.

116. *Smelts* are very delicate fish, but ought never to be plain boiled; being confident of the good use they may be turned to as a diet for the sick, I shall here give two receipts for dressing them very plainly, yet still very palatable. Choose them rather large,—if so, two would be sufficient for a meal,—having previously drawn and cleansed them, put a gill of water into a small stewpan, with a little salt, a saltspoonful of powdered sugar, and four small sprigs of parsley; when boiling lay in your smelts, which let simmer five minutes, or more, if larger than usual, keeping the stewpan well covered; then take them out carefully, lay them upon a dish, and pour the broth over; both fish and broth are excellent. They may be cooked the same way in the oven.

Another way is to add a little arrow-root, mixed with a drop of cold water, to the above, when half cooked; it makes it very soothing to the chest. Be extremely careful not to let the fish or liquor burn at the bottom of the stewpan; there should be about three parts of the quantity of liquor when cooked as you first put in water, allowing one quarter to evaporate whilst boiling.

117. *Broiled Smelts.*—When cleansed and wiped dry with a cloth, dip them lightly into flour, and put them upon a gridiron over a slow fire, for five, or six minutes, turning them carefully when half done; serve plain, or with a little sauce, if allowed, as many patients are forbidden moist food. I can highly recommend any kind of white fish cooked in this manner; and it is well known that nothing in the way of food is more digestible than fish.

Water souchet of flounders, soles, and slips may also be served to invalids, by proceeding the same as above.

Meat, Game, and Poultry, of every kind, for invalids, ought to be served as free from fat as possible.

118. *A Mutton Chop.*—Choose one from a lean loin of mutton, or if one in the house rather fat cut the greater part of it off; your chop should be about six ounces in weight, and cut off an equal thickness; lay it upon a table, and beat it lightly with the flat part of your chopper, then lay it upon a gridiron, over a good clear fire; season with a little salt, if allowed, and turn it four or five times whilst broiling; it will require about eight minutes over a good fire, but of course longer over an indifferent one; if by pressing it with a knife it feels firm, it is done; serve upon a very hot plate, for if partly cold, the least fat would immediately set, and be very unpleasant, especially to a person unwell.

119. *Plain Mutton Cutlet, from the Neck.* — An invalid will frequently be tired of a mutton chop; and for my own part I must say a cutlet is far superior in flavor, and

has a much neater appearance; cut off a rib from the neck, of the same thickness as a mutton chop; cut away the skin upon each side of the bone, to the chine, which chop off; trim away the greater part of the fat, cut a piece at the end of the bone, which scrape off, leaving about half an inch of the bone bare; then beat it lightly with the flat of the chopper; season; broil and serve very hot, as in the last.

120. *Stewed Chop or Cutlet.*—Put it into a stewpan or small saucepan, with a pint of water, and a little salt and sugar; let it stew as gently as possible from an hour and a half to two hours, skim off all the scum and fat, and the patient may partake of both chop and broth; if seasoning is allowed, put a teaspoonful of pearl-barley, with a little celery, leek, and turnip, cut up very small, into the stewpan with the water, when you first put the chop on, and proceed as before; serve the broth in a soup basin, with the chop in it; should the meat happen to be tough, let it stew rather longer; the broth should be reduced to about half a pint.

121. *Beef, Rump Steak.*—The tenderest part of the rump should be selected, about half a pound, not cut too thick, and very even; place it upon your gridiron over a moderate fire, turning it frequently; when done, sprinkle a little salt over; ten minutes would cook it thoroughly, but if wanted underdone, as in many cases where the patient only sucks the gravy, less time must be allowed.

122. *Stewed Beef.*—Put the same quantity of beef as in the last into a saucepan, with a quart of water, which place over the fire, and when beginning to boil, well skim, then add a little celery, turnip, and carrot, the whole weighing about an ounce, and cut very small, let stew gently about three hours, by which time the broth will be reduced to one quarter; skim all the fat off carefully; serve the meat upon a plate, and the broth in a basin.

123. *Lamb Chops or Cutlets.*—Proceed as just described for mutton, but being more delicate, they will require but little more than half the time to cook.

124. *Lambs' Feet* are very nutritious; purchase them ready cleaned; lay them ten minutes in boiling water, by doing which you will be able to draw out the leg-bone with facility; then put them in a stewpan (two would be sufficient), and pour over a pint of water with which you have mixed smoothly a tablespoonful of flour, and half a teaspoonful of salt; place them upon the fire, stirring frequently until boiling, when add a small onion, with a celery, parsley, and parsnip; boil gently for two hours, and when done, serve plain upon a plate, or with a little melted butter and parsley poured over. By using a little white broth from any meat instead of water, you make a delicious soft soup, which may be partaken of freely.

Calves' feet are dressed in the same manner, but using a double proportion of everything, and stewing them double the time; they are served precisely the same.

POULTRY FOR INVALIDS.

125. *Roast Chicken.* — Procure a nice plump chicken, which draw and truss, and cut the sinews; pass the spit through under the skewer as usual, and set it down before a clear fire; after being there five minutes, have ready a pat of butter, in the bowl of a wooden spoon, with which rub the chicken all over; if the fire is too fierce, put it back a short distance, that it may roast of a yellowish-brown color; when a light smoke arises from the chicken, which will be in about twenty minutes from the time it was put down, it is done; but to be quite sure whether a bird is done, the better way is to press it lightly, with your finger and thumb; should it feel quite set, it is sufficiently cooked.

126. *Boiled Chicken.* — Put a quart of water to boil in a saucepan, with a saltspoonful of salt, and two ounces of butter; when boiling, lay in the chicken, which keep gently simmering for twenty minutes, when it will be done.

By adding a few vegetables of each description to the water, and straining it when you take out the chicken, you have a very excellent broth either for the sick or healthy, especially after skimming off the fat you add a little vermicelli, which must be boiled in it five minutes.

As it is very improbable that a sick person would eat the whole of a chicken at once, I have annexed a few receipts, by which a chicken would suffice for four meals.

First, put a tablespoonful of rice in a stewpan, with half a pint of light broth; let it boil gently until the rice is in pulp, then put in the wing or leg of the previously-cooked chicken, which let remain to warm about five minutes; should the rice be too dry, add a little more broth; serve the fowl and rice together upon a hot plate. Secondly, if wanted plain, set it in a stewpan, with a few spoonfuls of stock, and let it warm gently. Thirdly, it may be folded in a sheet of paper lightly oiled, and warmed very gently upon a gridiron. Or fourthly, plain broiled upon a gridiron, and served with a little light gravy.

127. *Partridge.* — Proceed in every manner to roast as just directed for the chicken; a young one would require about ten minutes, or an old one fifteen, but then the breast only ought to be eaten; whatever remains may be served in either of the ways directed for chickens.

128. *Pigeons* may be roasted the same as partridges, but would not require so long. A pigeon may also be stewed as follows: — Put half a pint of mutton-broth into a stewpan, with a pigeon trussed as for boiling, let it stew gently twenty minutes, if young; both the pigeon and broth ought to be partaken of. Pigeons may

also be broiled, by cutting them open from the bottom of the breast to the joint of the wings, but not separating them; rub over with a little butter, broil twenty minutes over a moderate fire, and serve with a little gravy.

129. *Pulled Fowl.* — With the remainder of a roast or boiled fowl or chicken you may make a very light dish, by pulling off all the flesh with a fork, and putting it into a stewpan, then in another stewpan place all the bones (previously broken small with a chopper), with a little parsley, salt, sugar, and half a pint of water; let it boil gently until the water has reduced to a gill, then strain it over the flesh of the chicken in the other stewpan, which place over the fire until quite hot, and serve; should it be too thin, a small piece of butter and flour rubbed together may be added, and boiled a minute. Old or young fowls may be used, as it is not always convenient to get a young fowl, especially in the country, where everything must be turned to account and properly used: you would proceed with an old fowl the same as for a chicken, but stewing it three times as much, and adding more water in proportion; it would be here impossible to name the exact time required, as the fluctuation is so great, but by feeling the thigh of the fowl with the finger and thumb, you may ascertain, for if done sufficiently it will feel tender to the touch, and leave the bone with ease.

CULINARY CORRESPONDENCE.

LETTER NO. VI.

DEAREST ELOISE,—I here inclose you the last receipt which I intend to give you for invalids. You will, no doubt, fancy that my diet is extravagant; but let me teach you that when you must pay the doctor's bill, which I consider an extra and painful tax upon humanity, it is ours and their duty to try to restore health as soon as possible, which my receipts might, if well coupled with the science of a medical man, cause a prompt restoration, and have the desired effect of increasing the butcher's bill by diminishing that of the doctor. But I must also tell you that I intend this part of our little work, if ever published, to be useful to all classes of society, and that, among those receipts, the rich as well as the humble, may partake and benefit by them in selecting according to their means and their requirements. I am confident that you will agree with me that even here I have closely studied the rules of economy.

I shall therefore close the sick-room door to open the one of the parlor, and to witness the merry faces of the million who have abandoned their industrious occupations for the day, and partake, in the family circle, their simple but substantial Sunday meal. I always used to say, when in business, that he who works well deserves to live well,—I do not mean to say extravagantly, but that devoting one hour a day to their principal meal ought to be classified as a matter of business in regard to economy. We, therefore, must be very positive upon this important question, and make them perceive that dining well once or twice a week is really unworthy of such a civilized and wealthy country as ours, where provisions cannot be excelled by any other, both in regard to quantity and quality. Yours, etc.

HORTENSE.

LETTER NO. VII.

My dear Mrs. B.—Your observation upon the way many people live in this country is no doubt very correct, but do you not think that if you were not quite so abrupt on the subject, we should probably be more likely to succeed in bringing our friends round to your style of management; of which, for my part, I very much approve. But as it is a matter of importance, I should like you to describe in your next communication what are the principal and most useful joints in a family, and to discourse on them, in pointing out the good which may be achieved, and the evils to be avoided. Ever yours, &c.

ELOISE.

LETTER NO. VIII.

Many compliments to you, my dear Mrs. L.

At your request I here inclose the list you require, and which will show you how circumscribed the middle classes are in respect to the variation of their meals, in the way of meat and manner of cooking it. I do not disapprove of your idea in wishing me here to give a series or list of those provisions; but, on the other hand, I must tell you frankly my opinion, it being a subject which for some years I have made a study, indeed quite a hobby. If I am wrong, let any one who knows better correct me; you will allow I am always open to conviction and improvement, no matter how trifling, which often leads to an important one.

I shall therefore name all joints of meat which, though numerous, offer but little variation when continually dressed the same way, and observe that everybody has the bad habit of running only upon a few which are considered the best. They are as follow:

Those in beef are the sirloin, ribs, round, silver-side, aitch-bone.

In mutton—leg, saddle, haunch, loin.

Lamb—fore-quarter and leg.

Veal—fillet, loin.

Pork—leg, sparerib, loin.

Every one of these joints are of the most expensive parts, because generally used, although many of the other parts are equally as good, as I shall prove to you, in the receipts which I shall write for the dinner, what can be done in the way of made dishes out of those parts which are rarely or never used in this country by the middle classes, which will more clearly develope to you my ideas on the subject Besides, there is this advantage, that if a small tradesman were to follow these receipts, and buy every other time he goes to the butcher what he now considers a second-class joint, he would not only be conferring a public benefit, but also one on himself, and be the means of diminishing the price of those now considered the first class, which at the present moment bear too high a price in proportion, but which his pride causes him to purchase.

To prove to you that my argument is correct, look carefully over the inclosed list, which contains all the joints that are cut from beef, veal, mutton, lamb, pork, and you will find that ten of the prime are in daily use to one of the other, and principally for a want of the knowledge of cookery; leaving the science of cooking our food to a fierce or slow fire, or plunging our expensive provisions into an ocean of boiling water, which is thrown away, after having absorbed a great portion of the succulence of the meat. Try the receipt for the Pot-au-feu; taste the broth and eat the meat, and tell me which plan you consider the best. Do not think that I object to our plain joint, because, now and then, I am rather partial to them; but why not manage to make use of the broth, by diminishing the quantity of water, and simmering them, instead of galloping them at a special railway-train speed? Were the middle classes only but slightly acquainted with the domestic cookery of France, they would certainly live better and less expensively than at present, very often, four or five different little made dishes may be made from the remains of a large Sunday's joint, instead of its appearing on the table of a wealthy tradesman for several days cold, and often unsightly, and backed by a bottle of variegated-colored pickles, made with pyroligneous acid, which sets my teeth on edge merely in thinking of it, and balanced by a steaming dish of potatoes, which, seen through the parlor window by the customers in the shop, would make them think there was a grand gastronomic festivity taking place at Mr. A.'s or B.'s, the butterman or greengrocer; this may be excusable once or twice, on a hot summer's day, with an inviting salad, seasoned with merely salt, pepper, oil, and vinegar, but the continual repetition of that way of living in winter is, I consider, a domestic crime.

You will, perhaps, say that, in large firms, where forty or fifty, or more young men dine every day, or even in public establishments still more numerous, many professed cooks would be required to dress the dinner, if my plan was adopted; not at all, if the kitchen is properly constructed: but in these establishments, joints, of necessity, must be the principal viand, and there is very little left; what there is, is consumed cold for supper; but even there an amelioration might take place, although only a plain joint, either boiled or roasted, roasted or boiled, which is generally the yearly bill of fare, and so simple, yet seldom well done, and often badly, which, in a large establishment, must create great waste, and make bad food out of good meat, and that for want of care or a little more knowledge, which may appear to you but a trifling matter, but not so to thousands of poor old people, with toothless gums and fatigued stomachs, made comfortable within walls erected by the good feelings of government, or by public charity. I have often thought, when visiting these establishments, that a professed cook ought to be appointed, as well as a medical man, to visit all such in the metropolis, not only to inspect the quality of the provisions, but superintend the arrangements of the dietary table, and see that the viands are properly cooked, and thus correct the lamentable ignorance which exists at the present day; I am confident that tons of meat are daily wasted in such institutions throughout the country, which, if well employed, would feed a great part of the starving poor of the United Kingdom. The same system ought to be adopted in all the provincial towns; and, if it was in existence, we should not have to deplore such lamentable scenes which we had latterly to witness at Tooting, where, no doubt, many were to blame; for, by the calculation I have made, the allowance, though rather limited, was amply large enough to allow for good provisions, and leave sufficient remuneration for any reasonable and not covetous man. Why should not these poor children be watched over, and made as comfortable in every respect as the wish of those who pay to support them require? besides, it has an effect upon after generations; for upon the food at the period of growth depends the nature of the mind at a more advanced age, as well as the stature of the man. Do we not evince our care to objects of the brute creation, and feed, with the greatest attention, the race-horse? compare him with others of his species not so humanely treated, and note the difference: so it is with the human race; and I might almost say the prosperity of a country depends upon the food of its youth. You will perhaps think that I am rather sharp in my remarks, and probably longer than is required, but still it will be gratifying to both of us, should we find that these remarks prove beneficial to such establishments as above-mentioned; and it is only by giving notoriety to these important details, and being positive in exposing the truth, that we can be believed and followed, and you must not mind displeasing the few, if you are to be useful to the many. Forever, &c.

HORTENSE.

LETTER NO. IX.

MY DEAR HORTENSE,—After the receipt of your last observations, which, on first seeing, I thought too long, but after having read them over again, I am convinced that I shall not be able to shorten them; at all events, there is a great deal of truth in them, and, as you justly say, they are the observations of a person who has constantly studied domestic comfort and economy; I shall therefore copy them in the journal just as you send them to me. Truly yours,

ELOISE.

LETTER NO. X.

MY DEAR ELOISE,—I am glad to hear that you will not alter any of my last copy sent, because I assure you I wrote with a full conviction that I was right, and from facts which experience alone can engrave on the memory; but, however, we will now proceed: but I think it will be necessary to alter our original intention, namely, in order to save any confusion, to class all the receipts for the dinner together, and thus form a large bill of fare, and follow, on a small plan, what M. Soyer, of the Reform Club, has done on a large scale, in his 'Gastronomic Regenerator,' by which the most inexperienced hands may easily provide a large or small dinner adapted for all classes, without committing a blunder, and thus make a selection from soups, different dishes of fish, and an innumerable number of removes; entrées, roasts, savory dishes, vegetables, sweets, dessert, &c., and having chosen one or two of each series, and, on referring to the receipt, an idea of their cost, within a few pence of the market-price, may be gained.

Let me know, dear, by return of post, if you approve of my new idea, as it is rather deviating from our original one; but observe, that having so very distinctly given the Breakfast Receipts, and also for Invalids, it will be more clearly understood than by repeating the same over and over again, which would be unavoidable if following our first proposition. Yours truly, in haste,

HORTENSE.

LETTER NO. XI.

MY DEAR HORTENSE,—Never were you inspired by a better idea respecting your new plan; it is so clearly explained, that I fancy our labor is over; but I must tell you that, on the receipt of your last, I wrote to M. Soyer, to inquire if he would object to our taking a few hints from his "Kitchen at Home," which forms the last part of his work. His answer was immediate, short, and as follows:

"DEAR MADAM,—It would be entirely deviating from the preface of my

'Gastronomic Regenerator' to refuse you anything in my power; and as your simple demand lies within that scope, you are quite welcome to take a few hints, if you require them for your little work, from the part entitled 'My Kitchen at Home.'

"Wishing your exertions may be well appreciated, I am, dear madam, most sincerely, your humble and devoted,

"Reform Club.

A. Soyer."

As you have his book, you, no doubt, know to which part he alludes. He says, in his preface, that he has made it a rule never to refuse ladies anything in his power; so far he has kept his word with us: so you may, dearest, if you require, make use of his offer. I shall expect, by the next post, the commencement of the Dinner Receipts, which I am confident you will make as simple and as short as possible. With kindest regards, yours,

ELOISE.

ROASTING, BAKING, BOILING, STEWING, BRAISING, FRYING, SAUTÉING, BROILING.

ROASTING being the most general in use, we will first describe it, although not that which was first put in practice in cooking, it being evidently an improvement on broiling: we can easily understand how, in the early primitive times, man, finding that his food got covered with the ashes with which he cooked his meat, he would invent a species of grate upon which he could raise the fire, and cook his meat before it: this primitive mode of cooking has lasted, in many countries, up to the present day, and even in London to within a few years; for I remember seeing, in the old Goldsmith's Hall, a fire-place, consisting of stages, on which was laid the wood, and when the meat, &c., was spitted and arranged before it, the wood was lighted, and a man turned the spits. (It was, no doubt, from arranging the wood thus in stages that the name of range was derived.) In many noblemen's castles and ecclesiastical establishments, dogs were kept to turn the spit, from whence we have those of the name of turnspit; whilst in others, where there happened to be a person of a mechanical turn of mind, they applied a water-wheel to the purpose, and the water from it formed a stream in the kitchen, which served as a reservoir for live fish. Different opinions exist as to the mode and time required for roasting, but this must all depend upon the nature of the fire and the meat. In the Receipts will be found the time which each requires. My plan is to make up as large a fire as the nature of the grate will allow, because I can place my joint near or not, as may be required, and thus obtain every degree of heat.

BAKING is a branch of the art of cooking which, although one of the oldest, is the least understood. (As I shall have to refer to this subject again, I will give the reason why in a future letter.) It is performed in various kinds of air-tight chambers, called ovens, the best of which have the same form as in the time of the Egyptians. Previous to the art of baking being practised, boiled pulse and corn were the food of the people; even Rome contained no bakers until near six hundred years after it was founded. Of late years, great improvements have been made in the construction of ovens for baking of meat, called roasting ovens, which cause great economy in the expenditure of fuel; and, in large public establishments, where a number of the same kind of joints are required, it is the best plan of cooking. In the Receipts will be found the time required by each for baking, but, in a general way, for meat, hot ovens are the best; for poultry, not so hot as meat; and pastry, according to its kind. In using dishes or utensils for the oven, they ought, if of metal, to be of galvanized iron, and separate ones for meat and fish.

BOILING is the next branch of the art which is of the most importance and appears the most simple, yet, at the same time, the most difficult, and is a subject upon which, if I were to dilate, would occupy a good quarto volume; it is one of those easy things which it is supposed everybody can do, and therefore no attention is paid to it, and it is generally done badly. According to the way in which it is done, meat may be rendered hard and tough or tender, lose or retain its flavor or nourishment; great difference of opinion exists amongst medical men which are the easiest of digestion—roasted or boiled meats. I say it is a subject quite impossible to decide, as it must depend upon the different constitutions and climate; for we might as well say that the food of the Esquimaux is adapted for the native of Italy.

STEWING ought to be the best understood, on account of its economy; pieces of coarse meat, subjected to stewing, if properly done, become tender, as the gelatinous parts become partly dissolved; it should be done slowly, the pan partly uncovered, and frequently skimmed. Great cleanliness should be observed in all the vessels used for stewing.

BRAISING is the next and most important part of the art of cooking, and, like the sauté, belongs entirely to the French school, from whom it takes its name, *braise* being the remains of wood burnt in the oven, or live charcoal: and as this plan of cookery requires the action of the fire under and over the braising-pan, which is air-tight, in order that the aromatic flavor arising from its contents may be imbibed by the meat or poultry, and give it that succulence so much esteemed by epicures. The braise is put on the cover, which, in some cases, is made deep on purpose to hold it. Its origin is stated to be owing to a gastronomic society which was formerly in existence in Paris, whose object was to benefit and improve the art of cookery, and who offered a reward of a silver gridiron to any culinary artist who would discover a new mode of dressing a turkey. Although a gridiron was, no doubt, intended to be used, yet a young artist named La Gacque, warmed by the offer, directed his imagination to quite a different mode, and used the pan instead of the gridiron, and thus composed the braise, which was unanimously approved of by that scientific, gastronomic, and epicurean body, who awarded him the prize. The chief art in braising is to do it slowly, taking care that the ingredients are well-proportioned, receipts for which will be found in their proper place.

FRYING.—Of all the apparently simple modes of cookery there is none more so than that of frying, but yet how rare to meet with it done properly. I believe it is to be attributed, in a great measure, to the idea that, to do it well is expensive. I have therefore made a series of experiments upon a plan such as should be followed in every private house, and I am convinced that to do it well is cheaper than doing it badly; but, in the first place, we ought to consider, What is frying? It is the insertion of any substance into boiling oil, or grease, by which the surface of that substance becomes carbonized, and the heat which effects this object is sufficient to solidify the albumen and gelatine, or, more commonly speaking, cooked; to do this properly, the substance ought to be covered by the liquid, so that the heat acts all over it at the same time, or otherwise the osmazome, or gravy, will be dried out of that part which is not covered, and the succulence and flavor of the viand lost; or, should the liquid not be of that degree of heat which would carbonize the surface on the moment of its immersion, it would then enter into the substance, render it greasy, and destroy its flavor, which no degree of heat afterwards could remedy. Those articles which are fried are generally those which have a coating of materials (such as bread-crumbs and batter) which are quickly carbonized, and thus form a crust which prevents the grease penetrating, concentrates the liquids, and preserves the flavor of the article; the carbonization once effected, the fire should be immediately moderated, particularly if the article is large, in order that the interior may become properly solidified. All articles properly fried are generally much liked, as they are agreeable to the eye, and afford a pleasing variety.

The plan that I recommend you to adopt is, to obtain an iron or copper pan long enough for a good-sized sole, and 6 to 8 inches deep, and fill three to four inches of it with fat—the skimmings of the stock-pot, or, if that should not be sufficient, the kidney-fat of beef, cut up, melted, and strained. In wealthy establishments, lard, and, in some, bacon-fat melted is used, and, for some articles, olive oil, which can only be used once; but in our less luxurious homes I think the above is sufficient, besides, it has the advantage of not requiring that great attention which the other does. When you have the fat on, before immersing the substance you intend to fry, see that it is sufficiently hot by dipping your finger (not in the fat), but in a little water, and then hold it over the fat, so that a few drops go into it; if it spits and throws back the water, it is sufficiently hot: or, throw in a small dice of bread and take it out immediately; if it is firm or colored, it is hot enough: or, in frying of fish, before putting it in, lay hold of the head and dip the end of the tail, and, if it crisps it, then let the remainder go in. I have found, if due attention is paid to the pan to prevent it from burning, forty articles may be fried in it before it wants renewing; and I am certain it will be found cheaper than the common way of putting a little fat into the frying-pan and turning the sole over and over, for you are then almost certain of sending the grease up to the table, where it is not wanted. When the fat is not used, it should be emptied, whilst hot, through a sieve, into an earthen pipkin, and covered with paper to prevent the dust going in it. For the purpose of frying, an iron wire-basket, with a handle, is used, in which the object to be cooked is placed, and thus inserted in the liquid. The cost of this instrument is trifling.

SAUTEING.—You will perceive, dearest, by the following, that the word fried is often wrongly used in cookery instead of the word sauté, which process is totally different, and produces quite another effect on food. Sauté means anything cooked in a very small quantity of butter, oil, lard, or fat, one side of the article at a time, whilst the other requires about 100 times more of the above-named materials to cook properly. You will see, in these remarks, that it is not frying a pancake, omelette, or still less a chop, steak, or cutlet, but that they are sautéd; and how to explain that word, to use it instead of the misapplied word fry, puzzles me considerably, as I am quite ignorant of its origin as regards its application to cookery. All the researches I have made in English and French Dictionaries and Encyclopædias, have not enlightened me in the least on the subject. In French, it means to jump, hop, skip, understood by our boys at school, as well as by the grasshopper tribe, called in French sauterelles, from the word sauter, to jump. I well remember at school we had a French emigré for a dancing-master, who used to get into a passion when we did not dance to his professional taste; and used to say, in shaking his powdered wig, as holding his fiddle in one hand and his bow in the other, making all kinds of grimaces and contortions, which used to remind me of the principal figure in the group of the Laocoon, — "Mon dieu, mon dieu, young miss, vous sautez très bien, mais vous dansez fort mal;" which means, "You jump very well, but you dance very badly." It also reminds me of an expression made by a friend of ours from Havre, who was on a visit to us last November. Seeing some Guy Fawkes carried about the street, he asked me what it meant; when I told him, that in the year 1605, an attempt was made to destroy by gunpowder the King and Parliament in the House of Lords, as well as — —. "Oui, oui, madame, I know, I remember reading of it in English history; it was that little brute qui a voulut faire *sauter* le Parlement," replied he very quickly. "*Sauter, sauter,*" I said; "no, sir, not sauté—blow up." "Oui, oui, madame, I know, it is the same thing." "Same thing," replied I. This of course puzzled my culinary imagination still more; and I perceived, that if the word was translated to his meaning, it would sound most absurd and ridiculous; as, for example, on being at a festive board, and a polite young gentleman, or even your own husband, might gallantly offer to give you a *blow-up* cutlet, instead of a cotelette sauté, as they say in fashionable circles. I can easily conceive, that if the cotelette was blown up, it would stand a chance of coming down on the other side, thus saving the cook the trouble; but if Guy Fawkes had unfortunately succeeded, it would have produced quite another effect. Having failed in my literary researches, I tried to find it in practice. I therefore went to my kitchen, and put two spoonfuls of oil in a sautépan; I took a nice spring chicken prepared for broiling, put on the fire; and, as it began to act upon it, the oil began to jump, and also slightly the chicken. I then perceived that the way my French friend used the word was right; and that, after all, there was not such a great difference in Guy Fawkes's plan of cooking the Parliament and that of a cutlet or chicken, for both were doomed to destruction, the one by falling in awful ruins on the fire, and the other devoured by a ravenous stomach on the dinner-table. Now, dearest, having found no means of translating it to my satisfaction, I see no other plan but to adopt it amongst us, and give it letters of naturalization, not for the beauty of the word, but for its utility. The process of sautéing is at once quick, simple, and economical, and to be well done furnishes a pleasing article of food. The art of doing it well consists in doing it quickly, to keep the gravy and succulence in the meat, which a slow process would nullify, and is of course confined to small articles of every kind of food.

BROILING is, without doubt, the earliest and most primitive mode of cookery, it being that which would present itself to man in a state of nature. It is one of the easiest parts of cookery, and therefore should be done well; it entirely depends upon the fire, which must be exceedingly clear, and the best gridiron is that having round bars, which should be placed slanting over the fire, to prevent the fat going into it; the bars should be greased, and the gridiron should be placed on the fire to get hot before the object to be cooked is placed on it I have heard that great difference of opinion exists in cookery books upon the proper broiling of a steak, if it should be turned only once or often. My plan is to turn it often, and my reason is, that, if turned but once, the albumen and the fibrine of the meat get charred, and the heat throws out the osmazome or gravy on the upper side, which, when turned over, goes into the fire; by turning it often, so as at first only to set the outside, the gravy goes into the centre, and it becomes evenly done throughout. (*See* "Soyer's Mutton Chop.") As regards the thickness of the meat to be broiled, that depends in a great measure on the intensity of the fire, but the quicker the better, and also the sooner it is eaten after taken from the fire the better. I have latterly, in broiling rump-steaks, added that which, by a great many, is considered an improvement; it is, on turning them the last time, to dredge them out of a dredger with fine holes, in which has been placed four tablespoonfuls of fine biscuit or rusk-powder, one tablespoonful of salt, one teaspoonful of pepper, a saltspoonful of either eschalot-powder or mushroom-powder, or finely-pulverized salts of celery, well mixed together, and the steak to be placed in a very hot dish, with a little mushroom-ketchup and a small piece of butter, and served immediately.

SAUCES.

SAUCES in cookery are like the first rudiments of grammar, which consists of certain rules called Syntax, which is the foundation of all languages: these fundamental rules are nine, so has cookery the same number of sauces, which are the foundation of all others; but these, like its prototype the grammar, have two—brown and white, which bear a resemblance to the noun and verb, as they are the first and most easily learnt, and most constantly in use; the others are the adjuncts, pronouns, adverbs, and interjections; upon "the proper use of the two principal ones depends the quality of all others, and the proper making of which tends to the enjoyment of the dinner; for to my fancy they are to cookery what the gamut is in the composition of music, as it is by the arrangement of the notes that harmony is produced, so should the ingredients in the sauce be so nicely blended, and that delightful concord should exist, which would equally delight the palate, as a masterpiece of a Mozart or a Rossini should delight the ear; but which, if badly executed, tantalize those nervous organs, affect the whole system, and prove a nuisance instead of a pleasure. I will therefore be very precise in describing the two, in order that when you make them, you will not cause your guests to make grimaces at each other, when partaking of them at your festive board, for the present age is a little more refined than at the time of Dr. Johnson, and we are often obliged to swallow what we do not like; for it is reported of him, that being at a ceremonious dinner-party, and indulging in his usual flow of wit, he unconsciously partook of a spoonful of very hot soup, which he immediately returned to the plate he had taken it from; and observing the astonishment of some of his neighbors, he very coolly remarked, "A fool would have burnt his mouth."

When we are at home alone, I very seldom trouble myself by making white or brown sauce, which I can avoid by selecting simplified dishes, which easily produce their own sauce whilst cooking them. But when I expect a little company, the first I order of my cook is to make me half of the quantity of the following receipts for white and brown sauces:—

130. *White Sauce.*—Cut and chop a knuckle of veal, weighing about four pounds, into large dice; also half a pound of lean bacon; butter the bottom of a large stewpan with a quarter of a pound of butter, add two onions, a small carrot, a turnip, three cloves, half a blade of mace, a bouquet of a bay-leaf, a sprig of thyme, and six of parsley, add a gill of water, place over a sharp fire, stirring round occasionally, until the bottom of the stewpan is covered with whitish glaze, when fill up with three quarts of water, add a good teaspoonful of salt, and let simmer at the corner of the fire an hour and a half, keeping well skimmed, when pass it through a hair sieve into a basin; in another stewpan put a quarter of a pound of butter,

with which mix six ounces of flour, stirring over the fire about three minutes, take off, keep stirring until partly cold, when add the stock all at once, continually stirring and boiling for a quarter of an hour; add half a pint of boiling milk, stir a few minutes longer, add a little chopped mushrooms if handy, pass through a hair sieve into a basin, until required for use, stirring it round occasionally until cold; the above being a simplified white sauce, will be referred to very often in the receipts.

131. *Brown Sauce.*—Put two ounces of butter into a stewpan, rub it over the bottom, peel two or three large onions, cut them in thick slices, lay them on the bottom, cut into small pieces about two pounds of knuckle of veal,[3] all meat, or three pounds if with bone, a quarter of a pound of lean bacon cut small, two cloves, a few peppercorns, a tablespoonful of salt, two bay-leaves, a gill of water; set it on a brisk fire, let it remain ten minutes, when stir it well round, subdue the fire, let it remain a few minutes longer, and stir now and then until it has a nice brown color; fill your pan with three quarts of water; when boiling, set it on the corner of the stove, with the lid three parts on the saucepan; when boiling, skim fat and all; after one hour, or one hour and a half simmering, pass it through a sieve into a basin. To make the thickening or roux for it, proceed as follows:—Put two ounces of butter into a pan, which melt on a slow fire, then add three ounces of flour, stir it until getting a thin deep yellow color; this in France is called roux, being very useful in cookery, and will be often referred to in these receipts. This process will take five minutes, when remove from the fire for two minutes to cool, then add at once three and a quarter pints of the above stock, very quickly set it on the fire to boil, remove to corner to simmer, and skim; it ought to be entirely free from grease, and of a light chestnut color.

132. *Demi-Glaze—Thin Brown Sauce for Made Dishes.*—When I have a small dinner-party, I always, as I told you before, make small quantities of white and brown sauce as above, but this is a nice way of clarifying a brown sauce without much trouble, and makes it a beautiful transparent brown color: but although I have made it quite a study, that each *entrée*, or made dish for daily use, should make its own sauce, yet I must impress upon you that this sauce is the real key to cooking a good and ceremonious dinner. Put a pint of brown sauce in a middle-sized stewpan, add to it half a pint of broth or consommé, put it on the stove, stir with wooden spoon, let it boil as fast as possible, take the scum off which will rise to the surface, reduce it until it adheres lightly to the spoon, pass it through a sieve or tammy into a basin, stir now and then until cold, to prevent a skin forming on the top, put it by until wanted for use. It will keep for a week in winter, by adding half a gill of white broth every other day, and giving it a boil; the addition of a tablespoonful of tomatos, gives it a beautiful color; use where indicated.

133. *Thin Brown Sauce of Mushrooms.*—Put twelve tablespoonfuls of thin brown sauce in a small stewpan to boil, then have six or eight small mushrooms well cleaned and washed, chop them fine, and place in sauce, and boil for five minutes; taste if it is to your liking; the addition of a little sugar is an improvement: a little cayenne, if liked, may be introduced. This sauce is good for cutlets, broiled fowl

---

[3] Half veal and beef can be used; or if no veal, all beef.

and game, &c.

134. *Eschalot Sauce.*—Chop fine about a good tablespoonful of eschalot, wash them by placing them in the corner of a napkin, and pouring water over them; press them until dry, put them in a small stewpan with two tablespoonfuls of vinegar, one clove, a little mace; boil two minutes, add ten tablespoonfuls of demi-glaze, boil a little longer, add a little sugar, and serve.

135. *Piquant Sauce.*—Put two tablespoonfuls of chopped onions, or eschalots, cleaned as above, into a stewpan; put also four tablespoonfuls of vinegar and a bay-leaf, and boil; then add ten tablespoonfuls of brown sauce, half a one of chopped parsley, ditto of green gherkins; boil five minutes, skim, add a little sugar, taste if well seasoned, take out bay-leaf and serve.

136. *Tarragon Sauce.*—Put eight tablespoonfuls of demi-glaze, and four of broth, into a stewpan; boil for a few minutes, add a tablespoonful of vinegar, have ready picked twenty leaves of fresh tarragon, put in to simmer two minutes, and serve with any kind of poultry, but especially spring chickens.

137. *Brown Cucumber Sauce.*—Peel a small fresh cucumber, cut it in neat pieces, put in a stewpan with a little sugar, add half an ounce of butter, set it on a slow fire, stir it now and then, add twelve tablespoonfuls of brown sauce, and four of broth; let it simmer till tender, skim the butter off, remove the cucumbers into another stewpan, reduce the sauce a little, taste it and serve.

138. *Mince Herb Sauce.*—Put two tablespoonfuls of finely chopped onions in a stewpan, add a tablespoonful of oil, place it on the fire, stir a few minutes, add ten tablespoonfuls of demi-glaze and four of broth or water; boil, skim; if too thick, and the scum should not rise, add half a gill of broth or water; boil, and reduce to a proper thickness, and add a tablespoonful of chopped parsley if handy, one of mushrooms, and season with a little cayenne, the juice of a quarter of a lemon; serve. I often introduce a little garlic in this.

139. *Italian Herb Sauce.*—Proceed in the same way as the above, only add a little chopped thyme and a small glass of sherry.

140. *Robert Sauce.*—Peel and cut up two good-sized onions, put them in a stewpan with an ounce of butter till they are a nice yellow color, then add eight tablespoonfuls of demi-glaze, and two of water or broth; skim, boil quick; when a proper thickness, add a good tablespoonful of French mustard; season it rather high; if no French mustard, use English, but it completely changes the flavor, though still very palatable.

141. *Ravigote Sauce.*—Put in a stewpan one middle-sized onion sliced, with a little carrot, a little thyme, bay-leaf, one clove, a little mace, a little scraped horseradish, a little butter, fry a few minutes, then add three teaspoonfuls of vinegar, ten tablespoonfuls of brown sauce, four of broth; when boiling, skim, add a tablespoonful of currant jelly; when melted, pass all through a tammy, and serve with any kind of meat or poultry; with hare or venison it is excellent.

142. *Brown Mushroom Sauce.*—Clean and cut twelve small mushrooms in slices, place them in a stewpan with a little butter, salt, pepper, the juice of a quar-

ter of a lemon, set it on a slow fire for a few minutes, then add ten spoonfuls of demi-glaze; boil till they are tender, and serve. A little mushroom catsup may be introduced.

143. *Orange Sauce for Game.* — Peel half an orange, removing all the pith; cut it into slices, and then in fillets; put them in a gill of water to boil for two minutes; drain them on a sieve, throwing the water away; place in the stewpan ten spoonfuls of demi-glaze, or two of broth; and, when boiling, add the orange, a little sugar, simmer ten minutes, skim, and serve. The juice of half an orange is an improvement. This is served with ducklings and waterfowl: those that like may add cayenne and mustard.

144. *Garlic Sauce.* — Though many dislike the flavor of this root, yet those that like it ought not to be deprived of it. Put in a stewpan ten tablespoonfuls of demi-glaze, a little tomatos if handy; boil it a few minutes, scrape half a clove of garlic, put it in with a little sugar, and serve.

145. *Mint Sauce for Lamb.* — Take three tablespoonfuls of chopped leaves of green mint, three tablespoonfuls of brown sugar, and put into a basin with half a pint of brown vinegar; stir it well up, add one saltspoonful of salt, and serve.

146. *Liaison of Eggs.* — Break the yolks of three eggs in a basin, with which mix six spoonfuls of milk, or eight of cream; pass it through a fine sieve, and use when directed.

147. *Anchovy Butter Sauce.* — Put into a stewpan eight spoonfuls of demi-glaze, or three of broth; when boiling, add one ounce of anchovy butter; stir continually till melted: serve where directed.

148. *Soyer's Sauce.* — Put six spoonfuls of demi-glaze into a stewpan; when hot, add four spoonfuls of Soyer's Gentleman's Sauce; let boil, and serve with either chop, steak, cotelettes, poultry, or game.

149. *Papillotte Sauce.* — Scrape half an ounce of fat bacon, put it in a pan with four tablespoonfuls of chopped onions, stir over the fire for a few minutes, then add ten tablespoonfuls of brown sauce, and boil; then add a tablespoonful of mushrooms chopped, one ditto of parsley, a little nutmeg, a little pepper and sugar, a little scraped garlic; reduce till rather thickish; put on dish till cold, and use it for anything you may put up *"en papillotte."*

150. *Tomato Sauce.* — If fresh, put six in a stewpan; having removed the stalk, and squeezed them in the hand to remove pips, &c., add half an onion, sliced, a little thyme, bay-leaf, half an ounce of celery, one ounce of ham, same of butter, teaspoonful of sugar, same of salt, a quarter one of pepper; set on fire to stew gently; when all tender, add a tablespoonful of flour, moisten with half a pint of broth, boil five minutes, add a little cayenne, taste if highly seasoned, pass it through sieve or tammy, put it back in stewpan, until it adheres rather thick to the back of the spoon, and use it for any kind of meat or poultry. If preserved tomato, proceed as for poivrade sauce respecting the vegetables, omitting the vinegar, add the tomato, instead of brown sauce, add a tablespoonful of flour and broth to bring it to a proper thickness, and pass it through a sieve, and serve as above.

151. *Curry Sauce.*—This I generally keep ready-made in the larder, being very fond of what I consider such wholesome food as curry; but not liking to be troubled with making it often, I cause my cook to prepare a certain quantity at a time. Mr. B. is very partial to curry, but he likes it in winter; for my part, I prefer it in summer. After having partaken of some one very hot summer's day, I felt quite cool. Capt. White, who has been nearly twenty years in the East Indies, tells me that it will produce that refreshing effect; but I can enjoy it in any season.

Put into a pan four good-sized onions, sliced, and two of peeled apples, with a quarter of a pound of butter, the same of lean ham, a blade of mace, four peppercorns, two bay-leaves, two sprigs of thyme; stir them over a moderate fire until the onions become brown and tender, then add two tablespoonfuls of the best curry powder, one of vinegar, two of flour, a teaspoonful of salt, one of sugar; moisten it with a quart of broth or milk, or even water, with the addition of a little glaze; boil till in a pulp, and adhering rather thickly to the back of the spoon; pass all through a fine sieve or tammy, give it another boil for a few minutes, put it in a basin, and use when required. Any kind of meat, poultry, and fish, or parts of game, is excellent warmed in this sauce, and served with well-boiled and dry rice. I have kept this sauce in a cool place in the winter for a month, boiling it now and then. The quantity of powder may be omitted, and a spoonful of curry paste used, or some mangoes. (*See Curries.*)

152. *A very good and useful White Sauce (quite new).*—Put a quart of white sauce in a stewpan of a proper size on a fire; stir continually until reduced to one third; put two yolks of eggs in a basin, stir them well up, add your sauce gradually, keep stirring, put back in stewpan, set it to boil for a few minutes longer, then add one pint of boiling milk, which will bring it to its proper thickness; that is, when it adheres transparently to the back of a spoon; pass through a tammy into a basin, stir now and then till cold; if not immediately required, and I have any stock left, I use half of it with half of milk. I also try this way, which is very convenient: when the yolks are in, and well boiled, I put it in a large gallipot, and when cold, cover with pieces of paper, and it will keep good in winter for two or three weeks, and above a week in summer; and when I want to use a little of it, I only take a spoonful or two and warm it on the fire, and add enough milk or white broth to bring it to a proper thickness, and use where required. This sauce is very smooth, and never, turns greasy; it lies beautifully on fowl, or any white made dish; the addition of a drop of cream gives it a very fine white appearance.

153. *Onion Purée Sauce.*—Peel and cut six onions in slices; put in a stewpan, with a quarter of a pound of butter, a teaspoonful of salt, one of sugar, a half one of pepper; place on a slow fire to simmer till in a pulp, stirring them now and then to prevent them getting brown, then add one tablespoonful of flour, a pint of milk, and boil till a proper thickness, which should be a little thicker than melted butter; pass through a tammy, warm again, and serve with mutton cutlets, chops, rabbits, or fowl; by not passing it, it will do for roast mutton and boiled rabbit as onion sauce.

154. *Purée of Cauliflower Sauce.*—Boil a cauliflower well in three pints of water, in which you have previously put one ounce of butter, two tablespoonfuls of salt;

when done, chop it up, having prepared and slowly cooked in a stewpan an onion sliced, a little celery, half a turnip, one ounce of ham, two of butter, a little bay-leaf, mace, add then the cauliflower, stir round, add a tablespoonful of flour, moisten as above for onions, pass and finish the same way.

155. *Jerusalem Artichoke Sauce.*—Peel twelve, and well wash, boil till tender, and proceed as above.

156. *Turnip Sauce Purée.*—Boil six middle-sized ones, press all the water you can out of them, and proceed as the above.

157. *White Cucumber Purée.*—Peel two, or one large one, cut in slices, put in the stewpan with the same vegetables, &c., as for the cauliflower; when tender, add a tablespoonful of flour, three gills of milk or broth, boil, and finishing as the cauliflower.

158. *Sorrel Sauce, or Purée.*—Wash well four handfuls of sorrel, put it nearly dry into a middle-sized stewpan, with a little butter; let it melt, add a tablespoonful of flour, a teaspoonful of salt, half one of pepper, moisten to a thick purée, with milk, or broth, or cream; pass it through a sieve, put it back in a stewpan, warm again, add two whole eggs, two ounces of butter, and stir well, and serve where directed.

159. *Spinach Purée (see Vegetables, 2d Course).*—Endive is often used in France, and called chicorée. This purée may be made like the cauliflower, or only plainly chopped, put into a pan with two ounces of butter, a gill of white sauce, a little grated nutmeg, and a little salt, pepper and sugar.

160. *Stewed Peas and Sprew Grass.*—For cutlets, sweetbreads, fowls, or any dishes, they are applicable (see Vegetables, second course), also French beans, only using one third of the quantity that you would for a made dish for an entremet.

161. *Scooped Jerusalem Artichokes.*—Scoop with a round cutter twenty-four pieces of artichoke, of the size of half an inch in diameter, wash them, put them in a small stewpan with half an ounce of butter and a quarter of an ounce of sugar; put it on a slow fire for a few minutes, add two tablespoonfuls of white sauce, six of white broth or milk, let them simmer till tender, skim, mix a yolk of an egg with two tablespoonfuls of milk, pour in stewpan, and move it round very quick, and serve; it must not be too thick, and the artichokes must be well done; they must not be in purée; they are good with or served under any white meat.

162. *Scooped Turnips.*—Proceed exactly the same, only serve a little thinner: they will not do if stringy.

163. *Button Onions.*—The same, only make the sauce thinner, and boil longer, according to their size.

164. *Young Carrots.*—Scrape and trim to shape twenty small and young carrots, pass in sugar and butter, add white or brown sauce, but keep it thinner, as it requires a longer time boiling; when tender, if for white sauce, add a tablespoonful of liaison, stir, and serve.

165. *White Mushroom Sauce.*—Use small white ones; cut the dark part out and remove the tail, wash in several waters, put in a stewpan with a little butter, salt,

pepper, juice of lemon, sauté it for a few minutes, add a gill of white sauce, four table-spoonfuls of broth, milk, or water; boil and serve under any white meat.

166. *White Cucumber Sauce.*—Peel two cucumbers, divide each lengthways into four, remove the pips, and cut into pieces one inch long; add, in stewpan one ounce of butter, a teaspoonful of sugar, half of salt, let it stew on the fire for fifteen minutes, then add a gill of white sauce, six spoonfuls of milk, broth, or water, simmer gently and skim, add a tablespoonful of liaison, and serve where directed, but observe that all these garnitures ought to be served under the meat and over poultry.

167. *Ragout of Quenelles.*—Make twelve nice small quenelles (see *Quenelles*), warm half a pint of white sauce, in which you have put four tablespoonfuls of milk, and half a teaspoonful of eschalot; when well done, pour on the liaison over with the juice of a lemon, and serve. A few English truffles or mushrooms may be added to this sauce.

168. *Maître d'Hôtel Sauce.*—Put eight spoonfuls of white sauce in a stewpan, with four of white stock or milk; boil it five minutes, then stir in two ounces of maître d'hôtel butter; stir it quickly over the fire until the butter is melted, but do not let the sauce boil after the butter is in; this sauce should only be made at the time of serving.

169. *Green Peas Stewed.*—Put a pint of young peas, boiled very green, into a stewpan, with three table-spoonfuls of white sauce, two ounces of butter, a little sugar and salt, and two button onions, with parsley, tied together; boil them ten minutes; add two tablespoonfuls of liaison, stir it in quickly, and serve.

170. *Green Peas, with Bacon.*—Put a pint of well-boiled peas into a stewpan, with five spoonfuls of brown sauce, two of brown gravy, a teaspoonful of sugar, two button onions, and a bunch of parsley; let it boil about ten minutes; have ready braised about a quarter of a pound of lean bacon, cut it in dice about a quarter of an inch square, add it to the peas, take out the onions and parsley, season with an ounce of butter and half a teaspoonful of sugar; mix well together, stew twenty minutes, and serve.

171. *Blanched Mushrooms.*—Get a pottle of fresh mushrooms, cut off the dirt, and likewise the heads (reserving the stalk for chopping), wash the heads in a basin of clean water, take them out and drain in a sieve; put into a stewpan two wine-glasses of cold water, one ounce of butter, the juice of half a good lemon, and a little salt; turn or peel each head neatly, and put them into the stewpan immediately, or they will turn black; set your stewpan on a brisk fire, let them boil quickly five minutes, put them into a basin ready for use; chop the stalks and peel very fine, put them into a stewpan with three tablespoonfuls of the liquor the mushrooms have been boiled in; let them simmer three minutes, put them into a jar, and use where indicated.

Observe: Turning or peeling mushrooms is an art that practice alone can attain; if they are very fresh and white, wash them quickly, and wipe them on a cloth; throw them into the liquid above mentioned.

172. *Onions Stuffed.*—Peel twelve large onions, cut a piece off at the top and bottom to give them a flat appearance, and which adds a better flavor if left, blanch them in four quarts of boiling water twenty minutes, then lay them on a cloth to dry; take the middle out of each onion, and fill them with veal forcemeat (with a little chopped eschalot, parsley, and mushroom, mixed in it), and put them in a sauté-pan well buttered, cover them with white broth, let them simmer over a slow fire until covered with a glaze, and tender; turn them over and serve where required.

173. *Hot Tartar Sauce.*—Put two table-spoonfuls of white sauce in a small stew-pan, four of broth or milk, boil a few minutes, then add two tablespoonfuls of the tartar sauce (see Salads) in it, stir it very quick with a wooden spoon, make it quite hot but not boiling; put it on a dish, and serve where described.

174. *Mephistophelian Sauce.*—Do not be afraid of the title, for it has nothing diabolical about it; the first time I tried it was at Mr. B.'s birthday party; and some of his friends having over and over again drank his health, till he had hardly any health left to carry him to the drawing-room, where the coffee was waiting, about eleven o'clock, having asked for some anchovy sandwiches, but, from a mistake, not having any in the house, I composed this ravigotante sauce, which partly brought them back to their senses.

I cut up the remains of the turkey, rubbed some mustard over it, sprinkled a little salt and plenty of cayenne, put it on the gridiron on the fire, and made the following sauce: I chopped six eschalots, washed and pressed them in the corner of a clean cloth, then put them into a stewpan with one and a half wine-glassful of Chili vinegar, a chopped clove, a piece of garlic, two bay-leaves, an ounce of glaze, and boiled all together for ten minutes; then added four tablespoonfuls of tomato sauce, a little sugar, and ten of gravy or brown sauce; boiled it a few minutes longer, then added a pat of butter, stirring it well in, removed the bay-leaf, and poured over turkey, and served.

SOUPS.

IN France, no dinner is served without soup, and no good soup is supposed to be made without the pot-au-feu (see No. 215), it being the national dish of the middle and poorer classes of that country; thinking it might be of service to the working classes, by showing the benefits to be derived from more frequently partaking of a hot dinner, as I have previously observed, especially in a cold climate like ours. Clear light soups are very delicate, and in this country more fit for the wealthy; whilst the more substantial thick soups, such as mock turtle, ox-tail, peas, &c., are more in vogue, consequent to being better adapted to the million; therefore, after giving a few series of clear soups, I shall proceed to give a greater variety of the thicker sorts, being careful that every receipt shall be so plain as to give a correct idea of its cost.

175. *Stock for all kinds of Soup.*—Procure a knuckle of veal about six pounds in weight, which cut into pieces about the size of an egg, as also half a pound of lean ham or bacon; then rub a quarter of a pound of butter upon the bottom of the stewpan (capable of holding about two gallons), into which put the meat and bacon, with half a pint of water, two ounces of salt, three middle-sized onions, with two cloves in each, one turnip, a carrot, half a leek, and half a head of celery; put the cover upon the stewpan, which place over a sharp fire, occasionally stirring round its contents with a wooden spoon, until the bottom of the stewpan is covered with a white thickish glaze, which will lightly adhere to the spoon; fill up the stewpan with cold water, and when upon the point of boiling, draw it to the corner of the fire, where it must gently simmer for three hours, carefully skimming off every particle of grease and scum; pass your stock through a fine hair sieve, and it is ready for use when required.

The above will make a delicious broth for all kinds of clear soups, and of course for thick soups or purées; by boiling it rather faster about five minutes before passing, you will be better enabled to take off every particle of grease from the surface. In making a stock of beef proceed as above, but allow double the time to simmer; mutton or lamb, if any trimmings, might also be used; if beef, use seven pounds; if mutton, eight; or lamb, seven, of course bones and all included; with care, this broth would be quite clear. To give a little color, as required for all clear soups, use a little brown gravy or browning, but never attempt to brown it by letting it color at the bottom of the stewpan, for in that case you would destroy the greater part of the osmazome.

176. *Another way, more economical.*—Instead of cutting up the knuckle of veal so small, cut it in four or five pieces only, and leave the bacon in one piece; then,

when the broth is passed, take out the veal, which is very excellent served with a little of the broth for gravy, and the bacon with a few greens upon another dish. This is as I always eat it myself; but some persons would probably prefer a little parsley-and-butter sauce or sharp sauce, served with it. Should any of the veal be left until cold, it might be cut into thin slices, and gradually warmed in either of the before-mentioned sauces. Should you make your stock from the leg or shin of beef, stew it double the time, preserve the vegetables boiled in the stock, and serve with beef, or serve the beef with some nice sharp sauce over; the remainder, if cold, may also be hashed in the ordinary way. If of mutton, and you have used the scrags of the neck, the breast, head, or the chump of the loin, keep them in as large pieces as possible; and, when done, serve with a few mashed turnips, and caper sauce, separately; if any remaining until cold, mince it. Lamb would be seldom used for stock, being much too expensive; but in case of an abundance, which there sometimes is in the country, proceed the same as for mutton.

177. *Brown Gravies.*—Rub an ounce of butter over the bottom of a stewpan which would hold about three quarts; have ready peeled four onions, cut them into thick slices, with which cover the bottom of the stewpan; over these lay about two pounds of beef from the leg or shin, cut into thin slices, with the bone chopped very small, add a small carrot, a turnip cut in slices, and a couple of cloves; set the stewpan upon a gentle fire for ten minutes, shaking it round occasionally to prevent burning; after which, let it go upon a slow fire for upwards of an hour, until the bottom is covered with a blackish glaze, but not burnt; when properly done, and ready for filling up, you will perceive the fat that runs from the meat quite clear, fill up the stewpan with cold water, add a teaspoonful of salt; and when upon the point of boiling, set it on a corner of the fire, where let it simmer gently about an hour, skimming off all the fat and scum which may rise to the surface; when done, pass it through a fine sieve into a basin, and put by to use for the following purposes:—For every kind of roast meat, poultry, or game especially; also to give a good color to soups and sauces. This gravy will keep several days, by boiling it every other day. Although beef is the most proper meat for the above purpose, it may be made of veal, mutton, lamb, or even with fresh pork, rabbits, or poultry.

178. *Browning.*—When in business, and not so much time to devote to the kitchen, I used to make shift with a browning from the following receipt, using, however, but a very few drops: put two ounces of powdered sugar into a middling-sized stewpan, which place over a slow fire; when beginning to melt, stir it round with a wooden spoon until getting quite black, then pour over half a pint of cold water: leave it to dissolve, and take a little for use when required.

179. *Glaze* is an almost indispensable article in a *cuisine bourgeoise*, and should be kept by all persons in the middle classes of life, the advantage being that it will keep for months together, is very simple to make, and is always useful in cookery, however humble; in fact, with it you can dress a very good dinner with very little trouble.

Make a stock as directed in No. 175, but omitting the salt, which, when done, pass through a cloth into a basin; then fill the stewpan up a second time with hot water, and let boil four hours longer to obtain all the succulence from the meat, then pass it through a cloth the same as the first; then pour both stocks in a large stewpan together, set it over the fire, and let it boil as fast as possible, leaving a large spoon in, to stir occasionally and prevent its boiling over; when reduced to about three pints, pour it into a smaller stewpan, set again to boil at the corner, skimming well if required; when reduced to a quart, place it quite over the fire, well stirring with a wooden spoon until forming a thickish glaze (which will adhere to the spoon) of a fine yellowish-brown color; pour it into a basin, or, if for keeping any time, into a long bladder, from which cut a slice and use where directed.

Where, however, only a small quantity is required, reduce only the second stock, using the first for either soup or sauce; but in that case the salt must not be omitted from the first stock, but from the second only. Veal at all times makes the best glaze, but any kinds of meat, game, or poultry will produce more or less.

180. *To clarify Stock, if required.* — In case, by some accident, your stock should not be clear, put it (say three quarts) into a stewpan, and place it over a good fire, skim well, and, when boiling, have ready the whites of three eggs (carefully separated from their yolks), to which add half a pint of water; whisk well together; then add half a pint of the boiling stock gradually, still whisking the eggs; then whisk the boiling stock, pouring the whites of eggs, &c., in whilst so doing, which continue until nearly boiling again, then take it from the fire, let it remain until the whites of eggs separate themselves, pass it through a clean fine cloth into a basin; this must be taken as a rule for every kind of clear soup, which must be strictly followed by every person wishing to profit by this little work. These principles, once learned, would be useful at all times, and save a great deal of useless reference in the perusal of these receipts; and no persons can make themselves answerable for the success of any individual in making soups if the instructions recommended be not strictly followed. The following rule should be therefore punctually attended to.

All clear soups ought not to be too strong of meat, and must be of a light brown sherry or straw color. All white or brown thick soups should be rather thin, with just sufficient consistency to adhere lightly to a spoon when hot, soups of fish, poultry, or game especially. All purées, no matter whether of meat or vegetables, require to be somewhat thicker, which may be ascertained by its adhering more thickly to the spoon. Every Italian soup must be very clear, rather stronger of meat, and the color of pale sherry.

By following the few foregoing observations, experience will teach you volumes; for as there is a great difference in the quality of different materials (flour, for instance, which, if strong, would tend to thicken, but, if weak, actually almost turns to water by boiling), therefore your judgment, with the above few important remarks, will make you more perfect than the most precise quantities of weights and measurements, upon that important point.

181. *Clear Vegetable Soup.* — Peel a middling-sized carrot and turnip, which cut first into slices, then into small square pieces about the size of dice; peel also eigh-

teen button onions; wash the whole in cold water, and drain them upon a sieve; when dry, put them into a stewpan with two ounces of butter and a teaspoonful of powdered sugar; set them upon a very sharp fire for ten minutes, tossing them over every now and then until the vegetables become covered with a thin shiny glaze, which may take rather more than the before-mentioned time; care, however, must be taken, for should you let them get brown, the flavor of the soup would be spoiled; whilst, upon the other hand, if put in whilst surrounded with a whitish liquid, your soup would look white and unsightly; with a little attention, however, success is certain; and, once accomplished, there would be no difficulty in making any vegetable soups or sauce, therefore it is very desirable to know how to do it properly. When done, pour two quarts of clear broth over them, set it upon the fire, and when upon the point of boiling, place it at the corner to simmer, until the vegetables are quite tender (the onions especially), carefully skimming off all the butter as it rises to the surface; it will require about half an hour's simmering, and there should be half a pound of vegetables to two quarts of stock; taste if properly seasoned, which it ought to be with the above proportions, but use your own judgment accordingly.

By following the last process correctly, the only difference to be made in those descriptions of soup is in the shape the vegetables are cut.

182. *Printanière Soup.*—Cut a small quantity of vegetables as in the last, but rather less carrot and turnip, introducing a little celery, leek, and young spring onions, instead of the button onions; proceed exactly as before, but ten minutes before taking it from the fire, wash a few leaves of sorrel, which cut small and put into the soup, with six sprigs of chervil; in summer, a few fresh-boiled peas or French beans served in it is an improvement.

In whatever shape you may cut the vegetables for soup, always be cautious not to cut some pieces larger than others, and the whole of them rather small than large; for if some pieces should be small and others large, the smaller pieces would be quite in purée, whilst the larger ones would still be quite hard, which would cause your soup not only to eat badly, but give it an unsightly appearance, for the vegetable boiled to a purée would make the soup thick. The above remark, although simple, is still very important.

183. *Julienne Soup.*—This soup is entirely the hereditary property of France, and is supposed to be so called from the months of June and July, when all vegetables are in full season; and to make it in reality as originally made, a small quantity of every description of vegetables should be used, including lettuce, sorrel, and tarragon; however, some few sorts of vegetables mixed together make a most estimable soup. Weigh half a pound of the vegetables in fair proportions to each other; that is, carrots, turnips, onions, celery, and leeks, which cut into small fillets an inch in length, and of the thickness of a trussing-needle; when done, wash dry, and pass them in butter and sugar as before, proceeding the same with the soup, adding just before it is done a little sorrel, cabbage-lettuce, and chervil or peas, if handy, but it would be excellent without either.

184. *Clear Turnip Soup.*—Cut, with a round vegetable scoop, about forty pieces

of turnip, of the shape and size of small marbles, which put into a stewpan, with sugar and butter as before, but fry them of a light brownish color, and finish the soup, as in the previous receipts. A tablespoonful of Italian paste, previously half boiled in water, then drained and finished in the soup, is also an improvement.

185. *Clear Artichoke Soup.*—Peel twelve Jerusalem artichokes, which well wash, then cut as many round scoops as possible, the same as in the last, proceeding exactly the same. The remainder of either turnips, artichokes, or carrots may be boiled, and mashed with a little butter, pepper, and salt, and served as a vegetable, or reserved to make a soup purée; the remains of other vegetables from the previous soups should also be reserved for flavoring of stock, instead of using the fresh vegetables.

186. *Vermicelli.*—Put a quart of clear stock into a stewpan upon the fire, and when boiling add two ounces of vermicelli; boil gently ten minutes, and it is ready to serve.

187. *Italian Paste.*—Procure some small Italian paste, in stars, rings, or any other shape, but small; put on a quart of stock, and when boiling, add two ounces of the paste; boil twenty minutes, or rather more, when it is ready to serve.

188. *Semoulina.*—When the stock is boiling, add two tablespoonfuls of semoulina; boil twenty minutes, and it is then done. Proceed the same also with tapioca and sago.

189. *Macaroni.*—Boil a quarter of a pound of macaroni, in a quart of water, for ten minutes, then strain it off, and throw it into two quarts of boiling stock; let simmer gently for half an hour, when serve, with grated cheese, upon a plate separately.

190. *Rice.*—Well wash two ounces of the best rice, strain off the water, put the rice into a stewpan, with a quart of cold stock, place it upon the fire, and let simmer about half an hour, until the rice is very tender, but not in pulp.

191. *Mutton Broth.*—Any description of trimmings of mutton may be used for broth, but the scrag ends of the neck are usually chosen; put two scrags into a stewpan (having previously jointed the bones), with three onions, three turnips, and one carrot, fill up the stewpan with a gallon of water, and place it upon the fire; when boiling set it at the corner, where let it simmer for three hours, keeping it well skimmed; then cut a small carrot, two turnips, an onion, with a little leek and celery, into small square pieces, which put into another stewpan, with a wineglassful of pearl-barley; skim every particle of fat from the broth, which pour through a hair sieve over them; let the whole boil gently at the corner of the fire until the barley is tender, when it is ready to serve; the meat may be trimmed into neat pieces and served with the broth, or separately with melted butter and parsley, or onion sauce. Half or even a quarter of the above quantity can be made by reducing the ingredients in proportion.

192. *Irish Soup made of Mutton Broth.*—This soup is made similar to the last, adding ten or twelve mealy potatoes, cut into large dice, omitting the other vegetables, which, being boiled to a purée, thickens the broth; just before serving, throw

in twenty heads of parsley, and at the same time add a few flowers of marigold, which will really give it a very pleasing flavor.

193. *Scotch Cock-a-leekie.*—Trim two or three bunches of fine winter leeks, cutting off the roots and part of the heads, then split each in halves lengthwise, and each half into three, which wash well in two or three waters, then put them into a stewpan, with a stock previously made as directed (No. 175), and a fowl trussed as for boiling; let the whole simmer very gently at the corner of the fire for three hours, keeping it well skimmed, seasoning a little if required; half an hour before serving add two dozen French plums, without breaking them; when ready to serve, take out the fowl, which cut into neat pieces, place them in a tureen, and pour the leeks and broth over, the leeks being then partly in purée; if too thick, however, add a drop more broth or water. Should the leeks happen to be old and strong, it would be better to blanch them five minutes in a gallon of boiling water previous to putting them in the stock.

I prefer a young fowl; but, should an old one be most handy, stew it a short time in the stock before passing it. This soup will keep good several days, and would improve by warming a second time.

194. *Ox-tail Soup.*—Cut up two ox-tails, separating them at the joints, put a small piece of butter at the bottom of a stewpan, then put in the ox-tails, with a carrot, a turnip, three onions, a head of celery, a leek, and a bunch of parsley, thyme, and bay-leaf; and half a pint of water, and twelve grains of whole pepper, set over a sharp fire, stirring occasionally, until the bottom of the stewpan is covered with a thickish brown glaze, then add a quarter of a pound of flour, stir it well in, and fill up the stewpan with three quarts of water, add a tablespoonful of salt, and stir occasionally until boiling, when set it upon the corner of the stove, skim well, add a gill of good brown gravy, or a few drops of browning, and let simmer until the tails are stewed very tender, the flesh coming easily from the bones, then take them out immediately, and put them into your tureen; pass the soup through a hair sieve over them, add a head of celery, previously cut small, and boiled in a little stock, and serve.

Ox-tail soup may also be made clear by omitting the flour, and serving with vegetables, as directed for the clear vegetable soup (No. 181).

195. *Ox-cheek Soup.*—Blanch in boiling water two ox-cheeks, cut off the beard, take away all the bone, which chop up, and cut the flesh into middling-sized pieces, leaving the cheek-part whole; put all together into a stewpan, with four quarts of water, a little salt, ten peppercorns, two carrots, two turnips, one leek, one head of celery, and a bunch of parsley, thyme, and bay-leaf; let it stew at the corner of the fire six hours, keeping it well skimmed, then take out the fleshy part of the cheeks, and pass the broth through a hair-sieve into another stewpan; mix a quarter of a pound of flour with a pint of cold broth, which pour into it, and stir over the fire until boiling, when place it at the corner (adding two heads of celery, cut very fine, and a glass of sherry); when the celery is tender, cut the meat into small square pieces, keep them warm in the tureen, and when the soup is ready, pour over, and serve; give it a nice color with browning.

Sheeps' or lambs' heads also make very good soup by following the above receipt, and adding two pounds of veal, mutton, or beef to the stock: two heads would be sufficient, and they would not require so long to stew.

196. *White Mock-turtle Soup.* —Procure half a calf's head (scalded, not skinned), bone it, then cut up a knuckle of veal, which put into a stewpan, well buttered at the bottom, with half a pound of lean ham, an ounce of salt, a carrot, a turnip, three onions, a head of celery, a leek, a bunch of parsley, and a bay-leaf, add half a pint of water; set it upon the fire, moving it round occasionally, until the bottom of the stewpan is covered with a white glaze; then add six quarts of water, and put in the half head, let simmer upon the corner of the fire for two hours and a half, or until the head is tender, then take it out, and press it between two dishes, and pass the stock through a hair sieve into a basin; then in another stewpan have a quarter of a pound of butter, with a sprig of thyme, basil, marjoram, and bay-leaf, let the butter get quite hot, then add six ounces of flour to form a roux, stir over a sharp fire a few minutes, keeping it quite white; stand it off the fire to cool, then add the stock, stir over the fire until boiling, then stand it at the corner, skim off all the fat, and pass it through a hair sieve into another stewpan; cut the head into pieces an inch square, but not too thick, and put them into the soup, which season with a little cayenne pepper; when the pieces are hot, add a gill of cream, and pour it into your tureen.

The above quantity would make two tureens of soup, and will keep good several days, but of course half the quantity could be made.

197. *Brown Mock-turtle.* —Proceed the same as in the last article, only coloring the stock by drawing it down to a brown glaze, likewise adding half a pint of brown gravy (No. 177), omitting the cream, and adding two glasses of sherry.

198. *Mulligatawny Soup.* —Cut up a knuckle of veal, which put into a stewpan, with a piece of butter, half a pound of lean ham, a carrot, a turnip, three onions, and six apples, add half a pint of water; set the stewpan over a sharp fire, moving the meat round occasionally, let remain until the bottom of the stewpan is covered with a brownish glaze, then add three tablespoonfuls of curry powder, one of curry paste, and half a pound of flour, stir well in, and fill the stewpan with a gallon of water; add a spoonful of salt, the half of one of sugar, when boiling, place it at the corner of the fire, and let it simmer two hours and a half, skimming off all the fat as it rises, then pass it through a tammy into a tureen; trim some of the pieces of veal, and put it back in the stewpan to boil, and serve with plain boiled rice separate. Ox-tails or pieces of rabbits, chickens, &c., left from a previous dinner may be served in it instead of the veal. The veal is exceedingly good to eat.

199. *Giblet Soup.* —Clean two sets of giblets, which soak for two hours, cut them into equal sizes, and put them into a stewpan, with a quarter of a pound of butter, four pounds of veal or beef, half a pound of ham, a carrot, a turnip, three onions, two ounces of salt, and a bunch of parsley, thyme, and bay-leaves; place the stewpan over a sharp fire, stirring the meat round occasionally; when the bottom of the stewpan is covered with a light glaze, add a quarter of a pound of flour, stir well in, and fill up with a gallon of water, add about a pint of brown gravy (No.

177), stir occasionally until boiling, then set it at the corner of the stove to simmer, keeping it well skimmed; when the giblets are tender, take them out, put them into your tureen, pass the soup through a hair sieve over, and serve; twenty cooked button onions, or any small-shaped vegetables served in it, is very good, as is also a glass of port wine.

200. *Oyster Soup.*—Put four dozen of oysters into a stewpan with their liquor, place them upon the fire, when upon the point of boiling, drain them upon a sieve, catching the liquor in a basin; take off the beards, which put into the liquor, putting the oysters into a soup tureen; then put a quarter of a pound of butter into another stewpan over the fire, and when melted add six ounces of flour, stir over a slow fire for a short time, but keeping it quite white; let it cool, then add the liquor and beards of the oysters, a quart of milk, and two quarts of stock (No. 175), stir over the fire until boiling, then season with a teaspoonful of salt, half a saltspoonful of cayenne pepper, five peppercorns, half a blade of mace, a tablespoonful of Harvey sauce, half ditto of essence of anchovies; let boil quickly at the corner for ten minutes, skim it well, add a gill of cream, if handy, strain through a hair sieve over the oysters, and serve.

201. *The Fisherman's Soup.*—Put a quarter of a pound of butter into a stewpan, and when melted add six ounces of flour, stir well together over a slow fire a few minutes, when cool, add one quart of milk, and two quarts of stock (No. 175), stir over a fire until boiling; having previously filleted two soles, add the bones and trimmings to the soup, with four cloves, one blade of mace, two bay-leaves, one spoonful of essence of anchovies, one ditto of Harvey sauce, half a saltspoonful of cayenne, a little sugar and salt if required; let the whole boil quickly at the corner for ten minutes, keeping it well skimmed; cut each fillet of sole into six pieces, put them into another stewpan, with half a handful of picked parsley, pass the soup through a hair sieve over, boil again ten minutes, add a gill of cream, if handy, and it is ready to serve.

202. *Autumn Soup.*—Cut up four cabbage-lettuces, one cos ditto, a handful of sorrel, and a little tarragon and chervil, when well washed and drained, put them into a stewpan, with two cucumbers finely sliced, and two ounces of butter, place them over a brisk fire, stirring occasionally, until very little liquid remains, then add two tablespoonfuls of flour, stirring it well in, then pour over three quarts of stock, made as directed (No. 175), adding a quart of young and fresh green peas; half an hour's boiling will suffice for this delicious soup, and the flavor of the vegetables will be fully preserved; season with a teaspoonful of salt, and two of sugar.

203. *Hodge Podge.*—Cut two pounds of fresh scrag of mutton into small pieces, which put into a stewpan, with three quarts of cold water and a tablespoonful of salt, set it upon the fire, and when boiling place it at the corner to simmer, keeping it well skimmed; let it simmer an hour, then add a good-sized carrot, two turnips, two large onions cut into small dice, and six cabbage-lettuces, if in season (the whole well washed), and let simmer until quite tender; skim off all the fat, and serve either with the meat in the soup or separately. If in season, a pint of green peas boiled in the soup is a great improvement.

204. *French Cabbage Soup.*—This is a soup very much in vogue amongst the middle classes of the French people; it is very economical, and may satisfy a numerous family at a trifling expense. Put a gallon of water into a saucepan, with two pounds of streaky pickled pork or bacon, whichever most convenient, to which add a couple of pounds of white cabbage, cut in strips (using every part but the stalk, and previously well washed), two large onions, a carrot, a turnip, and a head of celery; let the whole boil three or four hours, until the pork is tender, skimming off all the fat, season with a little black pepper, brown sugar, and salt, if required (which is not very frequently the case, the pork or bacon generally being sufficiently so), lay slices of bread in your tureen (about one pound), pour the soup over; keep the tureen covered ten minutes, until the bread is soaked, and it is ready to serve. The pork or bacon may be either served separate or cut into small square pieces, and served in the soup. A few mealy potatoes are sometimes introduced, or a quart of large green peas, or a pint of dry split peas. You must observe that vegetables in France are much more used than in this country, as there are but few poor people there who do not possess a little garden, in which they grow their own.

It is also frequently made *maigre* by omitting the pork or bacon, adding more vegetables of all kinds, and a quarter of a pound of butter, and frequently where they have nothing else but cabbage, they make it only of that; now setting all national feeling aside respecting the poverty of their meals, I have known strong healthy men make a hearty meal of it, preferring it to meat, of which they scarcely ever partake.

205. *Purée of Vegetable Soup.*—Peel and cut up very finely three onions, three turnips, one carrot, and four potatoes, which put into a stewpan, with a quarter of a pound of butter, the same of lean ham, and a bunch of parsley; pass them ten minutes over a sharp fire, when add a good spoonful of flour, which mix well in, add two quarts of stock, and a pint of boiling milk, stir it until boiling; season with a little salt and sugar, rub it through a tammy, put it into another stewpan, boil again, skim and serve with croutons of fried bread as for Palestine Soup. It ought to be thickish.

206. *Palestine Soup, or Purée of Artichokes.*—Have a quarter of a pound of lean bacon or ham, as also an onion, a turnip, and a little celery, cut the whole into small thin slices, and put them into a stewpan, with two ounces of butter; place them over a sharp fire, keeping them stirred, about twenty minutes, or until forming a whitish glaze at the bottom, then have ready washed, peeled, and cut into thin slices, the artichokes, which put into the stewpan with a pint of broth or water, and stew until quite tender, then mix in two tablespoonfuls of flour quite smoothly, add two quarts of stock made as directed (No. 175), and half a pint of milk; keep it constantly stirred until boiling; season with a teaspoonful of salt, and two of sugar, then rub it through a tammy, place it again in a stewpan; let it boil five minutes, keeping it well skimmed, and serve with very small croutons of bread (fried in butter, and dried upon a cloth) in the tureen; a gill of cream, stirred in at the moment of serving, is a great improvement, although it may be omitted.

207. *Purée of Cauliflower Soup.*—Proceed as described for the purée of artichokes, but omitting the artichokes, and substituting four middling-sized cauli-

flowers, previously boiled and chopped fine.

A purée of turnips is likewise made in the same manner as a purée of artichokes, substituting turnips for artichokes, and adding half a tablespoonful more of flour. A purée of white Belgian carrot, called "Crécy à la Reine," is made in the same way, and is uncommon and delicate.

208. *Crécy Soup, or Purée of Carrots.*—Procure five or six large carrots, as red as possible, which well scrape, then shave them into very thin slices, taking off all the exterior red, but not using the centre, then peel and slice a large onion, a turnip, a quarter of a pound of lean ham, a few sprigs of parsley, and two bay-leaves; put them into a stewpan, with four ounces of butter, fry the whole of a light yellowish color, then add the carrot, with a pint of water, and let them stew until perfectly tender, mix in two ounces of flour quite smoothly, and add five pints of stock (No. 175); season with a little salt and sugar, and stir upon the fire until boiling, a quarter of an hour, when pass it through a tammy, and finish and serve as in the preceding; no cream, however, must be added. This soup ought to be of a red color.

209. *Green Pea Soup.*—Put two quarts of green peas into a stewpan with a quarter of a pound of butter, a quarter of a pound of lean ham, cut into small dice, two onions in slices, and a few sprigs of parsley; add a quart of cold water, and with the hands rub all well together; then pour off the water, cover the stewpan close, and stand it over a sharp fire, stirring the contents round occasionally; when very tender, add two tablespoonfuls of flour, which mix well in mashing the peas with your spoon against the sides of the stewpan, add two quarts of stock, or broth from the Pot-au-feu, a tablespoonful of sugar, and a little pepper and salt, if required; boil all well together five minutes, when rub it through a tammy or hair sieve; then put it into another stewpan, with a pint of boiling milk; boil five minutes, skim well, and pour it into your tureen. It must not be too thick, serve with croutons of bread as for Palestine.

210. *Winter Pea Soup.*—Wash a quart of split peas, which put into a stewpan, with half a pound of streaky bacon, two onions in slices, two pounds of veal or beef, cut into small pieces, and a little parsley, thyme, and bay-leaf, add a gallon of water, with a little salt and sugar, place it upon the fire, and when boiling, stand it at the side until the peas are boiled to a purée, and the water has reduced to half, then take out the meat, which put upon a dish, to be eaten with the bacon, keeping it hot, rub the soup through a hair sieve or tammy, put it into another stewpan, and when boiling, serve. The meat may also be served in the tureen if approved of. Maigre pea soup may also be made by omitting the meat, adding half a pound of butter, one quart of milk, and omitting a quart of water.

211. *Lentil Soup.*—Cut three onions, a turnip, and the half of a carrot into very thin slices, which put into a stewpan, with a quarter of a pound of butter, a few sprigs of parsley, a sprig of thyme, and two bay-leaves, add also two pounds of leg of beef, cut into small dice; set the stewpan upon the fire, stirring with a wooden spoon, until its contents are fried rather brownish, when add one quart of lentils, and three of water, let the whole simmer until the lentils are very tender, when season with nearly an ounce of salt, and half that quantity of sugar; it is then ready

to serve.

To make a purée of lentils:—when the soup is made, strain off the broth, add a good spoonful of flour to the lentils, which mash with a wooden spoon against the side of the stewpan; then again put in the broth, boil all up together, keeping it stirred with a spoon; rub it through a tammy or hair sieve, again boil and skim, and it is ready; serve with a few croutons of bread, as directed for Palestine soup.

212. *Maigre Soup.*—Cut two onions into very small dice, and put them into a stewpan, with two ounces of butter; fry them a short time, but not to discolor them; have ready three or four handfuls of well-washed sorrel, which cut into ribands and put into the stewpan with the onions, add one tablespoonful of flour, then mix well a pint of milk and a quart of water; boil altogether twenty minutes, keeping it stirred; season with a teaspoonful of sugar and salt, take it from the fire, and stir in quickly a liaison of two yolks of eggs mixed with a gill of cream or milk (it must not boil afterwards), put the crust of a French roll, cut into strips, in the tureen, pour the soup over, and serve very hot.

213. *Onion Soup Maigre.*—Peel and cut six large onions into small dice, put them into a stewpan, with a quarter of a pound of butter, place them over the fire until well fried, when well mix in a tablespoonful of flour, and rather better than a quart of water; boil until the onions are quite tender, season with a spoonful of salt and a little sugar; finish with a liaison, and serve as in the last.

214. *Hare Soup.*—Put half a pound of butter into a stewpan, and, when melted, add three quarters of a pound of flour, and half a pound of streaky bacon, cut into very small pieces; keep stirring over the fire until becoming lightly browned. You have previously cut up a hare into neat smallish pieces; put them into the stewpan, and keep stirring round over the fire, until they are set; then fill it up with five quarts of water, add two onions, a head of celery, a bunch of parsley, thyme, and bay-leaves, a blade of mace, and four cloves; when boiling, season with one ounce of salt and a little pepper, and let it simmer at the corner until the pieces of hare are done, which would be in about an hour if a young hare, but double that time if a very old one; the better plan is to try a piece occasionally. When done, take out the best pieces, and the inferior ones pound in a mortar, removing the bones, put it back in the soup, and pass all through a tammy, boil for ten minutes, and put it again into a stewpan, and serve. The above quantity would be sufficient for two tureens. A glass of wine may be added. Rabbit, pheasant, grouse, partridge, and other game soups, may be made in the same way.

215. *French Pot-au-feu.*—Out of this earthen pot comes the favorite soup and bouilli, which has been everlastingly famed as having been the support of many generations of all classes of society in France; from the opulent to the poorest individuals, all pay tribute to its excellence and worth. In fact this soup and bouilli is to the French what the roast beef and plum-pudding is on a Sunday to the English. No dinner in France is served without soup, and no good soup is supposed to be made without the pot-au-feu.

The following is the receipt:—Put in the pot-au-feu six pounds of beef, four quarts of water, set near the fire, skim; when nearly boiling add a spoonful and a half of salt, half a pound of liver, two carrots, four turnips, eight young or two old leeks, one head of celery, two onions and one burnt, with a clove in each, and a piece of parsnip, skim again, and let simmer four or five hours, adding a little cold water now and then; take off part of the fat, put slices of bread into the tureen, lay half the vegetables over, and half the broth, and serve the meat separate with the vegetables around.

Crab Soup.—We add to the list of M. Soyer's soups, a receipt for a purely American soup, a great favorite at the South, and esteemed a great luxury by those who have eaten of it—Ed.

[Open and cleanse twelve young fat crabs (raw), and cut them into two parts; parboil and extract the meat from the claws, and the fat from the top shell. Scald eighteen ripe tomatos; skin them and squeeze the pulp from the seed, and chop it fine; pour boiling water over the seed and juice, and having strained it from the seed, use it to make the soup. Stew a short time in the soup-pot three large onions, one clove of garlic, in one spoonful of butter, two spoonfuls of lard, and then put in the tomatos, and after stewing a few minutes, add the meat from the crab claws, then the crabs, and last the fat from the back shell of the crab; sift over it grated bread-crumbs or crackers. Season with salt, Cayenne and black pepper, parsley, sweet marjoram, thyme, half teaspoonful lemon juice, and the peel of a lemon; pour in the water with which the seed were scalded, and boil it moderately one hour.

Any firm fish may be substituted for the crab.]

FISH.

OF all aliments that have been given to the human race for nourishment, none are more abundant or more easy of procuring than this antediluvian species, and yet of how few do we make use, and how slight is our knowledge of their habits, for it is only within the last few years that the idea was exploded that the herrings made an annual migration from the Arctic seas to deposit their spawn on the shores of the British islands. It possesses, according to its kind, a greater or less degree of nourishment, depending, like the animal, in a great measure on those beautiful meadows at the bottom of the ocean, where it feeds; for even those which live upon some of a smaller kind, as the cod on the haddock, that on the whiting, and that again on the mussel, or other crustaceous fish, which move but little from the place where they were originally spawned, derive their nourishment from the herbs and the animalculæ which those herbs produce that lay around them; the cod on the southeast of the Bank of Newfoundland is as fine again in flavor as that on the north-west side. Fish, of course, do not afford the same amount of nourishment as meat, as they contain but a slight quantity of osmazome; but its flesh is refreshing, and often exciting. A curious circumstance has been observed in respect to the animate parts of the creation which draw their nourishment from fish, as in birds and the human race, that they produce more females when doing so than males.

It ought to be made an article of diet more often than it is, as the particles it contains tend to purify the blood from the grossness it receives in partaking of animal food; and when taken at the commencement of dinner, tends to assist the digestion of those substances which form the more substantial part of the meal.

In the receipts will be found those which I consider fit for the table; but, as a general rule to be observed, as in the feathered tribe, all those of beautiful *variegated* colors are more unfit to eat than any other; as if the great Creator of all, in order to please man, had destined some for his nourishment, and others to gratify his senses by their melodious notes and beautiful plumage.

Nothing indicates its freshness so well as fish; the merest novice ought to know it; their gills should be difficult to open, be red, and swell well; fins tight and close; eyes bright, and not sunk: the contrary to this denotes their being stale.

Of the round fish, the SALMON is considered the best and most delicate in flavor, but varies considerably, according to the river in which it is caught; for there is no doubt but that it returns to the river where it was originally spawned, and its time of spawning varies in different rivers. The male is the finest flavored fish, and has more curd than the female. Of late years it has been considered that this fish should be eaten as fresh as possible, for which purpose it is crimped when alive, that it may be flaky, and the curd in it. In former times, it was considered best to keep it two or three days; it is certain that, in keeping it, the curd undergoes a change, which produces a volatile salt, oily and balsamic particles, render it nutritive and invigorating; it is diuretic, pectoral, and restorative, and if eaten too profusely produces vomiting; but when the curd is in it, the flesh is hard and dry, lies heavy on the stomach, and produces indigestion. This fish, when out of season, may be distinguished by having large scarlet, purple, and blue spots on its sides, the male snout long, the female snout hooked. When in season, the color ought to be a silvery pink gray; when cooked, the flesh should be of a dark rose color; when out of season it is pale; small-headed fish are the best.

This fish was known to the Romans, who received it from Aquitaine and the Moselle.

216. *Salmon, plain boiled.*—I prefer always dressing this fish in slices from an inch to two inches in thickness, boiling it in plenty of salt water about twenty minutes; the whole fish may be boiled, or the head and shoulders of a large fish, but they require longer boiling. Salmon eats firmer by not being put into the water until boiling. Dress the fish upon a napkin, and serve with lobster sauce, shrimp ditto, or plain melted butter in a boat, with fresh sprigs of parsley boiled a few minutes in it. A salmon weighing about ten pounds will require an hour's gentle boiling; a head and shoulders weighing six pounds, half an hour; the remains may be dressed à la crême, as directed for the turbot.

217. *Salmon, Sauce Matelote.*—Cook three good slices of salmon as directed in the last, or a large salmon peal trussed in the form of the letter S, dress it upon a dish without a napkin, having previously drained off all the water; have ready one quart of matelote sauce, under or over.

To broil salmon, dip each piece in flour, put it on a gridiron, fifteen minutes will give it a nice pale color; it should be served with Dutch or caper sauce.

Cod.—This fish, like the former, belongs to the northern parts of the world; its flavor and quality, like terrestrial animals, depend greatly on its feeding-place, a few miles making a marked difference; it is exceedingly voracious. Those are best with a small head and thick at the neck.

218. *To boil Cod Fish.*—Crimped cod, as I have before remarked, is preferable to the plain; it is likewise better cut in slices than cooked whole; to boil it well, have the water ready boiling, with one pound of salt to every six quarts, put in your fish, draw the fish-kettle to the corner of the fire, where let it simmer slowly from twenty minutes to half an hour, when done, the bone in the centre will draw out easily; if boiled too much, it would eat tough and stringy; should the fish not be crimped, add more salt to the water, it will cause the fish to eat firmer.

219. *Cod Fish sauced over with Oyster Sauce.*—Boil three slices of the fish as above, drain and dress them upon a dish without a napkin, blanch three dozen oysters, by putting them into a stewpan, with their juice, upon the fire, move them round occasionally, do not let them boil; as soon as they become a little firm, place a sieve over a basin, pour in the oysters, beard and throw them again into their li-

quor, put them into a stewpan; when boiling, add two cloves, half a blade of mace, six peppercorns, and two ounces of butter, to which you have added a tablespoonful of flour, breaking it into small pieces, stir well together, when boiling, season with a little salt, cayenne pepper, and essence of anchovies, finish with a gill of cream or milk, and sauce over. The remains of this fish may be taken from the bone and placed upon a dish, with a little of the above sauce (to which you have added the yolks of two eggs) over, sprinkle over with bread-crumbs, and place it twenty minutes in a hot oven, till the bread-crumbs become brown.

220. *Salt Fish.*—Choose the fish with a black skin, and be particular in soaking it well; to boil, put it into a fish-kettle, with plenty of cold water, place it over the fire, and the moment it boils remove it to the corner, to simmer until done, which, if a piece weighing about three pounds, would be in about twenty minutes; do not let it boil fast, or the fish would eat hard and thready; dish it upon a napkin, with plain boiled parsnips and parsley round, and serve egg sauce in a boat.

Haddock, the callarias and galeris of the Romans. This is also the fish that it is said St. Peter took the tribute money from, and thus gave the impression of his finger and thumb, where it remains in confirmation of the miracle. It has a very fine flavor when fresh and in season, which is when the roe is very small; the time depends on the place where taken, but generally about October. I think one weighing from six to seven pounds is the best size, although I have had them at twelve pounds. The same features as in the cod will tell if they are fresh.

221. *Haddock.*—This is a fish which I can highly recommend, both for its firmness and lightness; it is excellent plain boiled, and served with a cream sauce or any other fish sauce. But the better plan is to cut four or five incisions upon each side of the fish, an inch deep, then put it into a deep dish, and cover well with salt, let it remain about two hours, then put the fish in boiling water, to simmer from thirty to forty minutes; if a fish of five or six pounds in weight, dish it on a napkin garnished with plain boiled parsnips and parsley, with egg sauce in a boat.

222. *Baked Haddock.*—Fill the interior of the fish with veal stuffing, sew it up with packthread, and truss it with the tail in its mouth, rub a piece of butter over the back, or egg and bread-crumb it over, set it on a baking-dish, which put in a warmish oven to bake, if a Dublin bay haddock, it would take from three quarters of an hour to an hour, but a common haddock would require but half an hour; the better plan is to run the point of a knife down to the backbone, from which, if the flesh parts easily, it is done, when dress it upon a dish without a napkin, and serve a Beyrout sauce, or any other, round.

Sturgeon derives its name from the German *stoeren*, to stir, to rake up; it is from the same word we derive our word *stir*. It is the accipenser of the Romans. This fish has long been in use in England, but, from its scarcity, it has always been expensive—indeed, it has been considered as a royal fish; for every one caught in the rivers of England belongs to the Queen, with the exception of the river Thames, which belongs to the Lord Mayor. The flavor of the young sturgeon is extremely delicate, but that materially depends upon the river in which it is caught, as it feeds upon the insects and plants,—in fact, entirely by suction; those caught in rapid rivers and sandy bottoms, and where they have the advantage of salt and fresh water, are the best.

223. *Economical mode of cooking Sturgeon.*—Take a piece of sturgeon about two pounds weight, and on sending a piece of meat to the baker's to be baked on a stand in a dish, put the sturgeon under it, with a little water, salt, pepper, &c., and a little chopped eschalot may be used; you can also put potatoes round it. Peas, if in season, are a good accompaniment, with melted butter.

224. *To roast Sturgeon.*—Take the tail part, skin and bone it; fill the part where the bone comes from with some stuffing, as for a fillet of veal; put butter and paper round it, and tie it up like a fillet of veal; roast, and serve it with melted butter and gravy.

They may be cooked precisely as veal, in large or small pieces, as for fricandeau, papillote, &c., and even salted, in imitation of tunny.

Mackerel.—This is generally recognized as the scomber of the Romans, by whom it was much esteemed; at the present day it is not held in that high estimation that it was some years since: the great supply which is now received from different parts of the coast at all seasons of the year may have a tendency to cause this. It is a fish which requires to be eaten very fresh, and soon becomes tainted. The soft roe of this fish is highly esteemed, and I have no doubt but that it was equally so with the Romans, and I believe it was an ingredient of the garum. When fresh, their skin is of a sea-green color, and very beautiful; fine bright golden eyes, and gills very red; they should be plump, but not too large; they should be cleaned by cutting their gills, so that, when pulled, the interior of the fish will come with them; wipe them well, cut off the fins, and trim the tail.

225. *Mackerel* are generally served plain boiled; put them in a kettle containing boiling water, well salted, let simmer nearly half an hour, take them up, drain, and dish them upon a napkin; serve melted butter in a boat, with which you have mixed a tablespoonful of chopped fennel, boiling it a few minutes.

226. *Mackerel à la Maître d'Hôtel.*—Cut an incision down the back of a mackerel, close to the bone, season it with a little pepper, salt, and cayenne, if approved of, butter the skin well, and place the fish upon a gridiron over a moderate fire, for about twenty minutes, turning it over when half done; when done, have ready two ounces of maître d'hôtel butter, half of which put in the incision at the back, previously putting the mackerel upon a hot dish without a napkin, spread the other half over; place it in the oven a few minutes, and serve very hot.

227. *Mackerel au Beurre Noir.*—Split the mackerel open at the back, making it quite flat, season with a little pepper and salt, and butter it all over, lay it upon a gridiron over a moderate fire, turning it when half done, for about a quarter of an hour, when place it upon a dish without a napkin, then put six ounces of fresh butter in a stewpan, which place over a sharp fire until the butter becomes black, but not burnt, when throw in about fifty leaves of picked parsley, which fry crisp, and pour over the fish, put three tablespoonfuls of common vinegar into the stewpan, which boil half a minute, season with pepper and salt, pour this also over the fish, which put into the oven five minutes, and serve very hot.

228. *To stew Mackerel.*—Take off the heads, the fins, and tails, and, having opened the fish and taken out all the hard roes, dry them with a cloth and dredge them lightly with flour; place three or four of them in a stewpan, with a lump of butter, the size of a walnut, to each fish; put into a small basin a teacupful of water, a tablespoonful of finely-chopped onions, the same of chopped parsley, a blade or two of mace, a little pepper and salt, a tablespoonful of anchovy essence, and a small teacupful of ale or porter (if not bitter). Add a tablespoonful of grated bread-crust, not burnt, but a light brown; pour all these ingredients over the fish, and let them stew gently for twenty minutes; have ready the yolks of three eggs, well-beaten, and when the fish is sufficiently done, take some of the gravy and mix gradually with the eggs, and, pouring them on the fish, shake the stewpan a little over the fire to thicken the whole, but not to curdle the eggs; the soft roes added are an improvement: have ready more grated crust, and having placed the fish whole in the dish, shake a little of the grated crust over the whole, so as to make it of a handsome brown. The Receipt requires to be carefully followed. If the gravy is too thick, more water may be added; also a glass of sherry, if liked.

229. *Fried Whiting.*—The whiting is generally skinned, and the tail turned round and fixed into the mouth; dip it first into flour, then egg over and dip it into bread-crumbs, fry as directed for the sole; for whiting aux fines herbes, proceed as directed for sole aux fines herbes. I prefer the whiting fried with their skins on, merely dipping them in flour.

230. *Whiting au Gratin.*—Put a good spoonful of chopped onions upon a strong earthen dish, with a glass of wine, season the whiting with a little pepper and salt, put it in the dish, sprinkle some chopped parsley and chopped mushrooms over, and pour over half a pint of anchovy sauce, over which sprinkle some brown bread-crumbs, grated from the crust of bread, place it in a warm oven half an hour; it requires to be nicely browned; serve upon the dish you have cooked it in.

231. *Red Mullets.*—Procure two red mullets, which place upon a strong dish, not too large, sprinkle a little chopped onions, parsley, a little pepper and salt, and a little salad-oil over, and put them into a warm oven for half an hour, then put half a tablespoonful of chopped onions in a stewpan, with a teaspoonful of salad-oil, stir over a moderate fire until getting rather yellowish, then add a tablespoonful of sherry, half a pint of white sauce or melted butter, with a little chopped parsley; reduce over a sharp fire, keeping it stirred until becoming rather thick; when the mullets are done, sauce over and serve.

232. *Red Mullet en papillote.*—Cut a sheet of foolscap paper in the form of a heart, lay it on the table and oil it, put the mullet on one side, season with salt, pepper, and chopped eschalot, fold the paper over and plait both edges together, and broil on a slow fire for half an hour, turning carefully now and then; serve without a napkin; they are excellent done thus, without sauce, but, if any is required, use melted butter, cream Hollandaise, anchovy or Italian sauce.

233. *Red Mullets sauté in Butter.*—Put two ounces of butter in a pan; when melted, put in one or two small mullets, and season with a teaspoonful of salt, half ditto of pepper, and the juice of half a lemon; set it on a slow fire and turn carefully;

when done, dish and serve plain, or with any of the sauces named in the former receipt.

Herrings, when in season, that is, when the roe is just forming, are most excellent and wholesome fish, when eaten fresh; I have this day (the 25th of April) partaken of some, caught in twenty-four fathoms of water, about twelve miles off the coast of Folkestone, in which you could just distinguish the formation of the roe. The richness of the fish at this period is extraordinary, and renders it worthy the table of the greatest epicure.

As this fish is now of so great importance as an article of food, I shall refer more at length to it in my letters on pickling and preserving, and give you a description of my new plan of curing and smoking, and also what I consider its medicinal and other properties. Its different modes of cooking are as follows:

234. *Herrings boiled.*—Boil six herrings about twenty minutes in plenty of salt and water, but only just to simmer; then have ready the following sauce: put half a gill of cream upon the fire in a stewpan; when it boils, add eight spoonfuls of melted butter, an ounce of fresh butter, a little pepper, salt, and the juice of half a lemon; dress the fish upon a dish without a napkin, sauce over and serve.

235. *Herrings broiled, Sauce Dijon.*—The delicacy of these fish prevents their being dressed in any other way than boiled or broiled; they certainly can be bread-crumbed and fried, but scarcely any person would like them; I prefer them dressed in the following way: wipe them well with a cloth, and cut three incisions slant-wise upon each side, dip them in flour and broil slowly over a moderate fire; when done, sprinkle a little salt over, dress them upon a napkin, garnish with parsley, and serve the following sauce in a boat: put eight tablespoonfuls of melted butter in a stewpan, with two of French mustard, or one of English, an ounce of fresh butter, and a little pepper and salt; when upon the point of boiling, serve.

Smelts.—Many have confounded them with the salmon-fry or smelt of one year old, whereas the smelt has roe and the fry none; it ascends rivers to deposit its spawn in November, December, and January, and the rest of the year they are considered in season, but they vary like the salmon, according to the river. This fish, when fresh, has a beautiful smell of violets or cucumbers, but the Germans call it stinck fish, I know not why; they lose this perfume in about twelve hours after being taken; they should be very stiff and firm, bright eyes, and transparent skin. This fish is very delicate, and requires very great attention in cleaning, merely pulling out the gills, the inside will come with them; they should be wiped lightly. When split and dried, they are called sparlings.

236. *To fry Smelts.*—Dry them in a cloth, and dip them in flour; then have half an ounce of butter of clear fat melted in a basin, into which break the yolk of two eggs, with which rub the smelts over with a brush, dip them in bread-crumbs, fry in very hot lard, dress them on a napkin, garnish with parsley, and serve with shrimp sauce in a boat.

White Bait.—This is a fish which belongs especially to London; although it is obtainable in other rivers in Great Britain and the Continent, yet it is not sought for; great difference of opinion exists amongst naturalists as to what fish this is the young of; in my humble opinion, I think it is a species distinct of itself, having a life of short duration. It is caught only in brackish water, floating up and down the river, according to the tide,—in very dry summers as high up as Greenwich, and in very wet as low as Gravesend. They spawn in winter, and make their appearance, about one inch in length, early in March. They should be cooked as follows:

237. White Bait.—Put them in a cloth, which shake gently so as to dry them; then place them in some very fine bread-crumbs and flour mixed; toss them lightly with the hands, take them out immediately and put them in a wire basket, and fry them in hot lard; one minute will cook them; turn them out on a cloth, sprinkle a little salt over, and serve very hot. Should you not have a wire basket, sprinkle them into the pan, and as soon as they rise take them out.

Turbot we consider the finest of flat-fish; and so it was, no doubt, considered by the Romans: hence the proverb, "Nihil ad rhombum," although Linnæus, from his classification, would make us believe it was the brill or bret, but I do not think so meanly of the epicures of those days as to imagine it. Its flavor depends greatly upon the place where taken, resulting from its food, feeding principally upon young crabs and lobsters; therefore it is not surprising that lobster sauce accompanies it when cooked. I prefer them of a middling size, not too large, but thick, and if bled when caught, so much the better. Should you be at the seaside, and buy one rather cheap, because it has red spots on the belly, remove them by rubbing salt and lemon on the spot. In my opinion they are better, and more digestible, and of finer flavor, forty-eight hours after being killed, than when fresh.

238. *Turbot.*—To cook it; cut an incision in the back, rub it well with a good handful of salt, and then with the juice of a lemon; set it in a turbot kettle, well covered with cold water, in which you have put a good handful of salt; place it over the fire, and as soon as boiling, put it at the side (where it must not be allowed to more than simmer very slowly, or the fish would have a very unsightly appearance). A turbot of ten pounds weight will take about an hour to cook after it has boiled (but, to be certain, ascertain whether the flesh will leave the bone easily); take it out of the water, let it remain a minute upon the drainer, and serve upon a napkin, with a few sprigs of fresh parsley round, and lobster sauce or shrimp sauce, in a boat.

239. *Turbot, the new French fashion.*—Boil your turbot as in the last, but dress it upon a dish without a napkin, sauce over with a thick caper sauce (having made a border of small new potatoes), sprinkle a few capers over the fish, and serve.

240. *Turbot à la Crême* is made from the remains of a turbot left from a previous dinner; pick all the flesh from the bones, which warm in salt and water, and have ready the following sauce: put one ounce of flour into a stewpan, to which add by degrees a quart of milk, mixing it very smoothly; then add two peeled eschalots, a bouquet of parsley, a bay-leaf and a sprig of thyme tied together, a little grated nutmeg, a teaspoonful of salt, and a quarter ditto of pepper; place it over the fire, stirring until it forms rather a thickish sauce, then take it from the fire, stir in a quarter of a pound of fresh butter, and pass it through a tammy; lay a little of it upon the bottom of a convenient sized dish, then a layer of the fish, season lightly

with a little white pepper and salt, then another layer of sauce, proceeding thus until the fish is all used, finishing with sauce; sprinkle a few bread-crumbs over, and put it into a warm oven half an hour; brown with the salamander, and serve upon the dish it is baked on. Any remains of boiled fish may be dressed the same way.

241. *Soles fried.* —Have about four pounds of lard or clean fat in a small fish-kettle, which place over a moderate fire, then cut off the fins of the sole, and dip it into flour, shake part of the flour off, have an egg well beaten upon a plate, with which brush the fish all over, and cover it with bread-crumbs; ascertain if the lard is hot, by throwing in a few bread-crumbs, it will hiss if sufficiently hot, put in the fish, which will require nearly ten minutes cooking, and ought to be perfectly crisp, drain it on a cloth, dish upon a napkin, garnish with parsley, and serve shrimp sauce in a boat.

The above quantity of lard or fat, if carefully used and not burnt, would do for several occasions, by straining it off each time after using. All kinds of fish, such as eels, smelts, whitings, flounders, perch, gudgeons, &c., are fried precisely in the same manner.

242. *Soles, sauté in Oil.* —Trim the fish well, dip it into a couple of eggs, well beaten, put six tablespoonfuls of salad-oil in a sauté-pan, place it over the fire, and when quite hot put in your sole, let it remain five minutes, turn over, and sauté upon the other side, ten or twelve minutes will cook it, according to the size; serve upon a napkin without sauce; they are excellent cold.

243. *Sole a la Meunière.* —Cut the fins off a sole, and make four incisions across it upon each side with a knife, then rub half a tablespoonful of salt and chopped onions well into it, dip in flour, and broil it over a slow fire; also have ready two ounces of fresh butter, mixed with the juice of a lemon, and a little cayenne, which rub over the sole, previously laid in a hot dish, without a napkin, turn the fish over once or twice, put it in the oven a minute, and serve very hot.

244. *Soles aux fines herbes.* —Put a spoonful of chopped eschalots into a sauté-pan, with a glass of sherry and an ounce of butter, place the sole over, pour nearly half a pint of melted butter over it, or four spoonfuls of brown gravy or water, upon which sprinkle some chopped parsley, place it in a moderate oven for half an hour, take the sole out of the pan, dress upon a dish without a napkin, reduce the sauce that is in the pan over a sharp fire, add a little Harvey sauce and essence of anchovy, pour over the sole, and serve.

Soles may also be plain boiled, using the same precautions as directed for turbot, and serve without a napkin, and a cream sauce poured over; or it may be served upon a napkin garnished with parsley, and a little shrimp sauce, or plain melted butter, in a boat.

245. *Flounders, Water Souchet.* —Procure four or six Thames flounders, trim and cut in halves; put half a pint of water in a sauté-pan, with a little scraped horseradish, a little pepper, salt, sugar, and forty sprigs of fresh parsley; place over the fire, boil a minute, then add the flounders, stew ten minutes, take them out and place in a dish without a napkin, reduce the liquor they were stewed in a little, pour over

and serve.

To fry flounders, trim them, and proceed precisely as directed for fried soles: three minutes is sufficient.

Skate, also called *Maid, Ray*, is not appreciated equal to what it ought to be; we generally have only the fin part, which is cut off and put into fresh water, where it curls up. It is a very invigorating fish, and I think deserves the attention of the medical profession. It is best cooked as follows:

246. *Skate.*—Procure two or three slices, tie them with string to keep the shape in boiling, put them into a kettle of boiling water, in which you have put a good handful of salt; boil gently about twenty minutes (have ready also a piece of the liver, which boil with them); when done, drain well, and put them upon a dish without a napkin; put three parts of a pint of melted butter in a stewpan, place it upon the fire, and when quite hot add a wineglassful of capers, sauce over, and serve.

247. *Skate au Beurre Noir.*—Boil a piece of skate as directed in the last; when done, drain it well, put it upon a dish without a napkin, and proceed exactly as directed for mackerel au beurre noir.

Skate may also be served upon a napkin, with a boat of well-seasoned melted butter, to which you have added a spoonful of Harvey sauce and one of anchovy.

Pike.—This fish spawns in March and April, according to the season. When in perfection, their colors are very bright, being green, spotted with bright yellow, and the gills are a bright red; when out of season, the green changes to gray, and the yellow spots assume a pale hue. It may be called the shark of fresh water. Those caught in a river or running stream are far superior to those caught in ponds, which often get too fat, and taste muddy. A middling-sized one, weighing about five pounds, would be best; when fresh, the eyes must be very transparent, the scales bluish, and not dry upon the back, or it would not clean well. The dressing is generally the making of the fish, as regards the approbation bestowed upon it. To clean them, have a sharp-pointed knife, put the point carefully under the scales (without piercing the skin) at the tail of the fish, pass the knife gently up the back to the head, dividing the scales from the skin carefully; you may then take off the whole of the scales in one piece (should this process appear too difficult, they may be scraped off in the ordinary way, it will not look so white, but would eat equally as good); then make two incisions in the belly, a small one close to the bladder, and a larger one above; pull out the gills one at a time with a strong cloth, and if the interior does not come with them, take it out from the incisions, and wash the fish well; the cutting off the fins is quite a matter of taste: it is usually done.

248. *Pike.*—Clean as directed above, stuff the interior as directed for haddocks, only adding some fillets of anchovies and chopped lemon-peel with it; curl round and put in a baking-dish, spread a little butter all over, put in a moderate oven, when about half done egg over with a paste-brush, and sprinkle bread-crumbs upon it; a middling-sized pike will take about an hour, but that according to the size and the heat of the oven; when done, dress upon a dish without a napkin, and sauce round as directed for baked haddock above referred to.

249. *Pike, Sauce Matelote.*—Cook a pike exactly as in the last, dress it upon a dish without a napkin, and sauce with a matelote sauce over, made as directed for salmon sauce matelote.

This fish may also be served with caper sauce, as directed for the skate; the smaller ones are the best; the remains of a pike placed in the oven the next day, with a cover over it and a little more sauce added, is very nice.

250. *Baked Carp.*—Procure a good-sized carp, stuff it, then put it into a baking-dish, with two onions, one carrot, one turnip, one head of celery, and a good bouquet of parsley, thyme, and bay-leaf; moisten with two glasses of port wine, half a pint of water, salt, pepper, and oil, and put it into a moderate oven about two hours to bake; try if done with a knife, which is the case if the flesh leaves the bone easily, dress upon a dish without a napkin, then have ready the following sauce: mince a large Spanish onion with two common ones, and put them into a stewpan with three spoonfuls of salad-oil, sauté rather a yellow color, add two glasses of port wine and one spoonful of flour, mix all well together, add a pint of broth (reserved from some soup) or water, with half an ounce of glaze, or half a gill of brown gravy, or a few drops of coloring, boil it up, drain the stock the carp was cooked in from the vegetables, which also add to the sauce; boil well at the corner of the stove, skim, and when rather thick add a teaspoonful of Harvey sauce, one of essence of anchovies, twelve pickled mushrooms, and a little cayenne pepper, pour all the liquor drained from the fish out of your dish, sauce over, and serve.

251. *Carp, Sauce Matelote.*—Put your carp in a small oval fish-kettle, with wine and vegetables as in the last, to which add also a pint of water and a little salt, with a few cloves and peppercorns; put the lid upon the fish-kettle, and stand it over a moderate fire to stew about an hour, according to the size; when done, drain well, dress upon a dish without a napkin, and sauce over with a matelote sauce, made as directed for salmon sauce matelote, or caper sauce, as for skate; small carp are very good-flavored, bread-crumbed and fried.

Trout.—There are several kinds, none of which, it seems, were known to the Romans. This is the salmon of fresh water, and bears a very close resemblance to it in flavor. They grow to a very large size; I partook of part of one weighing twenty-six pounds, which was caught in the Lake of Killarney, in July, 1848. They have different names in various parts of Great Britain, but there is the common trout, the white trout, and the sea trout; the white trout never grows very large, but the sea trout does, and is of a very fine flavor.

River Trout, when fresh, have the most beautiful skin imaginable, the golden and sometimes silvery tint of which makes me term it the sister fish of the red (sea) mullet; should the gills be pink instead of red, and the skin dry (which is frequently the case on the second day), they may still be eatable, but their succulence goes with their beauty. Clean them as directed for salmon.

252. *Trout à la Twickenham.*—When you have cleaned your trout, put them into a kettle of boiling water, to which you have added a good handful of salt, and a wineglassful of vinegar; boil gently about twenty minutes, or according to their size, dress upon a napkin, and serve melted butter, into which you have put a ta-

blespoonful of chopped gherkins, two sprigs of chopped parsley, salt and pepper, in a boat.

The remains of trout, salmon, or mackerel are excellent pickled:—put three onions in slices in a stewpan, with two ounces of butter, one turnip, a bouquet of parsley, thyme, and bay-leaf, pass them five minutes over the fire, add a pint of water and a pint of vinegar, two teaspoonfuls of salt and one of pepper, boil until the onions are tender, then strain it through a sieve over the fish; it will keep some time if required, and then do to pickle more fish by boiling over again.

253. *Trout à la Burton.*—Boil the trout as in the last; then put half a pint of melted butter in a stewpan, with two tablespoonfuls of cream, place it upon the fire, and when upon the point of boiling add a liaison of one yolk of egg mixed with a tablespoonful of cream (dress the fish upon a dish without a napkin), put two ounces of fresh butter, a pinch of salt, and the juice of a lemon into the sauce; shake round over the fire, but do not let it boil; sauce over the fish, sprinkle some chopped parsley, and serve.

Perch were known to the Romans, and those they received from Britain were considered the best. They do not grow to a very large size, four pounds being considered a large one. When fresh, are reddish at the eyes and gills. These fish, having a great objection to part with their scales, must be scraped almost alive, forming the fish into the shape of the letter S, and scraping with an oyster-knife; open the belly, take out the interior, pull away the gills, and wash well. When large, they are frequently boiled with the scales on, and they are taken off afterwards, which is much easier.

254. *Perch sautéd in Butter.*—Clean the fish as explained above, dry well, make an incision upon each side with a knife, put a quarter of a pound of butter in a sauté-pan over a slow fire, lay in the fish, season with salt, and sauté gently, turning them over when half done; when done, dress upon a napkin, and serve melted butter in a boat, or shrimp sauce. Small ones should be dressed thus.

255. *Perch, Hampton Court fashion.*—Cook the fish as above, and have ready the following sauce: put six spoonfuls of melted butter in a stewpan, with a little salt and the juice of a lemon; when upon the point of boiling, stir in the yolk of an egg mixed with a tablespoonful of cream; do not let it boil; blanch about twenty small sprigs of parsley in boiling water ten minutes, and some small pieces of rind of lemon for one minute, drain, and put them in the sauce, which pour over the fish, and serve.

Perch may also be served plain boiled or stewed as directed for tench, with sauce served separate.

256. *Stewed Tench.*—Put two onions, a carrot, and turnip, cut in slices, into a stewpan, or very small fish-kettle, with a good bouquet of parsley, a few sprigs of thyme, one bay-leaf, six cloves, a blade of mace, a little salt and pepper, and two glasses of sherry; lay your tench over (it will require four for a dish, and they may be either cooked whole or each one cut into two or three pieces), add a pint of water, cover down close, and stew rather gently over a slow fire for about half an hour; take them out, drain upon a cloth, dress upon a dish without a napkin, and

pour a sauce over made as directed for sauce matelote, cream sauce, or Beyrout.

257. *Tench with Anchovy Butter.*—Cook the tench as in the last, but they may be plain boiled in salt and water; dress upon a dish without a napkin, then put six spoonfuls of melted butter in a stewpan, with one of milk; place it upon the fire, and, when upon the point of boiling, add an ounce of anchovy butter; shake it round over the fire until the butter is melted, when sauce over and serve.

The *Eel* is greatly esteemed in all countries, but it differs in taste according to the river from whence it is taken; although we have some very fine eels in the river Thames, yet our principal supply is received from Holland, and the fish which come from thence are much improved in flavor by the voyage, and even increase in size. They arrive in the river Thames in vessels called eel scootes (schuyts), of which four have been allowed, for centuries, to moor opposite the Custom House, and the others are obliged to remain in Erith Hole until there is room for them, which greatly improves the fish: the value of those imported into London last year amounted to 132,600*l*. Nothing is more difficult to kill than eels; and it is only by knocking their heads upon a block or hard substance, and stunning them, that they suffer least. Take the head in your hand with a cloth, and just cut through the skin round the neck, which turn down about an inch; then pull the head with one hand, and the skin with the other, it will come off with facility; open the belly, take out the interior without breaking the gall, and cut off the bristles which run up the back. They are in season all the year round.

258. *Eels, fried.*—Cut your eels into pieces three inches long, dip the pieces into flour, egg over with a paste brush, and throw them into some bread-crumbs; fry in hot lard as directed for fried soles.

259. *Stewed Eels, Sauce Matelote.*—Procure as large eels as possible, which cut into pieces three inches long, and put them into a stewpan, with an onion, a bouquet of two bay-leaves, a sprig of thyme and parsley, six cloves, a blade of mace, a glass of sherry, and two of water; place the stewpan over a moderate fire, and let simmer about twenty minutes, or according to the size of the eels; when done, drain upon a cloth, dress them in pyramid upon a dish without a napkin, with a matelote sauce over, made as directed for salmon sauce matelote, but using the stock your eels have been cooked in to make the sauce, having previously well boiled it to extract all the fat.

260. *Eels à la Tartare.*—Fry as directed above, and serve on some Tartare sauce; or partly stew first, and, when cold, egg, bread-crumb, and broil gently.

261. *Spitchcocked Eels,* in some parts of England, are cooked with the skins on. They should be properly cleaned, and split down the back, and bone taken out, and cut into pieces of about four inches long; egg the inside and throw over some bread-crumbs, in which have been mixed some chopped parsley, a little dried thyme, and some cayenne; place them in a Dutch oven before the fire, and whilst cooking, baste them with butter in which some essence of anchovies has been mixed. The time they take cooking depends on the size, but may be known by the skin turning up.

262. *Conger Eel* is little appreciated in this country, although amongst the

working class of our neighbors, more particularly the French, it is an article of great consumption. If alive, its head should be cut off, and it should bleed as much as possible; but if dead, the pieces should be put into lukewarm water to disgorge previous to being cooked. The young fry are exceedingly good, and may be dressed like fresh-water eels. The large ones may be made into soup; and can also be cooked like sturgeon.

263. *French Angler's way of Stewing Fish.* — Take about four pounds or less of all kinds of fish, that is, carp, pike, trout, tench, eels, &c., or any one of them, cut them into nice middle-sized pieces, no matter the size of the fish — let the pieces be of equal size; put them in a black pot or stewpan, season over with nearly a tablespoonful of salt, half one of pepper, half one of sugar, four good-sized onions, sliced thin, add a half bottle of common French wine, or four glasses of port or sherry, half a pint of water, set it on the fire to stew, gently tossing it now and then; when tender, which you may easily ascertain by feeling with your finger the different pieces, mix a spoonful of flour with two ounces of butter, which put bit by bit in the pan, move it round by shaking the pan, not with any spoon; boil a few minutes longer, and serve, dishing the fish in pyramid, sauce over; if the sauce is too thin, reduce it till it adheres to the back of the spoon; taste, if it is highly seasoned, a few sprigs of thyme or bay-leaf may be added. Some of the fish may be done sooner than the others; if so, take them out first, and keep warm until all are done. The motive of mixing fish is, that it is supposed the flavor of all together is finer than one alone. Conger eel is also done in this way.

FISH SAUCES.

IN all ages and countries at all removed from barbarism, where fish has formed an article of diet, sauces of various kinds have been an accompaniment. With the Romans, in the time of Lucullus, great care was observed in their preparation; amongst others which they used, and the most celebrated, was the Garum and the Muria.

The *Garum* was the sauce the most esteemed and the most expensive; its composition is unknown. This is a subject well worth the attention of the epicures of the present day; they should subscribe and offer a premium for that which, in their opinion, may resemble it: it is a subject well worthy the attention of the Professors of our Universities. Perhaps some leaf yet undiscovered, that may have escaped the conflagration of Alexandria, might throw some light upon so interesting a subject. It appears, that mushrooms entered greatly into its composition; and that parts of mackerel, or of that species, formed another. The question is, at what time of the year were mushrooms in season there; and if at that period mackerel, or what species of mackerel have soft roes, as I think it probable that they entered into its composition, as an island near Carthaginia, where they were caught, was called Scombraria, and that which was prepared by a company in that town, and which was considered the best, was called Garum Sociorum.

The *Muria* was the liquid in which the tunny was pickled, and no doubt very similar to our essence of anchovies. Those most generally in use at the present day are the following, in addition to which there are various kinds made and sold in bottles, some of which are much cheaper to buy than to make.

264. *Melted Butter.*—Put into a stewpan two ounces of butter, not too hard, also a good tablespoonful of flour, mix both well with a wooden spoon, without putting it on the fire; when forming a smooth paste, add to it a little better than half a pint of water; season with a teaspoonful of salt, not too full, the sixth part that of pepper; set it on the fire, stir round continually until on the point of boiling; take it off, add a teaspoonful of brown vinegar, then add one ounce more of fresh butter, which stir in your sauce till melted, then use where required; a little nutmeg grated may be introduced; it ought, when done, to adhere lightly to the back of the spoon, but transparent, not pasty; it may also, if required, be passed through a tammy or sieve. If wanted plainer, the last butter may be omitted.

265. *Anchovy Sauce.*—Make the same quantity of melted butter as in the last, but omit the salt, and add three good tablespoonfuls of essence of anchovies.

266. *Fennel Sauce.*—This is a sauce principally used for boiled mackerel. Make the same quantity of melted butter as in the last, to which add a good tablespoon-

ful of chopped fennel; it is usually served in a boat.

267. *Egg Sauce* is generally served with salt-fish or haddock. Boil six eggs ten minutes, let them get cold, then cut them in pieces about the size of dice, put them into a stewpan, with three parts of a pint of melted butter, add an ounce more fresh butter, with a little pepper and salt; keep the stewpan moving round over the fire until the whole is very hot, and serve in a boat.

268. *Shrimp Sauce.*—Make the same quantity of melted butter as before, to which add three tablespoonfuls of essence of shrimps, but omitting the salt; add half a pint of picked shrimps, and serve in a boat. If no essence of shrimps, some anchovy sauce may be served with shrimps in it as a substitute.

269. *Shrimp Sauce* is also very good as follows: Pound half a pint of shrimps, skins and all, in a mortar, and boil them ten minutes in half a pint of water; pass the liquor through a hair sieve into a stewpan, and add a piece of butter the size of two walnuts, with which you have mixed a good teaspoonful of flour, stir it round over the fire until upon the point of boiling; if too thick, add a little more water; season with a little cayenne, and a teaspoonful of essence of anchovies; serve very hot; a few picked shrimps might also be served in it.

270. *Caper Sauce.*—Put twelve tablespoonfuls of melted butter into a stewpan, place it on the fire, and when on the point of boiling, add two ounces of fresh butter and one tablespoonful of capers; shake the stewpan round over the fire until the butter is melted, add a little pepper and salt, and serve where directed.

271. *Lobster Sauce.*—Put twelve tablespoonfuls of melted butter in a stewpan, cut up a small-sized lobster into dice, make a quarter of a pound of lobster butter with the spawn, as directed; when the melted butter is upon the point of boiling, add the lobster butter, stir the sauce round over the fire until the butter is melted, season with a little essence of anchovies, the juice of half a lemon, and a quarter of a saltspoonful of cayenne pepper; pass it through a tammy into another stewpan, and add the flesh of the lobster; when hot, it is ready to serve where required. This sauce must be quite red; if no red spawn in the lobster, use live spawn.

272. *New and Economical Lobster Sauce.*—Should you require to use the solid flesh of a lobster for salad, or any other purpose, pound the soft part and shell together (in a mortar) very fine, which put into a stewpan, covered with a pint of boiling water; place it over the fire to simmer for ten minutes, then pass the liquor through a hair sieve into a basin; put three ounces of butter into a stewpan, into which rub (cold) a good tablespoonful of flour, add the liquor from the lobster, place it upon the fire, stirring until upon the point of boiling, season with a little cayenne, and add a piece of anchovy butter, the size of a walnut; or, if any red spawn in the lobster, mix it with butter, as in the last, and add it, with the juice of half a lemon, just before serving. An anchovy pounded with the lobster-shells would be an improvement, and part of the flesh of the lobster might be served in the sauce.

273. *Lobster Sauce à la Crême.*—Cut a small lobster into slices the size of half-crown pieces, which put into a stewpan; pound the soft and white parts, with an ounce of butter, and rub it through a sieve; pour ten spoonfuls of melted but-

ter, and two of cream, over the slices in the stewpan, add half a blade of mace, a saltspoonful of salt, a quarter ditto of pepper, and a little cayenne; warm gently, and when upon the point of boiling, add the butter and two tablespoonfuls of thick cream, shake round over the fire until quite hot, when it is ready to serve.

274. *Lobster Sauce simplified.* — Put the slices of lobster, as in the last, into a stew-pan, with ten tablespoonfuls of milk, add a little pepper, salt, cayenne, two cloves, and half a blade of mace; set it upon the fire, and when boiling, add a piece of butter of the size of two walnuts, with which you have mixed a little flour; shake round over the fire, and when getting rather thick, add two spoonfuls of cream, if handy, and serve very hot.

275. *Beyrout Sauce.* — Put a tablespoonful of chopped onions into a stewpan, with one of Chili vinegar and one of common ditto, a pint of melted butter, four spoonfuls of brown gravy, two of mushroom catsup, and two of Harvey sauce; place it over the fire, keeping it stirred until boiling, then place it at the corner to simmer five minutes, skim well, then place it again over the fire, keeping it stirred until thickish, to adhere to the back of the spoon, when add two tablespoonfuls of essence of anchovies, and half a teaspoonful of sugar; it is then ready to serve.

The above, although a fish sauce, may be used for meat or poultry, by omitting the anchovy, and adding more Harvey sauce. If no brown gravy, add water and a little coloring.

276. *Oyster Sauce.* — Mix three ounces of butter in a stewpan, with two ounces of flour, then blanch and beard three dozen oysters, put the oysters into another stewpan, add beards and liquor to the flour and butter, with a pint and a half of milk, a teaspoonful of salt, half a saltspoonful of cayenne, two cloves, half a blade of mace, and six peppercorns; place it over the fire, keep stirring, and boil it ten minutes, then add a tablespoonful of essence of anchovies, and one of Harvey sauce, pass it through a tammy over the oysters, make the whole very hot without boiling, and serve. A less quantity may be made, using less proportions.

277. *Another method.* — Put a pint of white sauce into a stewpan, with the liquor and beards of three dozen oysters (as above), six peppercorns, two cloves, and half a blade of mace; boil it ten minutes, then add a spoonful of essence of anchovies, a little cayenne and salt if required; pass it through a tammy, or hair sieve, over the oysters, as in the last.

278. *A plainer method.* — Blanch three dozen of oysters, which again put into the stewpan, with their liquor (after having detached the beards), add six peppercorns and half a blade of mace; place them over the fire, and when beginning to simmer, add a piece of butter the size of a walnut, with which you have mixed sufficient flour to form a paste, breaking it in four or five pieces; shake the stewpan round over the fire, and when upon the point of boiling, and becoming thick, add half a gill of milk, or more if required; season with a little cayenne, salt, pepper, and a few drops of essence of anchovies; serve very hot.

279. *Mussel Sauce.* — Proceed exactly the same as for oyster sauce, using only the liquor of the mussels (not the beards) instead of the oysters, and serving the mussels in the sauce; about four dozen would be sufficient.

280. *Cream Sauce.*—Put two yolks of eggs in the bottom of a stewpan, with the juice of a lemon, a quarter of a teaspoonful of salt, a little white pepper, and a quarter of a pound of hard fresh butter; place the stewpan over a moderate fire, and commence stirring with a wooden spoon (taking it from the fire now and then when getting too hot), until the butter has gradually melted and thickened with the eggs (great care must be exercised, for if it should become too hot, the eggs would curdle and render the sauce useless); then add half a pint of melted butter; stir altogether over the fire, without permitting it to boil, pass it through a tammy into another stewpan; when wanted, stir it over the fire until hot. This sauce may be served with any description of boiled fish.

281. *Matelote Sauce.*—For about a pound-slice of salmon make the following quantity of sauce: peel thirty button onions, and put half a teaspoonful of sugar in a quart-size stewpan, place it over a sharp fire, and when melted and getting brown, add a piece of butter (the size of two walnuts) and the onions, toss them over now and then until rather brown, then add a glass of sherry, let it boil, then add half a pint of brown sauce, and a gill of broth, simmer at the corner of the fire until the onions are quite tender, skim it well, and add a few mushrooms, if handy, season with a little salt and sugar, and sauce over any kind of fish where described. The addition of a teaspoonful of essence of anchovies is an improvement. Use where directed.

282. *Matelote Sauce simplified.*—Proceed as above respecting the onions, only add a fourth more butter, and fry them a little browner; then add a glass of sherry and two teaspoonfuls of flour, which stir round gently with a small wooden spoon, add to it about a pint of water, stir now and then till boiling, add three saltspoonfuls of salt, two of sugar, one of pepper, and a bouquet garni, simmer and skim, add a few drops of coloring to give it a nice brown color; when ready to serve, add a good tablespoonful of anchovy essence; it ought to adhere lightly to the back of the spoon, but not be too thick; sauce over or under, as directed; small pieces of glaze, if handy, put into it is an improvement, also using broth instead of water; oysters and mushrooms may be introduced, also a little cayenne pepper. This sauce must be very savory.

283. *Lobster Butter.*—Procure half a lobster, quite full of spawn, which take out and pound well in a mortar; then add six ounces of fresh butter, mix well together, then rub it through a hair sieve, and put it in a cold place until wanted. The flesh can be used for any other dish.

284. *Anchovy Butter.*—Take the bones from six anchovies, wash the fillets, and dry them upon a cloth, pound them well in a mortar, add six ounces of fresh butter, mix well together, and proceed as in the last.

285. *Maître d'Hôtel Butter.*—Put a quarter of a pound of fresh butter upon a plate, with one good tablespoonful of chopped parsley, the juice of two lemons, half a teaspoonful of salt, and a quarter that quantity of white pepper; mix all well together, and put in a cool place till required.

286. *Ravigote Butter.*—Proceed as in the last, but instead of parsley, use one spoonful of chopped tarragon, and one of chervil, and add half a spoonful of Chili

vinegar.

REMOVES.

THESE are dishes which remove the fish and soup, served upon large dishes, and placed at the top and bottom of the table; great care should be evinced in cooking them, as they are the "pièce de résistance" of the dinner. I must also observe that a few of the receipts appear a little complicated, but which will not prove to be the case if tried once or twice. In the Entrées will be found how the remains of them may be dressed.

Since the science of analytical chemistry has become so perfect, and has shown us the elements of which every substance and liquid is composed, and that, in order to continue them in a state of action, and prevent decomposition, it is necessary to repair the loss which they are every moment undergoing, even from man, through every living thing, down to earth and water. But as I am not going to write you a lecture on chemistry, which will be so much more easy to read in Liebig, in order for you to choose your meat and viands with economy in regard to actual nourishment, it is necessary I should tell you, that, from infancy to old age, the human race must be continually imbibing elements of formation or reparation, even from the lime in the mother's milk, which forms the bones, to the osmazome extracted from animal matters, which creates a more lively circulation of the blood when it becomes sluggish and dull in old age. Each period, occupation, and station in life requires different substances of reparation, with which we ought to make ourselves intimately acquainted. Amongst the first, and that most generally in use with man, is the ox, the principal nourishment of which consists in the osmazome, which is that liquid part of the meat that is extracted by water at blood-heat. It is this which is the foundation and flavor of all soups, which gives the flavor to all meats, and which, on becoming candied by heat, forms the crust of roast meats.

The osmazome is found principally in all adult animals having a dark flesh, and to a very small extent in those having a white flesh; or even in the white flesh of fowls, but in their back and legs, in which parts lies their principal flavor. The bones of the ox contain gelatine and phosphate of lime. The gelatine is also found in the muscles and other cartilaginous parts of the animal; it is extracted by boiling water, and coagulates at the ordinary temperature of the atmosphere; it is the foundation of all jellies, blancmanges, and other similar preparations.

The albumen is also found in the flesh, and congeals as soon as the heat rises beyond that of the blood; it is this which is the scum on the pot when the meat is boiling.

BEEF.—All oxen should fast from twenty-four to forty-eight hours before being killed; when killed and skinned, they are opened and the inside cleaned; they are then hung up, and ought to be exposed to a draught until cold, and then divided down the back into two parts, leaving the head whole; these sides are then divided into two, called the fore and hind-quarters: the fore-quarter contains the shin, the clod and stickings, leg of mutton piece, chuck, middle rib, fore rib; the hind-quarter consists of the rump, sirloin, thin and thick flank, the veiny-piece, aitch-bone, buttock or round, and leg and foot; the head contains the tongue, palate, and brains; the entrails consist of the sweetbread, kidneys, skirts, and the double roll and reed tripe. When the meat is cut up, the following kernels are taken out: those in the neck, where the shoulder clod is removed; two from the round, the pope's eye, and one from the flap; one in the thick flap in the middle of the flank, and another between the rump and aitch-bone: these must be removed to preserve the beef, particularly in hot weather. The flavor and quality of the meat depend on the country from whence it comes, and the nature of its food.[4] As a general rule, the flesh ought to be of a dark red color, smooth, open-grained, with fat rather white than yellow running in thin streaks through the flesh. Ox-beef is the largest and richest, but heifer is better, if well-fed. It should be hung for two days previous to using, in a cool place, free from draught; it will keep good from three to six days, according to the weather.

287. *Sirloin of Beef* should never be less than three of the short ribs, and will weigh more or less according to the size of the ox from which they are taken; that from a small, well-fed heifer I consider the best, and will weigh about twelve pounds, and take about two hours to roast, depending much on the fire. Having spitted or hung the joint, cover it with buttered paper, and place it about eighteen inches from the fire; about one hour after it has been down, remove the paper and place the joint nearer the fire, and put half a pint of water, with a little salt, in the dripping-pan; about a quarter of an hour before removing from the fire, dredge it with flour and salt from the dredging-box; when taken from the fire, empty the contents of the dripping-pan into a basin, from which remove the fat; pour the gravy in the dish, and then place the joint on it; serve some scraped horse-radish separate. A Yorkshire pudding is very excellent when cooked under this joint.

288. *Ribs of Beef.* — This piece should consist of at least three ribs; the bones are generally sawn through about three inches from the top; these should be removed, leaving the flap, which fold under and fix with wooden skewers. This, in roasting, should be prepared and dredged as the sirloin. A drop of coloring gives the gravy an inviting appearance.

289. *Ribs of Beef braised.* — Take four ribs, not too fat nor too thick, remove the chine-bone neatly, and four inches of the tips of the rib-bones, run with a larding-needle several pieces of fat bacon through the thick part, trim over the flap and tie it well round, put it into the braising-pan; put a quarter of a pound of butter, one teaspoonful of pepper, and six teaspoonfuls of salt into the pan, cover it over, and place it on a slow fire for thirty minutes, stirring it now and then, then add two quarts of water; at the expiration of one hour and a half, add eighty small button onions and sixty small young carrots, or pieces of large ones cut in the shape, which place around the meat; a bouquet of ten sprigs of parsley, three bay-leaves,

---

[4] See future Letters.

and four sprigs of thyme tied together; half an hour after, add sixty round pieces of turnip; then place some live coals on the lid, and let it stew gently for one hour and a half longer, being altogether about four hours. Take out the meat, remove the string, and trim it. Skim off the fat from the liquor in the pan, remove the bouquet, &c., add a few pieces of butter in which have been mixed a tablespoonful of flour and a teaspoonful of sugar, two of browning, stir gently with a wooden spoon, and, when just on the boil, dress round the meat, and serve. In case it has reduced too much, add water.

The foregoing receipt may appear rather complicated, and may perhaps frighten you, and prevent you trying it; but I assure you, if you once try it, you will find it so good as to repeat it, particularly as many other receipts will be referred to this one. The vegetables and meat cold, are excellent.

290. *Stewed Rump of Beef.* — This is a very excellent and useful joint to be continually kept in a country-house, where you may be some distance from a butcher's, as, when hung up in a cool larder, it keeps good for a considerable time, and you never feel at a loss should some friends call unawares: after a third of it has been removed for steaks, pies, or puddings, the remainder makes an excellent joint, roasted or braised like the ribs, or stewed as follows:

Cut it away from the bone, cut about twenty long pieces of fat bacon, which run through the flesh in a slanting direction; then chop up the bone, place it at the bottom of a large stewpan, with six cloves, three onions, one carrot, a turnip, and a head of celery; then lay in the rump (previously tying it up with string), which just cover with water, add a tablespoonful of salt and two burnt onions (if handy), place upon the fire, and, when boiling, stand it at the corner; let it simmer nearly four hours, keeping it skimmed; when done, pass part of the stock it was cooked in (keeping the beef hot in the remainder) through a hair sieve into a basin; in another stewpan have ready a quarter of a pound of butter, melt it over the fire, add six ounces of flour, mix well together, stirring over the fire until becoming a little brownish; take off, and when nearly cold add two quarts of the stock, stir it over the fire until it boils; then have four carrots, four turnips (cut into small pieces with cutters), and forty button onions peeled, put them into the sauce, when again boiling draw it to the corner, where let simmer until tender, keeping it skimmed; add a little powdered sugar and a bunch of parsley: if it should become too thick, add a little more of the stock; dress the beef upon a dish, sauce round and serve. Brown sauce may be used, and the gravy will make excellent soup.

291. *Salt Round of Beef.* — This magnificent joint is, in general, too large for small families, but occasionally it may be used; the following is, therefore, the best method of cooking it: having folded the fat round it, and fastened it with skewers, tie round it, not too tight, some wide tape and a thin cloth, place it in a large stockpot with plenty of cold water, set it upon a good fire, and when beginning to boil, draw it to the corner, where let it simmer until done; five hours will be enough for a large one of thirty to thirty-five pounds; when done, remove the cloth and tape, and dish it up, previously cutting a slice two inches thick from the top, pouring a pint of the hot liquor over it when serving. To serve it cold, M. Soyer, in his "Regenerator," thus describes it:

"After receiving the above useful lesson, and being desirous of improving my profession in all its branches, I remembered that, amongst the number of joints boiled to serve cold for large civic, agricultural, or benevolent anniversary dinners, the round of beef was the most prominent, and having seen it standing in dishes to get cold, with the dish filled with the gravy that runs from it, particularly if a little over-done, caused me to hit upon the following expedient to prevent the meat losing so much of its succulence.

"Fill two large tubs with cold water, into which throw a few pounds of rough ice, and when the round is done, throw it, cloth and all, into one of the tubs of ice-water; let remain one minute, when take out and put it into the other tub; fill the first tub again with water, and continue the above process for about twenty minutes; then set it upon a dish, leaving the cloth on until the next day, or until quite cold; when opened, the fat will be as white as possible, besides having saved the whole of the gravy. If no ice, spring water will answer the same purpose, but will require to be more frequently changed; the same mode would be equally successful with the aitch-bone."

292. *Half-Round of Beef (Silver-side)* should be put into cold water, and let it come to a boil; simmer for two hours and a half, and serve the same as a round.

293. *Aitch-bone of Beef* (or, as I think it ought to be called, *Edge-bone*).—This is a very nice joint for a small family, but not so economical as is generally supposed; it should be pickled carefully, and cooked in the same way as the round; one weighing ten pounds will take two hours and a half; it should be trimmed on the top, and served with some of the liquor under it. It is very good when fresh and braised like the ribs.

294. *Salt Brisket of Beef.*—This is by no means an economical joint, as it loses considerably in cooking; it requires a long time to boil; should it be required as a large cold joint, the following is the best plan: procure a nice brisket with as little fat as possible, detach the whole of the bones from it, make a pickle (see Receipt), place it in it, previously rubbing it well with two cloves of garlic, leave it in the pickle from seven to nine days, rubbing and turning it every day; when ready to cook, cut it into two parts (one about two inches longer than the other), tie them together, and afterwards in a clean cloth, simmer it for about six or seven hours in a large stock-pot full of water; when done, take it out and let it drain, have ready a large dish-cover, place it upon a trivet, remove the cloth and string from the meat, and place it in the cover; have ready a piece of board to fit inside the cover, place it on the meat with a half-hundred weight on the top, and let it remain in a cold place until the next day, when take it out, trim it, garnish it nicely, and serve. This will keep good a considerable time, and is excellent for breakfast or luncheon; besides, it always keeps a "pièce de résistance" in the larder in case of accidents. It is also, when fresh, very excellent stewed like the rump of beef, or plain salted.

295. *Hamburgh Beef.*—The ribs are the best; they should be put to soak in soft water for twelve hours, and then put into cold water and boiled gradually; a piece of three ribs will take three hours; if intended to be served hot, the outside should be cut off, and the joint nicely trimmed and served up with the following garni-

ture round it: take four handfuls of brown kale, well washed, put a saucepan on the fire, with a gallon of water, and let it well boil; then add two tablespoonfuls of salt and half a saltspoonful of carbonate of soda, put the kale in, let it boil for ten minutes, drain it and squeeze all the water from it, put it on a chopping-board and chop it fine, then put it into a stewpan, with two ounces of butter, half a teaspoonful of pepper, one teaspoonful of salt, a little nutmeg, half a teaspoonful of sugar, and twenty roasted chestnuts cut in half, put it on the fire and keep stirring it for five minutes: if too dry, add a little milk or gravy, and place it on the side of the fire until wanted.

296. *To boil a pickled Ox Tongue.*—Put the tongue into a large stewpan containing two gallons of cold water, which set upon the fire until boiling, when draw it to the corner to simmer for three hours, if a tongue weighing about six pounds; but the better way to ascertain when done, is to try it with a trussing-needle, or the prongs of a fork, in the thickest part; if tender it is done, but if hard it must boil rather longer. A dried tongue should be soaked twenty-four hours previously to boiling; when done, skin it and trim the root, &c., and use where directed.

297. *To cook a fresh Ox Tongue.*—Put a tongue in lukewarm water for twelve hours to disgorge, then trim the root and scrape the tongue quite clean; have ready twenty pieces of fat bacon two inches long and half an inch square, which introduce with a larding pin into the most fleshy part in a slanting direction; then rub the tongue all over with salt, and run a long iron skewer through it, which tie upon, surround the tongue with vegetables, the same as directed for turkeys roasted and braised, and roast for two hours before a good fire; twenty minutes before it is done take away the paper and vegetables, to give a nice brown color; when done trim a little, to keep it steady in the dish, and garnish with any kind of stewed vegetables, or cut it in halves lengthwise to form a heart, and sauce over with piquante, tomatos, or any other sharp sauces found in their series. If no convenience for roasting, put into a stewpan a piece of leg of beef (cut small) weighing two pounds, with two onions, one carrot, two blades of mace, a little thyme and bayleaf, and a quarter of a pound of butter, sauté the whole twenty minutes, keeping it stirred over a moderate fire, then put in the tongue (previously prepared) and two ounces of salt, cover with water, and let boil gently four hours, skim and serve. The stock would be excellent for soup or brown sauce of any kind. The remains could be served in either of the methods directed for the remainder of pickled tongue.

298. *Rump Steak broiled.*—Procure a steak cut nice and even, of about half an inch in thickness (if well cut it will not require beating), which lay upon a gridiron over a sharp fire; have a good teaspoonful of salt, and half that quantity of pepper mixed together upon a plate, half of which sprinkle upon the side of the steak uppermost, after it has been upon the fire a couple of minutes, when turn, and sprinkle the remainder of the seasoning upon the other side; it will take about ten minutes to cook it to perfection, turning it occasionally, and serve upon a very hot dish, with a little scraped horseradish round. If properly done, it ought to be full of gravy, but a great deal depends upon the fire, which, if bad, causes the gravy to ooze from the meat and lie upon the top, which you lose in turning the steak over. A rump steak may also be served broiled as above, with a little maître d'hôtel, or

anchovy butter, rubbed, over as soon as done, and potatoes cut the size of half crown or shilling pieces, and fried crisp in hot fat; dress round. Or a steak may be served, with a few water-cresses, well washed, and dried upon a plate sprinkled with a little pepper, salt, and vinegar, and garnished round; a little oil might also be added.

Veal of about two to three months old is the best; the flesh ought to be white, approaching to pink, and the fat firm; it is cut up the same as mutton, except that, in the hind-quarter, the loin is cut straight, leaving the aitch-bone on it, which may be either dressed on the loin or separate. The fore-quarter consists of the shoulder, neck, and breast. The hind-quarter, the knuckle, leg, fillet, and the loin. The head and pluck consists of the heart, liver, nut, skirts, melt, and the heart, throat, and sweetbread.

The bull-calf is the best, the flesh is firmer grained or redder, and the fat more curdled than the cow-calf, which latter is in general preferred, being more delicate and better adapted for made dishes, as having the udder. Nothing can be worse than veal if not fresh; it should never hang more than two days in summer and four in winter. To be in full perfection, the kidneys ought to be covered with fat, and the veins in the shoulder bright red or blue. It is best from May to September, although it may be had good all the year. The head, when fresh, should have the eyes plump and lively; if stale, they are sunk and wrinkled.

299. *Fillet of Veal.*—Choose it of the best quality. Procure a leg, saw off the knuckle, take out the bone in the centre of the fillet, and fill up the cavity with some stuffing made as directed (see Receipt), fold the udder and flap round, which fix with three skewers; place half a sheet of buttered foolscap paper top and bottom, which tie over and over with plenty of string, run a spit through, fixing the fillet with a holdfast; set down to roast, placing it rather close to the fire ten minutes, rub well over with butter, then place it at least two feet and a half from the fire, to roast very slowly, giving it a fine gold color; a fillet weighing sixteen pounds would require three hours roasting, when done take it up, detach all the string and paper, trim the top and set it upon your dish; have a pint of melted butter in a stewpan upon the fire, to which, when boiling, add four spoonfuls of Harvey sauce, and two of mushroom catsup, mix well, and pour round the fillet; have also boiled nicely an ox-tongue, which skin and trim, dress upon a dish surrounded with greens or cabbage nicely boiled, and serve as an accompaniment to the fillet.

300. *Loin of Veal.*—One with plenty of fat and a good kidney, from which the chump and the rib-bone at the other end has been removed; fasten the flap over the kidney with a skewer, run a spit through lengthwise, commencing at the thick end, and fixing it with a holdfast, cover it with buttered paper; one of fourteen pounds will take about two hours and a half to roast. Serve with melted butter poured over.

301. *Chump of Veal* can be either roasted or boiled; one about four pounds will take one hour to roast, and one hour and a quarter to boil; roasted, serve like the loin: boiled, serve with either sauces, Nos. 122, 154, 160.

302. *Breast of Veal plain roasted.*—Paper the joint, and roast for about one hour,

and serve with gravy and melted butter; it may be roasted with the sweetbread skewered to it. By taking the tendons off, stew them for entrées.

303. *Shoulder of Veal.*—One weighing fourteen pounds will take about two hours and a half to three hours to roast or braise; if roasted, the same sauce as for the loin (No. 300), and braise (No. 310).

304. *Neck of Veal.*—Procure about eight pounds of a nice white neck of veal, containing six or seven chops; saw off under part of the chine-bone, so as to give it a nice square appearance, lard it thus: take about twelve pieces of fat bacon, two inches long and a quarter of an inch square, put the larding-needle through the flesh of the veal about one inch and a half, then put one third of the length of the piece of bacon in it, pull the needle out, and it will leave the bacon in the meat, showing a quarter of an inch of the bacon outside. Then braise as ribs of beef. Two hours will suffice.

305. *Neck of Veal with Peas.*—Proceed as in the former receipt, with the exception of leaving out the vegetables, and adding, half an hour previous to the meat being done, one quart of peas, twelve button onions, and a little more sugar; remove the fat, and serve as before.

306. *Neck of Veal with Haricots.*—Proceed as before, substituting the haricots for the peas, which must have been boiled in plenty of water for three or four hours previously. (See Receipt for Haricots.)

307. *Neck of Veal with New Potatoes.*—As before, using new potatoes in place of the peas. Any other vegetable, as French beans, broad beans, &c. may be served with it in the same way.

308. *Necks of Veal* can be larded or plain roasted, or braised in plain gravy as before, and served with either sauces, Nos. 150, 135, 137, 165.

309. *Knuckle of Veal* is a very favorite dish of mine: I procure two of them, which I saw into three pieces each, and put into a stewpan, with a piece of streaked bacon two pounds in weight, four onions, a carrot, two turnips, and six peppercorns, place over the fire, and when boiling add a little salt, skim well, and place at the corner to simmer gently for two hours, take up, dress them in your dish surrounded with the vegetables and bacon, and serve with parsley and butter over; very good soup may be made from the stock it was boiled in if required, or if not, into glaze, which put by until wanted.

310. *Loin of Veal braised.*—This joint generally weighs from twelve to fourteen pounds when off a good calf; have the rib-bones carefully divided with a saw so as not to hurt the fillet, prepare the braising-pan, and proceed as in receipt (No. 289); with the addition of one pint more water, but take care not to cover the meat, which might happen if your stewpan was small, which otherwise be boiling instead of braising; it will take about three hours: be careful about the fat, as this joint produces a great deal; taste the sauce before serving, in case more seasoning is required, which might be the case, depending on the nature of the veal. A good cook should taste all sauces before serving.

311. *Breast of Veal stuffed and stewed.*—Take about eight pounds of the breast

of veal, put your knife about half an inch under the skin, and open it about three parts of its width all the way down, then prepare some veal stuffing, and lay it in the opening you have made about one inch in thickness, sew it up, and proceed as receipt for shoulder.

Should half the size of either the above dishes be required, use but half the vegetables in proportion, and stew half an hour less.

The *Chump, Small Shoulder,* or pieces of the fillet may be dressed in the same way, but must be larded, like the neck.

All the above joints may be stewed in the same way, with less vegetables, and served with sauces (Nos. 131, 135); the gravy in which they are stewed will always be useful in the kitchen, or may be reduced and served with the joint.

312. *Shoulder of Veal stuffed and stewed.* —This is a very awkward joint to carve to advantage, and equally so to cook; by the following plan, it goes further than any other way.

Take the joint and lay it with the skin-side downwards, with a sharp thin knife carefully detach the meat from the blade-bone, then hold the shoulder edgewise and detach the meat from the other side of the bone, being careful not to make a hole in the skin; then cut the bone from the knuckle and take it out; you may at first be rather awkward about it, but after once or twice trying, it will become easy; you may also take out the other bone, but I prefer it in, as it keeps the shape better: then lard the lean part like the neck in (No. 304); mix some salt and a little mixed spice together, with which rub the meat from whence the bone has been cut, stuff with veal stuffing, or sausage-meat, or suet pudding; braise, garnish, and serve as (No. 289). This being the toughest part of the veal, it should be tried before taking up, to see if it is properly done, by thrusting a larding-needle in it; if it goes in easily it is done. This joint is excellent cold, and should be carved in thin slices crosswise.

313. *Calf's Head.* —Choose one thick and fat, but not too large; soak for ten minutes in lukewarm water, then well powder with rosin, have plenty of scalding water ready, dip in the head, holding it by the ear, scrape the hair off with the back of a knife, which will come off easily if properly scraped, without scratching the cheek; when perfectly clean, take the eyes out, saw it in two lengthwise through the skull, without spoiling the brain, which take carefully out, and put to disgorge for a few hours in lukewarm water; pull the tongue out, break the jawbone, and remove the part which contains the teeth, put the head into plenty of water to disgorge for one hour; make the following stock, and boil for about two hours and a half, and it will be ready to serve.

The stock is made by putting into a braising-pan two carrots, three onions, a quarter of a pound of butter, six cloves, a bouquet of parsley, thyme, and bay-leaves, set it on the fire for about twenty minutes, keep stirring it round, then add a pint of water, and when warm mix a quarter of a pound of flour, add a gallon of water, one lemon in slices, and a quarter of a pound of salt, then lay the head in; take care it is well covered, or the part exposed will turn dark: simmer gently till tender.

LETTER NO. XII.

MY DEAR ELOISE,—Do not make any mistakes in the way you describe the above receipts, which might be made very ridiculous if wrongly explained. For example: I once had an old French Cookery Book in my hand, which had the 15th edition stamped on its old brown leather cheek, in which a receipt of "Tête de Veau à la poulette," that is, a calf's head, with white sauce, in which small onions and mushrooms are introduced, reads as follows—but, before describing it, allow me five minutes to indulge in a hearty laugh at the absurd manner in which it is explained: it reads thus: "First choose your head as thick and fat as you can, then plunge it in two gallons of water, which must be nearly boiling in a pan on the fire; let your head remain about ten minutes, then take it out by the ears, and, after remaining a short time, scrape your hair off with the back of a knife without injuring your cheek, and pull your eyes out; break your jawbone and saw your head in two without smashing your brains, which take out carefully; set it in cold water, to get clean and white; then pull out your tongue, scrape and dry it, having previously boiled it with your head, which, after two hours' ebullition, will feel as soft as possible, when see that your head is in the centre of the dish; your tongue divided in two and placed on each side of it: sharp sauce, according to No.— is allowed to be served with either head or tongue." I assure you, dear, although I do not profess to be a first-rate scholar in that fashionable language—French, that I believe this to be as near as possible the true translation of the original. Then follows calves' feet, which is nearly as absurd as the former: "Pied de Veau an naturel," Calves Feet, the natural way.—"Choose your fine feet in the rough state, and, as with your head, place a pan of water on the fire; when hot, but not too much so, put your feet in the water for about ten minutes, try if you can easily clean them as your head with a knife, if not, add a spoonful of salt in the water, and let them remain a few minutes longer; then scrape like your head; when well cleaned wipe them dry, and they are ready for dressing, which may be done in almost twenty different ways. (See the series 'How to cook Pigs' Feet.') When your feet are tender, set them on a dish, take out the big bone, surround them with sausage-meat; wrap them up in caul, and form a heart with them; then place your feet on a gridiron, let them gently broil, and, when done, eat them for breakfast or luncheon." (After which a gentle walk might give you an appetite for dinner.)

Calf's Head (No. 313) may be dressed thus:—Half of the head will make a good dish for a remove; lay it in the dish very hot, having previously drained it well; have ready about a pint of Hollandaise or cream sauce, No. 280, pour it over and serve.

It may be surrounded with a dozen new potatoes, if in season, or some quenelles, or quarters of hard-boiled eggs; a little chopped parsley thrown on the head when the sauce is over it, makes it look very inviting. It can also be served "à la poulette," by putting a pint of white sauce in a stewpan; you have peeled and cooked about fifty button onions in white broth, to which you have added a little sugar and butter, and a few mushrooms; add the broth, onions, and sauce together, and when on the point of boiling, add a liaison of two yolks of eggs and the juice of a lemon; stir it well round; it ought to be the thickness of cream sauce;

pour over the head and serve.

It can also be egged and bread-crumbed, and placed in the cream for twenty minutes to get a nice brown color, and may be served with sauces, Nos. 150, 165.

MUTTON.—The sheep, when killed, is generally divided into two, by cutting across about two ribs below the shoulder; these are called the fore and hind-quarters: the former contains the head, neck, breast, and shoulder; the latter, the leg and loin; or the two loins together, the saddle or chine; or the leg and four ribs of the loin, the haunch. The entrails are called the pluck, which are the liver, lights, heart, sweetbread, and melt. When cut up, the kernel at the tail should be removed, and that in the fat in the thick part of the leg, and the pipe that runs along the bone of the chine. The flavor depends on the breed and pasture; that is best which has a dark-colored flesh, of a fine grain, well-mixed with fat, which must be firm and white. Wether mutton is the best; the meat of ewe mutton is of a paler color, and the fat yellow and spongy. To keep a loin, saddle, or haunch, the kidney-fat should be removed, and the place rubbed with a little salt. Mutton should never be cooked unless it has hung forty-eight hours after it is killed; and it can be kept for twenty-one days, and sometimes longer in a severe winter.

314. *Haunch of Mutton.*—Saw or break three inches from the knuckle-bone, remove all skin from the loin, put it on a spit, commencing at the knuckle, and bringing it out at the flap, avoiding the fillet of the loin; then cover it with three sheets of buttered paper, place it about eighteen inches from the fire, if a large one it will take two hours and a half; half an hour before being done, remove the paper, baste it with a little butter, and dredge it slightly; when done, dish it up with a frill round the knuckle, and pour a pint of hot gravy over. In summer time, French beans should be served with it, but always mashed potatoes.

315. *Saddle of Mutton.*—The same rule in regard to choice appiles to this as to the haunch. Take off the skin, run a lark-spit through the spinal marrow-bone, which affix to a larger one with a holdfast at one end and string at the other; then tie the skin over the back, and place it down to roast; it will not take so long a time to roast in proportion as another joint, one about ten pounds will take about one hour and twenty minutes; remove the paper ten minutes before taking it from the fire, dredge to give it a nice color, and make gravy as for beef, No. 287, or serve with gravy, No. 177.

316. *Saddle of Mutton, à la Polonaise.*—This is my economical dish, *par excellence,* and very much it is liked every time I use it. Take the remains of a saddle of mutton, of the previous day, cut out all the meat close to the bone, leaving about one inch wide on the outside, cut it with a portion of the fat into small dice; then put a spoonful of chopped onions in a stewpan, with a little butter; fry one minute, add the meat, with a tablespoonful of flour, season rather high with salt, pepper, and a little grated nutmeg; stir round, and moisten with a gill or a little more of broth, add a bay-leaf, put it on the stove for ten minutes, add two yolks of eggs, stir till rather thick, make about two pounds of mashed potatoes firm enough to roll, put the saddle-bone in the middle of the dish, and with the potatoes form an edging round the saddle, so as to give the shape of one, leaving the middle empty, fill it

with your mince meat, which ought to be enough to do so; if you should not have enough with the remains of the saddle, the remains of any other joint of mutton may be used; egg all over, sprinkle bread-crumbs around, put in rather a hot oven, to get a nice yellow color, poach six eggs, and place on the top, and serve brown gravy round; white or brown sauce, if handy, is an improvement. You may easily fancy the economy of this well-looking and good dish; the remains of a leg, shoulder, loin, neck of mutton and lamb may be dressed the same way, keeping their shape of course.

317. *Roast Leg of Mutton.*—Choose the same as the haunch. One about eight pounds weight will take about one hour and a half to roast: run the spit in at the knuckle, and bring it out at the thigh-bone; roast it some little distance from the fire at first, bringing it nearer as it gets done; baste it with a little butter whilst roasting, or cover it with a sheet of well-buttered paper, which remove just before it is quite cooked. The leg of doe mutton is the best for roasting; should it be ewe, and intended for roasting, I proceed thus two or three days before I want it. I make a small incision close to the knuckle, pushing a wooden skewer close down to the leg-bone as far as it will go; I then take one tablespoonful of port wine, if none handy I use catsup, and a teaspoonful of either treacle, apple or currant jelly, and mix them together; I then remove the skewer, and run the mixture in it, closing the hole with two cloves of garlic. This joint I prefer to dangle, rather than put on the spit.

318. *Boiled Leg of Mutton.*—This I prefer of the Southdown breed, and ewe is equally as good as doe. Cut the end of the knuckle from the leg, put it into an oval pan, in which there is sufficient water to cover it, throw in about one ounce of salt, place it upon a sharp fire until it is on the point of boiling, then remove to the side, and in five minutes remove the scum, and then let it simmer gently; if the turnips are to be boiled with it, peel and slice them, and put them into the pan half an hour before the mutton is done; it must be again put on the fire for a few minutes, as the turnips have stopped the boiling; dress it upon a dish with the turnips round it, or mash separate, and with caper or gherkin sauce: the broth may be reduced for soup.

319. *Leg of Mutton à la Bretonne.*—Choose one about six pounds weight, peel four cloves of garlic, make an incision with the point of a knife in four different parts around the knuckle, and place the garlic in it, hang it up for a day or two, and then roast it for one hour and a half. At the same time you have procured a quart of small dry French haricots, which after well washing put into a saucepan with half a gallon of water, add about half an ounce of salt, the same of butter, set them on the side of the fire to simmer for about three hours or till tender, when pour the liquor off into a basin, and keep the haricots hot; peel and cut two large onions into thin slices, put some of the fat of the dripping-pan into a frying-pan, put in the onions, and fry a light brown, add them to the haricots with the fat and gravy the mutton has produced in roasting, season with salt and pepper, toss them a little, and serve very hot on a large dish, put the leg on it, with a frill of paper on the knuckle. In case the leg is very fat do not add all of it to the haricots. This if well carved is an excellent dish for eight or nine persons; it is a dish very much

esteemed in France, and is considered cheap food from the nourishment afforded by the haricots, which can be purchased at sixpence per quart.

Shoulder and loin may be dressed in the same way.

320. *Shoulder of Mutton* is best if well hung; the spit should be run in at the flap and brought out at the knuckle; this should not be basted in roasting, but merely rubbed with a little butter; it is served occasionally with sauces, No. 158. This is sometimes boiled with onion sauce; or, as it is called, smothered in onions. It is also good by having the bone extracted, and its place filled with veal stuffing, and then put it on a trivet, in a baking-dish, with sliced potatoes under, and baked more or less in proportion to its size; one of six pounds will take one hour and a half—or as follows:

Put a small shoulder of mutton in a deep sauté-pan or baking-dish, season with a little pepper and salt, cover over with thin slices of fat bacon, then put in ten potatoes peeled and quartered, and the same quantity of apples, with half a pint of water, place in a moderate oven and bake for two hours, dress upon your dish, with the potatoes and apples round, skim all the fat from the gravy, which pour over and serve; it requires a little oil or butter over before baking.

321. *Shoulder of Mutton, Provincial Fashion.*—Roast a fine shoulder of mutton; whilst roasting mince ten large onions very fine, put them into a stewpan, with two tablespoonfuls of salad-oil, pass them ten minutes over a good fire, keeping it stirred, then add a tablespoonful of flour, stir well in, and a pint of milk, season with a little pepper, salt, and sugar; when the onions are quite tender and the sauce rather thick, stir in the yolks of two eggs and take it off the fire; when the shoulder is done, spread the onions over the top, egg over, cover with bread-crumbs, put in the oven ten minutes, and salamander a light brown color, dress upon your dish, put the gravy from it in your stewpan, with a pat of butter, with which you have mixed a little flour, boil up, add a little scraped garlic, pour round the shoulder, which serve. The shoulder may also be dressed in the housewife's method, as directed for the leg. A little browning may be added.

322. *Loin of Mutton.*—Take off the skin, separate the joints with a chopper; if a large size, cut the chine-bone with a saw, so as to allow it to be carved in smaller pieces, run a lark-spit from one extremity to the other, and affix it to a larger spit, and roast it like the haunch. A loin weighing six pounds will take one hour to roast.

323. *Leg of Mutton stewed with Vegetables.*—Have a good leg, beat it a little with a rolling-pin, make an incision in the knuckle, in which put two cloves of garlic, then put it into a stewpan, with a pound of lean bacon cut in eight pieces, set over a moderate fire half an hour, moving it now and then until becoming a light brown color, season with pepper and salt, add twenty pieces of carrots of the same size as the bacon, fifteen middling-sized onions, and when done add two bay-leaves, two cloves, and two quarts of water, replace it upon a moderate fire, moving round occasionally, stew nearly three hours, dress upon your dish with the carrots and onions dressed tastefully around, take off as much of the fat from the gravy as possible, take out the bay-leaves and pour the garniture round the mutton, which serve very hot. It can be braised like No. 289. A few drops of browning may be

required.

324. *Neck of Mutton.*—This is a very *recherché* dish, if off a good-sized sheep, and well hung; it must be nicely trimmed, sawing the bones at the tips of the ribs, which detach from the meat, folding the flap over; saw off the chine-bone, and carefully detach the remainder of the bone from the fillet; detach the skin from the upper part, fix the flap under with a couple of skewers, run a flat lark-spit from end to end, fix it to a larger one, cover it with buttered paper, and roast like the haunch; if of five pounds, nearly three-quarters of an hour to one hour. It should be served very hot, the plates and dish the same, and not one minute before it is wanted: serve gravy under.

325. *Boiled Neck of Mutton.*—Take one with little fat upon it, divide the chops, taking care not to cut the fillet, put it into a pan with cold water sufficient to cover it, place in it one ounce of salt, one onion, and a small bunch of parsley, boil it gently; when done, dish it up, and serve it with either parsley and butter made from the liquor in which it was boiled, caper or onion sauce, mashed turnips separate. Proceed as under receipt with the broth.

326. *Sheep's Head.*—Though this may be seen in every part of London inhabited by the working classes, and may be procured ready-cooked, I prefer always to prepare it at home, and very good it is. I choose a fine one, as fat as possible, and put it into a gallon of water to disgorge for two hours; wash it well, saw it in two from the top, take out the brain, cut away part of the uncovered part of the skull, and also the ends of the jaws, wash it well, put it into the stewpan, with two onions, one carrot, two turnips cut in slices, a little celery, four cloves, a bouquet of four sprigs of thyme, a bay-leaf, one ounce of salt, a quarter of an ounce of pepper, three quarts of water, set on the fire; when near boiling, add half a teacupful of pearl or Scotch barley; let it simmer for three hours, or till tender, which try with a fork; take out vegetables, cut in dice, remove bouquet, skim off the fat, and pour all into tureen. Or, lay the head on a dish, and serve with either onion sauce over, parsley and butter, or any sharp sauce; or egg and bread-crumb it over, put it in an oven for half an hour till getting a nice yellow color, and serve with sharp sauce under. Or, with the brain, thus: having boiled it for ten minutes in a little vinegar, salt, and water, cut it in pieces, warm it in parsley and butter, season it a little, and put it under the head and serve.

327. *Sheep's Head and Liver.*—Boil half a sheep's liver for thirty minutes in a quart of water, cut it into small dice, put two ounces of butter in the stewpan, and set it on the fire, then add a tablespoonful of chopped onions, cook it a few minutes, add the liver, season with salt, pepper, grated nutmeg, a spoonful of flour, half-pint of broth, stir when boiling, simmer for a few minutes, lay on dish, and put the head over just as it is out of the broth, or bread-crumb it, and put it in the oven.

LAMB.—The same rules for cutting up should be observed as in the sheep. The fore-quarter consists of a shoulder, neck, and breast together; if cut up, the shoulder and ribs. The hind-quarter is the leg and loin. The head and pluck consist of the liver, lights, heart, nut and melt, as also the fry, which is the sweetbread, bits and skirts, and part of the liver. The fore-quarter should be fresh, the hind-quarter should hang, it should be of a pale color and fat. The vein in the fore-quarter ought to be bluish and firm; if yellow or green, it is very stale. To ascertain if the hind-quarter is fresh, pass your finger under the kidney, and if there is a faint smell it is not fresh. If there is but little flesh on the shoulder it is not fine lamb; those that have short wool I have found to be the best flavored. Nothing differs so much in flavor and goodness as this: much depends upon the kind of pasture on which the ewe is fed; that which is obtained when it is the dearest has but little flavor, and requires the addition of lemon and cayenne to make it palatable.

328. *Neck of Lamb à la Jardinière.*—Plain roast the neck, as you would that of mutton; dish it up with sauce, and, whilst it is roasting, cut one middling-sized carrot in small dice, the same quantity of turnip, and thirty button onions; wash all in cold water, put them in a small stewpan, with one ounce of butter and half a teaspoonful of sugar, place on the fire till no liquid remains in the stewpan; add to it a gill of brown sauce, half a one of broth, add a small bouquet of parsley and bay-leaf; after once boiling, set it to simmer on the corner of the stove, skim off all the fat; when ready, taste if very palatable; it must be a nice brown color, and the sauce lightly adhere to the back of the spoon; serve on the dish, place the neck over: white sauce may be used instead of brown, only add a spoonful of liaison when ready to serve. This sauce is equally good with almost any kind of meat, game, and poultry: it will often be referred to, therefore be particular in making it; you can shape the vegetables in twenty different ways, by using either green peas, French beans, Brussels sprouts; sprey-grass may be added, when in season, but should be boiled separately, and added just previous to serving. Should you have no sauce-water cold, a little glaze may be used; or, for white sauce, use water and milk.

329. *Saddle of Lamb, Russian fashion.*—Roast a small saddle of lamb, keeping it pale; having had it covered with paper, take ten good-sized boiled potatoes, mash them with about two ounces of butter, a teaspoonful of salt, a quarter ditto of pepper, a tablespoonful of chopped parsley, and a little grated nutmeg; mix all well together with a fork, adding half a gill of milk and one egg; when cold, roll them into a long shape the size of plover's eggs, egg and bread-crumb twice, and fry light colored; dress the saddle, surround it with the potatoes, make a sauce of melted butter and maître d'hôtel butter, No. 285, put in it, and pour it round, and serve. All joints of lamb can be dressed thus.

330. *Leg or Shoulder of Lamb with Peas.*—These must be plain roasted; when done, serve with peas in the bottom of the dish, prepared as No. 169.

331. *Leg or Shoulder with French Beans.*—Plain roast as before; prepare beans as directed. (See Vegetables.)

332. *Boiled Leg of Lamb with Spinach.*—Procure a very small leg, and cut the end of the knuckle-bone, tie it up in a cloth and place it in cold water, with two ounces of salt in it, boil it gently according to size; when done, remove the cloth, and dish it up with spinach under it, prepared as directed. (See Vegetables.)

333. *Shoulder of Lamb braised.*—Take the blade bone from a shoulder of lamb,

and have ready ten long strips of fat bacon, which season rather highly, with pepper, salt, and a teaspoonful of chopped parsley, place the pieces, one after the other, in your larding pin, which draw quickly through the fleshy part of the shoulder, leaving the bacon in the meat; after having used all the bacon, roll the meat round, and tie it up with a piece of string; then put it into a stewpan containing a quarter of a pound of butter over a slow fire, stirring it occasionally until of a light golden color, when pour in a quart of water or broth, and add forty button onions, and a bunch of parsley; let simmer very slowly until the onions are quite tender, when take up the meat, pull off the string, and dress it upon a dish with the onions round; take the parsley out of the liquor, from which carefully skim off all the fat, and reduce it until forming a thinnish glaze, when pour it over the meat and serve. Mushrooms may be added ten minutes before sending to table.

334. *Breast of Lamb broiled.*—Saw off the breast from a rib of lamb, leaving the neck of sufficient size to roast or for cutlets; then put two onions, half a carrot, and the same of turnip, cut into thin slices, in a stewpan with two bay-leaves, a few sprigs of parsley and thyme, half an ounce of salt, and three pints of water, lay in the breast, which let simmer until tender, and the bones leave with facility, when take it from the stewpan, pull out all the bones, and press it between two dishes; when cold, season with a little salt and pepper, egg and bread-crumb it lightly over, and broil gently (over a moderate fire) of a nice yellowish color, turning it very carefully; when sufficiently browned upon one side, serve with plain gravy in the dish and mint sauce separately, or with stewed peas or any other vegetable sauce; tomato sauce is likewise very good served with it.

335. *Lamb's Head.*—See Sheep's Head (No. 324). This will take half the time to cook.

336. *Lamb's Fry.*—Take about a pound and boil for ten minutes in half a gallon of water, take it out and dry on a cloth; have some fresh crumbs, mix with them half a spoonful of chopped parsley, salt, pepper; egg the fry lightly with a paste-brush, dip it in the crumbs, fry for five minutes, serve very hot on a clean napkin in a dish, with fried parsley over.

337. *Lamb's Head with Hollandaise.*—If you want it very white, make stock as for sheep's feet, put it to stew when done, lay on dish with about twelve new potatoes (boiled) round it, pour over some cream sauce (No. 280), and serve.

338. *Lamb's Head, with Brain or Liver.*—Blanch the brain or liver, and mince them as for sheep's head, introducing only the yolk of an egg; mix with a little milk, stir in quick, add a tablespoonful of chopped parsley, the juice of half a lemon, lay it on the dish with the head over, and serve.

PORK.—The flesh of no other animal depends so much upon feeding as that of pork. The greatest care ought to be observed in feeding it, at least twenty-one days previous to its being killed; it should fast for twenty-four hours before. No animal is more used for nourishment, and none more indispensable in the kitchen; employed either fresh or salt, all is useful, even to its bristles and its blood; it is the superfluous riches of the farmer, and helps to pay the rent of the cottager. It is cut up the same as the ox. The fore-quarter is the fore-loin and spring; if it is a large pig, the sparerib may be cut off. The hind-quarter is the leg and loin. There is also the head and haslet (which is the liver, kidney, craw, and skirts), and also chitterlings, which are cleansed for sausages and black puddings. For boiling or roasting it should never be older than six months, and the leg must not weigh more than from six to seven pounds. The short-legged, thick-necked, and small-headed pigs are the best breed, a cross from the Chinese. If fresh and young, the flesh and fat should be white and firm, smooth and dry, and the lean break if pinched between the fingers, or you can nip the skin with the nails; the contrary if old and stale.

339. *Leg of Pork.*—Choose the pork as described at the commencement of this series, if a leg, one weighing about seven pounds; cut an incision in the knuckle near the thigh, into which put a quantity of sage and onions, previously passed in butter, sew the incision up with pack-thread, score the rind of the pork in lines across, half an inch apart, place upon a spit, running it in just under the rind, and bringing it out at the knuckle. If stuffed the day previous to roasting, it would improve its flavor; roast (if weighing seven pounds) about two hours and a half, and serve with apple sauce in a boat.

340. *Chine of Pork.*—Score it well, stuff it thick with pork stuffing, roast it gently, and serve with apple sauce.

341. *Sparerib of Pork.*—When spitted, rub some flour over the rind, roast it before a clear fire, not too strong, or cover it with paper; about ten minutes before taking it up, throw some powdered sage over it, and froth it up with some butter in a spoon, and serve with gravy under.

342. *Loin or Neck of Pork à la Piémontaise.*—The neck or loin must be plain roasted; you have peeled and cut four onions in dice, put them into a stewpan, with two ounces of butter, stir over the fire until rather brown, then add a tablespoonful of flour, mix well, add a good pint of broth, if any, or water, with an ounce of glaze, boil ten minutes, add two tablespoonfuls of French mustard, with a little pepper, salt, and sugar, pour the sauce upon the dish, and dress your joint upon it; serve with a little apple sauce separate in a boat.

343. *Loin or Neck of Pork, Normandy fashion.*—Procure a neck or loin, put it in a common earthen dish, having previously scored the rind, rub over with a little oil, place about twenty potatoes, cut in halves or in quarters, in the dish with the pork, ten onions peeled, and twenty apples, peeled and quartered, place in a warm oven for an hour and a half or more, then dress it upon your dish with the apples, onions, and potatoes around, and serve.

344. *Bacon and Ham.*—Bacon-pigs are cut up differently for hams, bacon, &c., but a poleaxe should never be used for killing them, as it spoils the head. To be good, the fat must be firm, with a slight red tinge, the lean a dark red, and stick close to the bone; the rind thin, if young; if old (should it be well fed it is sometimes better), it will be thick. For hams, choose one short in the hock; run the knife close under the bone, when it comes out, if not smeared and has a pleasant smell, it is good.

345. *Ham.*—This useful and popular dish, which is equally a favorite in the palace and the cottage, may be dressed in upwards of fifty different ways, with

as many different dishes, which are described in their place. They should be well soaked in water, and boiled gently for three or four hours. If to serve hot, take the skin off, except from the knuckle, which cut to fancy; trim the fat to a nice appearance, glaze and serve, or throw over some sifted raspings of bread mixed with a little chopped parsley. Serve where recommended.

346. *Bacon.*—A piece of good streaky bacon, not too salt, should be put into cold water and boiled for one hour and a half, and served with broad beans, when in season, round it, or any young peas.

347. *Sucking Pig* is merely plain roasted, stuffed with veal stuffing, but before putting it upon the spit it requires to be floured and rubbed very dry, otherwise the skin would not eat crisp; the usual method of serving it is to cut off the head, and divide the body and head of the pig in halves lengthwise; pour over some sauce made of the brains and a little brown sauce, or of white melted butter, nicely seasoned with salt, pepper, and sugar; serve apple sauce separate in a boat, if approved of.

348. *Hind Quarter of Sucking Pig (Yorkshire fashion).*—Cut off the skin, cover with paper, and roast before a quick fire about three quarters of an hour; ten minutes before being ready, remove the paper and baste it; serve with gravy under, and mint sauce and salad.

349. *Salt Pork.*—Pork is salted in the same manner as described for beef, omitting the sal-prunella, but of course not requiring so long a time; a leg weighing seven pounds would be well salted in a week, as also would a hand and spring weighing about ten pounds, and either would require two hours boiling, putting them in a stewpan, with cold water, and serving with carrots and greens and pease pudding.

350. *Pig's Cheek (a new method).*—Procure a pig's cheek nicely pickled, boil well until it feels very tender, tie half a pint of split peas in a cloth, put them into a stewpan of boiling water, boil about half an hour, take them out, pass through a hair sieve, put them into a stewpan, with an ounce of butter, a little pepper and salt, and four eggs, stir them over the fire until the eggs are partially set, then spread it over the pig's cheek, egg with a paste-brush, sprinkle bread-crumbs over, place in the oven ten minutes, brown it with the salamander, and serve.

351. *Pickled Pork (Belly part).*—Choose a nice streaky piece of about four pounds, it will take about three quarters of an hour boiling; serve, garnish with greens round it.

352. *Hand of Pork.*—Choose one not too salt; boil it for one hour. Serve as above.

VENISON is cut up the same as mutton, with the exception of the saddle, which is seldom or never cut; the flesh should be dark, fine-grained and firm, and a good coating of fat on the back. It should be well hung and kept in a dry, cold place. By running a skewer in along the bone, you will know when it is fit for eating; examine it carefully every morning to cut out any fly-blows.

353. *Haunch of Venison.*—A good haunch of venison, weighing from about twenty to twenty-five pounds, will take from three to four hours roasting before a

good solid fire; trim the haunch by cutting off part of the knuckle and sawing off the chine-bone; fold the flap over, then envelop it in a flour and water paste rather stiff, and an inch thick, tie it up in strong paper, four sheets in thickness, place it in your cradle spit so that it will turn quite even, place it at first very close to the fire until the paste is well crusted, pouring a few ladlefuls of hot dripping over occasionally to prevent the paper catching fire, then put it rather further from the fire, which must be quite clear, solid, and have sufficient frontage to throw the same heat on every part of the venison; when it has roasted the above time take it up, remove it from the paste and paper, run a thin skewer into the thickest part to ascertain if done; if it resists the skewer it is not done, and must be tied up and put down again, but if the fire is good, that time will sufficiently cook it; glaze the top well, salamander until a little brown, put a frill upon the knuckle, and serve very hot, with strong gravy, and plenty of French beans separate.

354. *Neck of Venison* should be cut like a neck of mutton, taking the breast off, leaving the neck about nine inches wide; detach the flesh from the chine-bone, and saw it off, leaving only the cutlet bones, then pass a lark spit through it, cover it with paste and paper the same as the haunch, and fix on spit, and roast, if about eight pounds, for two hours before a good fire.

POULTRY.

THIS is the best and most delicious of the various matters with which man furnishes himself as food; although containing but little nourishment, it gives a delightful variety to our repasts: from the sparrow to the turkey, we find everywhere, in this numerous class, that which gives a meal equally as good for the invalid as the robust.

Increasing every day in luxuries, we have arrived at a point unknown even to Lucullus; we are not contented with the beautiful qualities which Nature gives this species, but, under pretence of improving them, we not only deprive them of their liberty by keeping them in solitude and in darkness, but force them to eat their food, and thus bring them to a degree of fatness which Nature never intended. Even the bird which saved the capital of Rome is treated with still greater indignity, — thrust into warm ovens and nearly baked alive to produce those beautiful and delicious livers so well known to gourmets.[5]

The best way of killing poultry is to take the bird by the neck, placing the thumb of the right hand just at the back of the head, closing the head in your hand, your left hand holding the bird, then press your thumb down hard and pull the head and neck contrariwise; the neck will break instantaneously, and the bird will be quite dead in a few seconds, then hang it a short time by the legs for the blood to flow into the head, which renders the flesh much whiter. In France they are usually killed by cutting the throat close to the head; both methods are good with regard to the whiteness of the flesh, but I prefer the English method, not being so barbarous.

To pluck either game or poultry have the bird upon a board with its head towards you, and pull the feathers away from you, which is the direction they lie in; many persons pull out the feathers in a contrary direction, by which means they are likely to tear the skin to pieces, which would very much disfigure the bird for the table.

To draw poultry after it is well plucked, cut a long incision at the back of the neck, then take out the thin skin from under the outer with the crop, cut the neck bone off close to the body of the bird, but leave the skin a good length, make an incision under the tail just large enough for the gizzard to pass through, no larger; then put your finger into the bird at the breast and detach all the intestines, take care not to break the gall-bladder, squeeze the body of the bird and force out the whole from the incision at the tail; it is then ready for trussing, the method of doing which will be given in the various Receipts throughout this series. The above

[5] Foie gras de Strasbourg.

method of drawing poultry is equally applicable to game.

TURKEY.—The flesh of this bird depends greatly upon its feeding; it might be made much more valuable for table if proper attention was paid to it. A young one should have his legs black and smooth and spurs short, his eyes look fresh and feet limber.

It is singular that this bird should take its name from a country in which it was never seen; in other countries in Europe it is called the Indian cock, because, on the first discovery of America by Columbus, it was supposed to be part of the continent of India, and thus it received the name of the West Indies; and this bird, being brought over on the first voyage, was thus named. By many it is supposed to have been brought over by the Jesuits in Spain and Portugal. It is familiarly called so. It is also probable that they were the first who domesticated it. I have seen it stated that it was known to the Romans, and was served at the marriage of Charlemagne. From my researches I rather think they confound it with the pheasant. It has more flavor than any other of our domestic birds, and is, consequently, held in higher estimation and enjoys a higher price. Do not fear these long receipts, as each one contains several.

355. *Plain Roasted Turkey, with Sausages.*—This well-known dish, which has the joyous recollection of Christmas attached to it, and its well-known cognomen of 'an alderman in chains,' brings to our mind's eye the famed hospitality of this mighty city. The following is my plan of cooking it.—It must be first trussed as follows: Having first emptied it, break the leg-bone close to the foot, and draw out the sinews from the thigh; cut off the neck close to the back, leaving the skin long; wipe the inside with a wet cloth, cut the breast-bone through on each side close to the back, and draw the legs close up; fold a cloth up several times, place it on the breast, and beat it down until it lies flat; put a skewer in the joint of the wing, and another through the middle of the leg and body, one through the small part of the leg and body, close to the side-bones, and another through the extremity of the two legs. The liver and gizzard should be placed between the pinions of the wings, and the points turned on the back. When thus trussed, singe all the hair off that may remain, take about one pound of stuffing (see Receipt), and put it under the skin at the neck, tie the skin under, but not too tight or it may burst in roasting, put it on to a small-sized spit and fasten it with a holdfast, or hang it neck downwards from a bottle-jack, put it about eighteen inches from a good roasting-fire, let it turn about ten minutes, when the skin is firm and dry you press into the bowl of a wooden spoon, so that it sticks, about one ounce of butter, and rub the turkey all over with it; when all melted, remove the turkey eight inches further from the fire: one of about six pounds will take two hours to roast without pouring any fat over it. In case your fire is too fierce and likely to break the skin, draw it back still more; it will, with proper care, be of a golden color. I do not object to the gizzard being placed under the wing when roasting, but never the liver, which I cook in the dripping-pan, as the gravy which would run from it would spoil the color of the breast. When done, remove it, cut the strings, lay it on your dish, and pour under half a pint of good brown gravy, or make some with glaze; or, whilst the bird is roasting, butter the bottom of a small stewpan, pick and slice two onions,

lay them at the bottom, cut the neck in small pieces, add half a spoonful of salt, a quarter ditto of pepper, a little turnip, one clove, set on a slow fire till the onions are of a brown color, then add a pint of water, let it simmer for nearly one hour, then pass it through a sieve into a basin, skim off the fat, return the gravy again into a stewpan, give it a boil, and, when the turkey is ready to send to table, pour it under; if a little beef or veal handy, add it to the gravy if you require much.

This plan of roasting is adapted for all birds, and all my receipts for plain roasting of poultry will refer to this, with the alteration of the time which each takes to cook.

For *Sausages*, I seldom broil them; I prick them with a needle, rub the bottom of the frying-pan with a little butter, put twelve sausages in it, and set it on a slow fire and fry gently for about fifteen minutes, turning them when required (by this plan they will not burst), serve very hot round the turkey, or on a separate dish, of smoking-hot mashed potatoes; to vary the gravy I have tried the following plan: take off the fat which is in the frying-pan into a basin, then add the brown gravy, mix a good teaspoonful of arrow-root in a cup with a wineglassful of cold water, pour in the pan, boil a few minutes, pass it through a sieve, and serve with the turkey. The gravy this way is excellent.

356. *Turkey with flat Sausage Cake.* —Roast as before, fry thirty oval flat sausages (see Receipt), the same quantity of the same sized pieces of bacon, a quarter of an inch thick, make a border of mashed potatoes about the size of a finger, one inch inside the edge of the dish, dress your sausages and bacon on it as a crown alternately, put your turkey in the middle, and gravy over, or glaze, if handy; plain boiled tongue may, of course, be served with the turkey, or separate on a dish of greens; if any remains of tongue from a previous day, it may be served instead of the sausages, cut the same shape as sausages and warmed in a pan; if so, put a nice green Brussels sprout between each piece. Bread sauce is generally served with this dish; for my own part, I never eat it.

Boiled Turkey. —This is a dish I rarely have, as I never could relish it boiled as it generally is, by putting it into that pure and chaste element water, into which has been thrown some salt, the quantity of which differs as much as the individuals that throw it in. I often reflect to myself, why should this innocent and well-brought up bird have its remains condemned to this watery bubbling inquisition, especially when alive it has the greatest horror of this temperate fluid; it is really for want of reflection that such mistakes occur: the flavor of a roasted turkey, hot or cold, is as superior to the boiled as it is possible to be. But yet there is a kind of boiling which can be adopted, and which I sometimes practise, which makes a nice palatable dish, and the broth can be used for other purposes. I think, if you try it, you will never again resort to that bubbling system of salt and water. I proceed as follows: —

357. *Boiled Braised Turkey.* —I truss it thus: Cut the neck, leaving the skin on; cut the legs off; then run the middle finger into the inside, raise the skin of the legs, and put them under the apron of the turkey, put the liver and gizzard in the pinions, turn the small end of the pinions on the back, run a packing-needle with

string through the joint of the wing and middle joint of the leg, and through the body, and out at the opposite leg and wing, bring it round and tie it on the back, then run the needle and string through the ends of the legs or drumstick, press it through the back, and tie strongly; it is then ready. When the turkey is trussed, I then stuff it; and if I intend to have oyster sauce with it, I chop about two dozen of them into small dice and mix them with the stuffing, and place inside the breast. I then rub the breast with half a lemon, and put it into a two-gallon pan, and cover it with cold water, in which I add two ounces of butter, one ounce of salt, four onions, a stick of celery, one carrot, two turnips sliced, a large bouquet of parsley, two bay-leaves, two sprigs of thyme; set it on the fire, when beginning to boil, skim it, let it simmer two hours, or more if large; try the breast with a needle, if it goes in and out easily it is done; take it out and set it on a dish to drain, remove the string, serve on a fresh dish with a pint of good thick oyster sauce over it; by omitting the oysters in stuffing, you may serve the turkey with celery sauce, Jerusalem sauce, tomato ditto, mushroom ditto, or good parsley and butter; and, as an accompaniment, a piece of about two pounds of nice streaked bacon, which has been boiled with the turkey, and from which you have removed the skin, and serve on some greens, or Brussels sprouts, over which you have thrown a little salt, pepper, and two ounces of oiled butter. You see, dear — —, that this dish can be varied without much expense and trouble; observe, that this way, the broth is good for soup the same day, and by the addition of two pounds of veal cut in small pieces, a quarter of a pound of lean bacon, one onion, one blade of mace, one leek, a wineglass of water; put into a separate stewpan, stew on fire till forming a white glaze, then add it to the turkey when on the point of boiling; when done, skim off all fat, pass it through a tammy or cloth; you may use it for any clear soup by adding a little brown gravy or coloring, and also for any kind of purée; or, by reducing it a little, make white or brown sauce, adding to the last the proper color. I must observe, that this will be almost impracticable when you have a party; the only plan would be to get the turkey done one hour before you require it, keeping it hot with its breast in some of the stock; but, as the broth will keep well in small quantities, it can be reserved for the next day. That is my plan of boiling, but the following is my new way of giving the flavor of vegetables to all poultry, which is a decided improvement. The aroma from the bird when the cover is removed is quite inviting, and the appearance of it, which is as white as alabaster, and cuts also full of juice: I call it—

358. *Roast Braised Turkey.*—Peel and wash two onions, one carrot, one turnip, cut them in thin slices, also a little celery, a few sprigs of parsley, two bay-leaves, lay three sheets of paper on the table, spread your vegetables, and pour over them two or three tablespoonfuls of oil; have your turkey, or poularde, trussed the same as for boiling; cover the breast with thin slices of bacon, and lay the back of the bird on the vegetables; cut a few slices of lemon, which you lay on the breast to keep it white, tie the paper round with string, then pass the spit and set it before the fire; pour plenty of fat over to moisten the paper and prevent from burning, roast three hours at a pretty good distance from the fire; capons will take two hours, poulardes one hour and a half, fowls one hour, and chickens half an hour. This way it may be served with almost any sauce or garniture, as stewed peas, oyster

sauce, jardinière, stewed celery, cauliflower, stewed cucumbers, Jerusalem arti-chokes, which should be turned in the shape of a pear: these should be dished on a border of mashed potatoes; that is, an artichoke and a Brussels sprout alternately, or a small piece of white cauliflower, and a small bunch of green asparagus, or stewed peas, or stewed celery of two inches long, never more, or any other vege-table according to season, which taste or fancy may dictate. When I want to serve them with brown garniture or sauce, I remove the paper and vegetables twenty minutes before it is done, and give it a light golden color, then I serve it with either a ragout financier, or mushroom or English truffle. I also often stuff it thus: I put two pounds of sausage meat in a basin with a little grated nutmeg; I then take two tablespoonfuls of chopped onions, put them in a sauté-pan with a little butter, and let them do for two minutes, which add to the meat, also two eggs well beaten up, and a quarter of a pint of white sauce if at hand, and fifteen fine roasted chestnuts; add this to the stuffing, and fill the bird as usual, not too full at the breast; roast as above, giving half an hour longer for the forcemeat, put a quart of demi-glaze and a glass of sherry in a stewpan, reduce it to a pint and a half, add in it fifty button onions previously stewed, and twenty-five roasted chestnuts; sauce under.

359. *Turkey, if old.* — The French stew it exactly like the ribs of beef, the receipt of which you have; but as this is a large "pièce de résistance," I think I had better give it you in full as I do it: — Put a quarter of a pound of butter into a convenient-sized stewpan, such as will comfortably hold the old gentleman; cut one pound of lean bacon in ten or twelve pieces for a few minutes in the pan on the fire, then add your turkey trussed as for boiling, breast downwards; set it on a moderate fire for one hour, and until it is a nice color, add two tablespoonfuls of flour, and stir well round until it forms a roux, then add two quarts of water or broth; when you have it on the point of boiling, add fifty pieces of carrot the size of walnuts, the like of turnip, ten button onions, a good bouquet of sprigs of thyme, two bay-leaves, and ten of parsley, a small glass of rum, a clove, a piece of garlic, and let it stew gently for four hours. If you use water, season in proportion. Take your turkey out, and put the vegetables and sauce in a smaller stewpan, which ought to be nearly full; let it simmer on the corner of the fire, so that the fat rises and may be removed, and reduce it to a demi-glaze, dish up your turkey and serve with the sauce over it; small new potatoes, about twenty, when in season, may be added to the sauce or roasted chestnuts. The remains are excellent when cold, or will warm again with the addition of a little broth or water. The series of entrées will contain the dishes made from the remnants of the foregoing receipts.

FOWLS, in a general sense, mean all kinds of poultry, but, in a limited view, mean one species of bird, which is exceedingly common in all parts of Europe: there are an amazing number of kinds of this species produced by crossing the breed; great attention having been bestowed upon this subject of late years, that it is quite impossible to say which is the best. They are not originally natives of England, but were found there by the Romans, having probably been brought by the Phœnicians. We distinguish this kind in cookery as the chicken, capon, pullet, cock, and hen. Chickens from their age cannot be otherwise but tender; capons should have a fat vein on the side of the breast, thick belly and rump, comb short and pale, spurs short and blunt, and legs smooth. Pullets are best in the spring, just before they begin to lay. Cocks should have their spurs short, legs smooth, and comb short, smooth, and a bright color. Hens, legs and comb smooth, and full breast. Black legs are best for roasting and entrées, and white for boiling.

For preparing them for table, M. Soyer has invented a plan:—by cutting the sinews of the bird, it not only appears fuller and plumper when cooked, as the heat is liable to contract the sinews, but it also affords facility for carving when the sinews are divided; they are trussed in the usual way, only using string instead of skewers. The following is the ordinary plan of trussing—

For Roasting.—Having emptied the fowl and cleaned the gizzard, cut the skin of the wings, and put the gizzard and liver through it, and turn the pinion under; put a skewer through the first joint of the pinion and the body, coming out at the opposite side, and bring the middle of the leg close up to it; run a skewer through the middle of both legs and body, and another through the drumstick and side-bone, and one through the skins of the feet, the nails of which must be cut off.

For Boiling.—Prepare as before; put the finger in the inside, and raise the skin of the legs; cut a hole in the top of the skin, and put the legs under; put the gizzard and liver in the pinions, and run a skewer through the first joint; draw the leg close up, and run a skewer through the middle of the legs and the body, tie a string on the tops of the legs to keep them in their proper place.

360. *Poulards, Capons, and Fowls.*—These are the best at nine and ten months old; if after twelve or fourteen, are only fit to be stewed like the turkey, No. 369, but in less time, or boiled in broth or sauces, but when young serve as boiled turkey, No. 367. Roast, No. 365, less time, but take care to do it well, as white meat with red gravy in it is unbearable.

361. *Capon or Poulard roasted.*—Prepare it as you would a turkey, and it may be stuffed with the same kind of stuffing, tie over the breast a large slice of fat bacon, about a quarter of an inch thick, and two sheets of paper; ten minutes before being done, remove the paper and bacon, dredge it, and put a piece of butter on it, so that it is of a nice color, dish it up very hot with a gravy like the roast turkey.

362. *Capon boiled.*—The same as the turkey.

363. *Capon or Poulard à l'Estragon.*—I have been told many fanciful epicures idolize this dish. The bird should be trussed for boiling; rub the breast with half a lemon, tie over it some thin slices of bacon, cover the bottom of a small stewpan with thin slices of the same, and a few trimmings of either beef, veal, or lamb, two onions, a little carrot, turnip, and celery, two bay-leaves, one sprig of thyme, a glass of sherry, two quarts of water, season lightly with salt, pepper, and nutmeg, simmer about one hour and a quarter, keeping continually a little fire on the lid, strain three parts of the gravy into a small basin, skim off the fat, and pass through a tammy into a small stewpan, add a drop of gravy or coloring to give it a nice brown color, boil a few minutes longer, and put about forty tarragon leaves; wash, and put in the boiling gravy, with a tablespoonful of good French vinegar, and pour over the capon when you serve it; by clarifying the gravy, it is an improvement. All kinds of fowls and chickens are continually cooked in this manner in

France. They are also served with rice.

364. *Poulard with Rice.*—Having been braised as before, have a quarter of a pound of good rice washed, put in a stewpan, with a pint of broth, three spoonfuls of the capon's fat from the stewpan, a bouquet of parsley, let it simmer until it is tender, take the parsley out, add two ounces of butter, a little salt, pepper, nutmeg, stir it round, or form it into a delicate pulpy paste, lay some of it on a dish with the capon on it, put the remainder round it, making it smooth with a knife, leaving the breast uncovered; salamander the rice, and serve clear gravy separate; sometimes I add a little curry powder in the gravy, and egg and bread-crumb the rice, and salamander or make the rice yellow with curry powder, and make a border of half eggs round the dish, it looks well, and that is a great thing; and one fowl done thus will often go as far as two plain. It is generally the custom with us to send either ham, tongue, or bacon, as an accompaniment to poultry. I endeavor to vary it as much as possible; the following is one of my receipts.

365. *Poulards or Capons, with Quenelles and Tongue.*—When you are either roasting or braising, you make about twenty quenelles with table spoons, out of forcemeat of veal. Proceed and cook the same; when done, make a roll of mashed potatoes, which put round the dish you intend to serve it in, have ready cut from a cold tongue as many pieces of the shape of the quenelles, warm gently in a little gravy, then put the quenelles on the border; having cut a piece off the end, so that they may stand properly, with a piece of tongue between each, put the fowl in the centre, have ready made a quart of a new white sauce, which pour over the fowl and quenelles, glaze the tongue, and serve very hot. I found this dish at first rather complicated, but now my cook can do it well without my assistance; it looks and eats well, but is only adapted for a dinner of importance.

366. *The same with Cucumbers.*—Cut about four nice fresh cucumbers into lengths of two inches, peel and divide them down the middle, take the seedy part out, trim the corners, put about thirty of them into a stewpan, with two ounces of butter, a spoonful of eschalot, and the same of sugar; lay on a very slow fire for half an hour, or till tender; lay them on a border of mashed potatoes, with quenelles as above, and place the tongue between; in another stewpan you have put a little butter, and the trimmings of the cucumbers, then add a quart of white sauce, boil and pass through a tammy, adding a little sugar, or other seasoning if required, and finish with half a gill of good cream sauce over all except the tongue, which glaze. Cauliflower, sprue grass, Jerusalem artichokes, or Brussels sprouts, like the turkey, make excellent and inviting dishes.

367. *Capon with young Carrots.*—Scrape two bunches of young carrots, keep them in their original shape as much as possible, wash them and dry on a cloth, put them into a stewpan with two ounces of butter, a little sugar, salt, and pepper, set it on the fire for ten minutes, moving them now and then, add a quart of white broth, simmer gently until very tender and it comes to a demi-glaze; dish the carrots on a border of potatoes, the points towards the centre, cook some small button onions the same way, but very white, and dress them alternately; mix the two gravies together with a quart of demi-glaze, set it on the fire, boil fast, skim it, when forming a bright thinnish sauce, pour it over the capon and vegetables;

it being served with a brown sauce, it ought to be roasted brown like turkey (No. 355); turnips may also be added instead of carrots, or both.

368. *Fowls, Italian way.*—Prepare and cook the fowls as above, or re-warm some that may be left, cut the remains of a tongue into pieces one inch long and one quarter in thickness, cut three times the quantity of plain boiled macaroni the same way, with a few mushrooms, and add the whites of four eggs to it, with some broth and half a pint of white sauce; when boiling, add a quarter of a pound of grated Parmesan and half that of Gruyère, shake the stewpan so that the contents are well mixed, add a little salt and cayenne, put fowl on dish, sauce over and serve; or put the macaroni on the dish, mix bread-crumbs and a little grated cheese together and sprinkle over it, put it into the oven until it is a yellow-brown color, put the fowl on it very hot, and serve with a little white sauce over, and a strong gravy separate.

369. *Fowl à l'Ecarlate.*—Roast and braise two nice fowls, and boil a fine salted tongue, which trim so as to be able to stand it in a dish, when place it in the middle in a slanting position, place two fine heads of cauliflower at each end, and make a pint of cream sauce, pour over the fowl, and brocoli; glaze the tongue and serve. Fowls may be dressed in any of the ways before described, and dished up thus.

GEESE.—We have now arrived at your favorite dish, or, as your better half said on your return home from this, "What is better than a goose stuffed with sage and onion!" Of course many persons are of his idea, and I must say that I for one enjoy them occasionally when in season; yes, indeed I do, and with the original apple-sauce too; this last addition to our national cookery must have been conferred on it by the Germans, who eat sweets or stewed fruit with almost every dish; or, perhaps, from William the Conqueror, who left his land of apples to visit and conquer our shores; but never mind to whom we are indebted for this bizarre culinary mixture, I sincerely forgive them, and intend to have one for dinner to-day, which I shall have cooked as follows; but I must first tell you how they should be chosen. The flesh should be of a fine pink color, and the liver pale, the bill and foot yellow, and no hairs, or but few, on the body; the contrary will be observed in an old one, which will have the feet and bill red.

370. *Goose (to truss).*—Having well picked the goose, cut the feet off at the joint, and the pinion at the first joint; cut off the neck close to the back, leaving all the skin you can; pull out the throat, and tie a knot at the end; put your middle finger in at the breast, loosen the liver, &c., cut it close to the rump, and draw out all the inside except the soal,[6] wipe it well, and beat the breast bone flat; put a skewer in the wings, and draw the legs close up, running a skewer through the middle of both legs and body; draw the small of the leg close down to the side bone, and run a skewer through; make a hole in the skin large enough to admit the trail, which when stuffed place through it, as it holds the stuffing better.

371. *Roast Goose.*—Peel and cut in rather small dice six middle-sized onions, put in a pan, with two ounces of butter, half a teaspoonful of salt, a quarter ditto

---

[6] This word is not found in dictionaries, but is used by poulterers to denote that small piece of the lungs which is left in the bird.

of pepper, a little grated nutmeg and sugar, six leaves of fresh sage chopped fine, put on fire, stir with wooden spoon till in pulp, then have the goose ready trussed as under, and stuff it whilst hot, tie the skin of the neck to the back, pass the spit through and roast two hours before a moderate fire; baste the same as turkey (No. 355), give a nice yellow color, remove it from the spit, take off the string, and serve with half a pint of good brown gravy under and apple-sauce in a boat.

372. *The same, with another stuffing.* —I have tried it with the liver chopped and mixed it with the onions; I also at times add two cold potatoes cut in dice and a spoonful of boiled rice; it removes the richness of the fat, and renders it more palatable and digestive; and I also sometimes add twenty chestnuts cut into dice. The giblets should be stewed or made into pies. (See Receipt.) Where there is no gravy, broth, or glaze, still gravy is wanted, therefore put into the dripping-pan a teaspoonful of salt, half a pint of water, and dredge a little flour on it; when the bird is done, pour the contents of the pan into a cup, remove the fat, pour over the back of the bird, which serve on a very hot dish as soon as taken from the fire.

373. *Goose roasted (another way).* —Having the goose ready the day previous to using, take three cloves of garlic, which cut into four pieces each and place inside the goose, and stuff it as follows; take four apples, four onions, four leaves of sage not broken, four leaves of lemon-thyme not broken, and boil in a stewpan with sufficient water to cover them; when done, pulp them through a sieve, removing the sage and thyme, then add sufficient pulp of mealy potatoes to cause it to be sufficiently dry without sticking to the hand, add pepper and salt, and stuff the bird, having previously removed the garlic, tie the neck and rump, and spit it, paper the breast, which remove after it has been at the fire for twenty minutes; when done, serve it plain with a thickened gravy.

374. *Goose stewed.* —If an old one, stew it with vegetables, as duck (No. 378), only give it more time to cook. On the Continent they are dressed in different ways, but which are too complicated for both our kitchens.

375. *Goose Giblets, Ragout of, or of Turkey.* —Put them into half a gallon of warm water to disgorge for a few hours, then dry them on a cloth, cut into pieces not too small, put into a stewpan a quarter of a pound of good lean bacon, with two ounces of butter; when a little brown, add your giblets, and fry for twenty minutes longer, stirring it together; add a little flour, a good bouquet of parsley, twenty button onions, same number of pieces of carrot and turnip, two saltspoonfuls of salt, the same of sugar, stew together one hour until tender, skim off the fat, dish up the meat, reduce the salt if required, take bouquet out, and sauce over the giblets: both goose and turkey giblets take the same time to stew. If any remaining, they will make a capital pie or pudding, or merely warm up with broth or water, and a little flour.

376. *Preserved Goose for the Farm, or Country House.* —In case you have more geese in condition and season than what you consume, kill and cut them up into pieces, so that there shall be as little flesh left on the carcase as possible, and bone the leg; rub into each piece with your fingers some salt, in which you have mixed a little saltpetre, put them into an earthen pan, with some thyme, bay-leaf, spice, a

clove of chopped garlic, rub them for a couple of days, after which dip each piece in water and dry on a cloth; when you have chopped fine and melted all the fat you could get from the goose, and scraped a quarter of a pound of fat bacon and melted with it, pass through a sieve into a stewpan, lay the pieces in it, and bake very gently in a slow oven until a stiff piece of straw will go through it, then lay it in a sieve; when nearly cold put it in a bowl or round preserving jar, and press a smaller one on the top so that it all forms one solid mass, pour the fat over, when cold cover with a piece of bladder, keep it in a cold place, and it will be good for months together, and is excellent for breakfast, luncheon, or supper, having previously extracted the fat. Last winter I kept some for three months quite sweet; having half a one left, I put it by in the above way, bones and all, in a basin, and covered with the fat produced with roasting, and put in the larder, and it was excellent. Ducks may be served in the same way.

DUCKS.—There are several varieties of this bird, all, however, originating from the mallard. There has not been that care and attention paid to this bird as to the fowl; but I think it is well worthy the attention of farmers, it being one which is exceedingly cheap to rear; great care should be evinced in feeding it twelve days previous to its being killed. Ducklings are considered a luxury, but which, I think, is more to be attributed to their scarcity than flavor. The drake is generally considered the best, but, as a general rule, those of the least gaudy plumage are the best; they should be hard and thick on the belly, and limber-footed.

377. *Ducks roasted.*—Prepare them for the spit (that is, the same as geese, only leave the fat on), and stuff them with sage, onion, and bread-crumbs, prepared as for the goose, roast before a very quick fire, and serve very hot. There are many ways of cooking ducks, but this is the plainest and the best.

378. *Stewed Duck and Peas.*—Procure a duck trussed with the legs turned inside, which put into a stewpan with two ounces of butter and a quarter of a pound of streaked bacon let remain over a fire, stirring occasionally until lightly browned, when add a tablespoonful of flour (mix well) and a quart of broth or water, stir round gently until boiling, when skim, and add twenty button onions, a bunch of parsley, with a bay-leaf, and two cloves, let simmer a quarter of an hour, then add a quart of nice young peas, let simmer until done, which will take about half an hour longer, take out the duck, place it upon your dish (taking away the string it was trussed with), take out the parsley and bay-leaf, season the peas with a little pepper, salt, and sugar, skim the fat, reduce a little if not sufficiently thick, pour over the duck and serve.

379. *Duckling with Turnips* is a very favorite dish amongst the middle classes in France. Proceed as in the last, but instead of peas use about forty pieces of good turnips cut into moderate-sized square pieces, having previously fried them of a light yellow color in a little butter or lard, and drained them upon a sieve, dress the duck upon a dish as before, season the sauce with a little pepper, salt, and sugar, reduce until rather thickish, a thin sauce not suiting a dish of this description; the turnips must not, however, be in purée; sauce over and serve.

The remains of ducks left from a previous dinner may be hashed as directed for goose, and for variety, should peas be in season, a pint previously boiled may be added to the hash just before serving. The sage and apple must in all cases be omitted.

380. *Ducks à l'Aubergiste (or Tavern-keepers' fashion).*—Truss one or two ducks with the legs turned inside, put them into a stewpan with a quarter of a pound of butter; place them over a slow fire, turning round occasionally, until they have taken a nice brown color, add two spoonfuls of flour, mix well with them, add a quart of water, with half a tablespoonful of salt and sugar, let simmer gently until the ducks are done (but adding forty button onions well peeled as soon as it begins to boil), keep hot; peel and cut ten turnips in slices, fry them in a frying-pan in butter, drain upon a cloth, put them into the sauce, and stew until quite tender; dress the ducks upon your dish, skim the fat from the sauce, which has attained a consistency, add some fresh mushrooms, pour round the ducks and serve.

FLANCS.

AT this part of the dinner there are those dishes which are called Flancs, by which is understood, those dishes whose contents are not so large as the removes and not so small as the entrées, and the Receipts for which may be taken from either of those departments, with this difference;—instead of meat or poultry being cut up, it should be left whole: for instance, a loin of mutton, instead of being cut up into cutlets, should be served whole, with some sauce under it, and a duck, instead of being divided, should be left whole, with some sauce. It is also a great addition in the appearance of the table, and should always be served in a differently-formed dish to the entrées or removes; and are only required when eighteen or twenty persons dine, and four corner dishes are used.

ENTRÉES OR MADE DISHES.

ENTRÉES are, in common terms, what are called made-dishes; of course, these are dishes upon which, in the high class of cookery, the talent of the cook is displayed. Great care should be observed in dishing them up, for the eye is a great assistance to the palate; it often happens that the carelessness of the servant destroys the labors of the cook, by the manner in which the dish is taken from the kitchen to the dining-room. In some measure to avoid that, I direct a small thin border of mashed potatoes, about half an inch wide and a quarter of an inch deep, to be placed on the bottom of the dish, which keeps each object in its place: they should always be served exceedingly hot.

Made Dishes of Beef.—The remainder of any cooked joints of beef may be advantageously and economically dressed in the following ways:

381. *Hashed Beef.*—Cut the beef into small thin slices, which lay upon a plate, and to every pound of beef add half a tablespoonful of flour, a little chopped onion or eschalot, two salt-spoonfuls of salt, and a half one of pepper, mix the whole well together, and put it into a saucepan, with half a pint of water, stir it over the fire until upon the point of boiling, when set it at the corner of the fire to simmer for ten minutes; it is then ready to serve. A great improvement to the appearance of hash may be effected by adding a few spoonfuls of brown gravy (No. 177), or a teaspoonful of coloring (No. 178), which might always be kept in a bottle. The flavor of any kind of hash may be varied, by adding a few sprigs of parsley, or thyme, or a couple of bay-leaves, or a little tarragon, or a few spoonfuls of catsup, Soyer's, Harvey's, Soho, or Reading sauce.

382. *Miroton of Beef.*—Peel and cut into thin slices two large onions, put them in a stewpan or saucepan, with two ounces of salt butter, place it over a slow fire, keeping the onions stirred round with a wooden spoon until rather brown, but not burnt in the least, then add a teaspoonful of flour, which mix well in, and moisten with half a pint of water or broth if handy, season with three saltspoonfuls of salt, two of sugar, and one of pepper if water has been used, but if broth, diminish the quantity of salt, add a little coloring (No. 178), to improve its appearance; put in the beef, which you have previously cut into small thin slices, as free from fat as possible, let it remain a few minutes upon the fire to simmer, and serve upon a hot dish. To vary the flavor, a tablespoonful of vinegar might be added, or half a glass of sherry. The above proportions are sufficient for one pound and a half of solid meat, and of course could be increased or diminished, if more or less meat.

383. *Another way.*—Prepare the meat precisely as in the last, and when done put it into a pie-dish, sprinkle bread-crumbs lightly over, enough to cover the

meat, upon which lay a small piece of butter, put the dish in the oven for half an hour, or before the fire, with a screen behind it, turning the dish round occasionally. By grating the crust of bread you would obtain some brown bread-crumbs, which would do equally as well as bread rubbed through a sieve.

Should you have any cold from the first receipt, it may be served as here directed; but being cold, would require to be longer in the oven to become well hot through.

384. *Another way.*—If any left from a previous dinner, put it in a dish, placing the meat in the centre, rather higher, cover over with some delicate mashed potatoes, about two inches in thickness, to form a dome, rub some egg over with a paste-brush, and sprinkle crumbs of bread (either grated or otherwise) upon the top, and set in the oven until well browned, when serve.

385. *A quicker way.*—Cook a few slices of lean bacon in a frying-pan, but not too much, lay some of them in the bottom of the pie-dish, over which lay slices of beef cut thin, which season with a little pepper, salt, chopped parsley, and chopped eschalots (if not objectionable), sprinkle over a little flour, proceeding thus until the dish is pretty full, when pour over half a gill of broth or water, to which you have added a little coloring, No. 178, (more seasoning would be required if water was used), set the dish in the oven (having previously covered the meat over with mashed potatoes) for about an hour. By adding half the above quantity of liquor, the meat might be covered with a thin suet crust and served as a pie, as also might any of the former receipts, in which also a bay-leaf, chopped parsley, or even chopped gherkins, might be served, being a great improvement.

386. *Beef Palates.*—Although this is an article very seldom used in small families, they are very much to be commended; they may be dressed in various ways, and are not expensive, about four would be sufficient for a dish. Put them into a large stewpan of lukewarm water, where let them remain four or five hours to disgorge, after which pour off the water, cover again with fresh water, and place the stewpan upon the fire until the palates become hard, when take out one, which dip into cold water, scrape it with a knife, and if the skin comes off easily, take out the remainder, but if not, let them remain a short time longer, scrape them until you have got off all the skin, and nothing but the white half transparent substance remains. Then make a white stock as directed (No. 130), in which boil them three or four hours until very tender, which try with the point of a knife, then take them up, lay them flat upon a dish, covered with a little of the stock, and place another dish of the same size over, to keep them flat, let remain until cold, when they are ready to serve in either of the following ways:—

387. *Beef Palates à la Bretonne.*—Peel and cut two large onions into slices, which put into a stewpan, with an ounce of butter, stirring them over the fire until lightly fried, when add a teaspoonful of flour, which mix well in, and a gill of broth, season with a little pepper, salt, and sugar, add a few drops of brown gravy or browning (No. 179), and a spoonful of mustard; boil the whole, keeping it stirred until forming a thickish pulp, when cut the palates into square pieces, and put into it; when well hot through they are ready to serve; also make a curry sauce, as No.

151; cut your palate and warm in it, serve with rice separate, and it is delicious.

388. *Beef Palates à la Poulette.* — Make a little white sauce as directed, No. 130; after having prepared the palates, cut them into square pieces, and put them into a stewpan, just covered with some of the white sauce, season with a little white pepper, salt, sugar, chopped parsley, and the juice of half a lemon; let them simmer about five minutes, when pour in a liaison of one yolk of an egg, mixed with two tablespoonfuls of cream or milk, stir it in rather quickly, and not afterwards permitting it to boil, then turn it upon your dish, place sippets of toasted bread round, and serve: chopped parsley and a little lemon may be added.

389. *Beef Palates à la Maître d'Hôtel.* — Cut up the palates as in the last, and put them into a stewpan, just covered with melted butter, to which add a gill of milk, let simmer very gently about ten minutes, stirring it round occasionally; have ready two ounces of well-seasoned maître d'hôtel butter, which put into the stewpan, shaking it round until the butter is melted and well mixed, when serve as in the last.

390. *Ox-tails à la Jardinière.* — Cut and cook two ox-tails as directed for soup, but just before they are done, skim well, and take out the pieces of tails, which put upon a dish, then in another stewpan put two ounces of butter, to which, when melted, add three ounces of flour, stirring it over the fire until forming a brownish roux (thickening), then mix by degrees two quarts of the stock the tails were boiled in, and boil altogether ten minutes, then put in the tails, with one carrot and two turnips (cut into small dice, or any other shape, with a vegetable cutter), and about thirty button onions; let the whole simmer very gently upon the corner of the fire, keeping it well skimmed, until the vegetables are tender, and the sauce sufficiently thick to adhere to the back of the spoon, when dress the meat upon a dish, reduce the sauce, which pour over, and serve.

391. *Ox-tails au Gratin.* — Cook two ox-tails as before, and when cold, dry them upon a cloth, season with pepper and salt, have a couple of eggs well beaten upon a plate, into which dip each piece singly, afterwards throwing them into a dish of bread-crumbs, to cover every part, then beat them lightly with a knife, and again egg and bread-crumb them, broil them upon a gridiron, or place them in a very hot oven until of a brownish color, when serve with any sauce you may fancy, or with a little plain gravy.

392. *Ox-tails, Sauce piquante.* — Cook the tails as before, and when done dress them upon your dish pyramidically, then make about a pint of sharp sauce, No. 135, but omitting half the quantity of vinegar, and reducing it until rather thick; season rather highly, add three or four gherkins chopped very fine, pour the sauce over, and serve.

393. *Ox Heart.* — This dish, although not very *recherché*, is a good family one, and remarkable for its cheapness. Put it into lukewarm water one hour to disgorge, then wipe it well with a cloth, and stuff the interior with a highly-seasoned veal stuffing, tie it up in paper, and pass a small spit through the sides, set it before a good fire for about two hours to roast, keeping it well basted; when done, take off the paper, and serve with any sharp sauce, or a little plain gravy. Two hours would

be sufficient to roast a large heart; but if smaller, of course less time in proportion would be required. I have also stuffed a heart with sage and onion, and even ventured the apple sauce: both succeeded admirably.

I remember, when in business, upon one occasion, having a few friends pop in unexpectedly about luncheon-time upon a Saturday (which is a day I always contrived to keep my larder as short as possible), and having nothing but a heart as a meal to give them, I immediately gave orders to the cook to cut it into slices half an inch thick, dip each piece in flour, and afterwards egg and bread-crumb them, then to put four spoonfuls of oil in the frying-pan, lay part of the pieces in, and sauté of a nice color, then to keep them hot in a dish and sauté the remainder; and when all done, to pour off part of the oil, put a teaspoonful of flour in the pan, mixing it with the remaining oil and gravy, then pouring in a gill of water, season with a little pepper and salt, four spoonfuls of the vinegar from piccalilly, and a little of the pickle finely chopped; boil the whole a minute, pour over the heart, and serve very hot. It pleased very much, and I have since had some with a little plain gravy, and broiled bacon: in both instances it was very good.

394. *Potato Sandwiches.*—Sauté the slices of beef as directed for bubble and squeak, cover one side of each piece with mashed potatoes a quarter of an inch in thickness, egg and bread-crumb over, then proceed the same with the other sides, fry in hot fat of a light brown color, as you would a sole, and serve. Any kind of fresh meat may be used in the same way.

395. *Bubble and Squeak.*—I am certain you must know, as well as myself, of our hereditary dish called bubble and squeak; but, like the preparation of other things, there is a good way and a bad; and, as you prefer the former to the latter, proceed as follows:—Boil a few greens, or a savoy cabbage (which has been previously well-washed), in plain water until tender, which then drain until quite dry in a colander or sieve, put it upon a trencher, and chop it rather fine with a knife, then for a pound of salt beef you have in slices, put nearly a quarter of a pound of butter into a frying-pan, in which sauté the beef gently but not too dry; when done, keep it hot, put the cabbage in the frying-pan, season with a little salt and pepper, and when hot through, dress it upon a dish, lay the beef over and serve. Endive or large cabbage-lettuces may be used instead of cabbage, but care must be taken to drain off all the water.

396. *Stewed Beef or Rump Steak.*—Have a steak weighing two pounds, and an inch and a half in thickness, then put two ounces of butter at the bottom of a stewpan, when melted lay in the steak, with a quarter of a pound of lean bacon cut into very small square pieces, place the stewpan over the fire, turning the steak over occasionally until a little browned, when lay it out upon a dish, then add a tablespoonful of flour to the butter in the stewpan, which continue stirring over the fire until forming a brownish roux, then again lay in the steak, add a pint of water, with a glass of sherry if handy, and a little pepper, salt, and a couple of bay-leaves, let simmer slowly for one hour, when skim off all the fat, and add twenty button onions, let it again simmer until the onions are very tender, as likewise the steak, which dress upon a dish, take the onions and bacon out with a colander-spoon, and lay them upon the steak, pour the sauce round and serve. This slow process

must not alarm you.

397. *Ox Brains* are prepared exactly as directed for calf's brains, but being larger, require much longer to disgorge, as also a proportionate time longer to cook; when done, in addition to the sauce ordered for calf's brains, they may be served with strips of bacon broiled and dressed in a border round, sauce over with highly-seasoned melted butter and parsley sauce. You must observe, that all such kind of dishes being of themselves naturally tasteless, require to be highly seasoned: any sharp sauce is good with it.

398. *Beef à-la-Mode.*—Procure a small piece of rump, sirloin, or ribs of beef, about twelve pounds in weight, take away all the bone, and lard the meat through with ten long pieces of fat bacon, then put it into a long earthen pan, with a calf's foot, four onions, two carrots, cut in slices if large, a bunch of parsley, two bay-leaves, two sprigs of thyme, two cloves stuck into one of the onions, half a tea-spoonful of pepper, one of salt, four wine-glasses of sherry, four ditto of water, and a pound of streaky bacon cut in squares, place the cover over the pan with a piece of common flour and water paste round the edges to keep it perfectly air-tight, and place it in a moderate oven four hours, when take out of the pan, and dress upon a dish with the vegetables and bacon round, skim and pass the gravy through a hair sieve, which pour over and serve. But the above is best eaten cold, when it should not be taken from the pan, or the pan opened until nearly so.

A long brown earthen pan for the above purposes may be obtained at any china warehouse, but should you not be able to procure one, a stewpan must supply its place.

399. *Another method.*—Have ready six pounds of rump of beef, cut into pieces two inches square, each of which lard through with two or three strips of bacon; have also two pounds of streaky bacon, which clear from the rind and cut into squares half the size of the beef, put the whole into an earthen pan, with two calf's feet (cut up small), half a pint of sherry, two bay-leaves, a sprig of thyme, a bunch of parsley, four onions, with a clove stuck in each, a blade of mace, and half a pint of water, cover the pan as in the last, and put it in a moderate oven for three hours; when done, do not remove the lid until three parts cold, then take out the meat, lay some of the beef at the bottom of the stewpan (not too large), then a little bacon, then more beef, and so on alternately, press them lightly together, pass the gravy through a hair sieve over, and leave it until quite cold and set, when dip the stewpan into hot water, and turn it out upon a dish to serve. The calf's feet may be made hot in a little of the stock, to which add two pats of butter, with which you have mixed a teaspoonful of flour, season with a little chopped parsley and half a spoonful of vinegar, and serve as an entrée. The above is excellent either hot or cold.

400. *Fillet of Beef.*—Procure a piece of fillet of beef weighing about two or three pounds, which may be obtained at any butcher's, being cut from underneath the rump; trim off part of the fat, so as to round the fillet, which cut into slices the thickness of your finger, beat them lightly with a chopper, and cut the thin skin which covers the top of the fillet, to prevent their curling up whilst broiling; place

them upon a gridiron over a sharp fire, seasoning with a little salt and pepper, and turning three or four times to preserve the gravy: about six or seven minutes will be sufficient to cook them. Three or four slices would be sufficient for a corner dish; but if for a principal dish, of course more would be required. Fillet of beef dressed as above may be rubbed over with maître d'hôtel or anchovy butter, and served very hot.

401. *Fillet of Beef sauté.*—After having cut the fillet in slices as in the last, put two ounces of butter into a clean frying-pan, which set upon the fire, and when melted, lay in the meat, seasoned with a saltspoonful of salt and half that quantity of pepper to each piece; turn them over three or four times whilst cooking, and, when done, dress upon your dish, with either of the butters mentioned in the last spread over.

402. *Another method.*—When the fillets are dished up, put a tablespoonful of chopped onions into the pan they were cooked in, which cook for about a minute, but not letting them burn, then pour off part of the fat, if too much, and add two teaspoonfuls of flour; stir with a wooden spoon until becoming brownish, then add nearly a pint of water, a tablespoonful of vinegar, and a few drops of browning; let it boil a few minutes, seasoning with a little pepper, salt, and sugar; when of the consistency of thick sauce, pour over the fillets and serve. A few chopped pickles of any description (but not too hot) might be introduced, but then half the quantity of vinegar would be sufficient. A spoonful of Harvey's sauce may be added, and a little glaze improves it.

Mutton, lamb, or pork-chops, or veal-cutlets may be dressed in a similar manner.

403. *Minced Beef.*—Cut a pound and a half of lean cooked beef into very small dice, which put upon a plate; in a stewpan put a good teaspoonful of finely-chopped onions, with a piece of butter of the size of a walnut, which stir over the fire until the onions become lightly browned, when stir in half a tablespoonful of flour, with which mix by degrees half a pint of broth (or water) to which you have added a few drops of browning and a teaspoonful of vinegar; let it boil five minutes, stirring it the whole time; then throw in the meat, season rather highly with a little pepper and salt, and, when hot, pour it into a deep dish, and serve with sippets of toasted bread round, or poached eggs on it.

404. *Croquettes of Beef.*—Proceed precisely as in the last, but omitting the vinegar; when done, stir in two yolks of eggs quickly, stir another minute over the fire, then pour it upon a dish until cold; have a couple of eggs well beaten upon a plate, also some bread-crumbs in a separate dish, then divide the preparation into about a dozen pieces, which roll up into round balls, or any other shape, and throw them into the bread-crumbs, move them over until well covered, then roll them into the egg, then the bread-crumbs again, from which take them gently, patting the surface lightly with a knife, put them into very hot lard or fat to fry of a yellowish-brown color, being careful not to break them whilst frying; when done drain them upon a cloth, and serve either upon a napkin or with fried parsley.

405. *A Family French Salad for the Summer.*—I can assure you that, when in

France during the hot weather, I used to enjoy the following salads immensely, having them usually twice a week for my dinner; they are not only wholesome, but cheap and quickly done. Cut up a pound of cold beef into thin slices, which put into a salad-bowl with about half a pound of white fresh lettuce, cut into pieces similar to the beef, season over with a good teaspoonful of salt, half that quantity of pepper, two spoonfuls of vinegar, and four of good salad oil, stir all together lightly with a fork and spoon, and when well mixed it is ready to serve.

For a change, cabbage-lettuce may be used, or, if in season, a little endive (well washed), or a little celery, or a few gherkins; also, to vary the seasoning, a little chopped tarragon and chervil, chopped eschalots, or a little scraped garlic, if approved of, but all in proportion, and used with moderation. White haricot beans are also excellent with it.

406. *Potatoes and Meat Salad.*—Proceed as in the last, but omitting the lettuce; if any cold potatoes remain from a previous dinner, peel and cut them in halves if small, but in quarters if large, and then into pieces the size of a shilling but four times the thickness; put them into a salad-bowl with the meat, seasoning as before, but using more oil and vinegar, and adding a teaspoonful of chopped parsley. A small quantity of any description of pickles might be added to this salad, as also some anchovies or olives. The remains of any fowls, turkey, cold veal, lamb, or even mutton, may be mixed in salads, but, according to our habits, many persons would fancy they were not nutritious; of that I can assure them to the contrary.[7]

407. *Ox-Kidneys.*—Cut a nice fresh ox-kidney into slices, each being about the size of a half-crown piece, but double the thickness (avoiding the white part, or root, which is tough and indigestible), then put a quarter of a pound of butter into a stewpan upon the fire, and when very hot but not black, put in the pieces of kidney, stirring them round with a wooden spoon three minutes over a brisk fire; then add, for each pound weight of kidney, half a tablespoonful of flour, half a teaspoonful of salt, half the quantity of pepper, and a little sugar, moisten with a gill of water and half a glass of sherry, add a little browning if handy, and let simmer gently for five minutes, stirring them round occasionally; if too thick, add a few drops more of water, the same should be sufficiently thick to adhere to the back of the spoon, pour them out upon your dish, and serve very hot. Broth might be used instead of water if convenient, but then the seasoning should be a little diminished, a little chopped eschalot, parsley, or a few mushrooms, would be an improvement.

By cutting an ox-kidney lengthwise in three slices, it might be broiled or sautéd; if for gentlemen, season rather highly, but if ladies are to be the partakers, season more moderately; a little gravy may be served with it, to which you have added a little catsup; the root of the kidney must not be cut away in this case, although not eatable. Ox-kidneys are also an excellent addition to beef-steak puddings and pies.

[7] The quantity of the meat and vegetable should pretty equally balance with each other; after such a meal, a man's appetite is perfectly satisfied, and he is ready for an afternoon's work if required. It also does not require the aid of any fire, which we so ungratefully abhor in hot weather. Mr. B. very much approves of it once a week in summer.

408. *Ox-Feet or Cow-Heels* are very nutritious, especially when well boiled; they may be served in either of the methods directed for tripe, or with a plain parsley-and-butter sauce, to which, for a change, the juice of a lemon or a drop of vinegar may be added. Should any be left from the first day's dinner, it may be served à la Lyonnaise, as directed for cold tripe.

409. *Remains of Ox-Tongue.*—The remains of a tongue from a previous dinner may be again served thus:—Cut it into thin slices, put a small piece of butter into a frying-pan, lay the pieces of tongue over, which warm a few minutes in a sauté-pan, and serve with veal or fowl, if any; when at home alone, I frequently have it with mashed potatoes under, it makes a very good dish for luncheon. The pieces of tongue might also be egged and bread-crumbed previous to cooking as above, and served with a plain gravy, or any sharp sauce. (See Sauces.) Or should you have any tongue, and veal or beef remaining, sprinkle a little chopped eschalots at the bottom of a pie-dish, lay a layer of meat over, season with a little salt, pepper, and chopped parsley, then a layer of the tongue; have some yellowish crusts of bread grated, a teaspoonful of which sprinkle over the tongue, then again a layer of the meat, proceeding thus until the dish is nearly full, when sprinkle more of the brown bread-crumbs over the top, placing a small piece of butter here and there; pour in two wineglassfuls of water, set it in a warm oven half an hour, and serve very hot. Or instead of bread-crumbs, make a little good mashed potatoes, which spread over it smoothly with a spoon or knife, bake half an hour in a warm oven, and serve.

Should the remains of a tongue be but small, and if well pickled and boiled, the root and all would be excellent in any kind of beef, lamb, mutton, veal, or pork, hashed, or in pies or puddings made from those meats.

410. *Remains of Salt Beef.*—The remains of salt beef are very excellent, served in the few following ways, no matter from what joint, or from what part of the joint: cut as large and thin slices as possible, dip each slice into some vinegar from mixed pickles, previously poured upon a plate in small quantities; lay about a pound of the meat thus prepared upon a flat dish, pour a wineglassful of water over, warm it through in the oven, or before a small fire, and serve. Another way is, after having dipped the beef in pickles, roll them in flour and proceed as above, adding double the quantity of water. Another way is to sauté the slices with a little butter in a frying-pan, have ready some nice mashed potatoes very hot, lay the beef over, and serve.

Fricandeau of Veal.—This is a very favorite dish of mine. It is generally considered an expensive one, but the way in which I do it, it is not so; besides which, it gives a nice piece of veal at table, when a fillet would be too large. I proceed to prepare it thus:

411. Having the fillet prepared with the bone out as if for roasting, I lay it on a board with the skin side downwards, and then remove (not cutting it) that part of the outside which is separated from the thick fleshy part (in France called "la noix") of the fillet by a skin; I then place my hand on the top of the thick part, and cut away two thirds of it, leaving an inch to an inch and a half of flesh for the fillet.

I then take a chopper dipped in cold water, and beat the veal with the flat part, so as to make it of an equal thickness; I then lard it (see Larding). You may not succeed very well the first or second time, but now I am quite an artist in larding, as is also my cook, whom I taught, it being so much like sewing. But should you not be able to manage it, you must send it to the poulterer. The remains make an excellent fillet for another day's dinner. Having proceeded thus far, I then cook it in the following manner:

412. I take a stewpan of a convenient size, and lay on the bottom six or eight slices of bacon, and place the fricandeau on them; I then take two onions, two small carrots cut in slanting pieces, which place round it; I then make a bouquet of ten sprigs of parsley, two of thyme, two of bay-leaf, which I put in with two cloves, half a blade of mace, and about a pint of broth or water, so as not to cover the larding; if no broth, use water and a teaspoonful of salt, cover it with a sheet of buttered paper, set it on a moderate fire; when on the point of boiling, put it in a slack oven, where let it remain for two or three hours; be careful every twenty minutes to moisten or baste the fricandeau with the gravy which is in the stewpan; the slower it is done the better; ten minutes before it is removed from the oven, take off the paper, in order that the top may obtain a nice yellow color; if the oven should not be hot enough, place live coals on the lid of the stewpan until done, try also if it is tender with a pointed knife.

This dish ought to be carved with a spoon, being so tender; but I prefer to cut it with a very sharp knife, as it is more inviting in appearance. If you have no oven ready, stew gently on a hot plate, or by the side of the stove, with the lid on and live coals on the top. If you let it burn by any neglect or accident, do not tell your friends that I gave you the receipt, as it would eat so very bad, and I should lose my good name. It can be served with any sauce or purée, but the one I prefer is as follows: Take the gravy from the stewpan, which ought to be about half a pint, if not so much add water, pass it through a fine sieve into a basin, remove the fat from the top, put it into a small stewpan, reduce it a little to a demi-glaze, mix half a teaspoonful of arrow-root in a cup, with a little water, put it in the gravy, boil two minutes; it ought to be of a bright yellow color, and transparent; the fricandeau should be served with gravy under it. The following purées are excellent to serve with it: sorrel, endive, peas, beans, artichokes, and spinach; tomato, mushroom, and cucumber sauces, &c. If a piece of udder can be procured, stew it with the fricandeau, and serve it in the same dish. This receipt will well repay the trouble attending it. The following is very good, and more simple.

413. *Fricandeau Bourgeoise, in its Gravy.*—Cut as before from the fillet, cut the bacon the same as for the neck, and laid with about thirty large pieces, but in a slanting direction, leaving but little of the bacon to be seen, as the object is to give all the advantage of the bacon to the meat; put it into a stewpan with a quarter of a pound of butter, a quarter of an ounce of salt, and one tenth of that of pepper; set it on the fire for five minutes, turn it with a fork round and round, then rake some cinders over the coals or charcoal so as to make it go slow, and until it becomes of a nice yellow color; then add a gill of water, a bay-leaf, half an onion, stew until quite tender, turning it over and over now and then; put it on a dish, skim the fat off

the gravy, pour it over, and serve. It may also be served thus: by throwing into the stewpan about twenty mushrooms, well washed about ten minutes before serving; if the gravy is too thin, add a little arrow-root, and serve: it can also be served with the sauces named in the former Receipt. Nothing is nicer cold than this; if required to be re-warmed, put it into a little broth or warm water, and heat slowly.

414. *Calf's Liver sauté.*—Cut it into slices, put a little butter in the sauté- or frying-pan, when melted, lay the liver in season with salt, pepper, a teaspoonful of chopped eschalot, parsley, and grated nutmeg, sauté on a sharp fire, when rather brown on both sides dredge a tablespoonful of French vinegar, or a glass of wine, stir it well, and boil for a few minutes; dish the liver in crowns; if the sauce is too pale, add a little mushroom catsup or coloring, and it had better be too thin than too thick; taste if well seasoned, and serve: the above is for about two pounds of liver.

415. *Calf's Liver, English way.*—Cut the liver into thin slices, dip them in flour, and put in a sauté or frying-pan in which some slices of bacon have been previously cooked, and have left sufficient fat in it; sauté the liver until quite brown and rather crisp, when take out and place it upon a dish with the bacon, then dredge a spoonful of flour in the pan, or enough to absorb all the fat in it, then add a little broth or water so as to make it a thinnish sauce, season it, and add two spoonfuls of Harvey's sauce or mushroom catsup. If the above is nicely done, and the pieces cut the size of cutlets, it will make a nice entrée for an ordinary dinner. It should be served immediately, and very hot.

416. *Calf's Liver, dry.*—The same may be served dry with the bacon, or with any sharp sauce.

417. *Calf's Heart, roasted.*—Proceed exactly the same as for ox's heart, only this being more delicate and smaller requires less time to roast, from half an hour to one hour, depending on the size; they may also be cut in slices and sautéd like the liver above; or, by having four for a large dish they may be dressed exactly like the liver (No. 415), but white instead of brown; stuff them and sauté white in butter, which depends on a slow fire, and, adding the flour, just give a few turns and add the broth immediately, then the onions and mushrooms, season as described in the liver, stew very gently for one hour, take out the hearts, skim off the fat, let it be thickish, boil down a little if required, prepare two yolks of eggs well beaten, with a quarter of a gill of milk, broth, or water, which pour into the same, stir quick for half a minute, add the juice of half a lemon, trim the hearts, dish them in a dish with the points upwards, pour the sauce over, and serve.

418. *Roast Sweetbreads.*—Take the sweetbreads and lay them in water at blood-heat, to disgorge, for three to four hours; then blanch them for two minutes in boiling water, put them into a stewpan with a few slices of carrot, onions, turnip, a little parsley, thyme, bay-leaf, six peppercorns, a blade of mace, and a small piece of bacon, cover over with a little broth or water, and let it boil for twenty minutes; take them out and dry them in a cloth, egg and bread-crumb them, tie them on a spit, and roast a nice brown color for ten to fifteen minutes; or they may be browned in an oven, or fried in very hot lard for ten minutes, in which case they

should stew a little longer; they may be served with plain gravy and a piece of toasted bread under, or a little melted butter and some Harvey's, Reading, or Soyer's sauce, and a little catsup added to it, boiled and poured round it; or with any of the sauces fricandeau. The heart-bread being generally so expensive, I seldom make use of it, but it may be blanched, larded, cooked, and served like the fricandeau, diminishing the larding and cooking according to the size of the bread, or it may be dressed as above, or, if a large throat-bread, it may be larded.

419. *Sweetbreads sauté.*—Blanch two throat-sweetbreads as in the preceding receipt, cut them in slices, put some butter in a frying-pan, and melt; then put in the sweet-bread, season over with salt, pepper, juice of a lemon, parsley, and bay-leaf; turn them until done, and serve very hot, with maître d'hôtel sauce over.

420. *Another way.*—Prepare as above; add a little flour and a gill of broth, a few raw mushrooms, stir continually to prevent burning, add a few spoonfuls of cream and serve; if any remain, do them *au gratin*, that is, put them in a pie-dish or flat plated dish, brown, bread-crumb over, add a little broth, put into an oven, and, when very hot, serve.

421. *Veal Cutlets (old English method).*—See No. 157.

422. *Veal Cutlets aux Fines Herbes.*—Cut from the neck the same as you would from mutton, only of course larger; sprinkle with salt, pepper, and chopped eschalot, set them on a gridiron and broil like common chops, serve plain, or rub a little maître d'hôtel butter over them, set in a hot place for a few moments, and serve. They may also be sautéd, by putting them into a sauté-pan and sauté until a nice color, take them out and put in the pan a spoonful of chopped onions, parsley, and mushrooms (if handy), stir until done, then add a teaspoonful of flour; when it is a little brown, add half a pint of water, two spoonfuls of Harvey's sauce and one of vinegar, stir well round, dish up the cutlets, sauce over and serve. They may also be larded like the fricandeau, and served in the same way, and with the like sauces, only less time in cooking.

423. *Veal Cutlets en papillote.*—Prepare as the last, and put them in a pie-dish and pour the sauce over, and let them remain until cold; then cut a sheet of foolscap paper in the shape of a heart, and oil or butter it; lay one of the cutlets with a little of the sauce on one half of the paper, turn the other half over, then turn and plait the edges of the paper over, beginning at the top of the heart and finishing with an extra twist at the bottom, which will cause the sauce to remain in it; broil slowly on a gridiron for twenty minutes on a very slow fire, or place it in the oven for that time, and serve.

424. *Calf's Ears stewed.*—If you make mock turtle with half a calf's head, you may serve the ear; after having boiled the head as for mock turtle, cut out the ear (it should weigh about half a pound), lay it down on a board and make a few incisions through the thin gristly part about one inch long; should it require a little more doing, put it in the soup; when done, stand it on the dish in which you intend to serve it, turn the top of the ear over outside, so that it forms a round; if any brain to spare, put a piece in the centre, sauce over when very hot with parsley and butter, tomato, or any sharp sauce, and serve; or, instead of the brain, veal stuffing or

forcemeat may be used; egg all over, bread-crumb, put in an oven until very hot and a nice yellow color, dish and serve with plain gravy: or it may be served with any sauce or ragout.

425. *Made Dish from Joints that have been previously served.*—(If from braised veal, with vegetables.) Cut it into slices about a quarter of an inch in thickness, then put the remainder, vegetables and gravy, if any, in a pan; if not, with water and a piece of glaze; season with a little salt, pepper, sugar, a bay-leaf, and the juice of a quarter of a lemon, simmer gently for twenty minutes on a slow fire, dish the fillets in the form of a crown, lay the vegetables in the middle, pour gravy over, and serve. Or, what remains, cut into very small dice, leave none on the bones, put in a pan, shake a little flour over, season with a little salt, pepper, sugar, bay-leaf, and the juice of a quarter of a lemon, then moisten it with milk sufficient to make a sauce, warm it for ten minutes, add half an ounce of butter, stir it well, and serve very hot: or, if you prefer it brown, leave out the milk and throw a few chopped mushrooms and eschalots in, and moisten with a little water, to which add a few drops of browning, or a little catsup; it ought never to be too thick. Poached eggs may be served with these.

426. *Calf's Brains fried.*—Prepare them as for calf's head; cut them in pieces of about two inches square, dip them into batter, and fry them immersed in fat; serve with fried parsley.

427. *Calf's Brains à la Maître d'Hôtel.*—Prepare the brain as before, warm six spoonfuls of melted butter; when hot, add one ounce of maître d'hôtel butter, and, when melted, pour it over.

428. *Stewed Calf's Liver.*—Choose a nice fat one rather white in color, lard it through with bacon, put one quarter of a pound of butter in a pan, when melted add a tablespoonful of flour, keep stirring until a nice yellow color, then put in the whole of the liver, turn round now and then until it is a little firm, then add a pint of broth or water, and a glass of any kind of wine, a bouquet of parsley, thyme, bay-leaves, a little salt, pepper, sugar, and thirty button onions, simmer one hour; take the fat off and the bouquet out, dish the liver with the onions around it, reduce the sauce, so that it adheres lightly to the back of the spoon, sauce over, and serve. Any vegetables may be used, as carrots, turnips, peas, haricots; and if a little gelatine or isinglass is added to the sauce, and the liver with the sauce only put into a round basin and pressed down and left until cold, it will make a nice dish for supper, lunch, or breakfast. If required to be re-warmed, cut it into slices, put it in a pan, with a drop of water added to the gravy.

429. *Sheep's Brains.*—Proceed as for calf's brains: these being smaller do not require so long to cook; though very good, they are not so delicate as calf's brains.

430. *Sheep's Kidneys.*—For a small dish procure six fresh ones, take off the thin skin which covers them, and cut them into slices, put in a sauté-pan one ounce of butter, when melted and nearly brown, add the kidneys, with half a teaspoonful of salt, one quarter ditto of pepper, half a tablespoonful of flour, mix well together, add half a wine-glass of sherry and a gill of broth, simmer for a few minutes, and serve very hot; a nice crisp toast placed under them is an improvement; also,

a few raw mushrooms, cut in slices, added when being sautéd, are excellent. For broiled kidneys, see Breakfast. They can also be cut in half and cooked the same, and dished in a crown on a border of mashed potatoes.

431. *Sheep's Feet or Trotters.*—Previous to visiting the Continent, I had quite a dislike to the unfortunate *Pied de Mouton*, whose blackish appearance in stall and basket seemed to be intended to satisfy the ravenous appetites of the gentlemen with the slouched hat. But I must say since I have tasted them in France, cooked à la poulette, I have become of quite another opinion, and I have prepared them at home thus:—

I get a dozen of them from the tripe-butcher, all cleaned and ready, and beg of him to extract the long bone from them. I put a quarter of a pound of beef or mutton suet in a stewpan, with two onions and one carrot sliced, two bay-leaves, two sprigs of thyme, one ounce of salt, a quarter of an ounce of pepper, put on the fire, and cook five minutes; add two tablespoonfuls of flour, and stir it round; add two quarts and a half of water, then put in the feet, stir till boiling, simmer for nearly three hours, or until the feet are perfectly tender, when done, take them out, and lay on sieve, take a quarter of a pound of fresh butter, a teaspoonful of salt, the same of flour, a quarter of one of pepper, a little grated nutmeg, the juice of a lemon, mix all these well together on a plate with the back of a spoon; put the feet with a gill of milk in a stewpan on the fire, when very hot, put in the butter, stir continually till melted, having previously well mixed two yolks of eggs with five tablespoonfuls of milk or cream, which put in the stewpan, keep moving the pan round over the fire continually for one minute, serve in a very hot dish with croutons of fried bread cut in triangular pieces round the dish. The stock may be used for any purée or thick soup.

432. *French Ragout of Mutton.*—Take about two pounds of the scrag of the neck, breast, chump, or any other part, with as little fat as possible, cut it into pieces of about two inches square, put into a pan two ounces of butter, or good fat, when melted, add two tablespoonfuls of flour, stir with a wooden spoon till forming a brownish roux, add the meat, and stir it round for twenty minutes, add a little water, but not enough to cover the meat, one saltspoonful of pepper, four ditto of salt, and four ditto of sugar, a bouquet of six sprigs of parsley, stir till boiling, set it to simmer. Having previously peeled a few turnips, cut in large dice of one inch square about thirty pieces, put some fat in a frying-pan, and fry the turnips until rather brown, take them out, and put them in a stewpan with the meat when it is done, which will be in about one hour from the time it was put on; when ready to serve, take out the meat and turnips, squeeze the bouquet, which throw away, skim off the fat, if too thick, add a little broth or water, or, if too thin, boil it a little more, dish it up by placing the pieces in a circle and the turnips in the centre, sauce over, and serve very hot—if not it is spoilt. For those that like it, a small piece of scraped garlic may be added. Onions, carrots, peas, &c., may be used in place of the turnips.

This is a very favorite dish in France; I learnt it from an old French émigré, who used to visit us about ten years since. When I have company, I use the chops of the neck, dress them in a crown, placing the vegetables in the centre; I find them very much liked. I have at some houses partaken of harico-mutton which has been tolerably good, but nothing in flavor to this plan. If there is any left, it is good warmed again, or even cold.

433. *Irish Stew.*—Cut up about two pounds of the neck of the mutton into small cutlets, which put into a proper sized stewpan with some of the fat of the mutton, season with three spoonfuls of salt, half an ounce of pepper, the same of sugar, six middle-sized onions, a quart of water; set them to boil and simmer for half an hour, then add six middling-sized potatoes, cut them in halves or quarters, stir it together, and let it stew gently for about one hour longer; if too fat remove it from the top, but if well done the potatoes would absorb all, and eat very delicate; any other part of the mutton may be served in the same way. I hope dearest — —, that you will not blame my apparent common taste in saying that I am fond of an Irish stew. I always recommend it to my friends; I often add a bay-leaf to it, which varies the flavor.

LETTER NO. XIII.

DEAREST ELOISE,—I certainly here must avail myself of M. Soyer's kind permission by taking from his 'Gastronomic Regenerator' a very simple receipt, it is true, but one which, in my estimation, has a great deal more merit than that of a sumptuous dish—a new mutton chop; yes, dearest, that is all. Many will very likely laugh at me, and think I am joking to take notice of a dish of such trifling importance, but, indeed, I assure you that I am far from that, because I have tried it for my dinner to-day, and in my opinion it is as far superior to the other as silver is to copper; and it was only in an enlightened era of wonders like ours that such a novelty in the culinary department could have been produced; where steam, gas, railways, electric light, suspended bridges, which seem to fly like zephyrs across the bosom of our mighty, wealthy, old Father Thames, and the subterranean promenade under his gutta-percha bed, where, as the French say, the fishes from their windows make faces at the English while walking below, as well as (and more wonderful still) the electric telegraph, which, even more freely than free-trade itself, carries like lightning the flashes of the genius of a Cobden from our great commercial town of Manchester to Printing-house square and various offices the sparks of a speech, which, if printers were careless, might set the paper on fire, by acquainting the metropolis not only of his love for freedom, but of his enthusiastic action, motion, commotion, and almost his thoughts; even the cheerings of the *convives* are actually in print, and read with the greatest anxiety by the multitude in town, while the report of the last and most powerful line just put to press is still roaring with echo throughout the vast cupola of the Free Trade Hall as well as in the ears of thousands of guests present who have been favored by partaking of the monster banquet; and as well, but not so wonderful, the invention, insurrection, and demolition of the Chartists—the last effected by special order and special constables; the Satanic bottle, double sight, and ethérienne suspension of the inimitable Robert le Diable, by mistake called Robert Houdin; Banyard's Yankee cabinet picture, 3000 miles long, out of which 2999 and three quarters are out of sight; more so than all, the discovery of rocky dust, called gold, in the bar-

barian land of California, where the humble and convalescent potato would be worth its weight of the precious metal, a loaf of bread three times as much, and a basin of poor man's soup a guinea instead of a penny as here. Have we not also heard of the great sea serpent, which a very serious American, who appears to have been in company with him, says that he was so tarnation long, that whilst engaged in dining out upon 4000 or 5000 turtles in Honduras, the end of his tail was at the same time hunting the white bear in the crystallized mountains of the North Pole for his supper, being something of an epicure, and consequently fond of a change? These, dearest, are FACTS that no one can deny," I guess; "and still it was to be among all these marvellous wonders that the innovation of a new mutton chop should emanate from the brain of a simple individual, while, for a century previous, the ancestors of our great grandfathers were, as we were till the present day, often obliged to satisfy their voracious appetite with a fat and clumsy mutton chop. Even now, dear, you will hardly be able to comprehend the meaning of my enthusiasm for this simple innovation: it is then for its great simplicity and cheapness, and that if in general use (as I sincerely hope it will be), thousands will be able to partake of it and enjoy it, and probably will keep a friendly remembrance of the name of its inventor, because any one who invents, or tries so to do, attempts to conquer the greatest difficulty to obtain fame and wealth, and which by others is always envied and tried to be surpassed; such is the world. While here, the humble, unassuming, disinterested inventor of the said mutton chop will not even have the honor of opposition, though he may be copied. Believe me, dearest, that is the only cause of my admiration. Now for this wonder.

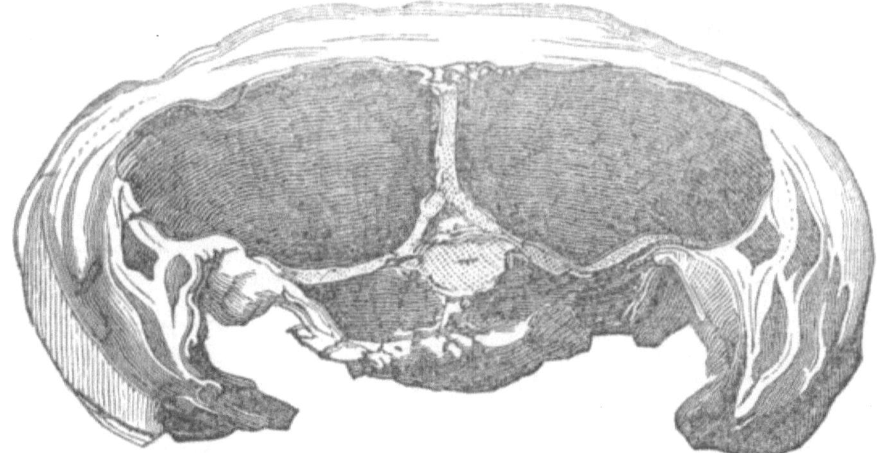

434. *Soyer's New Mutton Chop.* — Trim a middling-sized saddle of mutton, which cut into chops half an inch in thickness with a saw, without at all making use of a knife (the sawing them off jagging the meat and causing them to eat more tender), then trim them to the shape represented in the drawing, season well with salt and pepper, place them upon a gridiron over a sharp fire, turning them three or four times; they would require ten minutes cooking; when done, dress them upon a

hot dish, spread a small piece of butter over each (if approved of), and serve: by adding half a tablespoonful of Soyer's Gentlemen's or Ladies' Sauce to each chop when serving, and turning it over two or three times, produces an excellent entrée; the bone keeping the gravy in whilst cooking, it is a very great advantage to have chops cut after the above method. At home when I have a saddle of mutton, I usually cut two or three such chops, which I broil, rub maître d'hôtel butter over, and serve with fried potatoes round, using the remainder of the saddle next day for a joint. The above are also very excellent, well seasoned and dipped into egg and bread-crumbs previous to broiling. Lamb chops may be cut precisely the same, but require a few minutes less broiling.

You must remark that, by this plan, the fat and lean are better divided, and you can enjoy both; whilst the other is a lump of meat near the bone and fat at the other end, which partly melts in cooking, and is often burnt by the flame it makes; the new one not being divided at the bone, keeps the gravy in admirably. If well sawed it should not weigh more than the ordinary one, being about half the thickness. Do try them, and let me know your opinion.

Ever yours,
HORTENSE.

LETTER NO. XIV.

DEAR HORTENSE,—Yours of last night was received at our supper-table, which was surrounded by a few of our best friends, and I need not tell you the merriment it has created respecting your fantastic ideas of this age of wonders. A very sedate old gentleman, who happened to have met you at Mr. H.'s party about a week or two ago, and wished to be very courteous to you, and perhaps you did not notice his compliments, not only would he not give a smile to our hearty laugh, but actually swore that such comical nonsense was very dangerous to expose before the public, and especially if we intended to give publicity to it with the Receipts, the last of which he very much approved of. But respecting your fun on the review of our century,—"A woman," said he, "ought never to interfere with politics!" "Politics!" we all exclaimed, "where do you see anything political in it?" "In almost every word," replied he. "But in what part?" said we; "explain yourself." Unfortunately our hero stuttered very much. "Now, it-it-it is not one of-of-of you here, perhaps, who-who-who a-a-a-ve been in ann-y-pu-pu-public office like me in ma-ma-my youth. I was cla-cla-cla-clerk of the second cla-cla-clerk of the first cla-cla-cla-clerk of the private secretary's cla-cla-cla-clerk of the Home of-of-of——" Here, dear, we all burst out laughing, which made the old gentleman so mad that he rushed from the room into the passage, to the street-door, and out of the house, without his hat, Welsh wig, great coat, and umbrella, while the servant had a regular race to get hold of him. She at last found him talking to himself under one of our willow-trees in the garden, coming back for his tackle with his two hands over his red wig, and his thick head underneath. Being a wet night, after inquiring of the servant what he had said to her—"Ma-ma-ma-rie," said he, "you are a ve-ve-ve-very good girl indeed, very good girl, and I-I-I-I am ve-ve-ve-very sorry I have no money with me to gi-gi-gi-gi-give you something for your trouble, especially as you will ne-ne-ne-never see me here again, no, ne-ne-never." "Never mind, sir, about the money," said she to him, "I am no more disappointed than usual. Good night, sir." "Mary, you are a ve-ve-very sau-saucy huzzy, a ve-very saucy huzzy," was his answer. He then gradually disappeared in the fog. In a few seconds after, she heard some one sneezing most fearfully in the direction he was gone, which she believed to be our stuttering friend. So, you see, dear, there is quite an event on a mutton chop. But let me tell you that, though your receipt came rather late, we still had some for supper, and very good they were; every one was delighted with them; in fact, we did not eat hardly anything else, being so comically introduced to us. I had them brought up at three different times broiling hot from the gridiron. I made twelve chops out of a middle-sized saddle of mutton, weighing about seven pounds: is that right? and I have about three pounds of chump remaining, which, of course, I intend making broth, Irish stew, or pies with. But, dearest, let us go through the remainder of the Receipts without any more interruption.

My husband begs to be kindly remembered to you both. Ever yours,

ELOISE.

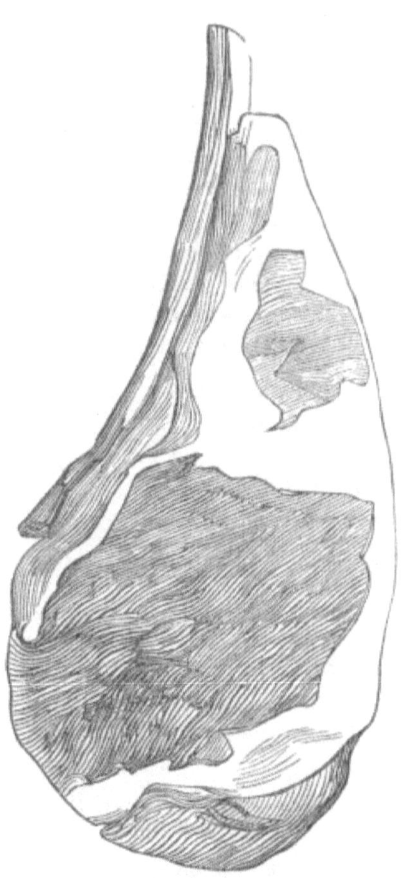

435. *Mutton Cutlets.*—Trim a neck of mutton by cutting away the scrag and sawing off three inches of the rib-bone, then cut about ten cutlets out of the neck, shape them by chopping off the thick part of the chine-bone, beat them flat to about a quarter of an inch in thickness with a cutlet-chopper, dipped in cold water, detach an inch of fat from the top of the rib-bone, and trim it like the following cut, season with a little salt and pepper, then well beat up one egg, dip a brush into it, and rub it lightly over the chop, dip it into bread-crumbs, form it into shape again, and dress in the following ways:—

Put two ounces of butter into a sauté-pan or very clean omelette-pan, melt it, and put the cutlets in; put it on the fire for five minutes till it is of a nice yellow color; turn them, let them remain four minutes longer, try if they are done by pressing with the finger, they ought to be firm and full of gravy; lay them on a clean cloth, and dress them in the form of a crown, that is, by keeping the thick part at the bottom, and the scraped part of the bone at the top, and each one resting half-way on the other. Every dish of cutlets must be served thus.

436. *Cutlets with Mushrooms.*—If for ten or twelve cutlets take about twenty fresh mushrooms, cut off the tails, wash them, and dry on a cloth, put two pats of butter in a stewpan, half a gill of water, the juice of a lemon, a little salt and pepper, set on the fire; boil for a few minutes, then add two tablespoonfuls of white sauce, when very hot add a liaison of the yolk of an egg made as follows:

Put the yolk in a cup, and mix well with two tablespoonfuls of milk, stir well for one minute, put it in the middle of your pan, if no white sauce, add a little milk to the mushrooms, and mix a little flour with half a pat of butter, and put it in, keep stirring until boiling; dish up the cutlets, add the liaison, and serve; or still plainer, take the same number of mushrooms, wash well, cut in thin slices, put into a stewpan, with two pats of butter, half a teaspoonful of flour, a little salt and pepper, the juice of a lemon, and a little water; stew gently for ten minutes, serve, pouring the sauce over, or in the middle of the cutlets.

They can be served as cutlets à la jardinière, with peas, with tomatoes, with artichokes, with spinach, à la poiverade, à la sauce piquante, with Brussels sprouts, and à la Soubise.

437. *Cutlets à la Maître d'Hôtel.*—When the cutlets are done, dish them up, put two ounces of maître d'hôtel butter in a clean sauté-pan, keep it moving until melted: put two spoonfuls of cream when very hot, pour over, and serve with fried potatoes in the middle.

438. *Cutlets, plainer way.*—Cut them from the neck, beat them down roughly without trimming, put them on the gridiron, when warm through, add salt, pepper, and very fine chopped onions, turn several times, they will take about ten minutes broiling; dish very hot, and serve. They may also be served on very white mashed potatoes.

439. *Sheep's Tongue, Demi-Glaze.*—For one dish, take six, put them in water to disgorge, then dry them, put them in a stewpan with two onions, half a large carrot, a bouquet of two bay-leaves, one sprig of thyme, a quart of broth if handy, or water, half a spoonful of salt, put them on to boil, and simmer for two hours till

done; try if tender with a pointed knife, if so take them out, skin them, trim out all the roots, cut the tongue in two, lengthwise, giving it a little of the shape of cutlets, skim the fat from the stock, reduce the whole or part to a demi-glaze, put your pieces on a dish, when ready to serve, make a thin roll of mashed potatoes, and dish them round it, add a little sugar to the demi-glaze, and a small piece of butter, stir round till melted, add the juice of half a lemon, pour boiling hot over the tongue, the sauce ought to adhere thickly to the back of the spoon. Observe, dear, how cheaply this dish may be procured, and I assure you it is very excellent: I have tried it with almost all the sauces I have described for cutlets, and have found it good with all; they are also very good in papillote, like veal cutlets.

440. *Sheep's Hearts.* — Proceed exactly as with the calf's heart, only diminish the time of cooking in proportion to the size, about thirty minutes will be sufficient; serve with any kind of sharp sauce, or any ragout of vegetables.

DISHES WITH THE REMAINS OF LAMB.

441. *Mince Lamb.* — (See Veal.) Serve with poached eggs over.

442. *Remains of roast or boiled Lamb with Peas.* — Cut up about two pounds, bones included, in rather small pieces, put into a convenient-sized stewpan, add to it two teaspoonfuls of flour, one of chopped onions, one of salt, a quarter ditto of pepper, half a pint of water, stir gently until near boiling, add one bay-leaf, and one pint of very green peas already boiled, simmer and serve. Half an hour is sufficient to prepare this dish; peas left from a previous day can be used, also cauliflower if not too much broken, and gently simmered, also a few mushrooms, or if no vegetables, add a little liaison, and the juice of half a lemon.

443. *Lamb's Feet* are much more delicate than sheep's trotters, but they are cooked and dressed the same, only in less time. If there are any left cold, cut them in two, put them in a basin, pour over a glass of vinegar, half of ditto of oil, one onion sliced, salt, pepper, fry them for twenty minutes, dip each piece in a batter, and fry a nice yellow color in fat; serve on a napkin.

444. *Lamb's Heart.* — Six will make a nice dish; stuff like calf's heart, only adding to it some bits of ham or red tongue; stew and serve with any kind of sauce.

445. *Lamb Cutlets.* — Ten cutlets would be sufficient for a dish, and might be cut from one neck, as described for mutton cutlets (page 182), but leaving them as large as possible; that is, about one third less than the mutton, season them lightly with salt and pepper, egg and bread-crumb them over, afterwards beating them gently with a knife, to put them again into shape; then have a little clarified butter upon a plate, into which dip each cutlet separately, afterwards throwing them into bread-crumbs, giving them another coat, and beat again. Then if wanted of a very nice color, put four spoonfuls of salad oil into a sauté-pan, lay in the cutlets and set them over a sharp fire, turning when required, six or eight minutes would be sufficient to do them nicely; when done, lay them upon a cloth a moment to drain, glaze, and dish them in crown upon your dish, and serve with cucumbers stewed in the centre.

Lamb cutlets may also be served with stewed peas, French beans, spinach, asparagus points, sauce jardinière, reforme, poiverade, piquante, or maître d'hôtel, which will be found in the series of sauces, or lamb cutlets may be broiled instead of fried, or served à la Maintenon, as directed for veal cutlets.

446. *Lamb Chops.* — Select a fine loin of lamb with the kidney in it, trim off the flap, and with a very sharp knife cut your chops from half to three quarters of an inch in thickness, cutting about eight chops from the loin, three of which should

have a piece of the kidney attached. I also cut two chops from the chump, which are very excellent eating, although clumsier in shape. Lay three of them upon a gridiron over a rather brisk but very clear fire, for if smoky it would entirely spoil the look and flavor of the lamb; and when just warmed through, season upon each side with a teaspoonful of salt, and a quarter of that quantity of pepper; broil of a nice yellow color, and serve with fried parsley over if convenient. Or lay some nice mashed potatoes upon your dish, and serve the chops upon it.

447. *Lamb Chops in paper, with fine herbs.*—Cut a piece of foolscap paper in the shape of a heart (and sufficiently large to fold a lamb chop in), rub a little oil over the paper, then season the chop with a teaspoonful of chopped eschalots, one of chopped parsley, a little pepper, salt, and grated nutmeg, wrap the chop in the paper, which plait down at the edges, lay it upon a gridiron over a slow fire, turning it frequently; it will take about twenty minutes to broil properly, when done serve in the paper very hot.

448. *Lamb Chop sauté.*—Put a piece of butter into a clean sauté- or frying-pan, and when melted lay in a chop rather highly seasoned with pepper and salt; fry it until thoroughly done and but lightly browned, and serve. Should gravy be required, pour off the greater part of the fat, and then stir in half a tablespoonful of flour, add a gill of broth or water, and a little coloring; stir with a wooden spoon, boiling five minutes, finish with an ounce of fresh butter and the juice of half a lemon; shake the pan over the fire until the sauce becomes rather thick, when pour over and serve.

449. *Pork Cutlets.*—Choose a small neck, cut eight cutlets out of it of the same shape as the mutton, only leaving a little more fat on it, season, egg and bread-crumb, fry in pan, serve with either sauces Robert, poiverade, piquante, tartare.

450. *Pork Cutlets with Pickle.*—Sauté, broil or fry, the chops, as in the preceding; make about a gill of melted butter, add to it two tablespoonfuls of liquor of piccalilly, and six or eight pieces of the pickle cut small; when very hot put on your dish, and dress your cutlets over, or if for a large dish, dress cutlets in a crown, and sauce in the middle.

451. *Pork Cutlets sauté.*—Cut six or eight good-sized cutlets from the neck of the same shape as the mutton, lay them in a buttered sauté-pan, season well with pepper and salt, place over the fire; when done lay them upon a plate, pour some of the fat from the sauté-pan, add a good tablespoonful of chopped onions, pass over the fire a minute, then add a teaspoonful of flour; moisten with half a pint of broth or water, with a piece of glaze added, season a little more, add a bay-leaf and a teaspoonful of vinegar, with one of mustard, mix well, lay in the cutlets until quite hot, when dress upon a dish, sauce over, and serve. This sauce is good with any kind of cutlets, but especially pork.

452. *Pork Cutlets aux Cornichons.*—Cut six or eight cutlets from a middling-sized neck of pork, season well with pepper and salt, dip in eggs well beaten upon a plate, and then into grated crust of bread (not too brown) put two ounces of lard or butter into a sauté- or frying-pan, lay in the cutlets and fry very slowly; when done place them upon a dish; keep hot, pour some of the fat from the pan, add

a good teaspoonful of flour, mix well, moisten with half a pint of broth or water with a piece of glaze, add half a wineglassful of vinegar, a little salt, pepper, and six gherkins in slices, place the cutlets in the pan to warm gently in the sauce, then dress them upon a dish, sauce over, and serve.

453. *Pork Cutlets sauce demi-Robert.*—Cut eight cutlets from a neck as before, season well with pepper and salt, sprinkle chopped onions and parsley over upon both sides, beating the cutlets lightly to make them adhere, then dip them into eggs well beaten upon a plate, and then into bread-crumbs; pat them lightly, have some clarified butter in a stewpan, into which dip the cutlets, and again into bread-crumbs, well covering them, place them upon a gridiron over a moderate fire, broiling a nice light brown color; when done dress them upon a dish; have ready the following sauce: cut two large onions into very small dice, put them into a stewpan with an ounce of butter, fry of a light yellow color, add a teaspoonful of flour, mix well, moisten with half a pint of broth and a spoonful of vinegar, season well, let boil, skim and reduce until rather thick, when add a spoonful of mixed mustard, a little coloring; sauce in the centre of the cutlets and serve.

454. *Excellent Sausage Cakes.*—Chop some lean pork very fine, having previously detached all the skin and bone, and to every pound of meat add three quarters of a pound of fat bacon, half an ounce of salt, a saltspoonful of pepper, the quarter of a nutmeg grated, six young green chopped onions, and a little chopped parsley; when the whole is well chopped put into a mortar and pound well, finishing with three eggs; then have ready a pig's caul, which cut into pieces large enough to fold a piece of the above preparation the size of an egg, which wrap up, keeping the shape of an egg, but rather flattened, and broil very gently over a moderate fire.

455. *Pigs' Feet.*—Procure six pigs' feet nicely salted, which boil in water, to which you have added a few vegetables, until well done, cut each one in halves, take out the long bone, have some sausage-meat as in the last, and a pig's caul, which cut into pieces each large enough to fold half a foot, well surrounded with sausage-meat, when well wrapped up broil slowly half an hour over a moderate fire, and serve. Or, when the pig's feet are well boiled, egg over, and throw them into some grated crust of bread, with which you have mixed a little parsley, broil a nice color and serve with a little plain gravy. This is called à la Ste. Menéhould.

456. *Pig's Kidneys.*—Cut them open lengthwise, season well with pepper and salt, egg over with a paste-brush, dip into bread-crumbs, with which you have mixed some chopped parsley and eschalot, run a skewer through to keep them open, and broil for about a quarter of an hour over a good fire; when done place them upon a dish, have ready an ounce of butter, with which you have mixed the juice of a lemon, a little pepper and salt, and a teaspoonful of French or common mustard, place a piece upon each of the kidneys, place in the oven for one minute, and serve. Pig's kidneys may also be sautéd as directed for ox kidneys.

457. *Hashed Pork.*—Put two spoonfuls of chopped onions into a stewpan with a wineglassful of vinegar, two cloves, a blade of mace, and a bay-leaf, reduce to half, take out the spice and bay-leaf, add half a pint of broth or water, cut some pork previously cooked into thin small slices, season well upon a dish with pepper

and salt, shake a good teaspoonful of flour over, mix all together, and put into the stewpan; let simmer gently ten minutes, pour out upon your dish, and serve with slices of gherkins in it; a little mustard may be added if approved of, or a little piccalilly with the vinegar is excellent.

The remains of salt pork, though very palatable cold, if required hot may be cut into large thin slices, and placed in a buttered sauté- or frying-pan, with a little broth, or merely fried in the butter, and served with a purée of winter peas, made by boiling half a pint of peas until tender (tied up in a cloth); when done put them into a stewpan with two ounces of butter; season with pepper and salt, add a gill of milk or cream, pour into the dish, and dress the pork over.

It may also be cut into thin slices and put into a soup plate, and pour some catsup or Harvey sauce over it, and let it remain for half an hour; butter the inside of a pudding basin, and lay some of the remains of peas pudding round it, and then place in the pork, cover it with some of the pudding, place it in a saucepan with a little water to get hot for about half an hour, and then turn it out and serve. Should you not have quite pork enough, you may make it up with a little sausage-meat, or any other kind of meat.

458. *Fritadella (twenty receipts in one).*—Put half a pound of crumb of bread to soak in a pint of cold water, take the same quantity of any kind of roast or boiled meat, with a little fat, chop it up like sausage meat, then put your bread in a clean cloth, press it to extract all the water, put into a stewpan two ounces of butter, a tablespoonful of chopped onions, fry for two minutes, then add the bread, stir with a wooden spoon until rather dry, then add the meat, season with a teaspoonful of salt, half the same of pepper, a little grated nutmeg, the same of lemon peel, stir continually until very hot; then add two eggs, one at a time, well mix together, and pour on a dish to get cold. Then take a piece as big as a small egg, and roll it to the same shape, flatten it a little, egg and bread-crumb over, keeping the shape, do all of it the same way, then put into a sauté-pan a quarter of a pound of lard, or clean fat, or oil; when hot, but not too much so, put in the pieces, and sauté a very nice yellow color, and serve very hot, plain, on a napkin, or on a border of mashed potatoes, with any sauce or garniture you fancy. These can be made with the remains of any kind of meat, poultry, game, fish, and even vegetables; hard eggs or cold mashed potatoes may be introduced in small quantities, and may be fried instead of sautéd, in which case put about two pounds of fat in the frying-pan, and if care is used it will do several times. This is an entirely new and very economical and palatable dish, and fit for all seasons, and if once tried would be often repeated; the only expense attending it is the purchase of a small wire sieve for the breadcrumbs. The reason I call it twenty receipts in one is, that all kinds of food may be used for it, even shrimps, oysters, and lobsters.

459. *Ramifolle.*—These are a little more expensive than the fritadella, and worthy the table of a crowned head. The flesh of fowls instead of lamb or veal, with the addition of one or two fat livers cut in dice. Proceed as in the former receipt, using the crumb of French rolls, and one or two truffles chopped fine: then make some pancake batter, and sauté two pancakes about one eighth of an inch thick, cover one with the meat, &c., and lay the other over, and put by until cold; when so cut

them to any shape you like, but if like cutlets add the small bone of fowl or pigeon, or the stalk of a sprig of parsley, egg and bread-crumb them, and sauté them in oil or lard of a nice yellow color, and dish them like cutlets, with any of the sauces or garnitures described for mutton cutlets; or if plain, with fried parsley. They may be made of any kind of meat, fish, or poultry. I have latterly had them sent up to table when we have had a few friends, and they have been very much liked; and, on inquiring the name, I baptized them Ramifolle, without any particular meaning, which name having pleased as much as the dish, therefore let them be called Ramifolles.

They may be made a plainer way with various meats or liver, and spread over one pancake, which roll over, and when cold cut it into three equal lengths, egg, bread-crumb, and sauté as above.

460. *Prussian Cutlets.*—Take a piece of veal, say one pound, from any part of the calf, as long as you extract the nerve, with a little fat, chop it up, but not too fine, add to it two teaspoonfuls of chopped eschalot, one of salt, half a one of pepper, little grated nutmeg, chop it a little more, and make it into pieces of the size of two walnuts, which give the shape of a cutlet; egg and bread-crumb each, keeping the shape; insert a small bone at the small end, sauté in fat, oil, lard, or butter, give it ten minutes on a slow fire till a nice brown color, dish and serve, with demi-glaze sauce, in which you have put a spoonful of Harvey's, and serve with any brown or white sauce or stewed vegetables you like. Any kind of meat may be used.

461. *Cutlets à la Victime, or Victimized Cutlets.*—Here, *ma belle amie*, is a terrific title for a receipt but do not fear it, as the time of the Inquisition is past, and you are not likely to become one in partaking of it. I do not recommend it to you on the score of economy, as it is the tip-top of extravagance; but forward it as a curiosity, and also in case similar circumstances should happen which caused its invention, which, you must know, was done by a culinary artist of Louis XVIII. of France, at the palace of the Tuileries, and first partaken of by this intellectual monarch and gourmet, who, at the end of his stormy reign, through a serious illness, was completely paralyzed, and, at the same time, the functionary organs of digestion were much out of order; being also a man of great corpulence, and a great admirer of the festive board, much food was required to satisfy his royal appetite; and the difficulty which his physicians experienced was to supply his want of food in the smallest compass. The head-cook, on being consulted, begged a few hours' reflection before he could give an answer to so important a question, as nothing but mutton entirely deprived of fat was to compose his Majesty's meal. After profound study by the chief and his satellites, a voice was heard from the larder, which was a considerable distance from the kitchen, crying, "I have found it, I have found it." It was a young man of the name of Alphonse Pottier, who, in saying so, made his appearance in the kitchen with three beautiful mutton cutlets, tastefully trimmed and tied together; he then, with a small skewer, fastened them to a spit, and placed them, to the astonishment of all present, close to the bars of the grate: two of the cutlets soon got brown (observe, not a word was to be said until the trial was made), from brown they soon turned black: every one gazed at each other in astonishment whilst Pottier, with quite a composed countenance, ter-

minated his scientific experiment, took them off the spit, drew the skewer out, cut the string, threw the two burnt cutlets away, and merely served the middle one, which seems to have received all the nutriment of the other two; it was served and greatly approved of by the physicians, as well as by the gourmet potentate, who in consequence of two being sacrificed for one, named it 'Cutlet à la Victime,' and often afterwards used to partake of them when in the enjoyment of health.

Cut three cutlets from the neck of mutton, about half an inch thick, trim one very nicely, free from fat, leave the other two as cut off, put the trimmed one between the two, flatten them together, so that the fat of the outside ones meet over the middle one; tie them together thus, and broil over a very strong fire for ten minutes; remove it from the fire, cut the string, and dish up the middle one only on a very hot dish, with a little salt sprinkled over it. If wanted roasted, proceed as above.

462. *Roast and Braised Chicken, for Entrées.* —Have a chicken trussed for boiling; put it on a spit, envelop it as for turkey (No. 358), roast half the time or little less, depending on the fire and the size of the chicken; when done, remove it from the spit, and take off the envelope, and serve with any of the following garniture:— jardinière, green peas, oysters, cucumbers, Jerusalem artichokes, white mushroom sauce, ragout of quenelles, juice of tarragon (No. 363), Dutch sauce, with a few heads of cauliflower well boiled, and cut small.

463. *Braised Chicken.* —If not convenient to roast, put a little bacon in a stewpan, then a chicken, a large onion, half a carrot, half a head of celery, two bay-leaves, two cloves, one peppercorn, one and a half tablespoonfuls of salt, a little pepper, a bouquet garni, and a quart of water, let simmer till tender; dish up, after having well drained it, take the string off, pour any of the above sauces over or under them; when the chicken is done, you can make, with the addition of a little more water, a very good purée, and even sauces, and by adding some trimmings of beef, veal, lamb, or mutton, it will make a first-rate clear broth, after being clarified giving it a proper color.

464. *Chicken plain boiled.* —Put two quarts of water into a stewpan, on the fire, or two ounces of butter, and a tablespoonful of salt and a few vegetables; when boiling, rub the breast of the chicken with half a lemon, and put it in to simmer from a quarter of an hour to twenty minutes; if a large fowl, increase the quantity of water, and boil longer; sauce over with parsley and butter, or celery sauce, or any of the above: use the broth.

The remains of any of the above, or of turkey, capon, guinea-fowl, or other poultry, may be dressed as hash, by cutting them into neat pieces; put them into a stewpan, put to it half a tablespoonful of salt, one of flour, half a one of chopped onions, ditto of parsley, a bay-leaf, half a pint of water, a few drops of coloring; set to simmer for twenty minutes, and serve; the addition of a few mushrooms is excellent.

465. *Poultry en Capilotade.* —Put with the pieces of fowl a tablespoonful of oil, and one glass of sherry, into a pan, and proceed as above; when ready to serve, chop a few gherkins, and put in.

466. *Indian Hash Fowl.*—Make a pint of sauce (p. 70), warm, put into it your pieces of fowl, and serve with rice plain-boiled.

467. *Fried Fowl.*—When you have cut the pieces as before, put them into a basin with a little salt, pepper, a spoonful of oil, and two of vinegar, and a little chopped eschalot, stir them well in it, and let remain for half an hour, have ready a quantity of batter, and take a fork and dip each piece one after the other into it, and then let it drop into the frying-pan, in which is sufficient hot fat to cover them; fry a nice color, and serve in a pyramid, with fried parsley over, or any sauce you like under.

468. *Blanquette of Fowl.*—Put half a pint of white sauce in a stewpan, with six tablespoonfuls of broth or milk, let it boil, having cut up about a pound of the remains of any kind of poultry, put it in the sauce, warm it, and add two spoonfuls of liaison to it; season with a little salt, pepper, the juice of half a lemon, stir it, and serve. Do not let it boil, or it will curdle, and be unsightly and unpalatable; a little cooked ham or tongue are good in it, also oysters, and served with bread sippets round. A little chopped parsley sprinkled over it makes it look very inviting.

469. *Minced Fowl.*—Cut the remains into small dice, with a little ham or tongue, add thick white sauce, season mildly; it can be served with poached eggs over.

470. *Sauté of Fowl.*—See the article Sauté, which is applicable to all kinds of poultry; if the fowl be old, it should be previously stewed.

471. *Broiled Fowl, with Sauce.*—Have a fowl ready plucked and drawn, open the back from one end to the other with a sharp knife, having previously cut the feet off at the second joint, make an incision in the skin, and pass the bone through to fix it internally; lay the fowl on the table, breast down, beat it as flat as possible with a chopper, take out the breast-bone, and also the rough part of the interior of the back, especially if a large or old fowl; after you have it in a nice shape, season all over with a teaspoonful of salt and half one of pepper, put it on a gridiron, over a slow fire, turning it every five minutes until done; if a young one, twenty-five minutes ought to do it well; but by trying with the finger on the thick part, it will easily be known by even an inexperienced hand, if firm under the finger, it is done, or by pressing the wing, and if tender, it is also done; put on dish, and pour over a brown mushroom sauce, or the following: put two spoonfuls of Chili vinegar, two of Harvey's sauce, two of catsup, one of chopped eschalot, ten of plain melted butter, put in a stewpan and boil for twenty minutes; skim and serve under or over.

472. *Another way.*—When the fowl is ready for broiling, put four tablespoonfuls of oil or fat, or one ounce of butter, into a sauté-pan, lay in the fowl, and sauté it gently until a nice yellow color, and then broil as above; or egg and bread-crumb it over, melting a little butter, and drop a little now and then when on the fire, and with care it will be gold color; serve with either sharp, mushroom, tomato, or poivrade sauce on.

473. *A la Tartare.*—By making about half a pint of the above sauce, and ornament an oval dish by placing on the border cut gherkins, beet-root, olives, place the sauce on it, and lay the fowl very hot over it; thus the fowl is hot and the sauce cold, but together very good.

474. *Croquettes of Fowl.* — Take the lean of the remains of a fowl from a previous dinner, and chop it up in small pieces, then put into a stewpan a teaspoonful of chopped eschalots with half an ounce of butter, pass them for about three minutes over the fire, add a teaspoonful of flour, mix well, then add the fowl, and a gill of white sauce, or more if not sufficiently moist; season with pepper, salt, and sugar; then stir in the yolks of two eggs very quickly, stir it a little longer on the fire, and turn it out on a dish to cool; when cold, take twelve pieces, each of the size of a walnut, roll them out an inch and a half in length, and bread-crumb thrice over; fry a good color, dress them on a napkin, or a border of mashed potatoes. Every kind of remains of game, meat, poultry, and fish, may be made the same way: if no sauce, add a little more flour, and use milk or broth.

475. *Fricassée of Fowl.* — Divide a fowl into eight pieces, wash it well, put the pieces into a stewpan, and cover with boiling water, season with a teaspoonful of salt, a little pepper, a good bouquet of parsley, four cloves, and a blade of mace, let it boil twenty minutes, pass the stock through a sieve into a basin; take out the pieces of fowl, trim nicely, then put into another stewpan two ounces of butter, with which mix a good spoonful of flour, moisten with stock, put in the pieces of fowl, stir occasionally until boiling, skim well, add twenty button onions, let simmer until the onions are tender, when add a gill of cream, with which you have mixed the yolks of two eggs, stir in quickly over the fire, but do not let it boil; take out the pieces, dress in pyramid upon the dish, and serve.

If you require to warm up the remainder of the above, put it into a basin, which stand in a stewpan in which you have placed a little water, put the cover over, and let it boil gently, by which means the contents of the basin will get warm without turning the sauce; when hot, dish up and serve. The same plan ought to be adopted to warm up any remains of dishes in which a liaison has been introduced; it prevents its turning, which is unavoidable in any other way.

476. *Fowl Sauté.* — Pluck and draw a fowl, cut it into pieces, seven or eight, as you like, that is, the two French wings, the two legs, the breast in one or two pieces, and the back in two; trim nicely, put into a sauté-pan two ounces of butter, put it on the fire; when hot, lay in your pieces, add a teaspoonful of salt, a quarter ditto of pepper, sauté gently, turn over; when of a nice gold color and tender, pour the fat of the pan, add a glass of sherry and ten spoonfuls of brown sauce, boil ten minutes longer but very slowly, and serve in pyramid; sauce over. This done in oil, with the addition of twenty mushrooms and a little garlic, is the celebrated dish of *poulet à la Marengo.*

477. *The Same, a plainer way.* — When prepared and cooked as above, instead of the sauce, which may not be handy, add a spoonful of flour, which dredge over till it is well mixed, then add half a pint of boiling water, a few drops of coloring or some mushroom-catsup, two teaspoonfuls of salt and a half of pepper, add a bouquet of parsley, let it simmer for twenty minutes, skim, taste if your sauce is well seasoned, dish your fowl, reduce your sauce until adhering to the back of the spoon, add the juice of half a lemon, and serve. A few mushrooms or English truffles may be added to it, which is a great improvement; the color of the sauce ought to be brownish; take out the bouquet which you have previously squeezed.

478. *Sauté of Fowl with Vegetables.*—Proceed exactly as above, only omitting the wine, add to the sauce fifty heads of young green scallions, or some small pieces of carrot and turnip, or a pint of green peas, or cucumbers cut in nice pieces, stew till tender, add a spoonful of powdered sugar, dish the fowl, skim the sauce, take out the parsley; when your sauce is thickish and of a nice color, pour over the fowl, and serve very hot.

479. *Blanquettes of Turkey.*—Cut off the flesh from the remainder of a roast or boiled turkey into as large slices as possible, then break up the bones, which put into a stewpan, with a little lean bacon and an onion, and a small bouquet of parsley, thyme, and bay-leaf, just cover them with water, and boil gently for three quarters of an hour, skim, and pass the stock through a cloth, and with it make a little white sauce as directed, then put the meat into another stewpan, lightly seasoned with a little pepper, salt, and grated nutmeg; just cover it with some of the sauce, and warm it gradually, not, however, permitting it to boil; when very hot, stir in three tablespoonfuls of cream, with which you have mixed the yolk of an egg, and when beginning to thicken, dress it upon a dish with toasted or fried sippets of bread around, cucumbers cut and dressed as directed p. 67, and added to the blanquette are a very great improvement, as are likewise button mushrooms or a few slices of cooked ham or tongue.

For a blanquette of fowl proceed precisely the same.

480. *Boudins of Fowl or Turkey.*—Cut up the remains of a turkey or fowls into very small dice, with a quarter of a pound of lean cooked ham to each pound of meat, make a stock with the bones as directed in the last; put a teaspoonful of chopped eschalots into a stewpan, with a piece of butter of the size of a walnut, which stir over the fire until the eschalots become a little yellowish, when stir in a good tablespoonful of flour, add the meat and about a pint of the stock, let boil gently a few minutes, season with a little pepper, salt, and sugar, stir the yolks of two eggs in quickly, and pour it out upon a dish until cold, when divide it into pieces of the size of eggs, which rub into long pieces of the shape and size of flat sausages, which egg and bread-crumb twice over, and fry of a nice brown color in hot fat or dripping, drain upon a cloth, and serve very hot.

481. *Turban of Croquettes à l'Epigramme.*—Croquettes are made from the same preparation as the last, but made up into small pieces, two inches in length and the thickness of your finger; egg, bread-crumb, and fry the same, dress in a circle upon a border of mashed potatoes, and serve with some blanquette of turkey or fowl in the centre.

482. *Hashed Goose.*—Put a spoonful of chopped onions into a stewpan with an ounce of butter, which fry over the fire until becoming rather browned, then stir a tablespoonful of flour, put in the remains of a goose, cut into neat pieces, and well seasoned with pepper and salt; add a pint of stock, let the whole simmer about ten minutes, and it is ready to serve. A little apple sauce may be served separately in a boat, or a couple of apples sliced, a few leaves of bruised dried sage may be stewed with the hash.

483. *Stewed Duck with Peas.*—Truss a duck with the legs turned inside, which

put into a stewpan with two ounces of butter and a quarter of a pound of streaked bacon, cut into small dice, set the stewpan over a moderate fire, occasionally stirring its contents until it becomes lightly browned, then add a good teaspoonful of flour, and when well mixed, a pint of stock or water, stir occasionally until boiling, when add twenty button onions and a bunch of parsley with a bay-leaf; let the whole simmer a quarter of an hour, keeping it well skimmed, then add a quart of young peas, and simmer half an hour longer, or until the peas are quite tender, when take out the duck, draw out the string, and dress it upon your dish; remove the parsley and bay-leaf, season the peas and sauce with a little pepper, salt, and sugar, pour over the duck and serve.

484. *Stewed Duck with Turnips.*—Proceed as in the last, but, instead of peas, use about forty pieces of good turnips, cut into moderately-sized squares, and previously fried, of a yellowish color, in a little lard or butter, dress the duck upon your dish, season the turnips and sauce with a little salt, pepper and sugar, and reduce it until thickish, not however to break the turnips; sauce over, and serve.

The remains of ducks left from a previous dinner may be hashed as directed for goose, but the sage and apple should in all cases be omitted; for variety, should peas be in season, a pint freshly boiled may be mixed with the hash at the time of serving.

485. *Fowl Sauté in Oil.*—Cut a fowl into eight pieces, that is, the two wings, two legs, two pieces of the breast, and two of the back, which put into a stewpan, with three tablespoonfuls of salad-oil, over a moderate fire, shaking the stewpan round occasionally, until the pieces of fowl are rather browned, when mix in a tablespoonful of flour, which moisten with a pint of stock or water, let it simmer at the corner of the fire twenty minutes, skimming off the oil as it rises to the surface; add a few blanched mushrooms in slices, season with a little salt, pepper, sugar, and a piece of scraped garlic the size of a pea; take out the fowl, which pile upon your dish, laying the worst pieces at the bottom; reduce the sauce over the fire, keeping it stirred until sufficiently thick to adhere to the back of the spoon, when pour over the fowl and serve. Use brown sauce, if handy.

486. *Fricassée of Rabbit.*—Cut a nice young rabbit into neat joints, and put them into lukewarm water to disgorge for half an hour, when drain and put them into a stewpan, with a large onion cut into slices, two cloves, a blade of mace, a little parsley, one bay-leaf, and a quarter of a pound of streaky bacon cut into small dice; cover the whole with water, and let it simmer twenty minutes, keeping it well skimmed; then pass the stock through a sieve into a basin, take out the pieces of rabbit with the bacon, then in another stewpan have two ounces of butter, with which mix a good tablespoonful of flour, moisten with the stock, and stir over the fire until boiling; then trim neatly the pieces of rabbit, which, with the bacon and twenty button onions, put into the sauce; let the whole simmer until the onions are tender, skimming off all the fat as it rises to the surface; then pour in a gill of cream, with which you have mixed the yolks of two eggs, leave it a moment upon the fire to thicken (but not to boil), take out the rabbit, which pile upon your dish, sauce over and serve.

487. *Gibelotte of Rabbit.*—Cut up a young rabbit into neat joints, as likewise a quarter of a pound of streaky bacon in small dice, put the bacon into a stewpan, with two ounces of butter, and when a little fried, put in the pieces of rabbit, which sauté of a light brown color, moving them round occasionally with a wooden spoon; then add a good tablespoonful of flour, working it well in, moisten with a pint of water, season with a little pepper and salt, and when beginning to simmer, skim off all the fat, and add thirty button onions, a few blanched mushrooms, and a little brown gravy or coloring; let simmer a quarter of an hour longer, when take out the rabbit, which dress upon your dish; reduce the sauce until it adheres to the back of the spoon, when pour it over the rabbit and serve.

488. *Compote of Pigeons.*—Put a quarter of a pound of lean bacon cut into small dice into a stewpan, with half an ounce of butter, and fry a few seconds over the fire, then have three pigeons trussed, with their legs turned inside, which place in the stewpan breast downwards, setting them over the fire until of a light brown color, moving them round occasionally; add a tablespoonful of flour, which work well in with a wooden spoon, until becoming browned, when moisten with a pint of water, add a good bunch of parsley, with a bay-leaf, and about thirty button onions, season with a little pepper and salt, let the whole simmer three quarters of an hour, keeping it well skimmed, then dress the pigeons upon a dish with the bacon and onions round, reduce the sauce to a proper consistency, take out the parsley and bay-leaf, sauce over and serve.

489. *Stewed Pigeon with Peas.*—Cook the pigeons precisely as described in the last, but omitting the onions and bay-leaf, and adding a quart of fresh green peas; when done, dress the pigeons in a dish, pour the sauce and peas over and serve.

490. *Hot Lamb Pie (raised).*—To make this an oval, a tin or copper pie mould would be required, which you would choose of a size most generally useful. Butter the interior of the mould, which stand upon a baking-sheet, then make the following paste: put a quarter of a pound of butter and the same of chopped suet into a stewpan, with half a pint of water, and let the whole boil together one minute, when strain it through a sieve into a basin containing two pounds of flour, mixing it first with a spoon, and when cool enough with the hand, until forming a smooth paste; when partly cold roll it out into a sheet half an inch in thickness, with which line the mould, pressing the paste evenly at all parts; have ready cut sufficient small lamb chops from the loin, neatly cut away the bones, and lay them round the interior of the pie alternately with slices of raw potatoes (a quarter of an inch in thickness), season rather highly as you proceed, with pepper, salt, chopped onions, and parsley; make a neat cover with the trimmings of the paste, and bake it rather better than two hours in a moderate oven; when done lift the cover, pour out as much of the fat as possible, add a little gravy and serve.

491. *Other various Pies.*—Hot raised pies may also be made with mutton by following the above directions. They are also very good made with fillet of beef cut into thin slices of the size of the lamb chops, or of rump steak, by laying a piece at the bottom, seasoning and filling alternately with potatoes and the meat; veal and ham pies are also excellent, but the potatoes in them had better be omitted, the veal however, seasoned and dipped in flour. Pies may also be made with veal

sweetbreads and ham, but then about three parts of a pint of white sauce should be poured in after the pie is baked. Fowls or rabbits may likewise be cut into joints, and put into a stewpan, with a piece of butter, previously well seasoning them with pepper, salt, and chopped eschalots; cover the stewpan close, and leave it twenty minutes over a slow fire, when add a pint of white sauce, and simmer ten minutes longer, when cold build them up in the interior of the pie, which cover and bake an hour in a warm oven. Pies of the above description can of course be made of any size, either large enough for a family meal, or very small and round, for a corner dish for a dinner party; most people who are in the habit of making them, keep two different-sized moulds for the purpose.

492. *Rump Steak Pie.*—Procure two pounds of rumpsteaks, which cut into thinnish slices, and season well with pepper and salt, dip each piece into flour, and lay them in a small pie-dish, finishing the top in the form of a dome; add a wineglassful of water, then have ready half a pound of half-puff paste, cut off a small piece, which roll into a band, and lay round the edge of the dish, having previously wetted it with a paste-brush, dipped in water, then roll out the remainder of the paste to about the size of the dish, damp the band of paste upon the dish, and lay the other piece over, make a hole with a knife at the top, press the edges evenly down with your thumbs, trim the pie round with a knife, egg over the top with a paste-brush, and ornament it with the trimmings of the paste, according to fancy: bake it rather better than an hour in a moderate oven, and serve either hot or cold.

493. *Veal and Ham Pie.*—Cut about a pound and a half of veal into thin slices, as also a quarter of a pound of cooked ham; season the veal rather highly with white pepper and salt, with which cover the bottom of the dish, then lay over a few slices of ham, then the remainder of the veal, finishing with the remainder of the ham, add a wineglassful of water, and cover and bake as directed for the beefsteak pie: a bay will be an improvement.

494. *Mutton pie.*—Procure the chumps of three loins of mutton, from which cut the meat in moderately thin slices, put a layer at the bottom of the dish, which season well with chopped parsley, eschalots, pepper, and salt; then put a layer of slices of raw potatoes, and again a layer of mutton, seasoning as before, proceeding thus to the top, which form in a dome, finishing with mutton, cover with paste, and bake as directed for rumpsteak pie.

495. *Another method.*—Cut six chops from a loin of mutton, from which trim as much of the fat as possible: season them well with salt and pepper, and lay them round in your pie-dish, the thick part uppermost, put two onions, in slices, in the centre, over which lay four middling-sized potatoes, each cut in halves, pour in a wineglassful of water, cover with paste, and bake as the last.

496. *Lamb Pie.*—Cut a small neck of lamb into chops, which must not be too fat, season them lightly with pepper and salt, and lay them in your pie-dish, with a few new potatoes in slices, pour in a little water, then cover and bake as directed for rumpsteak pie.

497. *Chicken Pie.*—Cut up a nice plump chicken into joints, which lay upon a dish, and season lightly with chopped parsley, white pepper, and salt, then lay the

back, cut into three pieces, at the bottom of a pie-dish, with the two legs on either side; have half a pound of cooked ham or bacon in slices, a layer of which cover over, then lay in the two wings, and over them the breast, cut into two pieces, which, with the remainder of the ham or bacon, form into a dome in the middle, pour half a pint of white sauce over, if handy, or a little broth or water, cover with paste, and bake as directed for the last. If no white sauce, dip each piece lightly in flour.

498. *Rabbit Pie.*—Cut a nice rabbit into joints, splitting the head in halves, and lay them in lukewarm water half an hour, to disgorge, then dry them upon a cloth, season well with pepper, salt, chopped eschalots, parsley, two bay-leaves, and a spoonful of flour; have also three quarters of a pound of uncooked streaked bacon, cut into square pieces the size of walnuts, build up the pieces of rabbit and bacon together, in a pie-dish, commencing with the worst pieces, and forming a dome; pour in a little water, cover with paste, and bake as directed for rumpsteak pie.

499. *Pigeon Pie.*—Line the bottom of a pie-dish with a pound of rumpsteak, cut into slices not too thin, seasoned with a little salt, pepper, and cayenne, and dipped into flour; have ready picked and drawn a couple of pigeons, cut off the feet, turn the legs in, fold up the pinions of the wings, and lay them breast to breast upon the meat, have the yolks of four hard-boiled eggs, which put at the sides, sprinkle a little pepper and salt over the pigeons, lay a bay-leaf upon the top, pour in a little water, cover with paste, stick the feet in the top, and bake as directed for the last.

500. *Partridge Pie.*—Line the bottom of a pie-dish with slices of veal, cut moderately thick, and rather lightly seasoned with white pepper and salt; have ready picked, drawn, and trussed a couple of young partridges, pour one glass of sherry over the veal, and lay in the partridges breast to breast, laying a piece of fat bacon over each, cover with paste, sticking the feet of the partridges in the top of the pie, and bake as before.

501. *Grouse Pie.*—Roast, very underdone, a couple of nice plump grouse; when cold, cut into joints, being the two wings, two legs, and the breasts into two pieces each, season them lightly, and lay them in a pie-dish, building them to form a dome, then break up the back-bone and other trimmings, which put into a stewpan, with a glass of sherry, a bay-leaf, an onion in slices, a few sprigs of parsley, three or four whole allspice, set the stewpan over the fire a few minutes until the wine boils, when add half a pint of brown sauce, and half a pint of broth, stir it over a fire until again reduced to half a pint, when strain it through a sieve, over the grouse; when quite cold cover with paste, as directed for rumpsteak pie, and bake in a warm oven; about half an hour would be sufficient, as the paste requires to be laid on thinner, the contents of the pie having been previously cooked.

Pies may be made from the remains of any poultry or game, in the same manner as here described; only, if poultry, use white sauce instead of brown, and omit the wine. If no sauce, roll each piece in flour, and make only the gravy, which place in it.

The remains of any joint of meat may likewise be served in a pie, by cutting the meat in slices, well seasoning, laying them in a pie-dish, and pouring half a pint of sharp sauce over; or use broth, or even water highly seasoned.

502. *Sea Pie.*—Put into a stewpan two pounds of beefsteak, season it with pepper and salt, a small bit of celery chopped up, or a pinch of ground celery seed, a pinch of pounded basil, a teaspoonful of chopped parsley, a small onion cut in slices; put on this six larks trussed for roasting, then make a piece of paste with suet, about one inch thick, and round like the stewpan; put half a pint of water or Hock in the stewpan, and cover the larks with the paste, pressing it against the sides of the stewpan; simmer for one hour, and serve, by putting a knife round the sides of the stewpan to detach the paste, and turn it over on a dish.

503. *Eel Pie.*—Skin and cleanse three good-sized eels, which cut into pieces about two inches in length, put a good-sized bunch of parsley, thyme, and three bay-leaves, all tied together, into a stewpan, with an onion, into which you have stuck six cloves, a glass of port wine, and a pint of broth, lay in the pieces of eels, and set them upon the fire to simmer for ten minutes, when take them out, laying them upon a cloth to drain, skim off all the fat from the stock the eels were cooked in, to which add rather more than half a pint of brown sauce, let the whole boil until reduced to three parts of a pint, when dress the pieces of eels up in a pie-dish, strain the sauce over through a sieve, and when cold, cover with paste as directed for rumpsteak pie, and bake about an hour in a moderate oven, serve it hot. If for a small pie, they may be used raw, and season accordingly, after having rolled each piece in flour.

504. *Beefsteak Pudding.*—Put a pound of flour upon a dresser, with which mix half a pound of beef suet, very finely chopped, make a hole in the middle, into which put a teaspoonful of salt, and sufficient water to form a rather stiffish paste, mix it well together, using a little more flour to dry it and prevent its sticking; then lightly butter the interior of a round-bottomed pudding-basin, roll out two thirds of the paste to half an inch in thickness, with which line the basin; have ready cut into slices, about the size of the palm of the hand and a quarter of an inch in thickness, two pounds of rumpsteak, with a little of the fat included, lay them upon a dish; season with two teaspoonfuls of salt, and one of black pepper, sprinkle a little flour over, move them about a little until each piece is well covered with flour and seasoning; then lay them within the paste, also putting in whatever seasoning may remain upon the dish, pour a gill of water over, moistening the edges of the paste; then roll out the remainder of the paste to form a lid, which place over, pressing it down with the thumb, then tie the basin in a pudding-cloth, and put it into a saucepan containing about a gallon of boiling water, and keep continually boiling for nearly two hours, adding a little more water occasionally, to keep up the quantity; then take it up, untie the cloth, run a sharp-pointed knife into the pudding, and if the meat feels tender, it is done (if not, it will require more boiling), turn it over upon your dish, lift the basin carefully from it, and serve, without opening the pudding to add gravy, as many persons do, for a pudding made as above will be full of gravy when cut at table.

505. *Mutton Pudding.*—Line a pudding-basin with paste, as directed in the last; then have ready cut into slices the meat from two loin-chumps of mutton, which lay upon a dish, and season with a teaspoonful of chopped onions, the same of

chopped parsley, rather more than half that quantity of black pepper, and salt in proportion; then put a layer of meat into the pudding, then a layer of raw potatoes cut into slices, proceeding thus until you have filled it up, but finishing with meat, cover it up as in the last, likewise tie it in a napkin, and boil, but rather better than two hours would be sufficient; serve as before directed.

506. *Lamb Pudding.*—If convenient, procure the entire ribs of lamb, sawing off the breast almost close to the lean part of the neck; the breast may be cooked as directed (No. 334); cut the neck into rather thin cutlets, which season lightly with white pepper, salt, and a little chopped parsley and onions: you have previously lined a pudding-basin with paste as before, fill it with the meat thus prepared, intermixing a few new potatoes cut in slices, finish the pudding, boil, and serve as before directed.

507. *Veal Pudding.*—Cut two pounds of veal from any part of the leg into slices, about the size of the palm of the hand and a quarter of an inch in thickness, put two ounces of butter into a frying-pan, and when melted lay in the veal, and a few slices of streaked bacon, season the whole with pepper and a little salt, add one bay-leaf, and a few sprigs of thyme; place the pan over a slow fire, sauté the veal gently for a quarter of an hour; then take it from the fire, and leave it in the pan until cold, then have a pudding-basin lined with paste as before, lay in the veal and bacon, pouring the gravy over, cover, and boil as before, but an hour would be sufficient.

508. *Pork Pudding.*—Line a pudding-basin with paste as before, and spread three quarters of a pound of sausage-meat of an equal thickness over the interior, have a pound and a half of lean pork, from the leg if possible, cut into square pieces of the size of walnuts, which season rather highly with pepper, salt, a teaspoonful of chopped eschalots, and half that quantity of dried sage; put the meat into the centre of the pudding, cover over with a quarter of a pound more sausage-meat, over which put on the cover of paste, tie it in a cloth, and boil two hours and a half, as directed for beefsteak pudding.

509. *Kidney Pudding.*—Procure one ox or eight mutton kidneys, which cut into slices the thickness of half-a-crown piece; lay them upon a dish, seasoning well with black pepper and salt, and shaking one ounce of flour over, mix all well together, to absorb the flour and seasoning; then have a pudding-basin, lined as directed for beefsteak pudding, finish, boil, and serve as there directed.

A pudding made with one pound of steak and a beef kidney is also very excellent, as is likewise a beefsteak pudding with two dozen of oysters (previously blanched and bearded) added.

510. *Rabbit Pudding.*—Cut a rabbit up in joints (splitting the head in halves), and lay them in a basin of lukewarm water an hour, to disgorge; line a pudding-basin with paste as directed for rumpsteak pudding, dry the pieces of rabbit upon a cloth, and lay them in the pudding with half a pound of streaked bacon, cut into square pieces, and seasoning rather highly with chopped eschalots, salt, pepper, and chopped parsley; cover, tie it in a cloth, boil it two hours, and serve as before directed.

511. *Suet Pudding.*—Put a pound of sifted flour in a basin, with half a pound of beef suet finely chopped, add two eggs, with a pinch of salt, and a quarter of a pint of water, beat well together with a wooden spoon, making a rather thick batter, flour a pudding-cloth, which lay in a small, round-bottomed basin, pour in the mixture, tie the cloth tightly, and put the pudding in to boil, with a joint of salt beef, if you have one, to serve the pudding with, or if not, in boiling water; an hour and a quarter would be sufficient to cook it; when done, untie the cloth, turn the pudding over upon your dish, and serve very hot.

512. *Yorkshire Pudding.*—Put six tablespoonfuls of flour into a basin, with six eggs, a pinch of salt, and a quarter of a pint of milk, mix well together with a wooden spoon, adding the remaining three quarters of a pint of milk by degrees; you have previously set a shallow tin dish under a piece of roasting beef before the fire; an hour before serving pour in the batter, leaving it under the meat until quite set and rather browned upon the top, when turn the pudding over upon the dish you intend serving it upon, and again place it before the fire until the other side is browned, when it is ready to serve with the meat.

This pudding is also very excellent baked under a small piece of beef of about five or six pounds. It is also frequently baked beneath a shoulder of mutton; also baked in an oven separate (with a few spoonfuls of gravy added), if the fire is not large enough.

513. *Toad in a Hole.*—Make a batter as directed for the Yorkshire pudding, but with the addition of a spoonful more flour and six ounces of chopped beef suet; butter a rather deep baking-dish, into which pour the batter, lay a solid piece of lean gravy beef, about three pounds, in the centre, and bake it an hour and a half in a hot oven.

Another method is to cut up about three pounds of rump-steaks into about six pieces, and putting them in the batter at various distances apart, but the former method is most common.

Any remains of cooked beef, veal, mutton, pork, roasted or boiled, salt or fresh, or game and fowl, cut in pieces, and seasoned to taste, may be used in this dish, by adding it to the batter when in the dish.

514. *Pease Pudding.*—Tie a pint of split peas in a cloth, leaving them room to swell, but not more; put them into a stewpan of cold water, where let them boil nearly half an hour until tender, but not at all watery (which they would not be if allowed only sufficient room to swell, and no more); then turn them out of the cloth, rub them through a hair sieve into a basin, after which add a quarter of a pound of butter, season with a little white pepper and salt, and mix all well together, with three yolks and one whole egg; lightly flour a pudding-cloth, which lay in a small round-bottomed basin, pour in the mixture, tie up the cloth, and put the pudding to boil for an hour in a saucepan of boiling water; when done, turn it from the cloth upon a dish, and serve with any joint of boiled pork.

515. *Fowl Pillau.*—Put one pound of the best Patna rice into a frying-pan with two ounces of butter, which keep moving over a slow fire, until the rice is lightly browned; then have ready a fowl trussed as for boiling, which put into a stewpan,

with five pints of good broth, pound in a mortar about forty cardamom seeds with the husks, half an ounce of coriander seeds, and sufficient cloves, allspice, mace, cinnamon, and peppercorns, to make two ounces in the aggregate, which tie up tightly in a cloth, and put into the stewpan with the fowl, let it boil slowly until the fowl is nearly done; then add the rice, which let stew until quite tender and almost dry; have ready four onions, which cut into slices the thickness of half-crown pieces, sprinkle over with flour, and fry, without breaking them, of a nice brown color, have also six thin slices of bacon, curled and grilled, and two eggs boiled hard; then lay the fowl upon your dish, which cover over with the rice, forming a pyramid, garnish with the bacon, fried onions, and the hard-boiled eggs cut into quarters, and serve very hot.

The bag of spice must be preserved, as it will answer the same purpose half a dozen times.

Fowl pillaus are frequently served with two ounces of Malaga raisins, which are added at the same time and stewed with the rice.

516. *Mutton Pillau.* — Trim a neck of mutton, by sawing off the tips of the ribs and taking away the chine-bone; then lay it in a stewpan, with a bag of spice as in the last, and cover with three quarts of stock, let it simmer very gently two hours; then take out the mutton, which keep hot upon a dish, skim off all the fat from the stock it was boiled in, to which add a pound of Patna rice, which stew until tender and very dry: then lay it over the mutton, garnish with fried onions, and hard-boiled eggs, as in the last, and serve very hot.

517. *Chicken Curry.* — Cut up a chicken into ten pieces, that is, two wings, two pieces of the breast, two of the back, and each leg divided into two pieces at the joints; then cut up a middling-sized onion into very small dice, which put into a stewpan, with an ounce of butter and a very small piece of garlic, stir them over the fire until sautéd well; then add two teaspoonfuls of curry powder and one of curry paste, which well mix in; then add half a pint of good broth, let it boil up; then lay in the pieces of chicken, cover it over, and put to stew very gently for half an hour, stirring it round occasionally, if getting too dry add a little more broth (or water); when done, the flesh should part easily from the bones, and the sauce should adhere rather thickly; season with the juice of half a lemon and a pinch of salt, and serve, with plain boiled rice, upon a separate dish.

Ducklings can be cooked in the same way.

518. *Chicken Curry with Paste.* — Cut a chicken up as described in the last, which put into a stewpan, with two ounces of clarified butter, put it over the fire, stirring occasionally until the pieces of the chicken are lightly browned; then pour off the butter and fat from the chicken, add three teaspoonfuls of curry paste and a pint of good broth, mix all well together, place the stewpan again upon the fire, stewing its contents slowly for about twenty minutes, when serve, as directed in the last.

519. *Rabbit Curry.* — Cut up a rabbit into smallish pieces, splitting the head in halves, cut up two large onions and one apple into very small dice, which fry in a stewpan with two ounces of butter; when nicely browned, add a good tablespoonful of curry powder, a teaspoonful of curry paste, half one of flour, and a pint of

stock, mix well together, then put in the rabbit, with half a pound of streaked bacon, cut into square pieces the size of filberts, let the whole stew very gently upon a very slow fire (or put the stewpan closely covered down into a warm oven) three quarters of an hour; when done, which you may ascertain by trying with the point of a knife if the flesh will leave the bone easily, pour off as much of the fat as possible, and turn it out upon your dish; serve with rice separately.

The curry sauce should be sufficiently thick to envelop each piece of the rabbit.

520. *Veal Curry.*—Cut up about two pounds of lean veal into small square pieces, half the size of walnuts, then put a large onion cut into small dice in a stewpan, with a clove of garlic and one apple cut into slices, and one ounce of butter; keep them stirred over a moderate fire until lightly browned, when stir in a good tablespoonful of mild curry powder, half one of flour, mix well, then add a pint of water, let it just boil up, put in the veal, which stir round two or three times, to mix with the curry, and put the stewpan over a slow fire, or in a warm oven for an hour and a half; when done (which you may ascertain by pressing a piece between the finger and thumb, if done it would be quite tender and separate), add the juice of a lemon and a little salt, stir the whole round three or four times very gently, to mix, and turn it out upon your dish, serve with rice separately.

Should you require a veal curry made in less time, the better plan would be to sauté the veal in butter previously, then putting it with its own gravy to the curry, and boiling the whole gently a quarter of an hour.

To make a veal curry with curry paste, sauté the veal in butter; when becoming slightly browned, add a good tablespoonful of the paste, with half a pint of water, leave it to stew about half an hour, when it will be ready to serve.

Beef, mutton, lamb, and pork curries are made precisely the same as directed for veal curries.

521. *Breast of Veal Curry.*—Procure a piece of breast of veal about three pounds in weight, with the bones and tendons attached, which chop into about twenty square pieces, and put into a stewpan, with two quarts of water, and a bunch of parsley, thyme, and bay-leaves; let it simmer three hours at the corner of the fire, skimming off all the fat, then take out the meat and strain the broth into a basin; in another stewpan have a middling-sized onion (cut into small dice), with an ounce of butter, sauté them rather brown, then add a good tablespoonful of curry powder, mix well, and pour in the broth, then add the meat, which let stew in the curry one hour longer, until the meat is very tender, and the sauce becomes rather thick; pour off as much fat as possible, season with a little salt and the juice of a lemon, which stir in very gently, take the meat out as whole as possible, dress them upon your dish, pour the sauce over and serve; rice separately.

522. *Breast of Mutton Curry.*—Cut up a breast of mutton, bones and all, into pieces about two inches in length and one in width, which put into a stewpan with two quarts of water, to simmer for about two hours, when proceed precisely as directed in the last.

523. *Breast of Lamb Curry* is made very similar to the preceding, and is con-

sidered a great treat to those who are fond of curries. Curry paste may be used to advantage, either by itself, or mixed equally with the powder. There being a great quantity of fat in the breast, great care should be taken to remove it from the curry every available opportunity.

524. *Lamb's Head Curry.*—Procure a lamb's head, which split in halves, break the bones at the nostrils, and put into lukewarm water an hour to disgorge, previously taking out the brains, which likewise disgorge in the water, then put the head into a stewpan well covered with water, let it boil two hours, when take it out, separate the bones from the flesh, which cut into small pieces. In another stewpan have a middling-sized onion cut into small dice, which set upon the fire, adding two ounces of butter, and sauté them a light brown color, when add a tablespoonful of curry powder, and half that quantity of curry paste, mix well together, then put in the pieces of head with half a pint of broth, and stew gently for half an hour. Whilst the curry is stewing, take the brains from the water, and put them into a stewpan of boiling water, let simmer five minutes, after which chop very fine, and put them into a basin, with a good handful of bread-crumbs, a little white pepper, salt, and chopped parsley, mix well together with an egg, and form it into six little round balls, which egg and bread-crumb twice over, and fry in a little hot lard, of a very light brown color, then dress the curry upon a dish, lay the brain croquets round, and serve with rice separately.

525. *Calf's Head Curry* is usually made with the remains left from a previous dinner; if about two pounds of meat remaining upon the bone, cut it whilst cold into thin slices, then cut two onions and two apples into small dice, which put into a stewpan, with an ounce of butter and half a clove of garlic cut in slices, stir with a wooden spoon over the fire until sautéd nice and brown, when add a tablespoonful of curry powder, half one of flour, mix well, then pour in a pint of broth, add a little salt, and boil twenty minutes, keeping it well stirred; then put in the calf's head, and let it remain upon the fire until quite hot through; add the juice of half a lemon, which stir in very gently, without breaking the meat, dress it upon a dish, and serve with rice separately. Curry sauce may be passed through a sieve previously to putting the head in.

526. *Calf's Feet Curry.*—After boiling a set of feet for calf's feet jelly, the feet may be served in curry as follows: separate the meat from the bones whilst the feet are warm; when cold, cut them into small square pieces, and proceed exactly as in the last; or use curry sauce.

527. *Calf's Tail Curry.*—Cut up calves' tails into joints, which put into a stewpan, with a small piece of lean ham and a bunch of parsley, thyme, and bay-leaf; cover them with three pints of cold water, and let simmer about two hours, until tender, keeping them well skimmed; when done, strain the stock through a hair sieve into a basin, and put the tails upon a plate; then proceed as directed for calf's head curry, but using the stock from the tails, and reducing the curry until rather thickish before adding the tails.

528. *Ox Tail Curry* is made precisely as in the last, but one tail would be sufficient, and it would require double the time to stew; or use curry sauce.

529. *Tripe Curry.*—Cut two large onions into very small dice, which put into a stewpan, with two ounces of butter, and stir over the fire until brown, when well mix in a tablespoonful of curry powder and half that quantity of paste; add a pint of broth, and two pounds of double tripe cut into strips; let the whole stew very slowly one hour, keeping it well skimmed, when dress it upon a dish, and serve with rice separately.

530. *Lobster Curry.*—Procure a large boiled lobster, break the shell, and take out the flesh in as large pieces as possible, cutting the tail into about six pieces, and the claws of a proportionate size; then cut two onions into small slices, which put into a stewpan, with an ounce of butter, fry them of a light yellow color, then mix in a good tablespoonful of mild curry paste (or half powder and half paste), and add a pint of good broth, then boil it up over the fire until becoming a little thickish, when put in the lobster, stir the whole round, then cover the stewpan closely, and put it into a moderate oven half an hour, by which time the curry would be of a proper consistency, and the lobster very delicately tender, add the juice of half a lemon, and serve with rice separately. If no oven it may be very gradually stewed over a slow fire, in which case it might want moistening occasionally.

531. *Crab Curry.*—Prepare the onions and curry precisely as in the last, but adding the flesh of a crab (broken small) instead of a lobster; let it stew over the fire about twenty minutes, add the juice of half a lemon, and serve as before.

532. *Oyster Curry.*—Blanch and beard six dozen of oysters, leaving the oysters in their own liquor; then cut two middling-sized onions into small dice, and sauté it in a stewpan, with an ounce of butter; when done, mix in two teaspoonfuls of curry powder and one of curry paste, then add the oysters with their liquor, and keep stirring over the fire until the oysters become enveloped in a thick sauce, when turn them out upon your dish, and serve with rice separately.

533. *Prawn Curry.*—Procure sufficient prawns to weigh about a pound; when picked, put half of a small onion chopped very fine into a stewpan, with half an ounce of butter, stir them over the fire until becoming rather yellowish; then add two teaspoonfuls of mild but rather piquant curry paste, mixing the whole gradually with half a pint of good broth; then put in the prawns, and stew gently about a quarter of an hour, when they will be ready to serve; rice separate.

If no curry paste, powder may be used, but the paste is far preferable.

Shrimps may also be curried in the same way, but they are in general so very salt.

534. *Salmon Curry.*—Have two slices of salmon, weighing about a pound each, which cut into pieces of the size of walnuts, cut up two middling-sized onions, which put into a stewpan, with an ounce of butter and a clove of garlic cut in thin slices, stir over the fire until becoming rather yellowish; then add a tablespoonful of curry powder and half that quantity of curry paste, mix all well together with a pint of good broth, put in the salmon, which stew about half an hour, pour off as much of the oil as possible; if too dry, moisten with a little more broth, mixing it gently, and serve as before.

Salmon curry may also be made with the remains left from a previous dinner, in which case reduce the curry sauce until rather thick before putting in the salmon, which only requires to be made hot in it.

The remains of a turbot might also be curried in the same way, and also any kind of fish.

535. *Fillet of Sole Curry.* — Fillet two nice soles, and cut each fillet into five pieces (slantwise); then in a stewpan have a small onion chopped fine and fried, to which add a tablespoonful of curry paste, or an equal quantity of paste and powder; when well mixed, put in the fillets of soles, with just sufficient broth to cover them; let it boil rather fast for ten minutes, when the sauce will become sufficiently thick to envelop the fish, season with the juice of half a lemon, and serve with rice separately.

Fillets of haddocks or whitings are curried precisely the same.

536. *Skate Curry.* — Plain boil about two pounds of skate with a piece of the liver, which put upon a dish without a napkin, previously well draining off the water; whilst the fish is boiling, cut two onions in slices, which put into a stewpan, with an ounce of butter, and fry of a lightish brown color; then mix in a tablespoonful of curry powder with a teaspoonful of flour, and a pint of good broth, set it upon the fire, keeping it stirred, and when boiling, put in a good-sized apple cut into slices, let boil until it is reduced to about half, when rub it through a tammy or hair sieve, pour it again into a stewpan, and when hot, pour over the fish, and serve with rice separately.

EGGS.

537. *Plain Baked Eggs.* —Butter with one ounce a plated dish, or common tart-dish, that will bear the heat of the oven; break carefully six eggs on it, season with one pinch of pepper, half a spoonful of salt, and add half an ounce of butter in small pieces over, put them in a slack oven until set, and serve.

538. *Baked Eggs with Asparagus.* —Cut twenty heads of sprue into small pieces, keeping only the tender part, boil them for fifteen minutes, put them into a stew-pan, with half an ounce of butter, set them on the fire for three minutes, season with a little pepper, salt, and sugar; when done, put them in the dish you intend to serve it in, break six eggs over, which season as above, put it into the oven until it sets, and serve; in case the oven is not sufficiently hot, place a salamander over the eggs.

539. *Mashed Eggs.* —Break four eggs into a stewpan, with one ounce of butter, half a teaspoonful of salt, and a pinch of pepper, put it on the fire, stir continually, and as soon as delicately set, serve.

These can be served with either green peas, sprue grass, or mushrooms, which must be stewed and prepared as if ready to serve; put some in the stewpan with the eggs, and proceed as before. If meagre, use cream instead of butter.

540. *Eggs with Burnt Butter.* —Put into a frying-pan two ounces of butter, which melt; as soon as it is on the point of browning, put in the eggs, which have been previously broken in a basin, and seasoned with pepper and salt; when well set, serve, with a teaspoonful of vinegar over the eggs.

541. *Eggs à la Tripe.* —Cut about two onions each into thin slices, put them in a stewpan, with half an ounce of fresh butter, and set them on a slow fire; when warmed through, put half a teaspoonful of salt, quarter ditto of pepper, a tea-spoonful of flour, a gill of milk, and a little sugar; let it boil, put in six hard eggs cut in quarters, and serve, after a little ebullition.

542. *Snow Eggs.* —Take half a pint of milk and a little sugar, and flavor it with orange-flower water, or any other essence, and put it in a stewpan on the fire, hav-ing previously beaten up the whites of six eggs to a stiff froth; if very hot weather, you must place the basin they are in on ice, or in cold water; whilst beating, add some powdered sugar lightly; when the milk is boiling, take the white up with a tablespoon, and drop it, one tablespoonful at a time, in the stewpan to poach, keeping the shape of an egg, which turn over when set; when done, remove with a colander on to a sieve, and dress them in a crown on the dish you intend to serve them on; when all done, beat up the yolks of four of the eggs in a stewpan, with a

little sugar and a few drops of orange-flower water, pour part of the boiling milk out of the stewpan into it, sufficient to make a good stiff custard, put it on the fire until rather thick, and pour over the white, and serve either hot or cold: the last is preferable.

543. *Eggs with Cheese.*—Put into a stewpan about two ounces of grated Parmesan, or Gruyère, or old Cheshire, with one ounce of butter, two sprigs of parsley, two spring onions chopped up, a little grated nutmeg, and half a glass of sherry; put it on the fire, and keep stirring until the cheese is well melted; break six eggs in a basin, put them in the stewpan, stir and cook them on a slow fire; when done, serve with fried sippets of bread round. Or,

Another way.

Put into a flat dish that will bear the oven a piece of butter the size of a walnut, the same of grated cheese, the yolks of two eggs, some grated cinnamon and nutmeg, mix these on the dish, put it either in the oven or in the hot plate, or, from want of either, before the fire, until it sets, then gently break six eggs on the dish, and cover with grated cheese, and salamander until a nice brown, or for want of one, keep it before the fire until it is so, and serve.

544. *Eggs in Cases.*—Cut up a sheet of paper into pieces of three inches square, turn up half an inch all around so as to form a kind of case, they will then remain but two inches square in the inside. Take a small piece of butter, a pinch of fine breadcrumbs, a little fine chopped parsley, spring onions, salt, and pepper, and mix them together, put a little into each case, then break one egg into each, put them on a gridiron over a slow fire, and do them gently, or place them in a dish in an oven; when well set, serve.

545. *Omelette with Herbs.*—Break six eggs in a basin or stewpan, and add to it a teaspoonful of chopped parsley, and one of chopped eschalot or spring onions, half ditto of salt, and a pinch of pepper, and beat it well up together. Put into an omelette-pan, that is, a small frying-pan six inches in diameter, two ounces of butter, which melt, then pour in the eggs, stir round with a spoon; as soon as it begins to set, lightly move it to that part of the pan opposite the handle, so that it occupies only one third, hold it so that that part of the pan is the lowest, move with a spoon the outside edges over, and let it remain half a minute, so that it obtains a good color, turn it over on to the dish so that the bottom is at the top. They must not be too much done, and served very hot. They may be served plain, or with the addition of any gravy.

Omelettes of ham, Parmesan, &c., are all made as the above, with the addition that these articles must have been properly cooked previously, and well chopped up, so as to mix well with the eggs, beat them up well together, and cook in a pan the same way, or a little grated cheese may be added. This I beg of you to practise; though simple, there is some art in making it.

GARNITURE FOR OMELETTES.

546. *Asparagus, Peas, and Green Peas.*—Put in a stewpan two spoonfuls of plain boiled sprue-grass that has previously been cut up, add to it half an ounce of butter, a little salt, pepper, and sugar, warm it on the fire, moving it continually; when warm, put it with a spoon in the centre of the omelette, turn over, and serve; the same with peas, and add melted butter or white sauce.

547. *Oysters.*—Open and blanch delicately twelve middle-sized oysters, and put them in a stewpan with their own gravy, beard them, add a tablespoonful of milk or cream, and give it a boil, then add half an ounce of butter in which you have mixed a saltspoonful of flour, stir it in without breaking the oysters, put over the centre of your omelette, and proceed as before.

548. *Lobster.*—Cut half or a small one in thin slices, put four tablespoonfuls of melted butter in a stewpan, a few drops of essence of anchovies, and a little cayenne; put in your lobster, warm it well, and put in the middle of the omelette, as above.

549. *Kidneys.*—Cook two kidneys as No. 430; when done, serve in centre of omelette, as above.

550. *Mushrooms.*—Wash about ten small fresh mushrooms, cut in slices, put in a stewpan, with half an ounce of butter, a little salt, pepper, and the juice of a quarter of a lemon, simmer for a few minutes on the fire till tender; if too liquid, add a little flour, place in centre of omelette, and proceed as above.

551. *Bacon.*—Cut two ounces of good lean bacon in small dice, put in pan to fry with the butter for one minute, then mix with the eggs prepared as for omelette of herbs, and cook the same way.

ENTRÉES OF GAME.

552. *Broiled Pheasant.*—Having drawn a pheasant, lay it upon its breast, and pass a knife down the back-bone, upon each side, taking it entirely out, then cut off the feet at the knuckle, break the leg and thigh-bones, turning the leg inside, separate the breast-joint of the wing, pressing the bird quite flat, then sauté it in a sauté-pan, with a little lard or dripping, and when browned on both sides, and about half done, place it upon a plate, season well with salt and pepper, egg and bread-crumb over, and broil it upon a gridiron over a moderate fire until sufficiently done, which would be in about a quarter of an hour, when serve with game, mushroom, or any piquant sauce.

The advantage of broiling or sautéing game or poultry is, that when you are alone, you need only cook the half of any large bird at one time.

Game Curries.—I have also made very good game curries, but not too hot with curry, as that would entirely destroy the flavor of the game.

553. *Pheasant stewed with Cabbage.*—The following is an excellent method for dressing a pheasant which should prove to be rather old, although a young one would be preferable. Procure a large savoy, which cut into quarters, and well wash in salt and water, after which boil it five minutes in plain water, then drain it quite dry, cut off the stalk, season rather highly with pepper and salt, have ready a middling-sized onion, and half a pound of streaky bacon, which, with the cabbage, put into a stewpan, covering the whole with a little good broth; let it simmer at the corner of the fire three quarters of an hour, then thrust the pheasant (previously three parts roasted) into the cabbage, and let them stew nearly three quarters of an hour longer, or until the stock has reduced to glaze, and adheres thickly to the cabbage, when dress the cabbage in a mound upon your dish, with the bacon, cut into slices, around, and the pheasant upon the top, half way buried in the cabbage; have a little game sauce, which pour round and serve.

554. *Joe Miller's stewed Pheasant.*—Roast a pheasant as directed (No. 582), but previously dipping it into flour, and occasionally flour over whilst roasting, thus making the exterior very crisp, and keeping it nearly white, then put the crumbs of two French rolls into a stewpan, with half a pint of milk, a small eschalot, a bay-leaf, an ounce of butter, and a little pepper and salt; let the whole boil a few minutes, when take out the eschalot and bay-leaf, place a piece of buttered toast upon your dish, pour the above over, dress the pheasant upon the top, and serve.

555. *Hashed Pheasant.*—Should you have any remains of pheasants from a previous day, cut them into as neat pieces as possible, then put an ounce of butter into a stewpan, with half an ounce of flour, which stir two or three minutes over the

fire, until becoming slightly browned; then add a glass of port wine, half a pint of water, season highly, boil at the corner of the stove, stirring and skimming occasionally, until sufficiently thick to adhere to the back of the spoon; then put in the pieces of pheasant, with a little coloring, let it remain ten minutes, at the corner of the stove, but not to boil, when dress the meat upon your dish, pass the sauce over through a sieve, and serve.

556. *A plain Salmi of Pheasant.* —Or, should you have a pheasant left that little has been cut from, cut and trim it into neat joints, which put into a stewpan, then in another stewpan put the bones and trimmings, chopped up very small, with an onion in slices, a little parsley, thyme, and bay-leaf, four peppercorns, and a glass of sherry, boil altogether two minutes, then add three parts of a pint of brown sauce, and half a pint of broth (if no brown sauce, add a spoonful of flour and a quart of broth or water and some coloring); let the whole boil until reduced to half, skimming it occasionally; place a fine hair sieve over the stewpan containing the pieces of pheasant, through which pass the sauce, warm altogether gently, without boiling, and when quite hot dress the pieces neatly upon a dish, pour the sauce over, and serve with sippets of fried or toasted bread (cut into the shape of hearts) around.

The remains of pheasant, or any other game, may also be minced and warmed in a little of the above sauce, and served with poached eggs upon the top, or likewise made into boudins and croquettes, as directed for turkey.

557. *Grouse.* —The Scotch method is to plain roast the grouse, dress it upon toast, and pour plain melted butter over.

But they may be dressed in any of the ways directed for pheasants, with the exception of being stewed with cabbage, as may be likewise every description of black game.

558. *Stewed Partridges with Cabbage.* —Have two nice partridges trussed as for boiling, and run five or six slices of fat bacon, of the thickness of a quill, lengthwise through the breast, but not to protrude, and roast them fifteen minutes before a moderate fire; have some cabbage stewed as directed for pheasant with cabbage, but stewed nearly dry before thrusting in the partridges; keep the whole hot, but not boiling, for about an hour; have ready two pork sausages, nicely broiled, dress the cabbage, which must be quite dry, upon your dish in a mound, with the partridges at the top, half buried in it, cut the bacon in halves, placing a piece at each end, with a sausage at each side; pour half a pint of game sauce round, and serve; good plain gravy is also very nice.

559. *Partridge sauté with Mushrooms.* —Have two young partridges, each of which cut in halves, and lay in a convenient-sized stewpan, into which you have previously poured two or three tablespoonfuls of salad oil, first seasoning them lightly with a little white pepper and salt, and a sprinkle of chopped eschalots; put a cover upon the stewpan, which place over a moderate fire, until one side of the partridges is browned, when turn them over, proceeding the same until browned on both sides; then pour off part of the oil, and add half a tablespoonful of flour, which well mix in, then add a glass of sherry, half a pint of broth, and twenty

small button mushrooms (previously blanched); let it simmer, skimming off all the oil which rises to the surface, until the partridges are tender, and the sauce thick enough to adhere to them; season the sauce a little if required, dress the partridges upon a dish, sauce over, and serve.

The remains of partridges may likewise be hashed or served in a plain salmi as directed for pheasants.

560. *Woodcocks, à la Lucullus.* — Plain roast the woodcocks as directed in Roasts, catching their trails upon toast, upon which, when done, dress the birds on a dish; have ready a little thick melted butter, with which mix the yolk of an egg and a little cream, pour this over the woodcocks, sprinkle lightly with bread-crumbs, salamander of a light brown color, and serve with a little gravy round.

561. *Woodcock, the Sportsman's fashion.* — Roast two woodcocks rather under-done, catching their trails upon a large piece of toasted bread, when done cut each bird into quarters, which place in a stewpan, with the remainder of the trail cut small, a little pepper, salt, a glass of sherry, a little chopped eschalot, the juice of half a lemon, and half a gill of broth, let the whole simmer very gently a few minutes; dress the pieces of woodcock rather high upon the toast, pour the sauce over, and serve.

562. *Hashed Woodcock.* — Should you have any remaining from a previous dinner, cut each one in four (or if not whole, into neat pieces), chop all the interior rather fine, which mix with a small piece of butter, a spoonful of bread-crumbs, and a little chopped parsley, make six croutons in the shape of hearts, from a piece of toasted bread, spread a piece of the above preparation upon each, and put them in a warm oven for a short time; hash the pieces of woodcock as directed for pheasant, and serve with the croutons round.

563. *Snipes à la minute.* — Put a quarter of a pound of butter into a stewpan, over which lay six snipes, breasts downwards, add a spoonful of chopped onions, the same of chopped parsley, a little grated nutmeg, half a teaspoonful of salt, and a saltspoonful of white pepper; set the stewpan over a brisk fire for seven or ten minutes (according to the size of the birds), stirring them round continually; then add the juice of one lemon, two glasses of sherry, the same of broth, and a spoonful of finely-grated crust of bread; let the whole simmer a few minutes longer, dress the birds upon a dish, stir the sauce well together, pour it over the snipes, and serve; a little glaze is an improvement.

564. *Plovers sauté with English Truffles.* — Procure four plovers, which lay breasts downwards in a stewpan, containing a quarter of a pound of butter, to which add eight raw truffles, well washed, peeled, and cut into very thin slices, two cloves, a bay-leaf, half a teaspoonful of salt, and a saltspoonful of pepper, pass the whole ten minutes over a sharp fire, stirring them round occasionally; then well mix in half a tablespoonful of flour, which moisten with half a pint of broth and a glass of white wine; let the whole simmer at the corner of the fire twenty minutes longer, keeping it well skimmed, dress the birds upon a dish, reduce the sauce to a proper consistency, season with a little sugar and the juice of a lemon, and pour it over the birds; serve very hot.

565. *Wild Duck, with Orange Sauce.*—Having trussed your duck as for roasting, rub it all over with the liver until quite red; then put it down before a good fire to roast for twenty minutes, after which cut eight incisions down the breast, and have ready the following preparation: put an ounce of butter into a stewpan, with a quarter of a saltspoonful of cayenne, the rind of an orange (free from pith, previously cut into strips, and blanched in boiling water, and well drained upon a sieve), and the juice of a lemon, warm all together, and when melted, but not oily, pour over the duck, and serve.

566. *Hashed Wild Duck.*—Cut up the remains of a duck or ducks into neat pieces, and put into a stewpan with half or a tablespoonful of flour (depending on the quantity), mix well, moisten with a glass or two of wine, and sufficient broth or water to make a thickish sauce, season well, add a little Harvey sauce, mushroom-catsup, a little sugar, and cayenne pepper; let simmer, but not boil, take out the pieces, which dress upon toast, reduce the sauce, pour over, and serve. A little coloring may be added, if approved.

567. *Widgeons.*—Rub the breast of a widgeon over with a part of the liver, chop up the remaining part, to which add a few bread-crumbs, a little chopped lemon-peel, chopped parsley, and an egg, with which stuff the interior, roast nearly as long as for the wild duck before a very sharp fire, dress upon toast on a dish, having ready the following sauce: put half a glass of port wine into a stewpan, with a teaspoonful of chopped eschalots, a little salt, pepper, and cayenne, boil a few minutes, add the juice of a lemon, and two ounces of fresh butter, sauce over, and serve. Widgeons are hashed the same as wild duck.

568. *Teal, a new method.*—Procure four, draw them; then put half a pound of butter upon a plate, with a little pepper, grated nutmeg, parsley, a spoonful of grated crust of bread, the juice of a lemon, and the liver of the teal, mix well together, and with it fill the interior of the teal; cover them with slices of lemon, fold in thin slices of bacon, then in paper, and roast twenty minutes before a sharp fire; take off the paper, brown the bacon, dress them upon a slice of thick toast, letting the butter from the teal run over it, and serve very hot.

569. *Teal à la sans façon.*—Roast four teal quite plain, prepare a quarter of a pound of butter as above, with the omission of the livers, which place in a stewpan over the fire, stirring quickly, until forming a kind of sauce, add some fillets from the pulp of a lemon, sauce over, and serve. The remains of teal also make excellent hash.

570. *Larks à la minute.*—Proceed as directed for snipes à la minute, previously stuffing them with their livers as directed for widgeons, adding a few mushrooms at the commencement; but do not let them stew too quickly, or the bottom will brown and give a bad flavor to the sauce; seven minutes are quite sufficient to stew them.

571. *Lark Pie.*—Cover the bottom of a pie-dish with thin slices of beef and fat bacon, over which lay ten or twelve larks previously rolled in flour, stuffed as above, season with a teaspoonful of salt, a quarter ditto of pepper, one of chopped parsley, and one of chopped eschalots, lay a bay-leaf over, add a gill of broth, and

cover with three quarters of a pound of half puff paste, bake one hour in a moderate oven, shake well to make the gravy in the pie form a kind of sauce, and serve quite hot.

572. *Jugged Hare.*—Put a quarter of a pound of butter, with a pound of bacon cut into dice, and the hare, cut into pieces, in a stewpan: set upon a moderate fire until the pieces of hare are becoming firm, when add six ounces of flour, mix well, and moisten with sufficient water to cover it: add two glasses of any kind of wine, and one of vinegar, season high with pepper and salt, let simmer until tender, keeping well skimmed; when done, and the sauce becoming rather thick, dress upon your dish, and serve.

573. *Jugged Hare (another way).*—Put about half a pound of butter, with ten ounces of flour, into a stewpan, put it on the fire, and keep stirring it round until it has a yellow tinge; then add a pound of bacon cut in square pieces, stir it a little longer on the fire; the hare having been previously cut up, put it into the stewpan and stir it about until it becomes firm, when add four glasses of port wine and sufficient water to cover it; season, and add two bay-leaves and four cloves, and when half done, about fifty button onions, or ten large ones in slices, a tablespoonful of brown sugar, let it simmer until it is well done and the sauce rather thick; dress up, sauce over, and serve. If an old one, it will take about four hours.

ROASTS—SECOND COURSE.

THESE dishes consist almost always of game, which require to be sent up immediately they are taken from the fire, and require great care and attention in cooking them. In the following pages will be found many which are scarce and rarely seen in London, and never mentioned in our various cookery books; but considering that many of our friends reside in the country, I have written it for them.

574. *Turkey Poults.*—Turkey poults, so called from being used when about the size of a large pullet, are trussed with the legs turned at the knuckle and the feet pressing upon the thighs, the neck is skinned and the head fixed under the wing; roast them the same as directed for turkeys, about twenty-five minutes or half an hour, according to their size, and in the same modes, but they are usually served, one larded and the other barded, with gravy and water-cresses in the dish.

575. *Roast Capon with Cresses.*—Roast and serve a capon in any of the ways directed for turkeys, roast of a nice gold color, and serve with water-cresses round; a capon weighing five pounds requires about three quarters of an hour to roast. Poularde au cresson, exactly as above.

576. *Roast Pullet.*—For a dinner of four entrées you would require two fowls, but not too large; truss and roast them as directed for a turkey, judging the time required according to their size, and serve with gravy and water-cresses; they may be larded, barded, or served in any way mentioned in the foregoing receipts. A fowl weighing two pounds and a half would require half an hour roasting, or three quarters of an hour, if larger.

577. *Spring Chickens* are served like fowls, generally plain roasted, but they may be larded as the poularde. Be particular in tying the legs upon paper to the spit, as directed for the turkey, as it so improves their appearance when roasted. About twenty minutes would be sufficient to roast them.

578. *Goslings.*—A green goose roasted plain, and served with a little gravy, is generally sent up for second courses; but if the larger ones are used, they must be stuffed with sage and onions, but very few would choose such a thing for a roast second course, whilst green geese in their season are great favorites; truss them by cutting off the leg at the knuckle, and the wing at the first pinion, fixing them at the side with skewers to throw the breast up; a full-grown goose will take one hour to roast, but a green one not more than half an hour.

579. *Ducklings* make a very favorite roast in the London season; they must have good fillets, white and plump, and require to be a little more underdone than

any other description of poultry; if too much done, the fat catches and gives a rank flavor to the flesh, besides causing the fillets to eat dry. They are usually served plain roasted for a second course, yet I have served them differently upon some occasions for the sake of variety, but it must be with a very thin sauce and one that invigorates the palate, although they never can be better than when served plain roasted. I shall here give one or two deviations: truss them by twisting the legs at the knuckles and resting the feet upon the thighs, cut the wing off at the first pinion and run a skewer through the bird, fixing the pinion and legs with it, place them upon a spit, and roast twenty minutes.

580. *Guinea Fowls.* — These birds must be very young, for, being naturally very dry, they are not eatable if more than twelve months old; they are generally larded or barded, and served plain roasted, rather well done; they are trussed like the common fowls, and require nearly three quarters of an hour to roast.

581. *Pea Fowls.* — These magnificent birds make a noble roast, and when young are very excellent; they are larded, plain roasted, and served with the tail stuck into the bird, which you have preserved, the head with its feathers being left folded up in paper, and tucked under the wing; roast about an hour and a half, take the paper from the head and neck, dress it upon your dish with water-cresses, and the gravy and bread-sauce separate in a boat.

GAME (CHOICE OF). — There is no article of food that is so deceiving in appearance to know if it is young, tender, and good, or not, as game; to a person living in the country, where a member of the family has shot them in his day's sport or have been received as presents, a knowledge how to distinguish them is requisite. Young birds may be distinguished by the softness of their quills; females will eat better than males, they are more tender and juicy. Old pheasants are known by the length and sharpness of their spurs, in young ones they are short and blunt. — Old partridges before Christmas have light-blue legs, instead of yellow-brown. — Wild fowl may be known to be old from their bills and the stiffness of the sinews of the legs, those that have the finest plumage are the worst eating. — Hares and rabbits: try if the ear will easily tear and the jaw-bone break between the finger and the thumb, if not they are only fit for soup or jugging. — On receiving birds of all kinds, put in their mouths three or four peppercorns bruised and one clove of garlic, and pepper the place where shot. In case you receive many, tie a piece of paper to them with the date on which they were received.

582. *Pheasants.* — At the present day there are great varieties of these birds, which differ as much in their flavor as their plumage. There are also a large quantity of hybrids sold in market as a genuine pheasant, and it is impossible to know them when plucked. The flavor of the bird will depend in a great measure on the nature of the country where it is killed.

Have them prepared and trussed: put them about eighteen inches from the fire for five minutes, then draw them close, and roast as quickly as possible, rubbing them all over with a little butter, serve up with bread-sauce separate, and good gravy under. They are also good larded, or one larded and the other barded.

583. *Partridges.* — The red-legged in this country are not so fine in flavor as the

gray; they are dressed like the pheasant, but all the time at a very quick fire, and serve very hot from the spit; it is better to wait a minute or two for it than to have it wait for you; dish it up with a little made gravy with it, and bread-sauces, as above.

584. *Grouse.* —These birds should be well kept, trussed like a fowl for roasting, and served with brown gravy under, or may be dressed as follows: truss as before, covering the breast with vine leaves and fat bacon, which tie on; roast from half to three quarters of an hour according to size, and serve with toast under, and melted butter over.

585. *Red Grouse, Gorcock or Moorcock—the common Moor Game (l'Attagas).* —Trussed like a fowl for roasting, which cook quick before a sharp fire, serve with toasted bread under.

586. *White Grouse or Ptarmigan (le Lagopède).* —They are to be trussed like the above, and plain roasted, and served with toast under and fried bread-crumbs, separate or dressed as follows:—Put two spoonfuls of currant-jelly in a stewpan, with the juice of a lemon and a little salt dissolved in it; when melted, pour over and serve.

587. *Wild Ducks (Canard Sauvage).* —The male is called the Mallard, and the young one Flapper. Under the above title a great many birds are sold.

They should all be cooked alike; they must be kept two or three days before they are dressed; they are trussed by twisting each leg at the knuckle, and resting the claws on each side of the breast, fixing them with a skewer run through the thighs and pinions of the wings; rub the liver over the breast, roast them before a quick fire from fifteen to twenty minutes, baste with butter, not basting them when first put down will keep the gravy in; one should be better done than the other, in order to suit the taste of those at table; serve with made gravy under, and a lemon separate.

588. *Widgeon, Whewer, or Whim (le Canard Siffleur).* —These should be eaten fresher than a Wild Duck, trussed, dressed, and served the same; fifteen minutes is sufficient before a good fire.

589. *Dunbird, Pochard, or Great-headed Widgeon (Pénélope, le Millouin).* —In some parts, *Red Heads, Parkers,* or *Half Birds*. These are dressed as above, but are not so good as the Widgeon.

590. *Teal (la petite Sarcelle).* —This is a delicious bird when fat, which they generally are after a frost. They must be trussed with care like ducklings; they will take about eight minutes to roast; serve with gravy, water-cresses, and lemon, separate, about six on a dish; or with sauces Nos. 141, 143.

591. *Garganey (la Sarcelle).* —These are called Summer Teal, resemble it in shape, and are dressed the same way.

592. *Plover.* —Of these there are several sorts, all of which are good to eat at certain seasons.

They should be well kept, but not too long, trussed gently, but not drawn, and put on a skewer, place them a little distance from a sharp fire, with a bit of toast under to catch the trail, baste with a little good butter, ten minutes is sufficient; dress them with toast under, and serve with gravy separate. They may also be served barded with vine leaves and very thin bacon.

593. — *Woodcock (la Bécasse).* — This is a most delicious bird when well cooked; they must not be kept too long; they are fit for cooking when they become black between the legs, and the feathers are rather loose; truss them with the legs twisted at the knuckles, and the feet pressing upon the thighs, bring the pinion of the wing to the thigh, having previously skinned the neck and head; bring the beak round under the wing, which pass through the pinions of the wings and thighs. Place four on a skewer, tie them on a spit, and roast before a sharp fire from ten to fifteen minutes, placing toast under to catch the trail; when done, serve on the toast and a very little gravy: they may also be barded with thin slices of bacon over the breast, and served with a sauce of *fumet de gibier*.

594. *Snipes.* — They are dressed in every respect like Woodcocks; and from seven to ten minutes is sufficient. They may likewise be fried in plenty of oil, and served with sauces Nos. 131, 143.

595. *Larks (l'Alouette).* — They are best in winter when very fat; they are roasted plain or with a thin slice of bacon and a leaf of celery tied over them; they require about eight minutes, and served with a little gravy and bread-crumbs, they are also used in pies (see *Pigeon Pie*); and may be dressed like Snipes.

596. *Quail (la Caille).* — Should be killed at least forty-eight hours before they are wanted; they should then be plucked, singed, drawn, and trussed by cutting off the wings at the first pinion, leaving the feet, and fixing the pinion and the wings with a very small skewer; cover the breast with vine leaves and a slice of fat bacon, and run a skewer through the pinions and thighs of each: tie on a spit and roast for ten to twelve minutes before a sharp fire. They should be served a nice gold color in a dish with a little gravy; they may also be trussed as above, and put into a pig's caul, and roasted and served with either sauces Nos. 141, 601.

597. *Rabbits.* — There are two sorts, the tame and wild; the wild or gray inhabits the mountainous districts; has the finest flavor, or on those places where it can feed on thyme, geneva, or other aromatic herbs, or on the sea coast, where he gets the lichen or wild moss. It has a much darker color than the tame. The tame rabbit, if properly fed 21 days before killing, may be made a very delicate article of nourishment; it should be kept from two to four days. When killed it should be removed to a cold place as quick as possible, that the fat may set.

If old, the claws will be long and rough, the coat rough and gray hairs mixed with it. If young, the claws and wool smooth. If stale, the flesh will be slimy and a bluish color; if fresh, it will be stiff, and the flesh white and dry.

598. *Hares.* — One is sufficient for a roast, skin and truss it nicely, stuff the interior with a good veal stuffing, sew it up, then put it on the spit, rub butter over the back and shake flour over it, roast it about forty minutes before a sharp fire, but that depends upon the size, of course; serve them with plain gravy in the dish and currant jelly separate. They are also served with a sauce poivrade, or sweet sauce;

they may also be larded.

599. *Leverets* are plain roasted and do not require stuffing, nor so long roasting, being smaller; they are usually served with plain gravy, but may be served with either of the sauces mentioned in the last; you require two for a roast. They will take from twenty-five to thirty minutes roasting. They may be larded, for a change.

600. *Wild Fowl Sauce.* — The following is a good sauce; the quantities are given for one wild duck.

Walnut catsup one tablespoonful; the same of Harvey's or Worcestershire sauce, the same of lemon-juice, a wine-glass of red wine, a good slice of lemon-peel, one eschalot minced, half a saltspoonful of cayenne pepper, one blade of mace, and a wine-glassful of gravy; boil ten minutes, serve very hot, and pour over the bird when cut up.

601. *Fumet de Gibier Sauce.* — Take the remains or bones of game (the backbones of grouse are best), chop them up small, put them in a stewpan, with a glass of white wine, an onion, a small piece of carrot and of turnip sliced, a leaf of celery, a sprig of thyme, the same of parsley, a bay-leaf, a clove, half a blade of mace; stir over the fire five minutes, then add a quart of brown sauce, if too thick add some water, boil for about twenty minutes, skim, strain, and serve; a little lemon-juice and cayenne pepper may be added if approved of.

SAVORY DISHES.

602. *Veal and Ham Pies (raised).* — The following few dishes will be found extremely useful for breakfasts, luncheons, second course in a dinner party, or for dinner in summer, but above all for supper when you give an evening party.

Having found a great difficulty in raising the crust for a pie with my hands, I purchased for a trifle a tin pie-mould, by the use of which the process is more simple, and the pie retains its shape whilst baking, and secures the gravy, much better.

Well wipe and butter the interior of the mould, then have ready two pounds of pâte fine, rather firm than otherwise, two thirds of which roll out to fit the mould, press it evenly over the interior, raising the paste half an inch above the edge of the mould, you have previously prepared six pounds of veal, cut from the fillet, as follows: cut four pounds into pieces an inch square, and as nearly as possible to the length of the pie; with the remainder make some forcemeat (see Receipt); then run eight pieces of fat bacon, each two inches in length, and a quarter of an inch square, through each piece of veal; have also two pounds of lean bacon, cut into pieces of nearly the same size as the veal, then put a quarter of a pound of butter into a frying-pan, and when melted over the fire, lay in the veal and bacon, season rather highly with a teaspoonful of salt, the same of pepper, half that quantity of grated nutmeg, and a tablespoonful each of chopped onion and parsley, sauté the whole a quarter of an hour, occasionally turning the meat, until getting of a nice color, and the bottom of the pan is covered with a thickish glaze; then line the interior of the pie with some of the forcemeat, to the thickness of half an inch, after which lay three pieces of veal at the bottom with two of the ham, alternately, which cover over with more forcemeat, to about an inch in thickness, then more veal and bacon, with forcemeat, again proceeding thus until full, finishing with the forcemeat, forming a dome about an inch above the edge of the paste, and lay a pat of butter with a bay-leaf at the top, then mould the remainder of the paste into a ball, which roll to the size of the top of the pie, wet the edges with a little egg, lay on the cover, which press down with the thumbs, working the edge up gracefully with the thumb and forefinger, to about an inch above the top of the mould, cutting some of the paste away where too thick, and crimp the extreme edge with a pair of paste nippers; then have ready half a pound of puff paste, which roll to about the thickness of about a quarter of an inch, from which cut a piece the size and form of the dome of the pie, upon which place it to form a lid (previously wetting the top with a little water), press it down lightly, egg over with a paste-brush, edges as well, make a small hole with a knife at the top, and carve any design upon the puff paste according to fancy; tie a band of buttered paper round the mould, an inch above the pie, put it into a moderate oven to bake about two hours, but to be certain if done, run a pointed knife or trussing needle into the centre, and if it feels tender it is sufficiently baked.

Then take it from the oven, and pour in a gill of strong gravy, in which you have dissolved a little isinglass (especially if in summer); when cold, take it from the mould (which opens at one end by drawing out a pin), and serve upon a napkin, garnished round with parsley. To carve, cut it into slices, the whole breadth of the pie and half an inch in thickness.

Such a pie as above would weigh four pounds when baked; but should you require a smaller one, diminish the proportions accordingly. If no puff paste, the top might be ornamented with a few leaves from the trimmings of the other paste. I have given you the above receipt very minutely, as the above applies to every description of raised pie, the difference only being its contents.

603. *Raised Pie of Fowls.*—Make the paste and forcemeat as in the last, but instead of veal and ham, bone a young fowl as directed for galantine, which lay flat upon a clean cloth, breast downwards, season the interior with a little pepper, salt, and chopped onions; spread a layer of forcemeat over, half an inch in thickness, have ten pieces of veal of the thickness of your finger, and the same length as the fowl, and the same number of pieces of fat bacon, lay half of the veal and bacon alternately upon the fowl, well seasoned with pepper and salt, cover over with more forcemeat, then another layer of veal and ham, cover with more forcemeat, then roll the fowl over, making the skin meet at the back, you have previously lined a raised pie-mould with paste, then line the pie with forcemeat, half an inch in thickness, lay in the fowl, sprinkle a little pepper and salt over, cover with the remainder of the forcemeat, to form a dome, place a pat of butter and two bay-leaves upon the top, finish and bake precisely as in the last: when done, pour in a gill of gravy made from the bones of the fowl; serve cold.

604. *Raised Pie of Pheasant.*—Proceed precisely as for the pie of fowl, but of course using a pheasant, an old one would answer the purpose if kept long enough, but all the sinews of the legs must be taken out in boning it, the fillets of the breast also, being very thick, may be partly cut out and used with the veal for the interior; if in a situation to obtain rabbits, the fillets of them might be used instead of veal for the interior, and the legs for forcemeat.

For gravy, break up the bones of the birds, which put into a stewpan with a glass of sherry, an onion, a few sprigs of thyme, parsley, and a bay-leaf; let it simmer a minute over the fire, then add a pint of broth and a little isinglass or gelatine, let the whole simmer for an hour, giving it a nice brown color, when pass it through a sieve into a smaller stewpan, place it again upon the fire, skim off all the fat, and reduce it to half a pint, and when the pie is baked, pour it in, shaking the pie a little to mix well; serve when cold.

Pies of grouse, partridges, moor fowls, &c. are made precisely in the same manner, using one or more according to the size you wish to make your pie. The fillets of hares are likewise excellent in pies, whilst the legs might be jugged or converted into soup.

Capons, poulards, green geese, or ducklings may also be served in a pie by proceeding as directed for fowls, but managing the size of the pie, and seasoning in proportion.

Pigeon pie can also be made in the same way, but then the meat with which the interior of the birds is filled must be cut much smaller, and require less time in cooking.

605. *Simple method of making Pies.*—Make two pounds of flour into a paste, as No. 602, and also two pounds of forcemeat, mould three quarters of the paste into a ball, which, with a rolling-pin, roll to about half an inch in thickness and of an oval shape; lay half the forcemeat in the centre, which spread over to within two inches of the rim, having prepared and sautéd some veal and ham as directed for the veal and ham pie, No. 602, lay them alternately upon the forcemeat, with which again cover the meat, laying a pat of butter and a bay-leaf upon the top; roll out the remainder of the paste of an oval shape, but much thinner than the other, damp the paste around with a little water, and lay the sheet of paste over, pressing it down with the finger and thumb, then wet the top, and bring up the paste at the sides, which will stick to it, thus forming a long square pie, with the trimmings of the paste form a few leaves, with which decorate it according to fancy, egg the whole well over, make a hole in the top, and bake two hours in a moderate oven; when done, pour in the gravy, as for pies made in moulds, and put by to serve cold. A square piece of puff paste laid upon the top, and ornamented previous to baking, is also a great improvement. Some gravy, as above, may of course be introduced.

You will perceive, my dear Eloise, from this one receipt, that any kind of poultry, game, or meat pies, might be made in the same manner. To carve, they should be cut across in thin slices through paste and all.

When we are alone I frequently make a very small one for luncheon, generally grating half a pound of sausage meat, with which I mix an egg and a little chopped eschalots, frying the veal or lean bacon or ham, and proceeding as for the larger ones; from three quarters of an hour to an hour would be sufficient to bake it; at times I make it with a pigeon, partridge, or two plovers stuffed, and surrounded with forcemeat, but boned: they are very excellent hot.

606. *Tureen of Game.*—I bought the other day a common earthen tureen, for which I gave ninepence; I made some forcemeat precisely the same as for pies, boned a grouse and stuffed it as for a pheasant pie, and seasoning the same; I then lined the tureen with the forcemeat, laid in the bird, which I again covered with the remainder of the forcemeat, put two pats of butter and a bay-leaf upon the top, then placed on the cover, fixing it down with a band of common paste laid inside upon the rim of the tureen, and baked it three hours in a moderate oven, and when I opened it about a week afterwards it was most delicious; when served to table the cover should be taken off, the bay-leaf removed, and a few fresh water-cresses laid over. All sorts of game, poultry, and meat, I have done in the same way; it is quickly done and very good and economical, as it will keep a long time.

607. *Galantines.*—Having twice failed in the attempt to make this difficult dish, I was about to relinquish the idea, but having received a small turkey about two

months back, I could not resist making another attempt, in which I succeeded; it is rather expensive, but it is a beautiful dish for supper. After having plucked, and singed off the hairs with a piece of lighted paper, I laid it breast downwards upon a clean cloth, and with a sharp-pointed knife boned it as follows: first, just pass the point of the knife through the skin, which cut open straight down the back-bone, then proceed to clear the flesh from the bones of the carcase until you come to the breast-bone, disjointing the wings and legs as you proceed; very carefully detach the breast-bone from the flesh without cutting through the skin, when you may remove the carcase with the interior of the turkey; then proceed to take the bones from the legs and wings, which is not quite so difficult; for the legs, scrape the first bone free from the flesh to below the first joint, where chop it off; cut the flesh round over the knuckle and pull the foot, when the remainder of the bone and sinews will come together; then cut off the wings at the first pinion, and the remaining bone is quickly scraped away.

I can assure you I found this quite a job the first and second time, but it is very essential to learn, as all kinds of poultry and game are boned in the same manner, and to this description all references upon the subject must be made throughout our little work.

You have prepared four pounds of forcemeat, as for pies, also have long strips of veal, ham, and fat bacon, which well season with salt, pepper, and chopped eschalots; put a layer of the forcemeat an inch thick down the bird, leaving two inches upon each side uncovered, then some of the veal, bacon, and cooked ham alternately, which again cover with forcemeat, but not exceeding half an inch in thickness (as too much forcemeat between the meat would spoil its appearance), proceeding thus until sufficient to fill the skin of the bird, when pull over the flaps, and sew it up tightly with a packing needle and small string, and tie it up in a napkin. If any, a few strips of cooked tongue, and blanched pistachios, laid in alternately with the veal and bacon, greatly improves its flavor and appearance.

To cook. Put in a stewpan with two onions, a carrot, half a head of celery, two cloves, a blade of mace, a good bunch of parsley, thyme, and bay-leaves, a knuckle of veal, the bones of the turkey, two calf's feet, two ounces of salt, add sufficient water to cover the whole, and set the stewpan upon the fire until upon the point of boiling; then draw it to the corner, skim, and let simmer for three hours; then take it from the fire, leaving it in the stock until nearly cold; then take it out, remove the string from the napkin, and roll the galantine up tighter, tying the napkin again at each end only; then place it upon a dish, the breast part upwards, set another dish upon it, on which place a fourteen pounds weight, which will press and cause it to cut firm; when quite cold it is ready to serve, having removed the napkin and the string with which it was sewed: the stock, however, should be clarified as direct-ed in the next receipt to make a savory jelly, which, when cold and firm, is cut in croutons and chopped, with which the galantine should be tastefully garnished.

Although at first I had some difficulty with this receipt, I can now see the va-riety to which it leads, as the same process answers for fowls, green geese, duck-lings, pheasants, grouse, partridges, &c., using game with the veal or pork for the interior, and stewing them according to their size, the bones of game being stewed with the stock would give the flavor to the savory jelly.

608. *To Clarify Meat Jelly.*—Having passed the stock (made as in the last) through a sieve into a basin, leave it until quite cold; then take off all the fat very carefully, ascertain if sufficiently or too stiff by putting a small piece upon ice; savory jelly requires to be rather stiffer than sweet, if too stiff add a little more broth, if the contrary, the stock must be reduced upon the fire until of the proper consistency. When the stock is boiling, and you are perfectly assured of its strength, have the white of four eggs with their shells in a basin, with half a pint of water, two spoonfuls of tarragon or common vinegar, and a glass of sherry, whisk all together; then whisk the stock quickly a few seconds, and pour in the other ingredients whilst whisking, continue whisking a few minutes until again upon the point but not boiling; then take it from the fire, and taste if palatable, place a cover upon the stewpan, which stand a little distance from the fire, putting a few red-hot cinders upon the lid for five minutes, tie a napkin by the four corners upon a jelly stand, through which pass the jelly, having a basin beneath to catch it, pour the first that runs through again into the napkin until it runs quite clear; when all through, pour it in a plain mould or sauté-pan, which place upon ice until the jelly is quite firm; then dip the bottom of the mould in hot water, turn the jelly out upon a cloth, and cut it into whatever shapes you please, to garnish and ornament any cold savory dish; the jelly when warm might be divided, one part kept white, and the other colored with a little brown gravy or coloring, thus enabling you to variegate in garnishing.

Should the jelly be required to ornament tongues, hams, pies, salads, or any article when no galantine is made; then to make the stock, cut the veal into small pieces, and split the calf's foot in two, put a quarter of a pound of butter in a convenient-sized stewpan, with the veal, foot, a small piece of lean ham, and the other ingredients as directed for galantine, pour in half a pint of water, put on the lid and stand it upon the fire until the bottom of the stewpan is covered with a white glaze; then add a gallon of water, let simmer three hours, keeping it well skimmed; then pass and clarify as above.

The knuckle of veal and foot may be served hot with a little parsley and butter, for a dinner previous to your party, with a little fried bacon separately, but for my own part I prefer them plain as they leave the stewpan.

609. *Cold Ham.*—Procure a very nice but small ham of about nine pounds in weight, which soak about ten hours in cold water, and simmer three hours in plenty of water; when done, take out and let remain until cold; then cut off the skin as thinly as possible, but without leaving the marks of it; let a piece remain upon the knuckle about two inches and a half in breadth, which either festoon or vandyke, carve the fat neatly to form a shell, and glaze it over lightly, serve with a paper frill upon the knuckle, and garnish with savory jelly, or if plain with a few bunches of fresh green parsley. A handful of fresh hay put in the water when boiling is an improvement.

610. *Cold Tongue.*—Boil a nice ox tongue for three hours, and, when done, take off all the skin, and truss it of a good shape, by placing the root against some fix-

ture, and running a fork through the middle of the thin part into the board upon which it stands; when cold trim and glaze it lightly over, cutting off the greater part of the root, place it upon a dish, garnished either with savory jelly or fresh sprigs of parsley.

611. *Galantine of Veal.*—When I do not like to go to the expense of a turkey or other poultry for a galantine, I procure a small breast of veal, and take out the tendons, which I stew; take out the remaining bones, and trim the meat to about fifteen inches in length and eight in width, using the trimmings for a ragout; season the interior of the breast, and proceed to lay on the forcemeat veal, ham, and bacon, as directed for the galantine of turkey, roll and sew it up, tie in a cloth, braise, and afterwards press it in precisely the same manner; when quite cold, glaze it nicely and serve, garnished with savory jelly; or, if for a large supper, six or eight small dishes might be made from it by cutting it into thin slices crosswise, and dressing six pieces in a border upon each dish, with a little jelly in the middle, or if no jelly, a sprig of parsley or water-cresses; but if served in the latter way, I introduce two ounces of blanched pistachios. When making the galantine, of course, the dishes must be placed at a distance from each other at various parts of the table. I have also made a galantine of a shoulder of lamb in the same way, previously taking out the bones.

612. *Cold Fillet of Veal.*—Roast braise as No. 358; when cold, trim neatly, and garnish with jelly or parsley.

A loin of veal larded through the fleshy part with raw ham, and fat bacon, and roasted as above, makes a very delicate dish.

A small shoulder of veal might be boned the same as a shoulder of lamb, and made into a galantine.

613. *Ribs of Beef larded.*—Choose a piece of beef with about four ribs, and cut very long, carefully take away the bones, lard the fleshy part through with strips of fat bacon, well seasoned with pepper, salt, and chopped parsley; spread some veal stuffing over, and roll it round, keeping the stuffing in the interior, tie it up with string, and roast in vegetables as in the last article, leaving it to cool in the vegetables; when cold, glaze and serve, garnished with sprigs of parsley.

The beef well rubbed with garlic and well seasoned with salt and pepper, previous to spreading on the stuffing, would be a great improvement.

I sometimes leave the bones in the meat, lard the fleshy part, and afterwards roast it in vegetables to serve cold.

614. *Pressed Beef.*—Procure a piece of brisket of beef, cut off the bones, and salt it as directed (No. 615), but adding a little extra sal prunella to the brine and a little spice; let the beef remain in pickle rather better than a week: when ready to cook, roll it round, tie it in a cloth, and let it simmer gently in plenty of water, about seven hours if a whole one, but four hours if only the thin end; when done take it up, remove the string, and tie the cloth at each end, put it upon a dish with another dish over, upon which place half a hundred-weight, leaving it until quite cold, then take the meat from the cloth, trim and glaze it lightly, and serve garnished

with a few sprigs of fresh parsley.

615. *Pickle for Beef à la Garrick.*—Take twenty pounds of salt, three quarters of a pound of saltpetre, four cakes of sal prunella, two pounds of moist sugar, two cloves of garlic, with which rub the meat well, and leave it rather more than a week, rubbing and turning it over every day.

This pickle is adapted for anything that is required red.

616. *Spiced Beef.*—Procure a piece of thin flank of beef about ten pounds in weight, which salt as the last for about a week; when ready, split it open with a knife and lay it out flat upon a dresser, having previously prepared six onions chopped very fine, with about ten sprigs of parsley, and the leaves of ten sprigs of thyme, the same of marjoram, two ounces of mixed spice (without cinnamon), and half an ounce of black pepper, mix altogether, spread half upon the beef as it lays before you, then fold it over to its original shape, lay on the remainder of the preparation, roll it up tightly in a cloth, boil, press, and serve as directed in the last article.

617. *Pig's Head in imitation of Wild Boar's Head.*—This you will say is not only a difficult dish to do, but a very expensive one. You are right when you are obliged to buy the pig to possess the head; but in a small farm-house where they kill a pig perhaps once a year at Christmas, the head can be very easily cut off for this purpose. Being on a visit some years since at a farm-house, I had the opportunity of having one, and trying my skill upon it; it was much approved of, both for its ferocious appearance, and its flavor, and it lasted good for three weeks.

The following is the way you should do it: procure the head with as much of the neck attached to it as possible (the hog must have been stabbed in the neck, not hit on the head as that would have broken the skull); then singe it well over the flame of a fire, then wipe it with a cloth, scrape well with a knife without scratching the skin, and place it on a cloth upon its skull; open it very carefully without piercing the skin, leaving no flesh whatever upon the bones; bone the neck of the pig, and cut it into small fillets two inches long, place the head on a board and rub it with half a pound of brown sugar, let it remain for one hour; then place it in a salting tub, and throw over it six pounds of salt, place in two quarts of ale, four bay-leaves, half an ounce of peppercorns, a quarter ditto of cloves, six blades of mace, eight sliced onions, ten sprigs of thyme, ten of winter savory, and two sliced carrots; stir it well up, and let it remain for two hours; then pour over the head, which turn every day for eight or ten days, rubbing it well; when sufficiently salted, take it out and dry it on a cloth, lay the head straight before you, skin side upwards; have ready six or eight pounds of forcemeat, but using pork instead of veal, with which cover the head an inch in thickness at the thinnest part; put the fillets cut from the neck in a layer lengthwise in the head, with a long piece of fat bacon, half an inch square, between each, sprinkle a little chopped eschalots, pepper, salt, and grated nutmeg over, and continue filling with forcemeat and the other ingredients until you have used the whole, finishing by covering forcemeat over; join the two cheeks together with the above in the interior, sew it up with pack-thread, giving it the shape of the head as much as possible, and fold it in one or two large thin cloths, leaving the ears out and upright.

Braise as follows: Put half a pound of butter in a large braising-pan or stock-pot, over which put four pounds of trimmings of pork or knuckle of veal, eight onions, two carrots, four turnips, eight bay-leaves, a tablespoonful of peppercorns, twelve cloves, ten sprigs of thyme, ten of marjoram, four blades of mace, half a bottle of bucellas wine, and four calf's feet, place it upon a sharp fire, stirring it occasionally, until the bottom is covered with a clearish glaze, then add four gallons of water and half a pound of salt; when boiling draw it to the corner of the stove, skim, and put in the head, the ears uppermost, and let simmer seven or eight hours, or according to the size and age of the pig; but the better plan would be to try it with a trussing-needle; if tender it is done; skim the stock, in which leave the head until half cold, when take it out, partly undo the cloths, and tie it again tighter if possible, and press it in a cover or upon a baking-sheet with three flat pieces of wood, one at each side, with a weight against them, and one upon the top between the ears, on which place a fourteen pounds weight, let it remain all night until quite cold, when take it out of the cloths, detach the thread it was sewn up with, cut a piece an inch in thickness from behind the ears (from which part it must be carved in as thin slices as possible), it will have a marbled appearance; trim the head a little, setting the ears in a proper position, glaze it with a brownish glaze, form the eyes with a little lard and a few black currants round, and the tusks with paste, baking them; have some very fresh tulips and roses, which stick tastefully in the ears and some around, but leaving space to carve; garnish boldly with croutons, aspic, made from the stock clarified as directed (No. 608); the meat and the calf's foot may be used for different dishes, see receipts.

The second one I had I boiled plainer, merely a little salt and a few vegetables; it was very good, but not so rich in flavor as the other; thus saving expense and trouble. They should be eaten with the following sauce:

Boar's Head Sauce.—Cut the rind (free from pith) of two Seville oranges into very thin strips half an inch in length, which blanch in boiling water, drain them upon a sieve, and put them into a basin, with a spoonful of mixed English mustard, four of currant jelly, a little pepper, salt (mix well together), and half a pint of good port wine.

LETTER NO. XV.

DEAR ELOISE,—To you, who are so fond of lobster, the following receipt will, I am confident, prove most valuable. To make sure of its quality, buy one heavy in proportion to its size; or, perhaps, *entre nous*, you would prefer to wait until a friend presented you with one.

LOBSTER.—This fish, which is continually before our eyes, and only looked upon as an article of food, is, without doubt, one of the wonders of the creation. A creature destitute of bones, yet furnished with a stomach capable of digesting the hardest substances, even its own shell, which it doffs once a year, when it is too small for it; without blood circulating through its body, yet strong and active. This is only one of those wonders of the mighty deep that we cannot but regard with awe and veneration, and yet the principal interest they do excite is when we visit a shell-fish shop to choose the largest and best for the smallest price. They are, without doubt, a very nourishing aliment, and are by many supposed to have a particular season, but which I believe not to be the case, as I have known them in and out of season on the same ground. When out of season, the pea or spawn is very large, and about being hatched; immediately after which it sheds its shell, and not its stomach, as is by many supposed. When in season, and fine-flavored, it should have no spawn, or very little, under the tail; and when its body is squeezed between the fingers it should not give, but be hard; its weight will also be a test, as it is a fish which wastes very much when kept long alive without food: great care must be observed in the boiling of it. A number should be placed at one time in a basket, and that placed in boiling water, adding half a pound of salt to every gallon of water, with a heavy weight upon it; if overdone, they eat tough and thready; if underdone, unwholesome and unpalatable. One weighing a pound will take fifteen minutes, and so on in proportion.

618. *Gratin of Lobster.* — Procure a good-sized lobster, cut it in half, detaching the head from the body; take out all the meat, and save the four shells; cut the meat into slices, then take a teaspoonful of chopped eschalots in a stewpan, with a piece of butter the size of two walnuts, pass them a few minutes over the fire, add a tablespoonful of flour (mix well in), half a pint of milk, stir over the fire, boiling about five minutes, then add the lobster, which season with a little cayenne, salt, chopped parsley, and essence of anchovies; stand it again upon the fire, stirring until boiling, then stir in the yolk of an egg; take off the fire, fill the shells of the lobster, sprinkle bread-crumbs over, with a little butter, put in the oven for twenty minutes; dish on a napkin and serve. To give it a nice color, use the salamander.

619. *Miroton Salad of Lobster.* — Prepare and ornament a border of eggs, like for that of game, put a thick layer of fresh salad in the centre, and dress over it in a crown, the lobster interspersed with slices of eggs and gherkins. The lobster must be divided in two across the back, extract the meat carefully out of it, and cut it in a round or slanting direction to the thickness of a crown piece, break the claws and cut the same way, and place on salad as above, so as to form a thick crown near the border of eggs, then take the interior of the lobster, pound it and pass it through a fine sieve, add to your sauce.

Any other kind of fish, as cod fish, &c., when cold, cut or break them in slices, lay them in a basin, season over with salt, pepper, nutmeg, slices of onion, parsley, a little oil and vinegar; put it in two hours before serving, and proceed as for lobster.

If there is any fish left from the previous day, I always make a salad of it, particularly in summer; there are many who object to so much oil, in which case it may be diminished.

620. *Salad Tartar.* — Make as usual the border of eggs and sauce, lay the salad in the middle and the lobster over, which has been previously cut in slices; pour over some of the same sauce as above, having added a tablespoonful of French mustard to it. Gherkins cut in slices, and a few stoned olives.

621. *Plain Salad.*—Take a lobster and any kind of salad, wash it well, dry in a cloth, cut the lobster up in a salad-bowl, sprinkle over it a teaspoonful of salt, half that of pepper, one of chopped tarragon or chervil, or parsley, if nothing better, four tablespoonfuls of oil, and two of common vinegar, but only one and a half if French, add the salad, stir lightly round with a wooden knife and fork, and it is ready.

622. *Lobster served plain.*—Break the tail from the body, cut the tail in two lengthwise, put the body in the middle of the dish, lay the half tail top and bottom, and the claws on the side; the shell previously broken, but not disfigured, and serve double parsley round.

623. *Lobster Salad.*—Dress a border of hard-boiled eggs, as directed in salad of game (No. 628), fill the centre with some nice fresh salad, then take the flesh from a middling-sized lobster, which cut into as large slices as possible, which put into a basin, and season with a little pepper, salt, oil, and vinegar, after which dress them pyramidically upon the salad, and have ready the following sauce: put the yolks of two fresh eggs in a basin, with the yolk of a hard-boiled one rubbed through a sieve, add half a saltspoonful of salt, and half that quantity of white pepper, and commence stirring round with a wooden spoon with the right hand, holding a bottle of salad oil in the left, dropping it in by degrees and continually stirring, and when becoming thickish add a couple of spoonfuls of common vinegar by degrees, still keeping it stirred, then more oil, proceeding thus until you have used three parts of a pint of oil, and a corresponding quantity of vinegar, by continually working, it will form a stiffish cream-looking sauce perfectly smooth; add a little more seasoning if required, and a teaspoonful of chopped parsley, with half that quantity of chopped eschalots, pour over the lobster and serve. Should the sauce curdle in making, the operation must be again performed, putting a yolk of an egg into another basin, working it with a little oil until forming a stiffish paste, when stir in the curdled sauce by degrees until the whole becomes smooth; always choose a cool place to make it in.

624. *Fish Salads.*—All fish salads are made precisely as in the last, but with the exception of fillets of sole salad, are made from the remains of fish from a previous dinner, especially turbot and salmon; but for fillets of soles they must be dressed thus:—

When filleted, melt an ounce of butter in a sauté-pan, lay the fillets in, season with pepper and salt, and the juice of half a lemon; sauté them on a slow fire until done, which may be from four to five minutes, and put by to get cold; cut in middle-sized pieces, and use as lobster.

625. *New Mayonnaise Sauce.*—Put a quarter of a pint of melted aspic upon ice in a stewpan, which keep whisking until becoming a white froth, then add half a pint of salad oil and six spoonfuls of tarragon vinegar, by degrees, first oil and then vinegar, continually whisking until it forms a white smooth sauce, to all appearance like a cream; season with half a teaspoonful of salt, a quarter ditto of pepper, and a little sugar, whisk it a little more, and it is ready to serve; it is usually dressed pyramidically over the article it is served with. The advantage of this sauce (which

is more delicate than any other) is, that you may dress it to any height you like and it will remain so for a long time; if the temperature is not too hot it will remain hours without melting or appearing greasy.

626. *Tartar Sauce.*—Rub the yolk of a cold hard-boiled egg through a hair sieve into a basin, to which add the yolks of two raw eggs, with a little salt and pepper; mix all together with a wooden spoon; have a pint of good salad oil in a bottle, hold it with the left hand over the basin, dropping it in very gradually, and with the right continue stirring it round until it becomes rather thick, then moisten it with a little tarragon vinegar, still keeping it stirred, then more oil, and so on until you have used all the oil, keeping it rather thick; then add a tablespoonful of finely chopped gherkins, half a ditto of chopped capers, half a ditto of chopped eschalots, and the same of chopped parsley, two of French mustard, a little cayenne pepper, sugar, and more salt if required; it is then ready for use. This sauce requires to be rather highly seasoned. Common vinegar may be used.

627. *Salmon in marinade.*—Have two good slices of salmon cut about four inches and a half in thickness, in a stewpan have three onions cut in slices, as also a turnip, a carrot, a head of celery cut small, a good half handful of parsley, two bay-leaves, and two ounces of butter; pass the whole ten minutes over a sharp fire, then add a pint of vinegar, a blade of mace, half a dozen peppercorns, and one ounce of salt; let simmer, then add three pints of water, put in the salmon, which simmer gently about half an hour, and leave in the marinade until cold, when serve with a little of the marinade strained through a hair sieve in the dish. Trout, mackerel, herrings, sprats, and fillets of sole or brill, are also very nice cooked in the same manner. A part of the above marinade may be made at any time, and almost any kind of fish remaining from a previous dinner may be done the same, and eaten cold.

628. *Salad of Game.*—Boil eight eggs hard, shell them, throw them into cold water, cut a thin slice off the bottom to facilitate the proper placing of them in the dish, cut each one into four, lengthwise, make a very thin flat border of butter about one inch from the edge of the dish you are going to serve them on; fix the pieces of egg upright, close to each other, the yolk outside, or alternately the white and yolk; you lay in the centre a layer of fresh salad that may be in season, and having previously roasted a young grouse rather underdone, which you cut into eight or ten pieces, then prepare sauce as follows: put a spoonful of eschalots, finely chopped, in a basin, one ditto of pounded sugar, the yolk of one egg, a tea-spoonful of chopped parsley, tarragon, or chervil, and a quarter of an ounce of salt, mix in by degrees with a wooden spoon, four spoonfuls of oil and two of Chili vinegar; when all mixed, put it on ice, or in a cold place; when ready to serve up, whip a gill of cream rather thick, which lightly mix with it, then lay the inferior parts of the grouse on the salad, sauce over so as to cover each piece, then lay over the salad and the remainder of the grouse; sauce over, and serve. The eggs may be ornamented with a little dot of radishes on the point, or beet-root. Anchovy and gherkin, cut into small diamonds, may be placed between, or cut gherkins in slices, and lay a border of them round, or in any way your fancy may dictate.

629. *Salad of Fowl.*—Proceed as for that of game, so far as the eggs and the salad

are concerned; then have a chicken, which has been previously plain roasted, or in vegetables, and cut it into ten pieces, put it into a basin, season with a teaspoonful of salt, quarter ditto of pepper, two tablespoonfuls of oil, one of vinegar, one onion sliced, and a few sprigs of chopped parsley, mix them well, and let them remain for a few hours, if time will permit. Take the pieces of chicken, and place in a dish with salad, as directed for grouse, with the sauce, &c., and serve. Nothing is better for ball-suppers than these kinds of dishes; they may be made of all kinds of solid fish, and the sauce is excellent; any kind of cold meat, dressed round with the sauce, may be served for supper or luncheon. It may be served with the same sauce or dressing as for Lobster Salad (or No. 623), or make the following one, which differs a little:—Put into a middle-sized, round-bottomed basin the yolk of two eggs, half a spoonful of salt, quarter of one of pepper, half a one of sugar, ditto of fine chopped onions, ditto of parsley, or of tarragon, or of chervil, stir with the right hand with a wooden spoon, while you pour some oil out of the bottle by keeping your thumb on its mouth, so that it runs out very slowly; when a few spoonfuls are in it, it will become quite stiff; pour also by degrees a few spoonfuls of vinegar, and so on until you have made enough for your salad; try if the flavor is good and relishing, as the quality of these two last ingredients varies so much, that I must leave it to your more simple and correct judgment. If you should fail at first, try again until you succeed, and I am certain you will be delighted with the result; it ought to be made in a cold place, particularly in summer. Great taste should be observed in the decoration of the border.

SHELL FISH.

Prawns are best when very red and have no spawn under the tail.

The *Escalop* is a fish very little used, but is exceedingly fine; it is in season at the same time as the oyster. It can be cooked in a variety of ways, but previous to doing which, it should be kept some time in salt water, so that it may free itself from any sand that may be in it; when opened, all the beard should be removed, and only the white, red, and black parts used; it may be cooked and used in every way like oysters, and is excellent with matelote of any kind of fish.

Razor Shell Fish or *Solen Fish.*—This is the aulo of the Romans, and a beautiful eating fish. It should also be cooked like oysters, and makes most excellent and strengthening soup.

OYSTERS.—No oyster should be eaten under four years old; their age is known by their shell—just the same as the age of a tree is known by its bark, or a fish by its scale, and the small oyster has the finest flavor.

630. *Escaloped Oysters.*—Put two dozen of oysters with their liquor into a stewpan, place over a fire, and when a little firm, drain them upon a sieve, catching the liquor in another stewpan; detach the beard from the oysters, and throw them again into their liquor; add half a blade of mace, place again upon the fire, and, when boiling, add a piece of butter the size of a walnut, with which you have mixed a teaspoonful of flour; shake round over the fire until becoming thick, season with a little cayenne, and salt if required; have an escalop shell, well buttered and bread-crumbed; place the oysters in, sprinkle bread-crumbs over, put it in the oven a quarter of an hour, pass the salamander over, and serve. The yolk of eggs may be added, and less flour.

631. *Stewed Oysters.*—Blanch and beard the oysters as above; when done, put them with their liquor in a stewpan, with four cloves, a blade of mace, and a teaspoonful of essence of anchovies, with a little chopped parsley and cayenne; let simmer a minute, stir in two pats of butter with which you have mixed half a teaspoonful of flour, let simmer a little longer, lay the oysters in your dish upon a piece of toast, and sauce over.

632. *Shrimps.*—Of these there are several varieties; a diversity of opinion exists amongst epicures of this little animal which is the best; but in my opinion a great deal depends on the manner of boiling, and their freshness.

The following is the plan: I prefer them boiled; to one gallon of water put two ounces of salt, one sprig of lemon thyme and one of mint, and let it boil; when boiling hard, put one quart of shrimps into an open wire or wicker basket with a handle, and place it in the water: the time they take to boil depends on the size of the fish, but may be known by their changing color; be particular not to boil them too much, or they will be tasteless and indigestible.

633. *Forcemeat.*—You will find this receipt so useful, and so often in use in made dishes, soups, fish, entrées, &c., that I must beg of you to devote to it your personal attention; and being rather difficult to execute, be present when your cook makes it, that she may follow strictly the receipt, which I flatter myself is rather original.

Take a pound and a half of lean veal, and cut it in long thin slices, scrape with a knife till nothing but the skin remains; put it in a mortar, pound it ten minutes, or until in a purée, pass it through a wire sieve (use the remainder in stock), then take one pound of good fresh beef suet, which shred and chop very fine, put it in your mortar and pound it, then add six ounces of panada (made as under) with the suet, pound them well together, and add the veal, season with a teaspoonful of salt, a quarter one of pepper, half that of nutmeg, work all well together, then add five eggs by degrees, continually pounding the contents of the mortar; when well mixed, take a small piece in a spoon, and poach it in some boiling water, and if it is delicate, firm and a good flavor, it is ready for use; if you require some very delicate, add two tablespoonfuls of white sauce, or even thick melted butter; you can vary the flavor by the addition of a spoonful of chopped parsley, eschalot, mushroom, &c., the flesh of rabbit or fowl, or hare, pheasant, grouse, &c., if plentiful, may be added, using the ingredients in proportion. One quarter of this quantity may be made if required.

634. *Panada for Forcemeats.*—Put two thirds of half a pint of water into a stewpan holding a quart, with nearly an ounce of butter; when boiling, stir in a quarter of a pound of flour; keep it moving over the fire until it forms a smooth and toughish paste; take it out of the stewpan, and when cold use it where directed.

635. *Forcemeats of Fish.*—These are much in use in France and other Catholic countries, especially in Lent, but they are a very excellent garnish for entrées of fish; they may be made of the flesh of almost all kinds of fish, more particularly the pike, salmon, trout, sole, haddock, and the whiting, which last is the most delicate.

636. *Forcemeat of Whitings.*—Take the fillets of three whitings, take off all the skin, and pound them well, then take them from the mortar, and form them into a ball; have a piece of panada (No. 634) one third the size of the ball, put the panada into the mortar, pound it well, then add two ounces of fresh butter, which mix well with the panada, then add the fish, season with pepper, salt, and a little grated nutmeg; mix all well together, then add by degrees three whole eggs and the yolks of two, try it in a little boiling water as directed for the forcemeat of veal. These are served generally as a meagre dish with a fish sauce, in Catholic families, especially in Lent time.

637. *Stuffing for Veal.*—Chop up half a pound of beef suet very fine, put it in a basin, with eight ounces of bread-crumbs, four ounces of chopped parsley, a tablespoonful of equal quantities of powdered thyme and marjoram, and a bay-leaf, the rind of a lemon grated, and the juice of half one; season with pepper and salt, and

one quarter of a nutmeg; mix the whole with three whole eggs; this will do also to stuff turkey or baked fish, adding some more chopped parsley.

VEGETABLES.

IN describing to you the different ways these may be dressed, I beg of you to make a constant use of them at your own table, as you will find they will be much better than partaking of half-raw greens, cabbage, turnip-tops, spinach, &c., and are less inviting in flavor, and, consequently, do not get consumed so much as they ought, which causes more meat to be eaten, and instead of refreshing the blood, as all vegetables will do in their season, only irritate it. Do not misunderstand me respecting our English way of partaking of plain boiled vegetables; I do not wish you to give them up entirely, but by adopting both plans, you will find it a great advantage in our domestic cookery. For my part, I do not object to our plain boiled vegetables, but merely to the neglectful way they are cooked and served up, often swimming in water. In France, no family in the middle station of life ever dines without a dish of dressed vegetables, upon which as much care has been bestowed in cooking as upon the principal dish of the dinner, and is often eaten alone.

638. *Asparagus.* — I cook it thus: I take a bundle and scrape lightly all the white part, beginning from the head down, and throw them when done into cold water, then tie them up in bundles of twenty-five each, if an ordinary size, if very large, half that number, keeping the heads together, and cut off the ends to make them the same length; have ready a pan containing one gallon of boiling water, in which has been thrown two ounces of salt, boil quickly for fifteen minutes, or till tender; dish them up with a piece of toast in the middle, keep the heads in the centre, and form a pyramid. Serve very hot, with rich melted butter, or cream sauce.

The queen of all vegetables, to my fancy, is asparagus. This may almost be said to be a modern vegetable in this country, and it is one which requires less cooking than perhaps any other, and is considered exceedingly wholesome.

639. *Young Green Peas.* — Young Green Peas! Do not those words sound pleasant to the ear, dearest? I fancy that by merely raising my eyes from the paper on which I am now writing, I shall see all our garden in buds and blossom; it not only seems to invigorate the sensitive part of one's appetite, but works upon the mind to that point that you may actually fancy you are breathing in a glowing atmosphere, and that the pearly dew is gracefully descending in small globules from heaven, to fix their sparkling eyes on the pinky bloom of myriads of roses. But, alas! how soon this charming illusion has disappeared since I have left for a moment the sight of my paper to give a peep through the garden window, where I perceive that though to-day is the 17th of April, the serious and uncheerful Father Winter has once more monopolized those delightful and variegated *nuances* of Nature, by laying out his universal snowy tablecloth over this for the present

ephemeral vision which the inviting words green peas had produced upon my senses; no doubt the effect of a good fire in my parlor, where I am now sitting, has had a great influence upon me respecting the summery temperature; but as a few weeks longer will realize my wishes, I shall here content myself by giving you the receipt how they ought to be cooked when you can get them.

When very young, I like them plain boiled, because their original flavor is so fresh and delicate, that any addition, except a little very fresh butter, would be certain to destroy their aroma; I even object to the introduction of green mint, though I do not want to deprive you of it, being only a matter of taste.

Put two quarts of water to boil, with half an ounce of salt, and then place in one pint of peas, boil a full gallop till tender (about ten minutes), put in a colander, drain one minute; lay them, raised in the centre, in a dish, put in them two pats of very fresh butter, and serve.

When older or larger, boil a little longer, add twelve leaves of green mint, which serve with it.

640. *Peas, French way.* — They do not look so inviting, not being so green; but I must say they are excellent as regards flavor. Choose them young and fresh; without both of these qualities, they would not cook properly. Put in a pint of cold water, mix the peas and butter well with your hand, add four button onions, a bouquet of six sprigs of parsley, one ounce of sugar, two saltspoonfuls of salt, one of pepper, put it over a tolerably good fire, moving them often; if getting rather dry, add a wineglassful of water, twenty minutes ought to be enough when tender; add one ounce of butter, in which you have mixed a teaspoonful of flour, which put in it, and stir it well; make a liaison of the yolk of one egg, a quarter of a gill of cream, which add and stir, take out the parsley and onions, and serve.

Another way. — When large, I stew them with two cabbage-lettuces cut in two, and stew longer, put in four wineglassfuls of water, or more if required, and finish as above.

To keep their color, I often proceed thus for entrées or second courses: I plain boil as above, and put them in a stewpan, with four small onions, a little mint, parsley, butter, sugar, and a drop of water, simmer a few minutes, add as above the flour, butter, and liaison, and serve; they are very good this way, but not so rich in flavor.

There are different kinds, but I prefer the Prussian Blue above all.

641. *Seakale.* — Proceed exactly as for asparagus for boiling, but previously to boiling cut out the black part of the roots, and well wash and tie it together, and serve with the same sauce as asparagus. There is a kind of seakale that is rank and stringy, and not worth eating; it may be known, when raw, by the outside near the root, which is very tough and hard.

642. *Sprue-grass.* — The longer the green part the better the sprue; take each piece and gently bend it, and it will break off at that part which you require, beyond it is too hard, and cannot be eaten; when you thus have the pieces, cut them into lengths of a quarter of an inch, which well wash; have one gallon of water,

into which put one ounce of salt, and boil, then put in the sprue and boil for ten minutes, or till tender, then drain on a sieve, put them in a stewpan, with two ounces of fresh butter, half a teaspoonful of flour, the same of salt, two pinches of pepper, and place on the fire, stir well together, and serve hot. The yolk of an egg, well beaten with two spoonfuls of cream, may be added to it; and when serving, also two spoonfuls of white sauce or melted butter,—but I always do it as the first.

643. *Celery.*—Cut about ten heads of large celery from six to seven inches long, trim the outside and cut the root to a point, wash it very well between the leaves, tie three together, put a gallon of water, with two ounces of salt, to boil, then add the celery, and boil for fifteen minutes, then drain it, put into a stewpan a small slice of bacon, and lay the celery on it, put it on the fire for two minutes, add one onion sliced, cover with broth until quite tender, then take it out, and dish on a piece of toast, pass the gravy through a sieve into a stewpan, skim off the fat, reduce it to a demi-glaze, add a little sugar and a small pat of butter, which you have rubbed into some flour, stir it well, and sauce over; it ought to be thick, and of a nice brown color, which produce, if required, by a little coloring. Marrow may be served with it, by taking two good pieces of marrow, and boil for a few minutes in a quart of water, and serve on each side the celery. It can also be cooked plain boiled, and served with melted butter over, and also boiled in eight tablespoonfuls of brown sauce, six of broth, and half a teaspoonful of sugar, in which it has boiled ten minutes, or until tender; sauce over and serve.

644. *Salsify.*—I do not know why this vegetable, which is held in such high estimation on the Continent, should be so little esteemed with us; I will here supply their manner of cooking it, and perhaps you will give it a fair trial. Take twelve middling-sized ones, scrape them well till quite white, rub each with lemon and put in cold water; put into a stewpan a quarter of a pound of beef or mutton suet, cut in small dice one onion, a little thyme, a bay-leaf, a tablespoonful of salt, and four cloves, put on the fire and stir for five minutes, add two tablespoonfuls of flour, and stir well, then add three pints of water, when just boiling put in your salsify, simmer till tender; they will take nearly one hour; dish on toast, sauce over with Dutch, maître d'hôtel, or onion sauce, or a very good demi-glaze, or Italian sauce. Should any remain, they may be made into fritters thus: put the sauce, if any, in a basin, add a little salt, pepper, two spoonfuls of vinegar, half a chopped eschalot, and a spoonful of oil, place in the salsify, and let it remain for some hours, when ready to serve, make a small quantity of batter, dip each piece in it, and fry for five minutes in lard or fat, dish up with fried parsley over.

645. *Vegetable Marrow.*—Choose eight young small ones, with smooth skin, and put them to boil in two quarts of water, in which you have put one ounce of salt, the same of butter, try with a needle if tender, then dish them tastefully on mashed potatoes in a dish, put half a pint of melted butter in a pan when near boiling, add a liaison of a yolk of an egg, two pats of butter, a little sugar, the juice of half a lemon, sauce over and serve; if they are rather large, cut them in two length-wise; if in smaller pieces, take all the inside out and boil till tender, and warm in the above sauce. You can also make a nice demi-glaze, as No. 132, and let them simmer in it for twenty minutes; do not break them, as they would then be unsightly; they can

be made into soup like cauliflower (No. 207).

646. *Cauliflower and Broccoli.*—Be very particular in cleaning them, choose them rather small, thick and firm, put them for one hour in salt and water, then rinse them well in water, that all the dirt may be removed from the interior; have a pan of boiling water, in which you have placed two ounces of salt and one of butter, drain and use where indicated; but if for second course, place them on a dish in the form of a dome, and cover over with some sauce as for vegetable marrow or plain melted butter, or Soubise sauce if preferred plain; serve it very hot, having drained it.

647. *The same gratiné with Cheese.*—Put into a stewpan ten spoonfuls of white sauce, No. 130, with a little chopped onions, which boil for a few minutes, add to it a quarter of a pound of grated Parmesan, or any mild English cheese; when boiling, add the yolk of one egg, and a little cayenne, mix quick, lay a little on a dish, put two or three heads of cauliflower or broccoli on it, pour the remainder of sauce over, and a little bread-crumbs and grated cheese; put in oven half an hour, give it a nice yellow color, and serve; if no white sauce, use melted butter, but do not boil it so long, or it will eat rather greasy.

648. *Jerusalem Artichokes.*—One of the best and most useful vegetables ever introduced to table, and anything but appreciated as it deserves to be. To prove to you that I am a great admirer of it, you will find it very often mentioned in my receipts. In using them for a second course, I choose about twelve of the same size, peel them and shape them like a pear, but flat at the bottom, wash them well, boil gently in three pints of water, one ounce of salt, one of butter, and a few sliced onions; when tender, I make a border of mashed potatoes on a dish, fix them on it point upwards, sauce over with either cream sauce (No. 280), white sauce (No. 130), melted butter (No. 264), maître d'hôtel, and place a fine Brussels sprout between each, which contrast is exceedingly inviting, simple, and pretty.

649. *Cucumbers* are most delicious stuffed and stewed, but very difficult to dress, and consequently chiefly used for entrées, in which series they will be found. They may, however, be treated like vegetable marrow.

650. *Artichokes.*—Pull the tail off four or six small artichokes, trim the bottom slightly with a knife, cut the point of every leaf, wash well in plain water, put them on in plenty of water, with a little salt, to boil, let them thus remain about half an hour, or until the leaves are easy to be removed, take them out and lay on a sieve to drain, and serve on a napkin, with melted butter separate.

651. *Beet-root.*—This is a very good dish, and, as I believe it has never been noticed in cookery, I must lay claim to its parentage; I have given the receipt to some friends, who highly approve of it. Take two nice young boiled beet-roots, which will take about from two to three hours to simmer in plenty of boiling water, peel when cold, cut in slanting direction, so as to make oval pieces, peel and cut in small dice two middling-sized onions, put in a pan, with two ounces of butter, fry white, stirring continually with a spoon; add a spoonful of flour, and enough milk to make a nice thickish sauce, add to it three saltspoonfuls of salt, four of sugar, one of pepper, a spoonful of good vinegar, and boil a few minutes; put in the slic-

es to simmer for about twenty minutes, have ready some mashed potatoes, with which make a neat border in your dish one inch high, then put the beet-root and sauce, highly season in the centre, and serve.

652. *French Beans.*—These are also a great favorite with many. To dress it, head and tail them, drawing off the back string, cut in long diamonds, boil till tender in water in which salt has been placed, a quarter of a pound to a gallon, try them after a quarter of an hour's boiling, drain them, lay them on a dish one inch thick, sprinkle with a little salt, pepper, and two pats of butter, then put in the remainder, proceed the same at top; serve very quickly, to prevent the butter oiling.

653. *The same, à la Maître d'Hôtel.*—When boiled as above, put in a stewpan, with a quarter of a pound of maître d'hôtel butter, when melted serve. They may be also served with white sauce thus: put in a stewpan eight spoonfuls of melted butter, season well, simmer gently, add the yolk of an egg, two ounces of butter, juice of half a lemon, and serve.

654. *Kidney Beans.*—Head and tail them, string and slit them down the middle, place them for half an hour in salt and water in which you have thrown a little culinary alkali, boil until tender, and serve with melted butter, or à la maître d'hôtel.

655. *Broad or Windsor Beans.*—Boil in salt and water: when done, serve with parsley and butter, or with a piece of bacon.

656. *Brussels Sprouts.*—Trim, wash, and boil about forty small Brussels sprouts; when tender, drain, dish, and sprinkle a little salt, pepper, and two ounces of butter over, and serve. Serve also in sauce, or with maître d'hôtel, like French beans. These are also very good for soups, sauces, or garnish.

657. *Spinach.*—This vegetable is very light and very good for invalids. It must be washed in several waters, after having been well picked; then put a quarter of a sieve of spinach to a gallon of water and three ounces of salt, boil for ten minutes till tender, drain on sieve, press a little with your hands to extract part of the water, chop it up fine, put in a stewpan, with a quarter of a pound of butter, a teaspoonful of salt, half ditto of pepper, put on a fire with a drop of warm broth for a few minutes, and serve.

658. *Spinach with Gravy.*—Proceed as before, but add a tablespoonful of flour and half a pint of strong gravy in it, as No. 177; serve with sippets of bread round.

659. *Spinach with Cream.*—Proceed as before, but putting half a pint of milk or cream instead of gravy, and the addition of a tablespoonful of sugar, cut three slices of bread, lay on dish, sift sugar over, put in oven, salamander over, cut in various shapes, and serve under or over the spinach.

660. *Young Haricot Beans.*—Take a pint, boil in two quarts of water, with a small piece of butter, and half an ounce of salt; when done, which will take only a few minutes, dish and serve; put butter over, sprinkle a little salt, and when on the dish, a gill of maître d'hôtel sauce or fennel sauce may be served over the larger one, or it is very delicious plain boiled, and with a piece of ham or bacon.

661. *White Haricot Beans.*—Nothing so cheap or so solid a food as haricot beans; get a pint of fine white beans, called the dwarf—I buy them for fourpence a quart.

I put them into half a gallon of cold soft water, with one ounce of butter; they take about three hours to cook, and should simmer very slowly, drain them and put into a stewpan with a little salt, pepper, chopped parsley, two ounces of butter, and the juice of a lemon, place on the fire for a few minutes, stir well, and serve. The water in which it is boiled will not make a bad soup by frying four onions in butter in a stewpan, adding a little flour, then the water poured over, and a slice of toasted bread, cut in pieces, and served in a tureen. Should the water in boiling reduce too fast, add a little more. They may be dressed for second course, à la Bretonne, as for leg. The longer sort requires to be soaked a few hours before boiling.

662. *Mushrooms.* — These are good every way when fresh; for a dish take about fifty button, cut the roots off, wash and rub the skin off with a cloth, cut them in slices the size of a shilling, tail and all, put them in a stewpan, with two ounces of butter, a small teaspoonful of salt, two pinches of pepper, and the juice of half a lemon, put them on the fire, simmer till tender, and dish them up on a nice crisp toast; should you require any sauce, add, when nearly done, half a spoonful of flour, a gill of broth, milk, or cream, or even water, stew a few minutes longer, pour over toast and serve.

If very large, they should have been carefully picked, for if the dirt should have got into the under part it is difficult to remove it; cut off the end of the tail and peel the top, put them on a gridiron, season moderately with salt and pepper, turn them, and when done serve them on a very hot dish, and put on each a piece of butter the size of a nut, and a squeeze of a lemon, put in a hot oven for a minute, or before the fire, and serve; a little Harvey's or Soyer's sauce is an improvement. They may also be put in an oven, by laying them in a sauté-pan or tin dish, put a little butter and season over each, and a drop of Harvey's sauce, and let them remain twenty minutes, and serve with gravy over.

663. *Lentils.* — Put into a stewpan one quart, add two quarts of cold water, one ounce of butter, a little salt, one onion sliced, a bouquet of parsley, set on the fire, simmer till tender, which may be in two hours; when done, drain in a sieve, and save the liquor, which can be made into a soup like the haricots (see receipt No. 661); put the lentils in a stewpan, with two ounces of butter, a little salt, sugar, pepper, and a tablespoonful of chopped eschalots, set it on the fire, put in butter and flour, mix well, boil ten minutes gently, and dish in a border of potatoes or in a deep dish. It may also be done thus: by frying till brown one onion, sliced in a stewpan, put in the boiled lentils, with two ounces of butter, a little flour, a gill of gravy, and season as above, stir well, boil, and serve hot.

Gabanza or Egyptian bean may be cooked in the same way.

664. *English Truffles.* — Put twelve of them to soak for four hours in lukewarm water; then with a hard hair-brush remove all the earth from them; then wash again, put them into a stewpan, with a few slices of bacon, two onions, half a head of celery, half a carrot, a clove of garlic, two bay-leaves, a sprig of thyme, four of parsley, a teaspoonful of salt, one of sugar, a half of pepper, two glasses of sherry, and a pint of broth; let them simmer for half an hour or more, but till tender; place them in the oven for twenty minutes longer, remove the truffles and place them on

a dish; have a little mashed potatoes, and make a border, and place the truffles on in pyramid to prevent them moving, strain the gravy they were in, skim off the fat, reduce it to about a gill, put in a teaspoonful of arrow-root in a cup, with a spoonful of water, mix it, and put to the gravy, boil a few minutes, pour over, and serve.

I peeled some of them, cooked the same way, they eat better; but they did not look so well.

665. *Sauté of the same.*—After having washed them, I peel them and cut into thin slices, and put about one pound of them into a stewpan; I then add a quarter of a pound of butter, a teaspoonful of salt, half one of sugar, a quarter ditto of nutmeg, warm over the fire, add a gill of broth, a little flour, mixed with a little butter, stir in, boil, and serve on toast;—or proceed as above, adding a gill of demi-glaze. They can be served with any entrées when properly done, and in all cases can be used instead of mushrooms.

666. *To cook Sourcrout.*—Put a quart of sourcrout, with a fat piece of bacon or pork, into an *earthen* pan, with sufficient water to cover it, stew for four or five hours, and serve with pork or fried sausages; it is better the second day. It may be procured in any good oil-shop in the winter.

667. *Sourcrout, Bavarian way.*—Well wash one quart of sourcrout, and put it into an earthen pan with a quarter of a bottle of Rhenish wine or any other light wine, and stew it for three hours; then add some veal gravy, well seasoned, and stew for three hours longer, and serve with sausages, or when you add the veal stock, put in a duck or a goose, and serve with it.

668. *Laver* is a marine plant (the *Ulvœ Lactuca*), which is obtained, in London, from the West of England; in Dublin, from Malahide; Edinburgh, from Aberdeen. It is merely washed, boiled, pulped, and potted by the fishermen's wives. It is considered wholesome, but I see nothing particular in it that can make it so unless it is the small quantity of iodine that it contains. It should be dressed like spinach (No. 658), and sent up very hot in a dish over a spirit-lamp, and is generally served with mutton. The following is a new plan I have introduced for cooking it, which has been liked by those persons who formerly disliked it.

Have some mashed potatoes as No. 672, roll it out the thickness of a quarter of an inch, cover it with some cold stewed laver nicely seasoned, put another layer of mashed potatoes over, and allow it to get quite cold, when cut it in square pieces, egg, bread-crumb, and proceed as for ramifolles.

POTATOES.—This root still bears its original American name, signifying earth-apple, and is divided into many species. Amongst those most common in use are the regent, ash-leaf, kidney; but, in the sister kingdom, Ireland, many other varieties are in use; as the lumper, reds, and blacks. There are as many different ways of cooking them as there are different species, which I will now describe.

669. *Plain Boiled or Steamed Potatoes.*—Well wash the potatoes and peel them, and throw them into cold water (that depends upon the kind, if new or young, or a kidney, they should be cooked immediately after they are peeled, whilst others require to remain a long time in soak); have ready a steamer with boiling water in

it, put the potatoes on the top, and steam for twenty to thirty minutes, and serve. Should you not have a steamer, and are obliged to boil them, do so by putting them into plenty of boiling water, and boil till tender or breaking, then pour them out into a colander, put a cloth over them, and put them in the screen, or before the fire, until you are ready to serve them; they ought always to be sent to table very hot.

670. *Baked Potatoes.*—This is a very favorite dish with many persons; they ought to be of a large size, called Regents, and when cooked very floury. Mr. B. tells me he sometimes lunches at a house in the city where the proprietor grows that sort in particular for the use of his customers, and he finds them better if he leaves them in the ground where they grow until wanted, and he has about three days' consumption taken up at a time. They are merely well washed, and put into a slow oven for about thirty minutes, or longer if large, and served with a pat of butter in a plate.

671. *Fried Potatoes.*—The long kidney potato is the best for this purpose; they should be washed and peeled, and cut into very thin slices, and thrown into boiling fat until a nice light brown color; dish up very hot, throwing a little salt over. The remains of cold ones may be cut into slices and fried in the same way, or they may be dipped into batter, and fried like fritters.

672. *Mashed Potatoes.*—Steam about ten fine potatoes for about thirty-five minutes, put them into a stewpan or bowl, with two ounces of butter, one teaspoonful of salt, a smaller spoonful of pepper, and half a pint of milk, and beat them very well up with a large fork, then add by degrees a gill of milk, and continue beating, and dish them lightly on a dish. Should you require to keep them warm, do so in a stewpan. I do not approve of putting them into moulds and then in the oven, as it makes them heavy.

673. *Potatoes à la Maître d'Hôtel.*—With young potatoes they are excellent. Boil ten middle-sized ones cut in slices of a quarter of an inch thick, put in the stewpan half a pint of milk or the same of broth, a little salt, pepper, grated nutmeg, and a tablespoonful of fresh chopped parsley, then simmer on fire; when boiling, add a quarter of a pound of fresh butter, the juice of a lemon, stir well for a few minutes; when each piece is well covered with the sauce, dish up, and high in the centre, as they must appear light.

674. *Lyonnaise.*—The remains of cold potatoes may be used thus:—Put three ounces of butter in an omelette pan, in which you fry rather white three sliced onions; put on the potatoes, cut in thin slices about the size of half a crown, and sauté them now and then until they have a nice yellow color; add a spoonful of chopped parsley, salt, pepper, and the juice of a lemon, sauté well that it should mix well together, dish and serve very hot; they are excellent to serve with chop, steak, or any joint.

675. *Irish way of boiling.*—In Ireland, where this root has been for so long a period the chief nourishment of the people, and where it takes the place of bread and other more substantial food, it is cooked so that it may have, as they call it, a bone in it; that is, that the middle of it should not be quite cooked. They are done thus:—

Put a gallon of water with two ounces of salt, in a large iron pot, boil for about ten minutes, or until the skin is loose, pour the water out of the pot, put a dry cloth on the top of the potatoes, and place it on the side of the fire without water for about twenty minutes, and serve. In Ireland turf is the principal article of fuel, which is burnt on the flat hearth; a little of it is generally scraped up round the pot so as to keep a gradual heat, by this plan the potato is both boiled and baked. Even in those families where such a common art of civilized life as cooking ought to have made some progress, the only improvement they have upon this plan is, that they leave the potatoes in the dry pot longer, by which they lose the *bone*. They are always served up with the skins on, and a small plate is placed by the side of each guest.

676. *To blanch Macaroni.*—Have half a gallon of water in a stewpan, in which put two ounces of butter and an ounce of salt; when boiling, throw in a pound of macaroni, which boil until tender, being careful that it is not too much done; the time of boiling depends principally upon the quality, the Genoa macaroni taking the longest time, and the Neapolitan the shortest, which last, if too much done, will fall in purée.

677. *Macaroni à l'Italienne.*—Boil half a pound of macaroni as above; when done, lay it on a sieve to dry for one minute, put it in a pan, with four spoonfuls of white sauce, add half a teaspoonful of salt, a quarter ditto of pepper, a little cayenne, toss the macaroni over the fire; when boiling, add two ounces each of grated Parmesan and Gruyère cheese, toss round and round until well mixed, then serve with a gill of very strong gravy around it.

678. *Macaroni au Gratin.*—Proceed the same as above; but after you have put the macaroni on the dish, omit the gravy, and cover it slightly with bread-crumbs, and about the same quantity of Parmesan cheese grated, a little butter, and then put in a hot oven for a quarter of an hour; if not hot enough, pass the salamander over it, and serve very hot.

679. *Macaroni à la Napolitaine.*—Boil half a pound of the best quality of macaroni for half an hour, as at No. 736; when tender, lay one quarter of it on the dish you intend to serve; have ready two ounces of grated Parmesan cheese, which you divide into four parts to lay over each layer of macaroni, then put over it two tablespoonfuls of strong gravy, made of half glaze and consommé, put the dish in the oven for ten minutes, and serve very hot.

680. *The real Italian method (called à l'Estoufade).*—Boil and proceed as before, but make the gravy as follows, and use it instead of the preceding. Take two pounds of rump of beef larded through, put in a small stewpan, with one quarter of a pound of butter, fry gently for one hour, turning almost continually; when forming a glaze add half a pint of broth, let simmer another hour, take the fat off, and use that gravy instead of that above described; a little tomato may be introduced if handy, serve the beef at the same time in a separate dish.

681. *Fried Mashed Potatoes in various shapes.*—Roast twelve fine potatoes; when done, take out the interior, which form into a ball; when cold, put them into a mortar, with a piece of butter half the size of the ball; pound them well together, season with a little salt, pepper, chopped eschalots, chopped parsley, and grated

nutmeg, mix them with the yolks of six, and two whole eggs; then form them into croquettes about the size and shape of a small egg, and bread-crumb them twice over, and fry them to a light brown color in a stewpan of hot lard, and serve as garniture where required.

682. *To boil Rice.*—Wash well in two separate waters a pound of the best Carolina rice, then have two quarts of water *boiling* in a stewpan, into which throw your rice, boil it until three parts done, then drain it on a sieve; butter the interior of a stewpan, in which put your rice, place the lid on tight, and put it in a warm oven upon a trivet until the rice is perfectly tender, or by the side of the fire; serve it separate with curry, or any other dish where required. Prepared thus, every grain will be separate and quite white.

683. *Chopping of Herbs, &c.*—This may appear a very simple thing to do well, yet it is often done badly, by which the flavor is lost. They should be well washed and dried, and then take the leaves in the left hand, pressing upon the leaves with your fingers, and chop as fine as possible, not by placing the point of the knife on the board and raising it and letting it fall, but with a good sharp cut, so that they are cut, not pressed. Onions should be peeled, and cut in halves lengthwise, and then with a thin knife cut each half in slices, leaving them joined at the root; again cut into slices contrarywise, and then from top to bottom; thus having cut into very small squares, chop it with both hands with the knife. You may also wash them; when half-chopped press them in a cloth, and chop them still finer.

OF DIFFERENT SORTS OF PASTRY.

THE variety of pastes is to the pastry what first stocks are to soups and sauces, and must be very properly first described, particularly as it is here I must refer my readers for paste even used for the hors-d'œuvre and entrées; to succeed you must be particular in your proportions, and very careful in the mixing; for, although there is nothing more simple if pains be taken, so will the least neglect produce a failure, nor is it only with the making of the paste that pains must be taken, but likewise with the baking, for as paste badly made would not improve in baking, neither will paste, however well made, be good if badly baked; should the oven be too hot the paste will become set and burn before it is done; and, again, if too cold it would give the paste a dull heavy appearance, but an oven properly heated (which can be readily known by a little attention on the part of those in the habit of using it) will give it a clear brilliant appearance.

For every description of pastry made from puff paste, try if the oven is hot by placing your hand about half-way in, and hold it there about a quarter of a minute, if you can hold it there that time without inconvenience it would not be hot enough; but if you cannot judge of the heat, the safest method would be, try a piece of the paste previous to baking the whole; I apply these few observations to all my friends, but particularly to the uninstructed, as a person of continual practice cannot fail to be aware of the truth of them.

684. *Puff Paste.*—Put one pound of flour upon your pastry slab, make a hole in the centre, in which put the yolk of one egg and the juice of a lemon, with a pinch of salt, mix it with cold water (iced in summer, if convenient) into a softish flexible paste, with the right hand dry it off a little with flour until you have well cleared the paste from the slab, but do not work it more than you can possibly help, let remain two minutes upon the slab; then have a pound of fresh butter from which you have squeezed all the buttermilk in a cloth, bringing it to the same consistency as the paste, upon which place it; press it out with the hand, then fold over the edges of the paste so as to hide the butter, and roll it with the rolling-pin to the thickness of a quarter of an inch, thus making it about two feet in length, fold over one third, over which again pass the rolling-pin; then fold over the other third, thus forming a square, place it with the ends top and bottom before you, shaking a little flour both under and over, and repeat the rolls and turns twice again as before; flour a baking-sheet, upon which lay it, upon ice or in some cool place (but in summer it would be almost impossible to make this paste well without ice) for half an hour; then roll twice more, turning it as before, place again upon the ice a quarter of an hour, give it two more rolls, making seven in all, and it is ready for use when required, rolling it whatever thickness (according to what you

intend making) directed in the following receipts. When I state that upwards of a hundred different kinds of cakes may be made from this paste, I am sure it will be quite sufficient to urge upon every cook the necessity of paying every attention to its fabrication, as it will repay for the study and trouble.

685. *Puff Paste, with Beef Suet.*—Where you cannot obtain good butter for making paste, the following is an excellent substitute; skin and chop one pound of kidney beef suet very fine, put it into a mortar and pound it well, moistening with a little oil, until becoming as it were one piece, and about the consistency of butter, proceed exactly as in the last, using it instead of butter.

686. *Half Puff Paste.*—Put one pound of flour upon your pastry slab, with two ounces of butter, rub well together with the hands, make a hole in the centre, in which put a pinch of salt and the yolk of an egg with the juice of a lemon; mix with water as before, then roll it out thin and lay half a pound of butter (prepared as for puff paste) rolled into thin sheets over, fold it in three, roll and fold again twice over, lay it in a cold place a quarter of an hour, give another roll, and it is ready for use where required; this paste is mostly used for fruit tarts, for which it is well adapted.

687. *Short Paste, or Pâte à foncer.*—Put a pound of best flour upon your pastry slab, make a hole in the centre, in which put an ounce of salt, half a pound of fresh butter, and sufficient water to form a stiff paste, mix well together, and it is ready for use where directed.

688. *Short Paste for Fruit Tarts.*—Put a pound of flour upon your pastry slab with six ounces of butter, and rub them well together; then make a hole in the centre, in which put two ounces of powdered sugar, two whole eggs, and a large wineglassful of water, mix the eggs, sugar, and water well, then drown in the flour and mix together, and work it lightly.

689. *Pâte d'Office, or Confectioner's Paste.*—Weigh half a pound of flour, which put upon your slab, make a hole in the centre, in which put six ounces of sifted sugar, mix it well with four eggs into a stiffish paste, having first well dissolved the sugar with the eggs, work it well, it is then ready for use.

This paste was very much used when pièces montés were so much in vogue, but in the several receipts in which it is referred to, it is used upon quite a new principle, and very much simplified; this paste, with the above proportions, ought to be very stiff, but still pliable enough to be worked without breaking; should it be too stiff add more eggs, or too soft more flour; the half or quarter of the above quantity may of course be made.

690. *Vols-au-Vent* of all things in pastry require the most care and precision; they that can make a good vol-au-vent may be stamped as good pastrycooks, although many variations in working puff paste, all others are of secondary importance. Make a pound of puff paste, giving it seven rolls and a half, leave it an inch in thickness, make a mark upon the top either round or oval, and according to the size of your dish; then, with a sharp-pointed knife, cut it out from the paste, holding the knife with the point slanting outwards; turn it over, mark the edges with the back of your knife, and place it upon a baking-sheet, which you have sprinkled

with water; egg over the top, then dip the point of the knife into hot water, and cut a ring upon the top a quarter of an inch deep, and half an inch from the edge of the vol-au-vent, set in a rather hot oven, if getting too much color, cover over with a sheet of paper, do not take it out before done, or it would fall, but when quite set, cut off the lid, and empty it with a knife; be careful to make no hole in the side or bottom; if for first course it is ready, but if for second sift sugar all over, which glaze with the salamander. Regulate the thickness of the paste from which you cut the vol-au-vent, according to the size you require it, the smaller ones of course requiring thinner paste. A vol-au-vent for entrées will take about half an hour to bake, and as the common iron ovens often throw out more heat upon one side than the other, it will require turning two or three times to cause it to rise equal; it ought to be when baked of a light gold color.

691. *Vol-au-Vent of Peaches.*—Put half a pound of sugar in a sugar-pan, with the juice of a lemon and about half a pint of water, place it upon the fire and boil till becoming a thickish syrup; then have eight peaches not quite ripe, which cut in halves, break their stones and blanch the kernels, throw six halves with the kernels into the syrup, boil three minutes, take them out with a skimmer, lay them upon a dish and take off their skins, stew the rest in syrup in like manner, four at a time; when all done pour what liquor runs from them again into the syrup, which reduce to a good thickness, pass it through a tammy into a basin, when cold pour a little over the peaches and leave until ready to serve; dress the peaches in your vol-au-vent with the syrup over. This is a receipt I learnt in France, where I got peaches for a sou each.

692. *Vol-au-Vent with Fruit.*—These are generally used for the second course, and do not require to be so high as the other, especially as the fruit ought to be dressed in the form of a pyramid, if they are cut about three quarters of an inch in thickness it will be enough; when nearly done, sift some powdered sugar over them, and put it back in the oven to glaze well, if not hot enough use the salamander; remove the interior, taking care not to make a hole in the bottom or sides, and fill with any kind of fruit you like, but never mix two kinds together, except currant and raspberry.

693. *Sweet Vol-au-Vent with Rhubarb.*—In the spring of the year, this makes a very inviting and wholesome dish, and its qualities purify the blood, which the winter's food has rendered gross; cut about twelve sticks of rhubarb into lengths of one inch, put it in a stewpan holding about two quarts, put over it a quarter of a pound of sugar, and a tablespoonful of water, set it on a sharp fire, stirring it, do not let it get brown, or it would spoil and lose its flavor; it will take but a few minutes to do; when tender, put it in a basin to cool; a few minutes before serving, fill the vol-au-vent with it, and serve cold.

694. *Ditto, with green Gooseberries.*—A quart of green gooseberries, a quarter of a pound of powdered sugar, the juice of half a lemon, and a tablespoonful of water, put on the fire and move it about for ten minutes, or till tender, and forming a thick green marmalade, put it in a basin till cold, serve in pyramid in the vol-au-vent; a little thick syrup, if handy, poured over, improves the appearance.

695. *Ditto, with Orange.*—Well peel six oranges, removing all the pith, divide each into six or eight pieces, put them in a pan, with a quarter of a pound of sugar, and the juice of one orange, set it on a slow fire, with the cover on, stir it now and then; ten minutes will be sufficient time for it, take out the pieces one after the other, lay them in a basin, reduce your syrup to a proper thickness, when ready to serve, dish your pieces of orange in it, and pour over the syrup.

696. *Another method.*—Make a thick syrup with half a pound of sugar, put in your pieces by a dozen at a time, just give them a boiling, remove them on a sieve, then add the other pieces, when all done, add the juice, which pass through a sieve, and back again to the pan, boil till a proper thickness, dish up and serve the syrup over.

697. *Ditto, a still plainer method.*—Have the pieces of orange ready, and put in a stewpan a quarter of a pound of sugar, a wineglass of brandy or rum, stir it well a few minutes, and serve with the liquor poured over.

698. *Ditto, with Cherries.*—Stone one pound of cherries, and put in a pan, with a quarter of a pound of powdered sugar, stew for five minutes, take them down, drain, then reduce the syrup till thick, and pour over at the moment of serving.

699. *Ditto, with Strawberries.*—Pick two pottles of very fresh strawberries, not too ripe, put them in with two ounces of powdered sugar, a teaspoonful of powdered cinnamon, toss them gently in a basin, and serve immediately in your vol-au-vent.

700. *Ditto, with Apples.*—This fruit being procurable all the year renders it one of very great convenience; Ripstone pippins are the best: cut in four, peel them, put a pint of syrup, when boiling, put in your apples, with the peel of half a lemon, and the juice of a whole one, let simmer till tender, put it in a basin, boil the syrup to a white jelly, let it stand till cold, put the apple in the vol-au-vent, and pour the syrup (cold) or jelly over; serve a few ornaments made with very green angelica.

701. *Another method.*—Cut any kind of apple, rather thin, put over a quarter of a pound of powdered sugar, the rind of a lemon chopped, the juice of the same, one ounce of butter, and a glass of sherry, put on the fire, toss till tender, but keep it very white, put it in a basin, when cold dish in your vol-au-vent; whip a gill of good cream, add ten drops of orange-flower water in it, cover over carefully and serve.

Apple sauté with butter, in this way may be served hot in the vol-au-vent. Any kind of plums or apricots, when plentiful, may be done the same as cherries, and served the same way.

702. *Little Fruit Rissolettes.*—I also make with the trimmings of puff paste the following little cakes: if you have about a quarter of a pound of puff paste left, roll it out very thin, about the thickness of half a crown, put half a spoonful of any marmalade on it, about one inch distance from each other, wet lightly round them with a paste-brush, and place a piece of paste over all, take a cutter of the size of a crown piece, and press round the part where the marmalade or jam is, with the thick part of the cutter, to make the paste stick, then cut them out with one a size

larger, lay them on a baking-tin, egg over, then cut a little ring in paste, the size of a shilling, put it on them, egg over again, place in a nice hot oven for twenty minutes, then sugar over with finely sifted sugar, so as to make it quite white all over, then put back into the oven to glaze: should the oven not be sufficiently hot, take a salamander, or, for the want of one, a red-hot shovel, full of live coals, may be used; serve in the form of a pyramid. A little currant jelly in the ring looks well.

703. *Flanc of Fruit.* — This requires a mould the same as No. 602; it must be well wiped with a cloth, butter it, then take the remains of puff paste, and roll it well so as to deaden it, then roll it out a size larger than your mould, and about a quarter of an inch thick, place your mould on a baking-tin, put the paste carefully in the mould and shape it well, to obtain all the form of the mould, without making a hole in it; put a piece of paper at the bottom, fill with flour to the top, and bake a nice color; it will take about half an hour, then take out the flour and paper, open the mould, and fill it.

704. *Flancs*, with any kind of fruit, like a vol-au-vent, are more easily made, and are equally as good a side dish. This may be made of half-puff or short paste, and fill with raw cherries and some pounded sugar over: bake together. Greengages, apricots, or any kind of plums, will require a hotter oven than for flour only in it, the fruit giving moisture to the paste; if baked in a slow oven will be heavy, and consequently indigestible.

705. *Another.* — If you have no mould, make a quarter of a pound of paste (No. 688), roll it round or oval to your fancy, a quarter of an inch thick, wet the edge all round about half an inch, raise that part and pinch it round with your thumbs and fingers, making a border all round, put on a baking-sheet, fill with fruit one row, if large two; remove the stones, and sift sugar over according to the acidity of the fruit; it will take less time, too, than if in a mould: you see what variation can be made with very little trouble or expense.

706. *Flanc of Apples.* — I just perceive that I had forgot to give you a few receipts in this way of cake, which I make very pretty when we have a party. Take eight Ripstone pippins, cut in four, peel a nice shape, rub with lemon, put half a pound of sugar in a pan, cover with cold water, juice of a lemon; boil till rather thick, then add half the apples, simmer till tender, put them on a plate, do the remainder the same way, reduce the syrup a little, put the apples in a basin, pour syrup over: when cold, dish in pyramid in the crust, which you have prepared as No. 703, pour over the syrup, which should be a jelly. I often cut in fine strips the rind of a lemon or orange, boil with the apples, and ornament also with pieces of young angelica preserved, cut in diamond, placing a piece between each apple. Flancs of pears may be made precisely the same way, but with good ripe eating pears cut in two lengthwise, leaving the stalk cut in half.

707. *A plainer way.* — Peel and cut eight apples in thin slices in a pan, with two ounces of pounded sugar, the rind and juice of a lemon, the rind well chopped, put on fire, stir till forming a thick marmalade, and tender, melt a little currant jelly, pour over and serve.

708. *Small Fruit Tarts.* — The next in order to sweet vol-au-vents, and which

are easier to make, are tartlets, their appearance being inviting, and their expense limited, and very easy to serve. They may be made from the trimmings of any puff paste which remains, should be enveloped in paper, and kept in a cold place, or in the flour tub. Make them as follows:—Have ready twelve or more small tartlet pans, which butter, line each with a bit of puff paste cut with a cutter the size of a crown piece, force up the edges with your thumb and finger, put a small ball (made of flour and water) in each, bake them nicely in a very hot oven; when done take out the ball (which may be kept for other occasions), the tartlets, and shake powdered sugar over the bottom of each, and glaze with a salamander, turn them over, and shake sugar in the interior, which also salamander; fill with any kind of preserve, marmalade, or fruit, for sweet vol-au-vents. They may be made with cream as follows:—Make your tartlets as before, placing cream instead of the ball of flour, made thus: put half a pint of milk in a stewpan, when boiling, add half a stick of vanilla, reduce the milk to half in another stewpan, have the yolks of two eggs and a quarter of an ounce of powdered sugar, and one ounce of sifted flour, with a grain of salt, pour in the milk, taking out the vanilla, place over a slow fire, keep stirring till it thickens; when cold, fill the tartlets, and bake nicely in a moderate oven; when cold, add a little jam, have ready a meringue of four eggs (see No. 711), lay a teaspoonful of each upon them, spreading it quite flat with a knife, ornament the top with some of the mixture, put into a paper cornet, sift sugar over, place in a slow oven till a light brown color, and the meringue quite crisp; if the oven is too hot, cover with a sheet of paper, dress, and serve in pyramid upon your dish. They ought to be of a light color.

709. *Rissole Fourrée.*—This is made as the rissole for entrées; it is a very simple receipt, and I vary it continually without the slightest difficulty; instead of making it with orange I substitute apricot marmalade, apple, raspberry, strawberry, or greengage jam; but no jelly, as currant or apple, as it would run through the paste and look bad. To vary the appearance at table, instead of egging, dust them lightly over with some coarse powdered sifted sugar, then bake them white instead of brown; if the oven is too hot cover with a sheet of paper, put a little marmalade or jam in a ring which you have selected, and serve. By blanching and chopping a few pistachios, and mixing with the sugar, makes them look very inviting, or even chopped sweet almonds changes the flavor; they may also be filled with any preparation of cream, rice, or vermicelli, prepared as for croquets. I also change them by sautéing, as they are much quicker done, and make a very nice dish. To remove the roast of the second course, I put six at a time in the sauté-pan (see page 62), which must be hot, and sauté a few minutes until a nice pale yellow color, serve with sifted sugar over, or egg and bread-crumb; serve very hot; if any left cold, warm in the oven.

710. *Flanc Meringue of Apple.*—Sometimes I make a meringue of three eggs, as No. 711; when it is hard I cover the apples with it half an inch thick, keeping the pyramid; then I put the remainder in a paper cornet; cut the point so that by pressing it the mixture may go out by degrees, with which I make various designs, according to fancy, sugar over, and put for half an hour to bake in a very slow oven; the color ought to be pale yellow; they are equally good hot or cold. If you

would keep it quite white, bake it in a still slower oven, and give it a quarter of an hour longer. When I do it so, I merely make dots all over, about a quarter of an inch distant from each other, of the size of small nuts, sugar over, and put a Corinth raisin in each knob, which gives it a good appearance, and bake as directed; when the eggs are just set, you may cover it with a sheet of paper, to prevent it taking too much color.

711. *Meringues à la Cuillerée.* — Pound and sift one pound of lump sugar, whisk the whites of twelve eggs very stiff, throw the sugar lightly over, and with a wooden spoon stir gently, perfectly mixing the sugar, then with a table or dessert-spoon lay them out upon white paper in the shape of eggs, sift powdered sugar thickly over, let them remain ten minutes, then shake off the superfluous sugar, place upon boards which you have wetted, and put them in a slow oven, just hot enough to cause them to be light and slightly tinged; when the outside becomes quite crisp, take off the papers, by turning them topsy-turvy and lifting the papers from them, dip your spoon into hot water, and with it clear out the best part of the interior, dust them with powdered sugar, lay them upon a baking-sheet, and put into the screen to dry; they may be made a day or two before they are required, if put away in a dry place; to serve, fill them with whipped cream flavored either with vanilla or orange-flower (but do not make it too sweet), stick two together, dress in pyramid upon a napkin, and serve. Should they happen to stick to the papers, moisten the papers with a paste-brush and water underneath.

712. *Gâteau Fourré.* — This style of cake is exceedingly simple, and admits of great variation. You must make a half pound of puff paste (No. 684), take one third of it and roll it out several times so as to deaden it, then mould it round with your hands to the shape of a ball, then roll it out flat to the thickness of half a crown, lay it on a baking-sheet, put on it marmalade a quarter of an inch thick, reserving about one inch all round of paste to fix the cover on, then roll out the remainder of the paste to the same shape, it will of course be thicker, wet the edges of the bottom and lay the cover on it, press it so that it sticks, cut neatly round the edges, and make a mark with the back of a knife about a quarter of an inch deep and half an inch apart all round, egg over, and lightly mark any fanciful design with the point of a knife on the cover, bake in a very hot oven for twenty minutes; when nearly done sprinkle some sugar over and salamander, and serve cold. It may be made with frangipane and cream and apple marmalade, and then can be served hot.

713. *Dartoise Fourrée.* — The former one must be made in proportion to the dish you intend to serve on, but the following is simple, and looks as well: prepare the paste as before, but roll the bottom piece square, put it on a baking-sheet, cover with jam, marmalade or frangipane, leaving one inch at the edge, roll the cover the same size, wet the edges, place it over, trim the edges, mark it down every three inches, and then crosswise every inch; bake in hot oven, sugar over, and salamander. When nearly cold, cut it where you have marked it; thus, a piece twelve inches square will give you forty-eight pieces; dish as a crown or pyramid, twelve pieces make a nice dish for a party. They may be made of any puff paste which is left, but will not be so light as if made on purpose; can be cut to any fanciful shape you please.

714. *Nougat of Apricot.*—Proceed as above, but lay apricot marmalade all over a quarter of an inch thick, blanched almonds, cut into fillets, mixed with two ounces of sugar, and the white of an egg added to it, bake in a moderate oven, and cut in true lozenge shapes (I do not mean those things called lozenges, but a diamond shape), dish up on a napkin in crown or pyramid; they ought to be of a nice transparent color. Orange, apple, or quince marmalade may be used instead of apricot. Red fruit preserve does not cook well.

715. *Crusts of Fruit.*—Put a quarter of a pound of butter in a sauté- or frying-pan, sprinkle a little sugar over, cut four or five slices of bread a quarter of an inch thick, three inches long, and one and a half wide, lay in your pan; take one dozen of greengages, open them in two, they must not be too ripe, lay the skin part on your bread, put a pinch of sugar in each, put it in a hot oven for twenty minutes; have ready a salamander or a hot shovel, and hold it over it for a few minutes, dish and serve hot or cold; the oven ought to be hot enough to give a nice yellow color to the bottom, which will eat crisp.

716. *Crusts with Madeira.*—Cut a French penny roll lengthwise in four or five slices, put the yolks of two eggs, with four spoonfuls of milk, mix it in a plate, dip quickly each piece in it, and sauté in a quarter of a pound of butter which you have previously melted in a pan, leave them on the fire until they have obtained a nice gold color on both sides, put a spoonful of apricot marmalade in a stewpan, with two glasses of Madeira, and place on the fire; when on the point of boiling, pour over the bread, which you have previously put in a plate, and serve very hot. Any preserve may be used, also any white wine; and should you have no French rolls, any fancy roll will do, or stale brioche (No. 11) is excellent for them.

717. *Cheesecakes.*—Under this head, in English Cookery Books, are a variety of Receipts, but in fact, there is only one; the others may all be denominated tartlets of one kind or the other, and require but little skill on the part of the cook to vary in an innumerable number of ways. The following is the plan in use in the farm-houses in the midland counties; some which I have received from Stilton, and also from Tuxford, in Nottinghamshire, are excellent.

Take four quarts of milk and turn it with some fresh rennet; when dry, crumble it and sift it through a coarse sieve into a bowl, beat it well up with a quarter of a pound of butter until it is quite smooth (it may require a little more butter, depending on the quality of the milk); mix in another bowl the yolks of four eggs and a quarter of a pound of very fine sifted biscuit powder, the rind of four lemons, the juice of two, a quarter of a pound of powdered sugar (some add a little grated nutmeg or cinnamon), beat these all well up together until forming a stiff cream, then put it by degrees into the bowl with curd, and mix them well together; line some tartlet-pans, previously buttered, with some paste (No. 686), and place some of the above mixture in, and bake quick. In some places milk is used instead of eggs. Should you not have rennet, procure some good milk, and turn it with the juice of a lemon or a teaspoonful of soda or culinary alkali to a quart of milk: drain the curd, and proceed as before.

718. *Richmond Maids of Honor.*—These delicious little cakes, which every in-

habitant of London who pays a visit to the most picturesque part of its environs knows so well, derive their name from a period when cookery was not thought to be a degrading occupation for those honored with that title. It is stated that they originated with the maids of honor of Queen Elizabeth, who had a palace at Richmond. I have a little work now before me, called 'The Queen's Delight,' in which are several receipts invented by the wives of the first nobles of the land, which I think is an excellent example for those housewives who honor this book by their perusal, to imitate. They are made as follows:

Sift half a pound of dry curd, mix it well with six ounces of good butter, break the yolks of four eggs into another basin, and a glass of brandy; add to it six ounces of powdered lump sugar, and beat well together one very flowery baked potato, cold, one ounce of sweet almonds, one ounce of bitter ditto pounded, the grated rind of three lemons, the juice of one, and half a nutmeg grated, mix these well together and add to the curds and butter; stir well up, and proceed as before, filling the tartlet pans.

719. *Lemon Cheesecakes.*—Take two large lemons, and rub the rind with one pound of loaf sugar, so that all the yellow part is removed; place the sugar in a basin, squeeze the juice of the lemons over, then add the yolks of six eggs, and beat it all well up, and put it by in a jar for use. It will keep for years. Any flavor, such as vanilla or cinnamon, may be added, if liked, when required for use. Having made the paste and lined the tins, mix one tablespoonful of the mixture with a teacupful of good milk, and place a little in each tartlet.

720. *Sweet Omelettes.*—Break six eggs in a basin, into which put a teaspoonful of sugar, three of cream, or a few small pieces of butter; put two ounces of butter in an omelette pan; when quite hot, pour in the eggs and proceed as for Omelettes of Herbs, turn over on your dish, sift some powdered sugar over, salamander, and serve.

721. *Omelettes of Preserved Fruits*, viz. Currant Jelly, Raspberry and Strawberry Jam, Apricots, Peaches, Cherries, &c., are made the same as the last, but, just before turning on your dish, put two spoonfuls of preserves in the centre, sugar over, salamander, and serve.

722. *Macedoine of Omelettes.*—Instead of making one with eight eggs, make four, with two eggs each, of different kinds of preserves; serve on the same dish, sugar over, &c., as before.

723. *Omelette with Rum.*—The same as sweet omelette, but, the moment of going to table, pour two glasses of rum round, and set it on the fire.

724. *Beignet Soufflé.*—Put in a stewpan a pint of milk or water, a teaspoonful of sugar, two ounces of butter, a few drops of essence of vanilla, or any flavor you please; give it a boil, throw in some flour, keep stirring all the time until it becomes quite thick and no longer tastes of the flour and detaches itself from the pan. It will take about half an hour, as the better it is done the lighter it is; withdraw it from the fire, stir in six eggs, one at a time, sift about two ounces of sugar, until the paste is of the stiffness of puff paste; have ready a pan of hot fat, into which you drop by a spoon small pieces of paste, it will increase their size; and when a nice color, take

them out, drain, and dish on a napkin, with sifted sugar over.

725. *Apple Fritters.*—Mix one pound of flour with half a pint of milk or water, then half a pound of butter melted in a stewpan, mix well together with a wooden spoon very smooth, thin it a little with table-beer or water, whisk the whites of three eggs very stiff, stir in gently; have six apples, peeled, cut in slices about a quarter of an inch thick, the cores taken out with a cutter, dip each piece in the batter, and fry in hot lard about six minutes; to fry well, the fat should not be too hot at first, but get hotter as it proceeds; they should be crisp, and of a nice golden color; serve on a napkin, and sift sugar over.

726. *Ditto, Peaches.*—Skim and cut in halves six ripe but fine peaches, take out the stones, have a batter prepared as the last, dip them in, fry, and serve the same.

727. *Ditto, Apricots.*—Cut in halves, and proceed as above, and sugar over until quite brown.

728. *Ditto, Oranges.*—Peel four oranges, divide them in quarters by the thin skin, without cutting the flesh, and proceed as before.

Any other fruit may be done in the same way, and can, if required, be soaked in wine or brandy previously, but they do not fry so well.

729. *Pancake with Marmalade.*—Put a quarter of a pound of sifted flour into a basin, with four eggs, mix them together very smoothly, then add half a pint of milk or cream, and a little grated nutmeg, put a piece of butter in your pan (it requires but a very little), and when quite hot put in two tablespoonfuls of the mixture, let spread all over the pan, place it upon the fire, and when colored upon one side turn it over, then turn it upon your cloth; proceed thus till they are all done, then spread apricot or other marmalade all over, and roll them up neatly, lay them upon a baking-sheet, sift sugar over, glaze nicely with the salamander, and serve upon a napkin; the above may be served without the marmalade, being then the common pancake.

730. *Apple Charlotte with Butter.*—For the few following receipts, the russet apple is the one I should recommend, it being the most suitable, not being so watery, or falling in purée, but in case they cannot be obtained, other sorts may be used, which will require to be more reduced in stewing.

Well butter the interior of a plain round mould, then cut twelve pieces of bread the size and thickness of a shilling, dip them in clarified butter, and lay them in a circle round the bottom of your mould; cut also eight small pieces in the shape of diamonds, dip them in butter, and with them form a star in the centre of the circle, cover the whole with a round piece of bread the size of the bottom of the mould, and the thickness of a penny-piece, cut about thirty other pieces an inch wide and four inches in length, dip one after the other in clarified butter, which stand upright, one half-way over the other, all round the interior of the mould; then have ready prepared two dozen or more russet apples, which peel and cut in slices, put them into a round stew or preserving-pan, with three ounces of butter and half a pound of broken lump sugar, with a little lemon-peel cut in strips, and a glass of sherry, place them over a sharp fire, tossing over occasionally, but keeping them together in a cake; when quite tender fill your mould (having previously well egged and bread-crumbed the interior), place another round piece of bread (also egged and bread-crumbed) over the apples, and stand the mould in a hot oven until the bread becomes well browned, take out and turn it over upon your dish, have a few spoonfuls of red currant jelly in a stewpan, with a glass of sherry, melt it over the fire, and when quite hot pour round the charlotte; sugar and salamander the top if not quite crisp, and serve. You may also, for a change, introduce a little sweetmeat of any kind in the middle of your charlotte, and use plain pieces of bread a quarter of an inch thick, instead of so many pieces for the sides.

731. *Apples with Rice.*—Peel and quarter twelve good-sized apples, put them into a preserving-pan, with three quarters of a pound of sugar, the thin rind of a lemon in strips, the juice of another, and a wineglassful of water, pass them over a sharp fire, and when tender lay them upon the back of a hair sieve to drain, then put six ounces of rice into a stewpan, with a quart of milk, place it upon the fire, stir until boiling, then place it upon a very slow fire to simmer very gently until quite tender, placing a little fire upon the lid, if it becomes dry before it is tender add a little more milk; then add a quarter of a pound of sugar, a quarter of a pound of butter, and four eggs, stir them well in, stir over the fire until becoming again thick; when put it upon a dish to get cold, then form a stand with it upon your dish eight inches in diameter and three in height, but hollow in the centre, where dress some of the apples, more rice over, then more apples, forming a pyramid; you have previously reduced the syrup drained from the apples, which pour over the whole, and garnish with some very green angelica, forming any design your fancy may dictate. Apples with rice may be served hot as well as cold.

732. *Pears with Rice.*—Peel and cut in halves eighteen small ripe pears, which put in a small preserving-pan, with three quarters of a pound of sugar, a little water, and the juice of two lemons, stew them till tender, then lay them upon a dish to cool, and mix three tablespoonfuls of apricot marmalade with the syrup, have some rice prepared as in the last, with which make a stand, but not quite so high, dress the pears in a border in the interior, and again in the centre dress the remainder of the rice in pyramid; when ready to serve pour the syrup over, and garnish tastefully with angelica round.

733. *Apples with Butter.*—Peel eighteen russet apples, which cut in quarters, and trim of a nice shape, put them into a small preserving-pan, with two ounces of butter and three quarters of a pound of sugar, having previously rubbed the rind of an orange upon it and pounded it, pass them over a sharp fire, moving occasionally until quite tender, have ready buttered a plain dome mould, put the apples into it, pressing them down a little close; when half cold turn it out of the mould upon a dish, and cover all over with apricot marmalade; when cold it is ready to serve.

734. *Apple Bread, Russian fashion.*—Put one pound and a half of lump sugar and a pint and a half of water into a round-bottomed copper preserving-pan, place it over a sharp fire and reduce it to a crack, have ready twenty-four good brown pippin apples peeled and cut into slices, which put into the sugar, keeping stirred until it becomes quite a thick marmalade, take off the fire and put it into a cylinder

mould, previously slightly oiled, shake it well down, and let it remain until quite cold; then turn it out of the mould upon your dish; have a few spoonfuls of currant jelly in a stewpan, which melt over the fire, add two glasses of good old rum, and when partly cold, pour over and serve with whipped cream in the centre, in which you have introduced a quarter of an ounce of candied orange-flowers; if any remain, it will be excellent to make croquettes.

735. *Apples sauté in Butter.*—Procure a dozen russet apples, which cut into slices a quarter of an inch in thickness, peel and take out the cores with a round cutter, then put two ounces of butter in a sauté-pan, spread it over the bottom and lay in your apples, with half a pound of powdered sugar and the juice of two lemons, stew gently over a moderate fire; when done, dress them rather high in crown upon your dish, melt three spoonfuls of red currant jelly in a stewpan, with which mix a glass of Madeira wine, which pour over when ready to serve.

736. *Croquettes of Rice.*—Well wash half a pound of the best Carolina rice, which put into a stewpan, with a pint and a half of milk, and a quarter of a pound of butter, place it upon the fire, stir until boiling, then place it upon a slow fire, cover the stewpan, and let simmer very slowly until quite tender; rub the rind of a lemon upon a lump of sugar, weighing a quarter of a pound, pound it in a mortar quite fine, add it to the rice, with the yolks of five eggs (mix well), stir them a few minutes longer over the fire until the eggs thicken, but do not let it boil, lay out upon a dish, when cold form it into a number of small balls, or pears, or into long square pieces, according to fancy; have three or four eggs in a basin well whisked, dip each piece in singly, and then into a dish of bread-crumbs, smooth them gently with a knife, dip them again into the eggs and bread-crumbs, put them into a wire basket, which put in a stewpan of very hot lard, fry a nice light yellow color, drain on a cloth, dress them pyramidically upon a napkin, and serve with powdered sugar sifted over them.

737. *Croquettes of Macaroni.*—Blanch six ounces of macaroni in two quarts of water until tender, then strain and put it in a basin of cold water; when cold cut it into pieces half an inch in length, and put it into a stewpan containing a pint and a half of boiling milk, in which you have infused a stick of vanilla, boil until it becomes thickish, add a quarter of a pound of powdered sugar, two ounces of butter, and the yolks of eight eggs, stir them well in over the fire until the eggs thicken, then pour out upon a dish, and proceed precisely as for the croquettes of rice.

738. *Pastry Cream sautéd.*—Put the yolks of six eggs in a stewpan, with two good tablespoonfuls of sifted flour, mix quite smooth with a wooden spoon; then add a pint of boiling milk or cream, stir in by degrees, and place it over the fire, keeping stirred until it thickens, add an ounce of butter, six ounces of sugar, two ounces of crushed ratafias, a little orange-flower water, and three whole eggs, mix the whole well together, and stir it a few minutes longer over the fire until the eggs set; then pour it out upon a sauté-pan, previously oiled, and when quite cold cut it into pieces one inch wide and two and a half long, dip them in eggs and bread-crumbs twice over, the same as for croquettes, sauté them in the same manner, dress upon a napkin as high as you can, with sifted sugar over, they may be flavored also with vanilla or lemon. They may be varied in shape according to fancy.

JELLIES.

NOTHING, I am confident, will give you more pleasure than trying the receipts which I am now about giving you; they are for jellies, that is, those made from gelatinous substances of animal production. They are the most wholesome productions of cookery, and are slightly nourishing and fortifying without being exciting. You will find the receipts as simple as possible; and you will perceive that, when you have made the foundation stock to perfection, they may be varied in twenty or more different ways, by changing the flavor, fruits, or colors.

739. *Jelly Stock*, made from calf's feet, requires to be made the day previous to being used. Take two calf's feet, cut them up, and boil in three quarts of water; as soon as it boils remove it to the corner of the fire, and simmer for five hours, keeping it skimmed, pass through a hair sieve into a basin, and let it remain until quite hard, then remove the oil and fat, and wipe the top dry. Place in a stewpan one gill of water, one of sherry, half a pound of lump sugar, the juice of four lemons, the rinds of two, and the whites and shells of five eggs, whisk until the sugar is melted, then add the jelly, place it on the fire, and whisk until boiling, pass it through a jelly-bag, pouring that back again which comes through first until quite clear; it is then ready for use, by putting it in moulds or glasses.

740. *Gelatine and Isinglass Jelly* is made as above, using one ounce and a half of either, and boil in one quart of water, reduce to half; if not required very clear, as for lemon jelly, it need not be run through a bag, but merely through a fine sieve.

741. *Hartshorn Jelly.*—Use half a pound of hartshorn shavings, boil in three quarts of water, and reduce to one; proceed as before. Also Arney's jelly powder can be used instead of any of the above, by dissolving in boiling water.

742. *Gold or Silver Jelly*, or both mixed, is made with eau de vie de Dantzic, mixing the gold or silver leaves with a little jelly, ornamenting the bottom of the mould with it, which place in ice till set, fill with very clear calf's foot jelly. It can also be made by cutting up a quarter of a sheet of gold leaf in a glass of pale brandy, and use as the former.

743. *Maresquino Jelly* is made by mixing six liqueur-glasses of maresquino with a quart of clarified calf's foot jelly; peaches or other fruits cut in quarters may be added.

744. *Rum-Punch, Curaçoa, Noyeau*, are made with the same quantity, and as the former.

745. *French Jellies* may be made with all kinds of fresh fruits, filling the mould by degrees, the jelly first, let it set, then the fruit, and so on till full, the mould

being buried in ice; when ready to serve dip in hot water, mix it well, and turn out carefully on your dish. In the winter, preserved fruits in syrup may be used, decorating the mould with them, pouring in a little jelly at a time until it is cold, and fill up by degrees; proceed as above.

746. *Orange Jelly.*—Procure five oranges and one lemon, take the rind off two of the oranges, and half of the lemon, and remove the pith, put them into a basin, and squeeze the juice of the fruit into it; then put a quarter of a pound of sugar into a stewpan, with half a pint of water, and set it to boil until it becomes a thick syrup, when take it off, and add the juice and rind of the fruits, cover the stewpan, and place it again on the fire; as soon as boiling commences skim well, and add one glass of water by degrees, which will assist its clarification, let it boil another minute, when add half an ounce of good isinglass, dissolved as directed (No. 740), pass it through a jelly-bag, add a few drops of prepared cochineal to give an orange tint, and then fill a mould and place it on ice; turn out as before.

747. *Lemon Jelly* is made the same way, only using six lemons and the rind of one; serve quite white, and add a gill of Bucellas, or any very pale wine.

Calf's foot stock, reduced and clarified, may be used instead of the isinglass.

748. *Whipped Jellies* are made from any of the above by placing some warm jelly in a large bowl or basin on ice, and when nearly cold whisking it; pour quickly in a mould set on ice and salt, where let remain till ready for serving; dip it in luke-warm water, strike gently, taking it in the right hand, place the left on it, turn it over, if it shakes in the mould, let it gradually slip off your hand on the dish, and remove the mould. All jellies are removed the same way.

749. *Bohemian Jelly Creams* may be made of any flavor as jellies, and either ripe fruit or with marmalade or jam, to which add the juice of two lemons, a pint of water, in which one ounce and a half of isinglass has been dissolved, or a pint of reduced clarified calf's foot jelly, stir together in a bowl placed on ice; when nearly cold, stir quickly in three parts of a pint of whipped cream, fill the mould, which should be kept on ice, and turn out as before. A small bottle of Crosse and Black-well's jelly may be used instead of the isinglass or jelly, by uncorking and placing the bottle in a stewpan of hot water till dissolved, or pour it in a clean stewpan, and reduce it one third. Cherries, raspberries, strawberries, currants, and gooseber-ries must be passed through a sieve; but apricots, peaches, apples, pears, quinces, pineapples, and marmalade may be used as they are. Creams may be made of any flavor, and of either ripe fruits, jams, or marmalade; they are made plain, thus: put the yolks of five eggs in a stewpan, with six ounces of sugar, beat it up with a spoon until white; in another stewpan have a pint of milk and one ounce of isinglass, boil ten minutes, stir continually to prevent burning, flavor with vanilla or anything to your taste, pour the milk on the eggs and sugar, put on the fire, stir well together, do not let it boil, pass through a tammy into a round bowl; when cold, set on ice, add two or three glasses of liqueur, keep stirring its contents, and when setting, add three parts of a pint of cream well whipped, mix well together, and pour into your mould in the ice, and keep there till required; turn out as before.

750. *Charlotte Russe.*—Line the inside of a plain round mould with Savoy bis-

cuits, cutting and placing them at the bottom to form a rosette, standing them upright and close together, fill with any of the above creams, omitting the fruits, place the mould in ice, let it remain till ready to serve, turn over on a dish, and remove the mould.

751. *Strawberry Charlotte.*—Line a plain round mould with ripe strawberries by burying the mould in ice to the rim, and dipping the strawberries in calf's foot jelly, first covering the bottom with them cut in halves, the cut side downwards, afterwards building them up the sides, the jelly (which must be cold, but not set) causing them to adhere; when finished, fill it with the cream as directed for the charlotte russe, and when ready to serve dip the mould in warm water, and turn it out upon your dish. The cream must be very nearly set when you pour it in, or it would run between the strawberries and produce a bad effect.

752. *Chartreuse Cake of variegated Fruits.*—Line a charlotte mould very tastefully with various kinds of fruits (such as stoned cherries, strawberries, pieces of peaches, apricots, &c.) by dipping them into jelly, forming some design at the bottom of the mould, and building them in reverse rows up the sides, having the mould previously placed in ice, when well set, terminate as in the last.

753. *Blancmange.*—To one quart of milk add one ounce of isinglass, a quarter of a pound of sugar, a quarter of an ounce of cinnamon, a little grated nutmeg, half of the peel of a lemon, and a bay-leaf, simmer over a slow fire, stirring till the isinglass is dissolved, pass it through a napkin into a basin, and pour into a mould. This can be made any color or flavor that will not curdle the milk; the milk of bitter almonds may be added to flavor it.

754. *Another.*—Put into a bowl about a pint of clear calf's-foot jelly warm, break six eggs, beat the yolks and pour them gradually into the jelly, beating all the time; put on the fire and whisk till nearly boiling, set it on ice or in cold water, keep stirring till nearly cold, and fill your mould. You may add whatever flavor you like.

755. *Trifles* should be made early in the day on which they are wanted; take a stale Savoy cake, cut it in slices of one inch thick, and lay it on the bottom of the dish; lay on that a thin layer of any kind of marmalade, jam, or jelly, have some macaroons and ratafia cakes and lay on, and cover the whole with some sponge cakes. For a dish nine inches in diameter, mix two glasses of sherry, one of brandy, half a one of rum, and the same of noyeau, and pour over, and let it remain until it is well soaked, then pour over about one inch thick of rich custard; put a pint of cream into a bowl, with some sifted sugar, a squeeze of a lemon, and about a tablespoonful of the wine, &c., you have put on the cake, whisk it well up. I use a trifle-blower, which saves some trouble; I also use it for all whipped cream; and as the froth rises remove it with a spoon on to a clean sieve, where let it drain, then place it on the custard until it is high and handsome.

I have occasionally, when being in a hurry, and having no cream by me, proceeded as above, and made the whip with the whites of eggs, and some very white peach or egg-plum marmalade together, until it makes firm froth or whip, which put on the custard; this may also be colored a nice pink.

Trifles are generally considered unwholesome; I think it is because they are often made too long before they are wanted, and no spirit is used in the cake, the consequence is, the cream turns sour.

The remains of this make an excellent pudding.

PUDDINGS IN MOULDS.

WE have already, in the Comforts for Invalids, given several of the most simple receipts. I prefer using, in these kinds of puddings, as the principal ingredient, stale Savoy cake, or sponge cakes, or ladies' fingers, and, if I cannot get them, crumbs of stale bread; they may be made in a hundred different ways, according to the fancy and taste of the cook; the mould should be buttered and papered; they may be either baked or steamed.

There is hardly any of our sex, from childhood to old age, but loves this truly English mixture, which appears upon our tables in a hundred different shapes, but always under the same name; and I should not fancy my labors complete if I did not produce a new one of my own invention; I therefore beg you to accept of the dedication, as I intend to call it—

756. *Pudding à la Eloise.*—It is made as follows: take half a pound of bread-crumbs, which put in a basin, with two ounces of sago, six ounces of chopped suet, six eggs, five ounces of moist sugar, and a tablespoonful of either orange, lemon, or apricot marmalade; mix all well together, and ornament the bottom of the mould with green angelica in syrup, and Smyrna raisins, and fill up with the mixture. Place the mould in a stewpan containing water to half the height of the mould, and boil gently for two hours; remove it from the mould, and serve with a sauce made of a tablespoonful of either of the marmalades, or of currant or apple jelly and two glasses of sherry poured over. This, I assure you, received great praise from the little party of juveniles that I had the other day.

757. *Pudding à la Reine.*—Butter and paper the mould, fill up with cake or bread-crumbs, when full pour some custard in until it will hold no more; this may be flavored with any white liquor or essence you please, for instance, citron (then it is called Pudding à la Reine au Citron), or orange; use peel thinly sliced, and so on for any flavor you may give it.

758. *Mince-meat Pudding.*—Butter and paper the mould, then put a layer of cake and a layer of mince-meat alternately, till full, then add the custard.

759. *Demi-Plum Pudding.*—Prepare the mould, then add a layer of plum pudding, broken in pieces, that has been left from the previous day, alternately, till full, fill up with custard, and steam or bake for three minutes. The remains of any kind of pudding may be used thus.

760. *Trifle Pudding.*—Prepare the mould, and fill with the same ingredients as directed for trifle, taking care that the wine, &c., is well soaked in before adding the custard. Steam or bake thirty minutes. The sides and tops of these puddings

may be ornamented with cut angelica, hops, or candied orange or lemon-peel, in any fanciful design you please, and they may be served with any kind of wine sauce.

761. *Carrot Pudding.*—Mix in a bowl half a pound of flour, half a pound of chopped suet, three quarters of a pound of grated carrot, a quarter of a pound of raisins stoned, a quarter of a pound of currants, and a quarter of a pound of sugar, brown or sifted white; place these in a mould or dish, beat up two whole eggs, the yolks of four in a gill of milk, grate a little nutmeg in it, and add it to the former; bake or steam forty-five minutes.

PUDDINGS BOILED IN CLOTHS.

THE principal one, and the most celebrated, is the plum pudding.

762. *Plum Pudding.*—Pick and stone one pound of the best Malaga raisins, which put in a basin, with one pound of currants (well washed, dried, and picked), a pound and a half of good beef suet (chopped, but not too fine), three quarters of a pound of white or brown sugar, two ounces of candied lemon-and orange-peel, two ounces of candied citron, six ounces of flour, and a quarter of a pound of bread-crumbs, with a little grated nutmeg; mix the whole well together, with eight whole eggs and a little milk; have ready a plain or ornamented pudding-mould, well butter the interior, pour the above mixture into it, cover a sheet of paper over, tie the mould in a cloth, put the pudding into a large stewpan containing boiling water, and let boil quite fast for four hours and a half (or it may be boiled by merely tying it in a pudding-cloth previously well floured, forming the shape by laying the cloth in a round-bottomed basin and pouring the mixture in, it will make no difference in the time required for boiling); when done, take out of the cloth, turn from the mould upon your dish, sprinkle a little powdered sugar over, and serve with the following sauce in a boat: Put the yolks of three eggs in a stewpan, with a spoonful of powdered sugar, and a gill of milk; mix well together, add a little lemon-peel, and stir over the fire until becoming thickish (but do not let it boil), when add two glasses of brandy, and serve separate.

The above sauce may be served, poured over the pudding, if approved of.

An excellent improvement to a plum pudding is to use half a pound of beef marrow cut into small dice, omitting the same quantity of suet.

763. *Rowley Powley.*—Roll out about two pounds of paste (No. 685), cover it with any jam or marmalade you like, roll it over and tie it loose in a cloth, well tying each end; boil one hour and serve, or cut it in slices and serve with sauce over.

764. *Plum Bolster, or Spotted Dick.*—Roll out two pounds of paste (No. 685), having some Smyrna raisins well washed, and place them on it here and there, roll over, tie in a cloth, and boil one hour, and serve with butter and brown sugar.

765. *Plain Bolster.*—Roll as above, sift some white or brown sugar over it, the addition of a little powdered cinnamon to the sugar is an improvement, roll over and proceed as before.

766. *Apple Dumplings.*—Peel and cut out the core with a cutter, cover it with paste (No. 685), tie in a cloth, and boil according to size; these are all the better for being boiled and kept in the cloth, hung up for four or six weeks, and re-warmed. They may likewise be baked. These kind of boiled puddings, containing a large

quantity of paste, should be made with flour, in which is mixed one saltspoonful of culinary alkali powder to four pounds of flour, which will cause them to be much lighter.

PLAIN BAKED PUDDINGS IN DISHES.

767. *Marrow Pudding* may be made in various ways; it is best with half a pound of ladies' finger cakes, and a quarter of a pound of beef marrow, chopped fine, a quarter of a pound of currants well cleaned, half an ounce of candied lemon-peel, a little nutmeg, a tablespoonful of powdered sugar, a saltspoonful of salt, and half a wineglassful of wine or brandy: put these on a dish, and fill up with custard, having previously put a border of paste on the rim; about half an hour will do it.

768. *Custard Pudding.*—Make a border of paste on the dish, and fill up with custard, grate a little nutmeg on the top.

Any kind of fruit puddings with custard may be made in the same way, by placing them in the custard, and sift some finely powdered sugar over, before going to the baker's.

769. *Fruit Puddings* are best made in a basin, the basin to be buttered and lined with the paste, and then filled with the fruit, which cover with the paste, the paste should be rolled round to the thickness of half an inch, and when the fruit is in, drawn to the centre and squeezed, and then tied up in a cloth kept on purpose, and boiled in plenty of water; when done, which will be according to the nature of the fruit you put in it, serve it either turned out of the basin or not. The cover should be of the same thickness as the sides. Sugar should be added before being covered.

770. *Apples* should be pared, cored, and cut in quarters, and put in with some sugar, a few cloves, and a bit of lemon-peel.

771. *Wall fruit—as Peaches, Nectarines, Apricots, and Plums,*—should he cut in half, and the kernels extracted from the stones and added, a little cream, according to the size of the pudding, in which a little grated cinnamon is added, may be put in at the same time as the fruit; use but little sugar.

772. *Gooseberry, Rhubarb, Currants, red, white, and black, Raspberry and Cherry, Blackberry, Whorts, Damson, and Greengage*—may all be made in a similar way.

773. *Mince Meat.*—Procure four pounds and a half of kidney beef suet, which skin and chop very finely; have also a quarter of a pound of candied lemon and orange-peel; the same of citron, a pound and a half of lean cooked beef, and three pounds and a half of apples, the whole separately, chopped very fine, and put into a large pan with four pounds and a half of currants, well washed and picked, two ounces of mixed spice, and two pounds of sugar; mix the whole well together with the juice of eight lemons and a pint of brandy, place it in jars, and tie down until ready for use; a pound and a half of Malaga raisins, well stoned and chopped, may likewise be added to the above. It is ready for use in a few days.

774. *Mince Pies.*—Have a piece of puff-paste, which roll out to the thickness of a penny-piece; have also a dozen tartlet-pans, which lightly butter, cut out twelve pieces with a round cutter from the paste, each the size of your tartlet-pans; lay them upon the slab, roll the trimming of the paste again to the former thickness, cut twelve other pieces, with which line the tartlet-pans; put a piece of mince-meat, made as under, in each, wet them round, place on the lids, pricking a hole with a pin in the centre, and close them well at the edges; egg over lightly, and bake about twenty minutes in a moderate oven.

775. *Fruit Pies.*—These are made in pie-dishes, the top of which is only covered with paste; the edge of the dish should be wetted, and a strip of paste, about one inch wide and a quarter of an inch thick, put on it, then fill the dish with the fruit, wet the paste on the edge, and cover with paste, mark the edge with a roller, or the back of a knife.

776. *Apple Pie.*—Pare, cut, and core sufficient apples to fill the dish, put a small cup in the middle or not, as you like, one clove, to every three apples, a pinch of pounded cinnamon, a small piece of chopped lemon-peel, and sugar; bake according to size.

777. *Rhubarb and Apple,* or *Rhubarb and Gooseberry, Currant and Raspberry, Cherry, Plum, Damson, Pear, Quince, Mulberry, Whortleberry,* or *Whorts and Raspberry, Dewberry and Raspberry,* or *Cranberry,* may all be made in the same way, in winter. A little whipped cream may be placed in the top, for a variety.

REMOVES—SECOND COURSE.

778. *Chestnut Pudding, Nesselrode fashion.* —Blanch four dozen chestnuts in boiling water, skim and place them in the screen, when dry take them out, and when cold put them into a mortar, with one pound of sugar, and half a stick of vanilla, pound the whole well together, and sift it through a fine wire sieve, put into a stewpan, with the yolks of twelve eggs, beat them well together; in another stewpan have a quart of milk, when boiling pour it over the other ingredients, mixing well, and stir over a sharp fire until it begins to thicken and adheres to the back of the spoon, then lay a tammy upon a large dish, pour the mixture in and rub it through with two wooden spoons; when cold place it in a freezing-pot and freeze as directed (No. 833); when frozen have a large high ice-mould, which closes hermetically, have also two ounces of currants and two ounces of Smyrna raisins, soaked in four glasses of marasquino from the previous day, with four ounces of candied citron cut in dice, put them into the freezing-pot, with a pint of whipped cream and half the meringue preparation directed in No. 711; freeze the whole well together and fill your mould, which bury in ice and salt until ready to serve, then dip it into lukewarm water, and turn it out upon your dish.

779. *Iced Cabinet Pudding.* —Have ready prepared, and rather stale, a sponge-cake as directed (No. 859), which cut into slices half an inch thick, and rather smaller than the mould you intend making the pudding in, soak them well with noyeau brandy; then lay some preserved dry cherries at the bottom of the mould, with a few whole ratafias, lay one of the slices over, then more cherries and ratafias, proceeding thus until the mould is three parts full; have ready a quart of the custard (No. 804), omitting half the quantity of isinglass, pour it lukewarm into your mould, which close hermetically, and bury in ice and salt, where let it remain at least two hours; when ready to serve dip it in lukewarm water, and turn it out upon your dish; you have made about half a pint of custard, which keep upon ice, pour over the pudding when ready to serve, and sprinkle a few chopped pistachios over.

780. *White Almond Pudding Ices.* —Blanch and skin a quarter of a pound of sweet almonds, with six or eight bitter ones, when dry and cold, place them in a mortar, with three quarters of a pound of sugar, and ten or twelve leaves of candied orange-flowers, pound well, sift through a wire sieve, and place it in a stewpan, with the yolks of eight eggs, beat them well together; then in another stewpan have boiling a pint and a half of milk, which pour over the other ingredients by degrees, keeping it stirred, place it upon the fire, stirring until it thickens and adheres to the back of the spoon, rub it through a tammy, add two glasses of noyeau; when cold put into your freezing-pot to freeze, and when half frozen add

a pint and a half of whipped cream, when quite frozen fill a mould, and serve as pudding Nesselrode fashion.

781. *Fruit, Chartreuse of, with Lemon Jelly.*—Make a chartreuse of fruit as directed (No. 752), in a round or oval mould, having a quantity of fruit left; having also about a quart of orange jelly, which place upon ice in a bowl, whisking it until on the point of setting, then place a layer of it in the chartreuse, then a layer of the fruit, the jelly, and so on until quite filled, place it upon ice, and when set and ready to serve, dip in lukewarm water, and turn it out upon your dish; serve garnished round with jelly in the skins of the oranges, cut in quarters after it has set, or leave out the garnishing.

782. *Soufflé of Orange Iced.*—Prepare about three parts of the quantity of ice as directed in the last, to which, when half frozen, add a pint and a half of whipped orange jelly just upon the point of setting, beat the whole well together with the spatula, working it until well frozen: have a dozen and a half of oranges, peeled, quartered, and passed in sugar as directed for vol-au-vent, and place them in a basin upon ice; when ready to serve, make a border of almond paste upon your dish, in the centre of which put a little of the ice, then a layer of oranges, then the same and oranges again, proceeding thus and finishing in pyramid; garnish round with various small ripe fruits.

783. *Punch Cake Soufflé.*—Break ten eggs, put the whites in a copper bowl, and the yolks in a basin, with four tablespoonfuls of powdered sugar, four of crushed ratafias, two of potato flour, a little salt, and a quarter of an ounce of candied orange-flowers, beat well together, whip the whites, which stir in lightly with the mixture; well butter and bread-crumb the interior of an oval plain mould, butter also and bread-crumb a band of paper three inches broad, which tie round at the top of the mould, pour in the mixture, and half an hour before ready to serve stand it in a moderate oven (it will take about the above time to bake), when done turn it out upon your dish; have ready a custard of three yolks of eggs, to which you have added two glasses of essence of punch, pour round the cake and serve.

The above mixture may be baked in twelve small moulds and dressed in pyramid, but then they would require more sauce.

SOUFFLÉ.

THESE dishes, being the last of the Dinner, require the greatest care and taste in executing, as, by the time they come on the table, the appetites of those around it are supposed to be satisfied; the eye and the palate require to be pleased, in order to sustain the enjoyments of the table; this is a period of dinner when another of the senses may be gratified by the introduction of music (and which is continually practised on the Continent), and all ought to be of a light and inviting character.

Formerly it was the custom never to give a dinner without a soufflé as the last dish, or professionally speaking, remove. I do not dislike them, but they require the greatest care and nicety, and are rather difficult to perform in our old-fashioned kitchens, but easy in my new stove; at any rate I must give you the receipt.

784. *Soufflé of Lemon, or any other flavor.*—Prepare a crust or croustade of fine paste (No. 687), or water paste, by lining a raised pie-mould with it, filling with bread-crumbs, and finishing the edges as for a raised pie; bake it (of a very light brown color) about an hour in a moderate oven, when done, empty out all the bread-crumbs without taking it out of the mould, then tie a band of buttered paper (four inches wide) round the top, and put it by until wanted. Put half a pound of butter in a stewpan, with which mix three quarters of a pound of flour without melting it, in another stewpan have rather more than a quart of milk, into which, when boiling, put two sticks of vanilla, place a cover upon the stewpan and let it remain until half cold, then take out the vanilla, and pour the milk upon the butter and flour, stir over a sharp fire, boiling it five minutes, then stir in quickly the yolks of ten eggs, and sweeten with half a pound of sugar; when cold, and an hour and a quarter before you are ready to serve, whip the whites of the ten eggs very stiff, stir them in with the mixture lightly, pour it into the croustade, and bake about an hour in a moderate oven; if going too fast, and liable to be done before required, open the oven door, as it ought to be served the moment it is done; when ready to serve take it from the oven, detach the band of paper, take it from the mould, dress it upon a napkin on a dish, and serve immediately.

These soufflés may be baked in a silver soufflé-case, if preferred, they will take considerably less time in baking, but fall quicker after being taken from the oven; any liquor or spirits may be introduced in soufflés of this description if approved of.

This is large enough for a dinner of eighteen; a quarter of that quantity will make a nice family one, baked in a plain tart-dish.

785. *Soufflé of Orange-flowers.*—Proceed exactly as in the last, but infusing an ounce of candied orange-flowers in the milk instead of the vanilla.

786. *Soufflé of Rice Cream* is made by using ground rice instead of the common flour, finishing the same, and using any of the flavors directed in the last three.

787. *Soufflé of Lemon.* — Proceed as directed for soufflé à la vanille, but infusing the rind of two lemons, free from pith, in the milk instead of the vanilla.

788. *Omelette Soufflé.* — Break six eggs, place the yolks in one basin and the whites in another; add to the yolks three tablespoonfuls of lump sugar, half one of fecule of potato or wheat flour, and ten drops of orange-flower water; beat well together; whip the whites, beginning rather slowly at first, increasing by degrees, until it forms a stiff froth; then add the yolks, very gently beating up the whites as you add it: have ready a silver or plated dish (for want of either, use tin), and butter it well; place the mixture on it, and put it into a hot oven; look that it rises; if so, run a knife round it; sift some sugar on it, place it in the oven again, and serve, when well raised, immediately.

789. *Omelette Soufflé Sauté.* — The mixture is prepared precisely as the last, but the appearance and flavor are very different, being produced by the different method of cooking them; put an ounce of butter into a very clean omelette-pan over the fire; when melted, pour in half the preparation, place it over a very brisk fire a few seconds, then twist it round in the pan, which give a jerk, tossing the omelette half-way over, stand it over the fire again, give the pan another jerk, tossing the omelette again over, and turn it out upon your dish, set it in the oven, and proceed the same with the remainder of the preparation, which when done turn over upon the other; leave it in the oven about a quarter of an hour, sprinkle sugar over, salamander and serve very quickly. The butter the soufflé is sauté in gives it a superior flavor to the last.

790. *Cream Omelette Soufflé.* — Proceed as in the last, deducting two of the whites of eggs, and adding a gill of whipped cream, sauté and serve as before.

791. *Soufflé Biscuits.* — Put the yolks of five eggs in a basin, and the whites in a copper bowl, add a pound of sugar, upon which you have rubbed the rind of a lemon previous to pounding, beat it well with the yolks of the eggs, then add a gill of cream, well whipped, and five ounces of flour; stir all together lightly, whip the whites of the eggs very stiff, and stir them into the preparation; have ready ten small paper cases, fill each one three parts full, and fifteen minutes before serving place them in a moderate oven; when done shake sugar over, dress in pyramids, upon a napkin, and serve.

792. *Soufflé, or Whipped Cream.* — Take one quart of cream, put it into a bowl, with a quarter of a pound of powdered sugar, and orange-flower powder of water, and have another bowl near you, over which you must place a sieve to receive and drain the cream, whip the cream with a whisk, or blow it up with a bellows made on purpose, and as it rises in a froth, take it off with a spoon, and place it on the sieve; continue till all is used, then put back the drainings, and continue until you have none left, then put it into your dish or in glasses, or on a trifle, and ornament with nonpareils, or with green citron peel or angelica cut very fine and tastefully. It can likewise be iced.

793. *Coffee Soufflé Cream.* — Take about a quarter of a pound of clean raw coffee,

heat it in a clean sauté-pan on the fire, so that it gets hot through, but does not burn, then put it into one quart of cream, and cover it up; let it cool as quickly as possible on ice, add five ounces of powdered sugar, and proceed as above.

794. *Vanilla Soufflé Cream.*—Cut a pod of vanilla small, pound it with sugar, sift it through a fine sieve, and add it to your cream, or add some drops of essence of vanilla, and proceed as directed above.

795. *Fondue of Parmesan and Gruyère, or any other grated Cheese.*—Put a quarter of a pound of butter and six ounces of flour in a stewpan, mix them well together (without melting the butter) with a wooden spoon, then add rather more than a pint of boiling milk, stir over the fire, boil twenty minutes, then add the yolks of five eggs (stir in well), half a pound of grated Parmesan, and a quarter of a pound of grated Gruyère cheese; season with half a teaspoonful of salt, a quarter do. of pepper, and half a saltspoonful of cayenne; if too thick add two or three whole eggs to give it the consistency of a soufflé, whip the five whites of egg firm, stir them gently into the mixture, have ready a croustade prepared as for the soufflé (No. 784), pour in the above mixture, and bake it in a moderate oven; it will require a little longer time than the soufflé; dish and serve the same.

796. *Neapolitan Fondue.*—Prepare half of the mixture as in the last, but previous to adding the whites of eggs stir in a quarter of a pound of good macaroni blanched, and cut into pieces an inch in length; add the whites, bake, and serve as before.

797. *Fondue (simple method).*—Put two ounces of Gruyère and two ounces of Parmesan cheese (grated) into a basin (or, if you have not got them, use English cheese), with a little salt, pepper, and cayenne, add the yolks of six eggs, with a quarter of a pound of butter melted (mix well), whip the whites of the six eggs, stir gently into the other ingredients, fill small paper cases with it, bake about a quarter of an hour in a moderate oven, dress upon a napkin, and serve very hot.

798. *Fondue of Stilton Cheese.*—Put six ounces of butter and half a pound of flour in a stewpan, rub well together with a wooden spoon, then add a quart of warm milk, stir over the fire a quarter of an hour, then add the yolks of eight eggs, three quarters of a pound of grated Parmesan, and half a pound of Stilton cheese in small dice, season rather highly with pepper, salt, and cayenne, add the white of the eggs whipped very stiff, which stir in lightly; have a dozen and a half of small paper cases, fill each one three parts full, place them in a moderate oven, bake about twenty minutes; when done dress them upon a napkin on your dish, and serve very hot.

799. *Cheese Raminole.*—Put a gill of water in a stewpan, to which add two ounces of Gruyère and the same quantity of Parmesan cheese (grated), two ounces of butter, a little cayenne pepper, and salt if required, set it upon the fire, and when boiling stir in two or three spoonfuls of flour; keep stirring over the fire until the paste becomes dryish and the bottom of the stewpan quite white, then add three or four eggs by degrees, until forming a paste like No. 724, butter a baking-sheet well, and lay the paste out in pieces upon it with a tablespoon, making them long, and half the size of the bowl of the spoon; egg over, and lay a small piece of Gruyère

cheese upon each, put them into the oven about twenty minutes before they are required; bake them a little crisp, and serve very hot, dressed in pyramid upon a napkin.

800. *Puff Cheesecake.*—Make half a pound of paste (No. 686), which roll very thin, have ready some grated Parmesan and Gruyère cheese mixed, throw half a handful over the paste, which fold in three, roll it out to the same thickness again, cover again with cheese, proceeding thus until you have used the whole of the cheese (half a pound), then cut them into any shapes you like with pastry cutters, set on a wet baking-sheet, egg them over, bake a nice color in a moderate oven, dress in pyramid upon a napkin on a dish, and serve very hot.

801. *Cheese Soufflé, or Diablotins.*—Put a gill of milk in a stewpan, with two ounces of butter; when boiling, stir in two spoonfuls of flour, keep stirring over the fire until the bottom of the stewpan is dry, then add four eggs by degrees, half a pound of Gruyère, and half a pound of grated Parmesan cheese; mix well in, season with pepper, salt, and cayenne rather highly, mould the paste into little balls with the forefinger against the side of the stewpan containing it, drop them into hot lard; fry of a nice light brown, dress in pyramid upon a napkin, and serve very hot; a quarter of that quantity may of course be made.

802. *Turban of Almond Cake Iced.*—This is a very good and useful second course remove. Make half a pound of puff paste, give it nine rolls, rolling it the last time to the thickness of a penny-piece, have ready blanched and chopped half a pound of sweet almonds, which put in a basin with half a pound of powdered sugar and the whites of two eggs, or a little more if required; spread it over the paste the thickness of a shilling, and with a knife cut the paste into pieces two inches and a half in length and nearly one in breadth, place them upon a baking-sheet, and bake nicely a very light brown color, in a moderate oven, dress them on a stiff border of any kind of stiff jam or marmalade, so as to form a large crown according to the size you require it; then fill the interior with vanilla cream, or any other, iced, but not too hard, and bring it up to a point; the cake may be cut in any shape you fancy, but never make them too large.

803. *Turban of Pastry.*—Observe that any kind of pastry fourrée, as No. 712, or meringue, No. 711, will, if dished as above, with iced cream, make a very nice remove.

804. *Custard for Puddings.*—Take one pint of milk, to which add the yolks of two eggs, and beat up, add a quarter of a pound of sugar, half a saltspoonful of powdered cinnamon and nutmeg, and a bay-leaf. For mould puddings, the mould should be filled first with the bread, &c., and the custard added; should it be wanted alone in glasses, it must then be put into a saucepan on the fire until it nearly boils, keep stirring it well during the time.

805. *Batter for Fritters.*—Take half a pound of flour, one ounce of butter, which melt, the whites of three eggs well beaten, half a glass of beer, and enough water to make a thick batter.

DESSERT.

LETTER NO. XVI.

Ma chere Eloise,—Remembering your admiration of the small dessert I put on the table at my last birth-day party, you will, I am confident, feel interested in the description of desserts in general, and I will give you a few more hints and receipts, which will tend both to economize as well as gratify the palate and sight; and very different in style from some of our visitors, who, though they spend their money freely enough when they give their Christmas party, but still keep up the old style of covering their table with dry sweet stuff, and, in the way of fruits, display oranges in their original golden skin, Ribston pippins in their mournful ones, American apples with their vermilion cheeks, large winter pears in their substantial state, the whole ornamented and crowned with laurel, no doubt to signify their immortality, being present upon almost every table from year to year, especially the unsociable pear, which no teeth can ever injure, but, on the contrary, it may injure the teeth. A very comical friend assured us, as a fact, that he had met one of the before-mentioned pears in three different parties in less than a week, having, for curiosity's sake, engraved his initial with a penknife upon one he was served with at the first party. "And, talk about pine-apples," said he, "many times I have had the pleasure of meeting with the same, and even as much as twice in less than twelve hours, quite in a different direction, that is, on a dinner-table in the west-end about eight in the evening, and, at midnight, on the supper-table of a civic ball; at dinner being perched on an elevated stand in the centre of a large wide table, so much out of reach that it would almost require a small ladder to get at it; and I must say that every guest present paid due respect to his high position, and never made an assault, or even an attempt to disturb, much less to uncrown his fruity majesty, though, now and then, one of the fair guests, as a compliment, would remark to the amphitrion, that she never saw in her life a finer pine-apple. 'Very fine, very fine indeed, madam! will you allow me to offer you part of an orange?' 'Not any more, I thank you, sir,' being the reply."

On the supper table this aristocratic and inaccessible pine still holds its kingly rank, and is still proudly perched on the top of a sideboard, surrounded by Portugal or Rhenish grapes, and to prevent its dethronement by removing the grapes the intelligent waiter has carefully tied it to the ornament that supports it. Our friend, who is a literary gentleman, has promised to write a small brochure, to be called the 'Memoirs of a Pineapple in London,' which I am confident, will not fail of being very interesting, having had the advantage of mixing in so many different societies.

I know, dearest, what will be your feeling after the perusal of the above, that I have given vent to a little scandal; but it is the truth, and of almost daily occurrence, so that there is no mystery about it. I do not mean that it is very general, but is certainly often practised; for my part, you know my style: I never attempt to astonish my guests with extensive wonders of nature and art in any shape of eatable, but simply follow the middle prices, by which I always can procure the best quality of article in comestibles; and nothing pleases me more when I give a party than that every dish on the table should be partaken of, and still more so when entirely eaten. I do not approve of meanness; though a great economist, I abhor it as much as I do extravagance; and we never, I assure you, give a single party without being perfectly satisfied that it does not interfere with our daily comforts, that is, as regards financial matters. For dessert in summer I confine it entirely to fresh fruit, compotes, ices, and a few almond cakes, and Savoy biscuits. Fruits, preserves, oranges, compotes, and biscuits in winter.

The list of names I here inclose to you consists of moderately priced articles, and will enable you to make a good appearance for your dessert, and at a trifling expense.

The first thing I wish you to be initiated in is, what is called in France "compote," which may be made almost from any kind of fruits, especially apples, pears, apricots, plums, greengages, peaches, cherries, gooseberry, oranges, &c. It was on my second visit to Havre that I took lessons in confectionery; I paid as much as ten shillings per lesson to M. Bombe Glacé, that being the "nom de guerre" of the first confectioner there; but you know, dearest, how quick I am learning, especially anything in the way of cookery. I really must say I do love cooking, so you may fancy that the clever artist, Monsieur le Confiseur, had not very many of our demi-souvereign, as he called them, from us; my Mr. B. thought at the time that it was quite ridiculous and extravagant to pay so much for a trifle like that; but let me tell you, dear, he had not then tasted them; but now all the wall-and tree-fruits from our garden, if I were to follow entirely his taste, would be converted into compote, he being so remarkably fond of it.

COMPOTE.

PROCURE a very clean tin stewpan or a small sugar-pan; it being more preferable for boiling sugar, why I cannot tell, never having asked the reason, being so anxious to know other things which I thought more serviceable. Since I have tried it in a common stewpan, it has answered very well; and knowing by experience that your culinary laboratory is still in its innocent infancy, you might be prevented from making an immediate experiment by waiting till you could get one; you may use that three-pint size stewpan for it, which I lent you for a pattern about three weeks ago, and after which I shall feel extremely gratified by its reappearance on my kitchen shelf at No. 5, being out of the middle row of them, because every time I enter my kitchen it puts me in mind of a very pretty woman minus one of her front teeth.

Excuse me if I claim it of you, but I want to teach you punctuality as well as economy.

806. *Winter Pears.* — To put an end to its long and hard existence, I would cut it into six or eight pieces lengthwise, peel and cut out the cores, giving them a nice shape; then put them into a stewpan, with a quarter of a pound of sugar, a gill of port wine, the thin rind of a lemon, a little cinnamon, and half a pint of water; let them simmer gently about an hour or until tender; when done, put them into a basin, reduce the syrup until thickish if required, and pour over; when cold they are ready to serve.

A little prepared cochineal mixed with the syrup very much improves their appearance. A dish composed half of these and half of the white has a very pretty appearance. By placing a layer of marmalade among them, at the bottom of the dish, you may dish them in crown, or any shape you like.

807. *Compote of Peaches.* — Put half a pound of lump sugar (broken into small pieces) into a stewpan, with a quarter of a pint of water, which set upon the fire to boil until forming a thickish syrup; you have previously cut four ripe peaches in halves, lay them carefully in the boiling syrup to simmer a couple of minutes, then carefully remove them with a colander-spoon on to a hair-sieve to drain, when remove the skins, and dress the peaches neatly upon your dessert-dish; reduce the syrup until of a good consistency, and when cold pour it over, and they are ready to serve.

808. *Compote of Apples.* — Procure six nice ripe apples, but not too large, which peel, cut in halves, and cut out the cores, rub each piece over with a little lemon, and put them into boiling syrup made as last directed, but with the juice of a lemon, and the rind cut into small fillets added; let the apple stew until tender, but not

broken, when drain them upon a sieve, reduce the syrup; and when both are cold, dress the apple neatly upon your dish, and pour the syrup over. A little green angelique, cut in various shapes, will make a pretty ornament on any white compote.

809. *Compote of small Apples, served whole.*—Select nine small golden pippins, each as nearly as possible of an equal size, and with a long round vegetable cutter, of the size of a sixpenny piece, cut out the cores, then peel them very thin and smooth, rub their surface with lemon juice, and throw them into a basin of spring water; have ready boiling half a pint of syrup, made as before directed, to which add the rind of a lemon (cut into thin strips), and the juice, lay in the apples, which let simmer very gently until quite tender, when drain them upon a hair-sieve, and reduce the syrup until thickish; when quite cold, dress the apples upon your dish, five at the bottom, three upon them, and one upon the top; when ready to serve, pour the syrup over.

810. *Compote of Green Apricots.*—Have a pottle of green apricots, from which pick off all the stalks, and throw them into a stewpan containing a quart of boiling water, and let them boil very fast for ten minutes, and drain them upon a sieve: have ready half a pint of syrup made as before directed, in which boil them until tender, but not to break, and thicken the syrup, pour the whole into a basin until quite cold; should the syrup then be too thin, strain it off into the stewpan to reduce to a proper consistency, pouring it again over the apricots when quite cold. Dish tastefully.

811. *Compote of Greengages.*—Procure twelve greengages, not quite ripe, each of which cut into halves; have ready boiling half a pint of syrup, as before directed, into which put half the fruit, let it simmer a couple of minutes, then remove them with a colander-spoon, draining them upon a sieve; then put in the remainder, with which proceed in the same manner; remove the skins, put the fruit into a basin, reduce the syrup until thickish, and when cold, pour it over the fruit, which is then ready to serve.

Any description of plums may be dressed in precisely the same method.

812. *Compote of Apricots.*—Procure six very fine ripe apricots, which divide into halves; have ready half a pint of boiling syrup reduced quite thick, in which let them simmer about a minute, when pour the whole into a basin until cold; should the fruit not be quite ripe, they would require longer time to simmer. I frequently break the stones and blanch the kernels to add to the compote; they are a great improvement, also, to cherries and plums.

813. *Compote of Cherries.*—Take a pound of fine cherries, not too ripe, and cut away half the stalks with a pair of scissors; have half a pint of syrup, which boil until very thick, when add half of the cherries, and boil them two or three minutes, take them out with a colander-spoon, drain them upon a sieve, and proceed the same with the remaining half; reduce the syrup until very thick, dress the cherries pyramidically upon your dish, stalks uppermost, and when the syrup is cold, pour it over, and serve.

814. *Compote of Oranges.*—Make a pint of syrup as before; have six fine oranges, which skin carefully, scraping off as much of the pith as possible; divide each

orange into eight entire pieces, without breaking the delicate skin with which they are divided; when the syrup is very thick, put in the pieces of oranges, which simmer gently for five minutes, when take them out with a colander-spoon, and drain them upon a sieve; reduce the syrup very quickly until thickish, and when cold, pour it over the oranges, which will be then ready to serve. Half the rind of the oranges, free from pith, cut into small fillets, are a great improvement boiled in the syrup.

815. *Compote of French Plums.* — Put half a pound of French plums into a stew-pan, with a gill of water, the same of wine, the rind of half a lemon cut thin, two cloves, and a good spoonful of sugar, let them simmer about twenty minutes, and when cold take out the lemon and cloves, and they are ready to serve.

COMPOTES OF FRUIT SIMPLIFIED.

AS I usually make them when alone, or, if not, for a very ceremonious dinner-party. The whole of the following must be done over a very slow fire.

816. *Pears.*—Cut six ripe middling-sized pears in halves, peel neatly, cut out the cores, and put them into a stewpan, with a quarter of a pound of powdered sugar, the juice of a lemon, the thin rind cut into strips, and a very little drop of water, set them upon the fire, stewing them until tender; they will form their own syrup; put them in a basin until cold, when they are ready to serve.

817. *Pippins.*—Peel and cut four apples into quarters, take out the cores, and stew them as directed for pears, but using the rind of an orange instead of the rind of a lemon.

818. *Oranges.*—Prepare four oranges as directed (No. 814), which put into a stewpan, with a quarter of a pound of powdered sugar, and the juice of another orange; set them upon the fire, and when the syrup becomes sufficiently thick to adhere to the pieces of orange, they are done; when cold, dress them in a circle upon your dish, with strips of angelica between each.

819. *Apricots.*—Cut eight unripe apricots into quarters, which put into a stewpan, with four ounces of sugar, the juice of a lemon, and a drop of sherry, set them upon the fire, shaking the stewpan round occasionally, until the apricots are tender, but not broken; a very few minutes would be sufficient to stew them, and when cold, they are ready to serve.

For Peaches, proceed exactly the same; but if too ripe, they must be done as directed for compote of peaches.

820. *Greengages and other Plums.*—Put twelve into a stewpan with a quarter of a pound of sugar, the juice of a lemon and a little drop of water, set them over the fire, shaking the stewpan round occasionally until the fruit is tender, but not mashed; when cold, dress them in pyramid, and pour the syrup over.

821. *Cherries.*—Cut the stalks of a pound of cherries rather short, and put the fruit into a stewpan, with a quarter of a pound of sugar and the juice of a lemon; place them over the fire (occasionally shaking the pan round), letting them simmer about two minutes, when take them out with a colander-spoon, and put them into a basin until cold, reduce the syrup, to which add sufficient isinglass to set it as a jelly, and pour it upon a large plate until set, when dress the cherries pyramidically, just dip the bottom of the plate containing the syrup into warm water, and turn it as a jelly over the cherries.

822. *Green Gooseberries.*—Put a pint of green gooseberries into a stewpan with

two ounces of sugar and a little sherry, place them over a sharp fire, as the quicker they cook the better color they will keep; when tender but not broken, pour them into a basin, and when cold they are ready to serve.

823. *Red Rhubarb.* — The small forced rhubarb (Mitchell's Royal Albert) is by far the best. Cut about half a pound of it into pieces half an inch in length, which put into a stewpan with a quarter of a pound of powdered sugar and a wineglassful of water; set it over a sharp fire, occasionally shaking the stewpan round, and when quite tender pour it into a basin until cold; when it is ready to serve, should the syrup be too thin, add sufficient isinglass to set it, and when cold dress it pyramidically upon your dish.

824. *Currants and Raspberries.* — Pick the stalks from a pint of currants, which put into a stewpan with half a pint of raspberries and a quarter of a pound of powdered sugar; set them upon the fire, shaking the stewpan round occasionally until boiling, when pour them into a basin to cool. Should the syrup be too thin, which would be the case if the fruit is too ripe, drain the fruit from it, reduce it by boiling, and when cold, pour it again over the fruit, which will then be ready to serve.

825. *Royal Iceing for Cakes.* — Have ready a pound of the best white sugar, which pound well and sift through a silk sieve, put it into a basin with the whites of three eggs, beat well together with a wooden spoon, adding the juice of half a lemon, keep beating well until it becomes very light and hangs in flakes from the spoon (if it should be rather too stiff in mixing, add a little more white of egg, if, on the contrary, too soft, a little more sugar), it is then ready for use where required.

826. *Chocolate Iceing for Cakes* is made similar to the last, but when finished have ready a piece of the common chocolate, which melt in a stewpan over the fire, keeping it stirred; when quite melted stir some of it in with the iceing until you have obtained the color required, moistening the iceing with a little more white of egg, and use where directed.

827. *Sugar in Grains* is made by pounding a quantity of sugar in a mortar, and sifting off all the fine through a hair-sieve, then again what remains in the sieve put into a rather coarse wire sieve, and that which passes through is what is meant by the above term.

828. *How to give color to Sugar.* — Prepare about half a pound of the sugar as in the last, which put upon a baking-sheet; have a spoonful of the essence of spinach, which stir in with the sugar until every gram is stained, then put them in a warmish place to dry, but not too hot: to color them red, use a little prepared cochineal or liquid carmine, instead of the spinach, and proceed exactly the same: sugar may be made of other colors by the use of indigo, rouge, saffron, &c.; but not being partial to such a variety of coloring, I have merely given the red and the green, which, with the white, I consider to be sufficient for any of the purposes for which they are used.

829. *Sugar of Vanilla.* — Chop a stick of well-frosted vanilla very small, and put it into a mortar, with half a pound of lump sugar, pound the whole well together in a mortar, sift through a hair sieve, and put by in a bottle or jar, corking it up tight, and using where required.

830. *Sugar of Lemon.*—Rub the rind of some fresh lemons upon a large piece of sugar, and as it discolors the part upon which it is rubbed scrape it off with a knife; when you have obtained a sufficient quantity, dry a little in the screen, and bottle for use where required. Orange sugar may be made in the same manner, substituting very red oranges for the lemons.

831. *How to make clear Sugar.*—Break three pounds of fine white sugar, the hardest and closest grained is the best, put it into a sugar-pan, with three pints of clear spring water, set over a sharp fire, and when beginning to boil place it at the corner to simmer, and squeeze in the juice of half a lemon, skim well and reduce to two thirds, it is then ready to use for jellies.

If not able to obtain the best quality of sugar, it would be necessary to use white of eggs as an assistance in the clarification, by putting the white of one egg in a basin and whipping it well with a pint of cold water, add half of it to the sugar, whipping it well in, let simmer, adding the remainder by degrees whilst simmering, and passing it through a fine cloth into a basin. The boiling of sugar is divided into seven different degrees, which may be ascertained by the following directions:—

The first degree is known by dipping a copper skimmer into it whilst boiling, turning it over two or three times, if the sugar falls from it in sheets it has attained the first degree.

The second is known by boiling your sugar rather longer, dipping your finger and thumb into cold water, then your finger into the boiling sugar, putting your finger and thumb together, and again opening them, it will form a kind of thread; if it is too weak boil a little longer, this is the most useful degree for fruit or water ices.

The third degree is attained by boiling it a little longer, and trying it in the same manner, upon the thread baking, should it form a kind of pearl, it has attained the above degree; the sugar in boiling would also be covered with a quantity of small bubbles resembling pearls.

The fourth degree is attained by boiling it still longer, dip a skimmer into it, turn, take out and blow it hard, when the sugar will form little bladders and float in the air, this degree is called the soufflé.

For the fifth degree boil still longer, trying it in the same manner, but blowing harder, the bladders will be larger and adhere together, forming feathers; this degree is called la plume, or the feather.

The sixth is called le petit casée, and is obtained by boiling the sugar a little longer: to know this degree have a pint of cold water in a basin, into which you have put a piece of ice, dip your finger into it, then into the boiling sugar, and then into the water again, take the piece which adheres to the finger and bite, if rather crisp, but sticking to the teeth, it has attained that degree.

The seventh and last requires great attention, to attain it boil rather longer, dip your finger in as before, if it cracks and does not at all adhere to the teeth in biting it is done, take from the fire, and it is ready for use for making any kind of sugar ornament.

When intended for such purposes, however, add a little tartaric acid when it arrives to the degree la plume and pour it into a smaller sugar-pan, allowing it to reach the rims, it will be then unable to burn round the sides as if in a larger pan; if such a thing should, however, happen in a larger pan, wipe the interior of the pan round with a sponge previously dipped in cold water, or it would discolor the sugar.

Ornaments of spun sugar I have a very great dislike to for a dinner; but, if required, the sugar must be boiled to the last degree. Should the sugar grain it may be brought back by adding more water, and when dissolved, boiling over again; in spinning sugar you must keep the bulk of it in a warm temperature, having a little in a smaller pan for use, which keep in a melted state by placing it in a bain-marie of hot water, or in a hot closet.

832. *Silk Thread, or Spun Sugar.*—Having boiled your sugar to the seventh degree, as in the last, oil the handle of a wooden spoon, tie two forks together, the prongs turned outwards, dip them lightly into the sugar, take out and shake them to and fro, the sugar running from them over the spoon forming fine silken threads, proceeding thus until you have as much as you require, take it from the spoon and form it with your hands into whatever may be directed for the garnishing of any dish, not, however, too thick, or it would look heavy. An experienced hand would prefer doing it from the lip of the sugar-pan.

Other kinds of ornaments from sugar are made in a similar manner by oiling a mould or shape and running fillets of the sugar from the lip of the pan over it as tastefully as possible, but as I have not referred to it in this work I will not enter into its details. These are more fit for suppers than dinners.

833. *Vanilla Ice Cream.*—Put the yolks of twelve eggs in a stewpan, with half a pound of sugar, beat well together with a wooden spoon, in another stewpan have a quart of milk, and when boiling throw in two sticks of vanilla, draw it from the fire, place on the lid and let remain until partly cold, pour it over the eggs and sugar in the other stewpan, mix well, and place it over the fire (keeping it stirred) until it thickens and adheres to the back of the spoon, when pass it through a tammy into a basin, let remain until cold, then have ready a pewter freezing-pot in an ice-pail well surrounded with ice and salt;[8] put the above preparation into it, place on the lid, which must fit rather tightly, and commence twisting the pot round sharply, keeping it turned for about ten minutes, when take off the lid, and with your spatula clear the sides of the interior of the pot, place the lid on again, turn the pot ten minutes longer, when again clear the sides and beat the whole well together, until smooth, it being then about half frozen, then add four glasses of noyeau or maresquino and a pint and a half of cream well whipped, beat the

[8] To freeze quickly any description of ice the freezing-pot must be well set, place it in the centre of the pail, which must be large enough to give a space of four inches all round, break up small twelve pounds of ice, which put round at the bottom six inches in depth, over which put two pounds of salt, beat down tight with a rolling-pin, then more ice, then salt, proceeding thus until within three inches of the top of your freezing-pot; saltpetre mixed with the salt will facilitate it in freezing.

whole well together, place the lid upon the top, keep twisting it round a quarter of an hour, clear well from the sides, beat again well together, proceeding thus until the whole is frozen into a stiff but smooth and mellow substance; should you require to keep it some time before serving, pour the water which has run from the ice out of the pail, and add fresh ice and salt; when ready to serve work it up smoothly with your spatula, fill the mould and proceed as No. 778.

834. *Coffee Ice Cream.*—Proceed exactly as in the last, but omitting the noyeau or maresquino, and making an infusion with coffee as directed (No. 40) instead of vanilla.

835. *Ice of Chocolate* is made similar to the vanilla ice cream, but omitting the vanilla and liqueur, in the room of which scrape a quarter of a pound of chocolate, place it in a stewpan over the fire and keep stirring until melted, then have ready boiling a quart of milk, which mix with the chocolate by degrees, finish with eggs and sugar, and freeze as before.

836. *Ice of Pine-apple.*—Procure a rather small pine-apple, take off the rind, which reserve, and cut the apple into pieces an inch in length and about the thickness of a quill, place them in a sugar-pan, with half a pound of sugar and half a pint of water, set it upon the fire and reduce to a rather thickish syrup, have ready a pint and a half of milk upon the fire, into which, when boiling, throw the rind of the pine-apple, cover it over and let infuse ten minutes; in another stewpan have the yolks of twelve eggs, to which add the milk by degrees (previously straining it), place over the fire, keeping it stirred until adhering to the back of the spoon, when pass it through a tammy into a basin, add the syrup and pine-apple, and freeze it as in the last, adding a pint and a half of whipped cream; when half frozen, use where directed.

837. *Lemon Ice Cream.*—Take the rind from six lemons as thin as possible and free from pith, squeeze the juice of the lemons into a sugar-pan, with half a pound of sugar and half a pint of water, place it upon the fire and reduce until rather a thickish syrup, have a pint and a half of milk upon the fire, into which, when boiling, throw the rind of the lemons, cover over and let remain until half cold; in another stewpan have the yolks of twelve eggs (to which you have added an ounce of sugar), with which mix the milk by degrees, and stir over the fire till it adheres to the back of the spoon, when stir in the syrup and pass it through a tammy; when cold, freeze as directed (No. 833), adding a pint of whipped cream when half frozen.

838. *Orange Ice Cream.*—Proceed precisely as in the last, but using the juice and rind of ten oranges instead of lemons as there directed.

839. *Apricot Ice Cream.*—Procure a dozen and a half of fine ripe apricots, which cut in halves, take out the stones, which break, extracting the kernels, which blanch in very hot water and skin, then put them with the apricots into a sugar-pan, with half a pound of sugar and half a glassful of water, let them boil until almost forming a marmalade, when put them by in a basin, have the yolks of twelve eggs in a stewpan, with which mix by degrees a pint and a half of milk, set over the fire, keeping it stirred until thick enough to adhere to the back of the spoon, when pass

it through a tammy into a basin, add the syrup and apricots, and, when cold, three glasses of noyeau, freeze as in No. 833, and, when half frozen, add a pint of good whipped cream.

840. *Strawberry Ice Cream.* — Procure about two pounds of fine ripe strawberries, which pick and rub through a hair-sieve with a wooden spoon, obtaining all the juice and pulp of the strawberries, with which mix half a pound of powdered sugar and put it by in a basin; in a stewpan have the yolks of twelve eggs, with which mix by degrees a pint and a half of milk, stir over the fire until it becomes thickish, adhering to the back of the spoon, when pass it through a tammy, and when cold add the juice from the strawberries and three glasses of maraschino, freeze it as directed (No. 833), adding a pint of whipped cream when half frozen and sufficiently prepared; cochineal, to give it a strawberry color, if approved of.

841. *Marmalade of Apple.* — Peel and cut thirty apples in slices, taking out the cores, and, if for preserving, to every pound of fruit put three quarters of a pound of broken sugar (but, if for immediate use, half a pound would be quite sufficient), place the whole in a large preserving-pan, with half a spoonful of powdered cinnamon and the rind of a lemon chopped very fine, set the pan over a sharp fire, stirring it occasionally until boiling, when keep stirring until becoming rather thick; it is then done: if for immediate use, a smaller quantity would be sufficient, which put by in a basin until cold; but if to keep any time put it in jars, which cover over with paper, and tie down until wanted.

842. *Marmalade of Apricots.* — Stone about eight pounds of ripe fleshy apricots, break the stones, and blanch and skin the kernels, which with the apricots put into a preserving-pan, add six pounds of sugar and place it over a sharp fire, stirring occasionally until boiling, when keep stirring until becoming rather thick, take it off, put it in jars, and when cold tie paper over, and put by until ready for use.

843. *Quince Jam Purée.* — Procure a sieve of fine ripe quinces, which peel and cut in four, taking out the cores, place them in a large preserving-pan and cover with cold water; set upon the fire, and when boiling and tender to the touch, place them in a large sieve to drain one hour, pass them through a tammy, then have ready a corresponding weight of sugar boiled to the sixth degree (No. 831) in the preserving-pan, to which add the purée of quinces, keep stirring over the fire till forming thin sheets, drop a little upon the cover of a stewpan, if it sets quickly take it from the fire, put it in small jars, and let remain a day until quite cold, when tie them down, and put by until wanted.

844. *Apricot Marmalade Jam.* — Procure a quantity of very ripe apricots, each of which cut into four or six pieces, break the stones and blanch the kernels, put the apricots in a preserving-pan with a small quantity of water, boil them until quite tender, when pass them through a sieve; to every pound of fruit have three quarters of a pound of sugar (in a preserving-pan) boiled to the sixth degree (No. 831), add the apricots with their kernels, and keep stirring over the fire, until forming thin transparent sheets, try when done as in the last, and put away in pots. The marmalade would be still more transparent if you were to peel the apricots first, but then you would lose some of their delicious flavor.

845. *Marmalade of Cherries.*—Procure a sieve of bright Kentish cherries, pull out the stalks and stones, and put the fruit in a preserving-pan, place over the fire, keeping it stirred until reduced to two-thirds; have in another preserving-pan, to every pound of fruit, half a pound of sugar boiled to the sixth degree (No. 831), into which pour the fruit when boiling hot, let reduce, keep stirring until you can just see the bottom of the pan, when take it from the fire, and fill your jars as before.

A plainer way is to take off the stalks and stone the fruit, place them in a pan over a sharp fire, and to every pound of fruit add nearly a pound of sugar, keep stirring until reduced as above, and let it get partly cold in the pan before filling the jars.

846. *Strawberry Jam.*—Pick twelve pounds of very red ripe strawberries, which put into a preserving-pan, with ten pounds of sugar (broken into smallish pieces), place over a sharp fire, keep continually stirring, boiling it until the surface is covered with clearish bubbles, try a little upon a cover, if it sets, fill the jars as before.

847. *Raspberry Jam.*—Pick twelve pounds of raspberries, and pass them through a fine sieve to extract the seeds, boil as many pounds of sugar as you have pounds of fruit to the sixth degree (No. 831), when add the pulp of the fruit, keep stirring over the fire, reducing it until you can just see the bottom of the pan, take it from the fire, and put it into jars as before.

848. *Jelly of Apple.*—Cut six dozen of sound rennet apples in quarters, take out all the pips, put them into a sugar-pan, just cover them with cold water, and place over the fire, let boil until the apples become quite pulpy, when drain them upon a sieve, catching the liquor in a basin, which afterwards pass through a new and very clean jelly-bag; to every pint of liquor have one pound of sugar, which boil to the sixth degree as directed (831); when, whilst hot, mix in the liquor from the apple with a very clean skimmer; to prevent it boiling over keep it skimmed, lift the skimmer occasionally from the pan, and when the jelly falls from it in thin sheets, take it up and fill the pots as before; the smaller pots are the best adapted for jellies.

849. *Jelly of Quince.*—Proceed exactly as directed in the last, but using quinces instead of apples.

850. *Sweetmeat of Currant Jelly.*—Put half a sieve of fine red currants in a large stewpan, with a gallon of white currants and a gallon of raspberries, add a quart of water, place over the fire, keep stirring, to prevent them sticking to the bottom, and let boil about ten minutes, pour them into a sieve to drain, catching the juice in a basin and draining the currants quite dry, pass the juice whilst hot through a clean jelly-bag, have a pound of sugar to every pint of juice, and proceed precisely as directed for apple jelly. Should you have time to pick the currants from the stalks previous to boiling, you would lose that bitter flavor, and have less difficulty in making your jelly clear.

851. *Currant Jelly* is made precisely as in the last, omitting the raspberries, the difference being in the use; the last being adapted for the garnishing of pastry, and this to use for sauces, or to serve with hares, venison, or any other meat, where required.

A more simple method of making currant jelly is to rub the fruit through a sieve, and afterwards squeeze it through a fine linen cloth, put it into a preserving-pan with, to every pint of juice, three quarters of a pound of white sugar; place over a sharp fire, stirring occasionally with a skimmer, keeping it well skimmed; it is done when dropping in sheets as before from the skimmer. For my own part, I prefer this last simple method, being quicker done, and retaining more of the full freshness of the fruit.

It is not my intention to give a description of the various methods of preserving fruits, which belongs to the confectionery department; that I shall do in the Letters from the Farm; I have, however, given the few foregoing receipts, they being required for reference from various parts of this work, and being all that are required for the garnishing of dishes for the second course; various other fruits may, however, be made into marmalades and jellies by following those few simple directions.

SALADS OF VARIOUS FRUITS.

YOU will perceive, my dear Eloise, that there is no end to the variation of dishing fruits for desserts; the following being more simple than any, and within the reach of almost every individual.

852. *Salad of Oranges.* — Select four good oranges, the thinnest rind ones are preferable; cut them crosswise into slices double the thickness of a crown-piece, dress them round upon your dish, one piece resting half-way upon the other; shake one ounce of sifted sugar over, pour over a good tablespoonful of brandy, and it is ready; to serve it out, put two pieces upon the plate of each guest, with a spoonful of the syrup. Slices of red Malta oranges, dressed alternately with the other, has a pleasing effect. Any kind of liquor may be used, as also might whiskey, rum, or that white cream or blue devil commonly called g— —; dear me, I quite forget the name.

853. *Salad of Strawberries.* — Pick the stalks from a pottle of very fine strawberries, which put into a basin with half a teaspoonful of powdered cinnamon, two glasses of brandy, and an ounce of sifted sugar, toss them lightly over, and dress them in pyramid upon your dish, pouring the syrup over; these should only be dressed a few minutes before serving; the brandy might be omitted. If handy, a glass of maraschino, substituted for brandy, makes them delicious.

854. *Salad of Peaches.* — Procure four ripe peaches, which peel and cut into quarters; put them into a basin with two ounces of sugar and a glass of sherry, toss them lightly over, dress upon your dish and serve. Apricots, greengages, and other plums are dressed in salads in the same manner, leaving their skins on.

855. *Salad of Currants and Raspberries.* — Put an equal quantity of each, making rather more than a pint, into a basin, with two ounces of powdered sugar-candy, and a little powdered cinnamon, toss them over lightly, and they are ready to serve.

856. *Pine Apples.* — I have tried several experiments with the West Indian pine-apples, many of which being rather stale when they arrive here, would make an unsightly appearance whole upon the table, but made into a compote or salad, they are really excellent, having also the advantage of being very cheap.

For a *compote*, peel one rather thickly, to leave no black spots upon it, make a syrup with half a pound of sugar, as directed (No. 831), cut your pine-apple into round slices a quarter of an inch in thickness, which put into the syrup, boiling them ten minutes; take them out with a colander-spoon, reduce the syrup until thickish, and pour it over the pine-apple; when cold it is ready to serve.

For a *salad*, peel and cut a pine-apple into small square dice, which put into a basin with two ounces of sugar-candy (powdered) and a glass of noyeau, toss all well together and serve.

For *marmalade*, pair and cut into small pieces several small pine-apples, and to every quart thus cut up add one pound of fine sugar, boil for half an hour, and put in a pot.

857. *Cake of Savoy in mould.*—Have ready a large high mould lightly buttered (with a soft brush, and clarified butter), turn the mould up to drain, and when the butter is quite set throw some finely sifted sugar into it; move the mould round until the sugar has adhered to every part, after which turn out the superfluous sugar, tie a band of buttered paper round at the top, and place it in a cool place until the mixture is ready. Place the yolks of fourteen eggs in a basin, with one pound of sugar (upon which you have rubbed the rind of two lemons previous to pounding), beat well together with a wooden spoon until nearly white, then whip the whites of the eggs very stiff, add them to the yolks and sugar, with six ounces of flour and six ounces of potato-flour, mix the whole lightly but well together, and fill the mould rather more than three parts full, place it in a very moderate oven one hour, keeping the oven-door shut; then try when done as directed in the last, if done take off the paper and turn it out upon a sieve until quite cold. The above mixture being more delicate than the last, would not do so well for removes, but may be used for that purpose by being made three or four days before it is required.

858. *Savoy Cakes, or Ladies' Fingers.*—Have the weight of nine eggs of sugar in a bowl, which put into a bain-marie of hot water, weigh the same weight of flour, which sift through a wire sieve upon paper, break the eggs into a bowl, and proceed as directed for sponge-cake; then with a paper funnel or bag, with a thin pipe made for that purpose, lay it out upon papers into biscuits three inches in length and the thickness of your little finger, sift sugar over, shaking off all that does not adhere to them; place them upon baking-sheets, and bake in rather a warm oven of a brownish-yellow color, when done and cold, detach them from the paper by wetting it at the back, place them a short time to dry, and they are ready for use for charlotte russe, or wherever directed.

859. *Sponge Cake.*—Put one pound of powdered sugar in a good-sized bowl, which stand in a bain-marie of hot water; sift one pound of flour upon a sheet of paper, then break twelve eggs into the bowl with the sugar, which whisk rather quickly until they become a little warm and rather thickish, then take the bowl from the bain-marie, and continue whisking until nearly or quite cold; then add the chopped rind of a lemon and the flour, which mix lightly with a wooden spoon; have ready your mould or baking-dish lightly buttered, into which you have put a little flour, knocking out all that does not adhere to the butter, pour in the mixture and place it one hour in a moderate oven, it may require longer or not so long, but that will depend entirely upon the compass you have it in; if done it will feel firm to the touch, but the surest method is to run a thin wooden skewer into the centre, if it comes out clean the cake is done, but if not some of the mixture would adhere to it; care should be taken not to disturb it until quite set, or it would sink in the

centre, and never properly bake; when done turn it out upon a sieve to cool. Serve where indicated.

860. *Small Sponge Cakes.*—Put six whole eggs into an earthen pan with half a pound of sugar, upon which you have previously rubbed the rind of a lemon, stand the pan in very hot water, keeping its contents well mixed until becoming rather warm, when take it from the water, continuing to whisk until quite cold and thickish, when stir in gently half a pound of sifted flour; have ready buttered, and dusted with sugar, about a dozen small sponge-cake tins, put a tablespoonful of the mixture into each, shake sugar over, and bake them in a moderate oven.

861. *Pound Cakes.*—Put one pound of butter into an earthen pan with a pound of powdered sugar, and a little grated nutmeg, beat them well together with the hand until forming a smooth lightish cream, when add by degrees eight eggs, beating it ten minutes after, when add a pound and a quarter of sifted flour, stir it in lightly, and put the mixture into hoops to bake.

862. *Queen's Cakes.*—Weigh of butter the weight of six eggs, and nine of powdered sugar, which put together in an earthen pan, heat well with the hand until forming a smooth cream, when add by degrees nine eggs, and when well beat, stir in the weight of nine eggs of flour and half a pound of currants; have ready buttered about a dozen little round cake pans, fill each one rather better than three parts full with the mixture, shake sugar over, and bake them in a moderate oven. If no cake pans, drop the mixture upon paper in pieces half the size of a walnut, and an inch and a half apart, shake sugar over, bake in a warm oven, and, when done, remove them from the papers.

863. *Almond Cakes.*—Procure one pound of ground almonds, to which add two pounds of powdered sugar, mixing the whole with the whites of nine eggs, beating the mixture well with a wooden spoon for about ten minutes, lay them out upon wafer paper of an oval shape with a tablespoon, put three or four strips of almonds upon the top of each, and bake them in a slow oven; when done, break away all the wafer paper but that which adheres to the bottom of the paper, and, when cold, they are ready for use.

864. *Cocoa-Nut Biscuits.*—Scrape four cocoa nuts, to which add the same weight of powdered sugar, mix with whites of eggs, beating with a wooden spoon until forming a softish but thick paste; lay the mixture out upon wafer-paper in small drops, baking them as directed in the last.

865. *Moss Biscuits.*—Weigh half a pound of flour, to which add an ounce and a half of butter and five ounces of sugar, rub them well together and mix with one whole and one white of egg and a teaspoonful of milk; then add two ounces of ground almonds, which rub well into the paste; afterwards rub the whole through a gauze wire sieve, taking it off in small pieces, which lay upon a lightly-buttered baking-sheet, and bake them in a moderate oven.

866. *Rout Cakes.*—Procure one pound of ground almonds, to which add one pound of powdered sugar, mixing them together with yolks of eggs until forming a stiffish but flexible paste, when form it into small biscuits of the shapes of coronets, bunches of filberts, birds' nests, or any other shapes your fancy may dictate;

let them remain five or six hours, or all night, upon the baking-sheet, and bake them in a warm oven.

867. *Rout Biscuits.*—Boil a pound and a quarter of lump sugar, upon which you have rubbed the rind of a lemon, in half a pint of milk; when cold, rub half a pound of butter with two pounds of flour, make a hole in the centre, pour in the milk with as much carbonate of soda as would lie upon a sixpence, and a couple of eggs, mix the whole into a smooth paste, lay it out upon your baking-sheet in whatever flat shapes you please, and bake them in a very warm oven.

The proper way to shape these biscuits is by wooden blocks having leaves, pine-apples, and other devices carved upon them.

868. *Cream Biscuits.*—Rub one pound of fresh butter into one pound of flour, make a hole in the centre, into which put half a pound of powdered sugar upon which the rind of a lemon was rubbed previously to pounding, and three whole eggs, mix the eggs well with the sugar, and then mix all together, forming a flexible paste; cut it into round pieces each nearly as large as a walnut, stamp them flat with a butter-stamp of the size of a crown-piece, and bake them in a slack oven.

869. *Shrewsbury Cakes.*—Weigh one pound of flour, into which rub half a pound of butter and six ounces of flour, make a hole in the centre, into which break a couple of eggs, and add sufficient milk to form a flexible paste, which roll out to the thickness of a penny-piece, and cut it into small cakes with a round cutter; bake them in a moderate oven.

Ginger Cakes are made precisely as the above, but adding half an ounce of ground ginger before mixing; and *Cinnamon Cakes*, by rubbing in an ounce and a half of ground cinnamon after the paste is mixed.

870. *Macaroons.*—Blanch and skin half a pound of sweet almonds, dry them well in your screen, then put them into a mortar with a pound and a half of lump sugar, pound well together, and pass the whole through a wire sieve; put it again into a mortar, with the whites of two eggs, mix well together with the pestle, then add the white of another egg, proceeding thus until you have used the whites of about eight eggs and made a softish paste, when lay them out at equal distances, apart upon wafer-paper, in pieces nearly the size of walnuts, place some strips of almonds upon the top, sift sugar over, and bake in a slow oven of a yellowish brown color; they are done when set quite firm through.

871. *Ratafias.*—Ratafias are made similar to the above, but deducting two ounces of sweet, and adding two ounces of bitter almonds; they are laid out in much smaller cakes upon common paper, and baked in a much warmer oven; when cold, they may be taken off the paper with the greatest ease.

These cakes are very serviceable in making a great many second-course dishes.

872. *Italian Drops.*—Have a mixture similar to the above, merely a liqueur glassful of best noyeau, lay it in round drops upon paper, and bake in a hot oven without sifting any sugar over; when taken from the papers, dry them a little in the screen, and they are ready to serve.

The bottoms may be spread over with apricot marmalade, and two stuck together just previous to being served, if approved of.

873. *St. James's Cake.*—Put one pound of very fresh butter in a good-sized kitchen basin, and with the right hand work it up well till it forms quite a white cream; then add one pound powdered sugar, mix well, add ten eggs by degrees; put to dry a pound and a quarter of flour, which mix as lightly as possible with it; blanch and cut in slices two ounces of pistachios, two ditto of green preserved angelica, add two liqueur glasses of noyeau, two drops of essence of vanilla; whip a gill and a half of cream till very thick, mix lightly with a wooden spoon.

LETTER NO. XVII.

THE DINNER-TABLE.

MY DEAR ELOISE,—I thank you for your kind compliment, but I have always been of opinion that the arrangements and serving of a dinner-table, have as much to do with the happiness and pleasure of a party as the viands which are placed upon it; this I had a practical proof of last week. Mr. B. and myself were invited to dine with Mr. D., a city friend, at Balham Hill; I had before met Mrs. D. at an evening party, at his partner's, at Hackney, and knew little of her.

Dinner was served pretty punctually, only half an hour after time. On my entrance in the room, my first glance at the table showed me that there was a want of *savoir-faire* in its management: the plate, very abundant and splendid, was of so yellow a cast that it looked as if it were plated, and the cut glass was exceedingly dim. My first surprise was that there were no napkins, the next the soup plates were quite cold, which I have found often the case in other houses; after being served with fish, and waiting until it was cold for the sauce to eat with it, I was rather sceptical how the rest of the dinner would progress. After the first, the second course made its appearance, which was heavy and too abundant; the plain things were well done, but there was only one servant in the room for the whole party of fourteen, and from the strict formality of the table, it would have been a sacrilege to have handed your plate for any vegetables, or anything else you might require. There were four saltcellars, certainly very massive silver ones, at each corner of the table, and a beautiful cruet-frame in the centre; the hot dishes of this course, like the previous one, became cold and tasteless before being eaten, and during the time the servant was serving the champagne, all the plates were empty; in fact it was a good dinner spoilt. The wine drank with less goût than usual, and the long pauses between the courses made the formality appear still greater than it really was, and made you wish for the time to arrive for the cloth to be removed, which was not done, only the slips, a most awkward undertaking for one servant, and should never be practised unless having at least two.

About half an hour after the cloth was removed, and just as the conversation was being thawed from the freezing it received at the dinner-table, Mrs. D. and the ladies withdrew, and for an hour and a half we had to bear the insipid conversation of the drawing-room, the hissing urn on the tea-table bearing a prominent part. Several messages were sent from time to time to the dining-room that coffee was ready; and when at last the gentlemen came, two had had quite wine enough, which caused them to receive sundry angry looks from their wives who were present, and who were glad to get them into their carriages which were waiting, and right glad indeed was I when ours was announced.

This all happened, my dear Eloise, not from meanness; for if money could have purchased it nothing would have been wanting, but solely from want of *management*; and every one should think before they invite their friends to partake of their hospitality, if they know how to entertain them. Money of course will provide delicacies of all kinds, but to know how to dispose of those delicacies to the best advantage, that your friends may appreciate them, is what is sadly wanting in more than one house I visit.

A very excellent remark is made in *Punch* by Mr. Brown, in his Letters to a Young Man about Town, on the subject of great and little dinners. He says: "Properly considered the quality of the dinner is twice blest; it blesses him that gives, and him that takes; a dinner with friendliness is the best of all friendly meetings—a pompous entertainment, where no love is, is the least satisfactory."

Our dinner on which you compliment me so much, we sat down twelve, for although the room and table would accommodate more, yet as my service of plate is for that number, and the arrangements of the kitchen are limited, that is the number I prefer, besides beyond which the conversation becomes partial, which is the bane of a dinner-table. You know we have no regular man-servant, but for these occasions I hire two, and place one on each side the table, and they each have their own side table with a change of everything that is required. The first thing to be looked to is the lights: these ought to be so placed as not to intercept the view of any person at the table, but at the same time they ought to be enough to show everything off to advantage; I prefer removing some of the lights from the table to the sideboard when the cloth is removed, as the light after dinner ought to be more subdued. In laying the cloth we place it over the baize, and remove it after dinner, as Mr. B. says he likes to see the mahogany, for when he asks a city friend to come and put his feet under his mahogany, it looks rather foolish if he never sees it. I have, as you know, my table rather wide, that is, six feet, and I generally place a vase of flowers in the centre, as I think their freshness and odor add greatly to the appearance of the table, and admit a flanc on each side. We prefer the old English plan of taking the top and bottom of the table, instead of I and Mr. B. being together at the side.

The cloth being laid with its proper side uppermost, I order a napkin, two knives, two prongs, two tablespoons, and two wine-glasses to be placed to each person, a saltcellar between every other, that being a condiment which every one uses, though often wrongly; the cruet-frames and other requisites are kept on the sideboards. I then have the fish and soup served together, the potatoes and sauce on the sideboard; I serving the soup, and Mr. B. the fish, and often a little dish of fried fish, such as smelts, &c., to remove the soups. This gives me an opportunity of seeing that my guests are properly attended to, and also leisure of taking wine with any gentleman who challenges me. During the time this course has been progressing, the cook has had time to dish up the removes nice and hot, and get all up close to the door, as I like as little time as possible to intervene in changing the dishes; and these consist generally of variously dressed chickens, which I have before me, as this gives an opportunity for the gentleman on my right to display his gallantry; but, thanks to Soyer's separator, this is an easy task. This affords me still further leisure to pay attention to my guests. Mr. B., who is a capital carver, either has a saddle or a haunch of mutton, or a quarter of lamb before him, the rest of the dishes consisting of a tongue and entrées. I select those most easy to carve, and also easy for the cook to prepare. This is a period of dinner where a great deal depends upon the attendants; they should know almost by the look what this lady or that gentleman require, and what kind of vegetables to hand them; a first-rate butler should be able to judge by the physiognomy to whom he should offer mint sauce with the lamb, and who prefers cayenne; on their attention and hot plates, depends the success of the substantial part of the dinner.

As soon as I see that all are served, and words are few in consequence of the organ which utters them being employed in another way, I give a look to the two servants, which they understand, and immediately two reports are heard,—they are from two bottles of champagne, opened at the same time by the attendants, who have each a salver with six glasses on it; this takes but a short time to serve, and prepares the palate for the entrées, which generally get praised; indeed my cook would think something was wrong if two of the dishes did not go down empty. By having the champagne thus, I find it goes much further than if only one bottle was opened at the time, there being sufficient left in the bottles for a gentleman to challenge a lady to take champagne with him. If I have game I remove the top and bottom dishes with them, and make the sweets a separate course, taking care to have *cold plates* for the jelly, and having the liquors handed round when the sweets are on the table; one cheese I place opposite Mr. B., and macaroni opposite myself. Objections have been made to the use of napkins, as being of no service at an English dinner-table, and only a copy of the dirty manners of our neighbors. If we are more cleanly at the table than they are (which I question), there is no reason why we should not use that which would make us still more so; but Mr. B. is so well pleased with the rose water which he has at the court dinners of his company, that he made me a present of those two beautiful dishes which you admired so much. The outside compartment holds rose-water, and the inner one a little eau-de-cologne; these are placed on salvers, and pass down each side of the table, the corner of each napkin being dipped into it. They seem to be absolutely required, and I must say they form a delightful adjunct to the dinner-table.

He[9] has also introduced at our table, but *only at Christmas*, another city custom, which the gentlemen seem very much to like,—I cannot say so for the ladies; it is what he calls a loving cup; he has it placed before him when the cheese is put on; and after filling the glass of the lady on each side of him, he rises and drinks to their health and the rest of the company, and then passes it to the gentleman on the left, who, in like manner, fills the glass of the lady on his left, rises, drinks to her health and the company, and thus it goes round the table. Your husband, my

----

[9] With regard to the wine, that is a matter I leave entirely to Mr. B., but his maxim is, that "the best is the cheapest."

dear Eloise, thought that the contents were exceedingly good, or, as he expressed it, nectar fit for the gods, and would like to have the receipt, — here it is as Mr. B. prepares it: — The cup holds two quarts; he places in it half a teacupful of capillaire; if he has none, he uses dissolved lump sugar, with a few drops of orange-flower water in it, one pint of brown sherry, one bottle of good *Edinburgh* ale, mixing these together, and a minute before placing on the table, adding one bottle of soda water, stirring it well up till it froths; he then grates some nutmeg on the froth, and places a piece of toast in it, and sends it to the table with a napkin through the handle of the cup. I must say, since we have had this, it has produced some most interesting conversation as regarded the antiquity of the custom, &c. In addition, Mr. B. bought the cup at a sale, and it is stated to have been drunk out of by Henry the Eighth: this of itself is a subject of conversation, and draws out the talents and conversational powers of our guests, and one in which ladies can join, as there is hardly one of our sex who has not read Miss Strickland's "Queens of England." You have often made the remark, that the time always appears short whilst we are at table; this is, no doubt, from the animated conversation which is kept up, for that is the real motive of meeting together, to enjoy the conversation of one another, to gain and impart information, and amuse ourselves with the wit and talent of those around us, and not for the sake of eating and drinking; yet without the assistance of both of these, the most sparkling wit would be as heavy as a bad soufflé, and the brightest talent as dull as my looking-glass on a foggy day.

In order to prolong the time, and to enjoy the gentlemen's society as much as possible, I do not have the dessert placed on the table until ten or twenty minutes after the cloth is removed; this also gives an opportunity for my guests to admire the beautiful Sevres dessert plates, containing views of the French chateaux; this of course gives a subject for conversation to those who have visited them. In the dessert I generally introduce some new importation, such as bananas, sugar-cane, American lady apples, prickly pears, &c.; these also give a subject for the gentlemen to talk about when the ladies have left, as free trade, colonial policy, &c. About half an hour after the dessert is on the table, and when I see that the conversation is becoming less general, I retire to the drawing-room; the servants then remove the dirty glass and plates, and Mr. B. introduces some of his choice claret or Burgundy in ice coolers.

You know, my dear Eloise, I allow very little more than half an hour for us to talk about the last new fashions, or of Mrs. A. and B.'s cap, and the young ones about their partners at the last ball, and other nothings, when the tea and coffee are brought up on salvers; it is always made down stairs, and sent up in cups to the drawing-room, although Mr. B. had a very handsome silver service presented to him just after we were married, for serving as an honorary secretary to some grand masonic festival, yet the milk ewer and sugar basin are all I allow in the room. This does away with the formality of the tea-table and the hissing of the tea-urn; it allows some young gentlemen with a Byron collar and a little down under his chin to turn over the pages of a music-book for a young lady at the piano, and make his coffee at the same time; it allows my dear mamma and Mr. P. to make up their whist table, and have their tea whilst playing; or, if we make up a quadrille, to have a few turns of a waltz or polka, the coffee is serving during the time; whilst this is going on the hand of the clock advances, and half-past ten soon arrives, and with it Mrs. C.'s fly; Dr. D.'s brougham is at the door; the party breaks up, delighted with the evening they have passed in each other's society: and this you see done with trifling management.

LETTER NO. XVIII.

DEAREST ELOISE,—You are right in your remark, that there is a great difference as to the manner and way in which evening parties or soirées are given in different houses, although being frequented by the same party or circle. I must say I have my own ideas on this subject, and I think the French understand this matter much better than we do, and that we could not do better than imitate them. We English are a plodding, matter-of-fact people, and carry our notions into every concern in life: our dinners and entertainments are given with an ulterior object, and with a view of what may be gained from it, even from the charitable dinner at the London Tavern to the man who asks another to partake of a pint of beer with him at a public-house. It is this, together with ostentation, which is the bane of society, by bringing together people of incongruity of ideas, destroying that free exchange of thought which constitutes the true pleasure of social réunions; we are also naturally of a reserved and cautious disposition: hence the reason why the pleasures of a soirée are not felt until after supper. Of these I am a great advocate, though not to the extravagant and outré manner many are given in the present day. Of course in the way most ladies are now educated, they would rather be attending to the adornment of their persons for the occasion than to the entertainment and amusement of their guests. Those who can afford it, are quite right to patronize a first-rate confectioner, and thus save themselves the trouble; but how many that cannot afford it do the same thing, and make a bargain for a bad supper with one, by which he gains little, and the guests great disgust, instead of doing it at home and ordering a few good things which would look and eat well. There are a variety of drinks which could be made at a moderate expense, good and wholesome, and infinitely better than bad Marsala, which you are often obliged to partake of. I will enclose you a few receipts for them, and some bills of fare for suppers for small soirées.

BEVERAGES FOR EVENING PARTIES.

874. *Lemonade.*—Peel six lemons free from pith, cut them up in small pieces, and put them with two cloves in a bottle, with half a pint of hot water, and place it in a bain-marie, or stewpan, with boiling water, and let it stand by the side of the fire for one or two hours, taking care it does not boil; remove it and let it remain until cold; then take half a pint of lemon-juice, half a pint of capillaire—if none, use sugar, that will make the same quantity of syrup—to which add a few drops of orange-flower water; add the infusion of the rind, stir well together, and add two quarts of cold water. The acidity of some lemons is greater than others, in which case, and also if using lime-juice, more capillaire must be used.

875. *Cold Punch.*—Proceed as above for lemonade, but add one pint of capillaire to half a pint of lemon-juice, one pint of pale brandy, one pint of pale rum, one tablespoonful of arrack, and five quarts of cold water; let it remain some time before it is decantered.

876. *Port Wine Negus.*—Take one quart of new port wine, of a fruity character, one tablespoonful of spirit of cloves, one teacupful of sugar, one lemon sliced, half a nutmeg grated, pour over these two quarts of boiling water.

877. *White Wine Fillip.*—Take one bottle of sherry or Madeira, or champagne, or any other good white wine, a gill of noyeau or maraschino, the juice of half a lemon, add to it one quart of calf's foot jelly well sweetened and boiling hot, and serve immediately.

878. *Sandwiches.*—In making a large quantity, a stale quartern loaf should be taken and trimmed free from all crust, and cut into slices the eighth of an inch in thickness, slightly buttered, and then thin slices of meat, nicely trimmed, may be laid on and covered with another slice of bread, and then cut into eight parts; should they be but some time before they are wanted, they ought to be put one over the other, as they thus keep moist,—a little mustard and salt may be added to the meat, if preferred. Some thin slices of gherkin may be added to the meat, and the same plan can be adopted with pickled fish, brawn or sausages.

The following varies the common mode of making sandwiches:

Take a small quantity of very fresh cream cheese, put it into a basin or a marble mortar, add some salt, pepper, and a little mustard, beat it well up until it is of the same consistence as butter; if too hard add a little of the latter, and use it as butter on the bread, with slices of meat between. Or make it into salad sandwiches:—cover the bread as before, and have ready some mustard and cress and water-cresses well washed and dried, put into a bowl with mayonnaise sauce, and when ready to serve place it neatly between the bread.

LETTER NO. XIX.

—— Farm, Essex, July —, 1849.

MY DEAR ELOISE,—You are no doubt surprised at receiving this from the above address, but you remember when you last called I thought my little Emily was unwell, the next day she seemed worse, I then had the Dr.—, who ordered her out of town, and a friend of Mr. B.'s being present recommended this place; so Emily and I have now been a week here, and she has already improved by the change of air; it has also done me good, and I am greatly amused with the various occupations going on in the farm, which is an old-fashioned one, tenanted by a good old English farmer, his wife, and son; the latter is gone to see a brother settled in Liverpool. The cleanliness and regularity of the house are quite charming; but what delights me more than all is the dairy—such delicious cream and butter that it makes me quite envy people living in the country!

I must describe the pretty dairy to you: it is situated at the back of the house, and sheltered by it from the mid-day and afternoon's sun, and from the morning's sun by a plantation, so that it is deliciously cool; it is about twelve feet long by ten wide, paved with flat stones, and the walls of plaster, like stone, a door at one end with a window above and a window high up at the other end, and two windows at the side; these have thin wire shutters and glazed sashes on hinges; the roof is of slate, with about two feet thickness of thatch over it; there are also several little openings for the admission of air, about one inch from the floor. A dresser, two feet wide, being two inches from the wall, is on both sides, and above these are two shelves of nine inches wide, also two inches from the wall, these are supported on iron brackets. At the end, and opposite the door, is the churn, which is turned by a wheel outside, with apparatus for a donkey or mule to work it, if required.

All the utensils are of sycamore wood and perfectly clean, never used twice without washing in hot water with soda put in it, and made perfectly dry.

There are as many ways of making butter as there are counties in Great Britain. I will now tell you how it is practised here. The cows are milked at a regular hour, not later than five, the milk taken as soon as possible into the dairy, and placed in the dishes about six quarts in each; is thus left for twenty-four hours; then it is skimmed, and the cream from each is placed in a deep bowl or pan, where it remains until the next day, when it is churned. Friday's milk is made into cheese; when churned it is gathered well together from the milk and laid in a clean bowl, with hard spring water in it, and worked to and fro until it is brought to a firm consistence; it is then laid out thin, and then what is called here a scotcher is taken—that is, a kind of five-pronged fork of wood, only each prong is as sharp as a knife, and drawn through every part of it; then whatever salt is required is added, and it is then formed into pats, or done any way they like. If intended as corned or salt butter, they then add one pound of fine salt to every fourteen pounds of butter; in some places the coarsest grained salt is used; in others two pounds of salt, one pound of saltpetre, and one pound of white sugar mixed together, one fourth of this for every fourteen pounds. If intended for keeping, it is put into stone crocks until it is wanted. The way in which they make the cheese here is as follows: all Friday's milk is taken, that of the morning is kept until the afternoon, and mixed with it; then two spoonfuls of rennet to every twelve quarts of milk are put to it and well mixed, it is then left all night. Very early the next morning the curd is removed with a strainer and equally broken into the cheese vat or mote until it is about one inch above the brim, a cheese cloth or strainer having previously been put at the bottom of the vat, and large enough to allow for part of it to be turned over the top when the vat is filled; when thus filled it is taken to the press, and left for two hours with a clean cloth under it; it is then turned over on the cloth, and pressed again; and the same process is continued three or four hours out of the twenty-four. It is then removed and placed on the shelf, and turned regularly every day for the first two months; after that occasionally.

I intend to try my hand at it shortly, and see what I can make of it.

I find that the butter which is made here and potted for winter use is not intended to be sold as salt, but as fresh, and the dairy-maid has just told me how it is done. For every quart of new milk from the cow, she takes one pound of potted butter, which has been treated thus the day previous: into two quarts of cold water two tablespoonfuls of vinegar are mixed, and the potted butter well broken and kneaded in it, and then taken out, and served the same in fresh water, in which it is left until the next morning, and then mixed with the milk, put into the churn and churned again, and then treated in the usual way as butter; by this plan there is a large quantity of sweet milk always in the farm, as it is exceedingly good when strained.

The following is the way they make the clouted cream:—

879. *Clouted Cream.*—Strain the milk as soon as it comes from the cow into wide pans, holding about six quarts each, so as to be about three inches deep, and let it remain for twenty-four hours; then gently place the pan upon a hot plate or slow charcoal fire, which must heat it very gently, for if it boils it is spoilt; as soon as the cream forms a ring in the middle, remove a little with the finger, and if there are a few bubbles rise in the place where you do so, it is done, which will be in half to three quarters of an hour; remove it from the fire, and let it remain twenty-four hours; then skim it, and throw a little sugar on the top.

CONVERSATION ON HOUSEHOLD AFFAIRS.

Mrs. R. After all the receipts and information which you have given me, there is one which you have not touched upon yet, which, perhaps, is of more importance than all the rest, it is the management of servants.

Mrs. B. You are right, my dear, it is of great importance, and more so than many of us imagine, as for myself I do not consider that I am a good manager, being perhaps of too forgiving a disposition; but there is one good quality which I possess which makes up for the want of others, that is exactitude; by enforcing this it causes all to know their place, and perform their work.

Mrs. R. But what surprises me is to see everything so well done and clean with so few servants; you seem to have but two maid servants, the cook, house-maid, and coachman.

Mrs. B. Yes, that is all, and I generally find that they are enough for the work, unless I have a dinner party, and then of course, as you know, I have extra men; but I will tell you how I pass the day, and then you will be able to judge.

We are what are called early risers, that is, Mr. B. is obliged to leave home every week day at twenty minutes past nine; our breakfast is on the table at half-past eight; the breakfast parlor having previously been got ready, as the servants rise at seven. We are, when we have no visitors, our two selves, the three children, and the governess. The children, in summer time, have had a walk before breakfast, but before leaving their room they uncover their beds, and if fine open the windows, if a wet morning about two inches of the top sash is pulled down. The servants get their breakfast at the same time as we do, as we require hardly any or no waiting upon, everything being ready on the table. In a former letter I told you what was our breakfast some years since when in business, now we have placed on the table some brown bread, rolls and dry toast; the butter is in a glass butter-dish, and the eggs are brought up when we have sat down to table. The urn is placed on the table, as I make my own tea and coffee; the cocoa is made down stairs.

You will perhaps be surprised when I say that I make the coffee for breakfast myself, but I have done so for some little time past, having found that when made in the kitchen it never came up twice alike, but now we always have it delicious.

I lately purchased a coffee-pot which enables me to do it in the very best manner, with no more trouble than I have in making the tea. I mentioned it in my receipts for coffee, and said it was invented by a Mr. S., which letter was inserted by mistake instead of C. which it ought to be. It is called Carey's Hecla. It makes the very best coffee at one short operation, and is so contrived as to produce it almost boiling hot; in fact, never permitting the great mistake of boiling the coffee itself at all.

Mr. B. generally leaves home in the brougham, which returns in time for me; in case I should be going out, he then goes in a cab or omnibus. Whilst we are at breakfast, I generally consult Mr. B. what he would like for dinner, and if he is likely to invite any friend to dine with him; the fishmonger has previously sent his list and prices of the day. I then write with a pencil on a slip of paper the bill of fare for the nursery dinner, luncheon, should any be required, and our dinner, which I send to the cook. At ten o'clock I go down stairs into the kitchen and larder, when the cook gives me her report, that is everything that is required for the next twenty-four hours' consumption, including the servants' dinner, which report is filed in the larder and made to tally with the week's list, for I must tell you that the week's consumption of all things that will not spoil is had in on the Saturday, on which day the larder is properly scoured out, and everything put again into its proper place, there being bins for all kinds of vegetables, &c. The larder is generally kept locked, the cook and I only having keys, because it is in fact a larder, and not, as in many houses, full of emptiness; this occupies about half an hour, during which time the chambermaids have been attending to the bed-rooms and drawing-room, &c. If I go out or not, I always get my toilet finished by twelve o'clock; I thus have one hour to write notes, or see tradesmen or my dressmaker, and Monday mornings check and pay my tradesmen's accounts, and to dress. If I stop at home, I amuse myself by reading, or going to see the children in the nursery, or sometimes go again into the kitchen and assist the cook on some new receipt or preparation, and often have several calls; during the course of the morning the two maids scour out alternately one or two of the rooms, according to size, except on Wednesdays, when one of them is otherwise engaged.

Mr. B. arrives home at twenty minutes to five, and at half-past five we dine: the cloth is laid, and everything prepared as if we had company; it may be a little more trouble for the servants; but when we do have any friends they find it less trouble; besides it is always uncertain but what Mr. B. may bring somebody home with him, and it prevents slovenly habits; the two maids, with the exception of Wednesdays, are always ready to attend on us. I never allow the coachman to defile our carpets with his stable shoes; all his duties in the house are—the first thing in the morning to clean the knives and forks for the day, for enough are kept out for that purpose, clean the boots and shoes, and those windows the maids cannot easily get at, and assist in the garden if required. Many have made the remark to me, that as you have a male servant why not have him wait at table. I reply that the duties of the stable are incompatible with those of the table, and if he does his duty properly he has enough to do. The servants dine at one, and have tea at quarter to five, by which time the cook has everything ready, all but to take it from the fire, and the maids the dining-room ready. The nursery dinner is at the same hour; after dinner, should we be alone, we have the children and the governess down; if we have company we do not see them; they go to bed at a quarter to eight, and we have tea and coffee at eight; the governess comes and passes the rest of the evening with us; eleven is our usual hour of retiring, before which Mr. B. likes his glass of negus, a biscuit, or a sandwich, which is brought upon a tray.

Mrs. L.—What you have described to me is all very well, yet I am certain, that if I go and try to do the same to-morrow, I shall not succeed; how is it that you have everything in its place, and I never hear a word said to the servants?

Mrs. B.—It is because they all know their duties, and if they should in any way neglect them, I think of the maxim, bear and forbear, for none of us are perfect, and I take an opportunity when I may be alone with them to tell them quietly of their faults. Some mistresses will go into the kitchen and be angry with them before the other servants; the consequence is, that as soon as her back is turned they all begin to laugh. A ridiculous incident of this kind occurred the other evening at Mrs. G.'s. We missed her out of the drawing-room just before tea, and it appeared that her young boy Fred, followed her; whilst we were at tea he was very communicative, as children sometimes will be (l'enfant terrible), and said, "We have been having such fun in the kitchen." On inquiry he said, "My mother has been down stairs scolding Jane, and I hid myself behind the door; and when my mother had gone up, Betsy the cook spoke and moved her hands just like mamma; it made us all laugh so, it was such fun." I need not tell you it was no fun for Mrs. G., who looked rather annoyed. We should ever remember, that we have our feelings, and should also think that others have theirs; and I think it is as much the mistress's fault when anything goes wrong in the house, as the servants'. I only lose my servants when they get married, or from ill health, and the only thing that I find bad, is, that they quarrel amongst themselves, but should this occur thrice with the same two, I dismiss them both. I am certain, that if you teach your servants to take care of themselves, they are certain to take care of you. I continually hear Mrs. M. complaining of changing her servants, and that seems to be her sole occupation. Poor thing, she has no children, and nothing to occupy her mind, and without occupation the mind becomes diseased, and the least action throws it into fever. Mrs. N. complains of the extravagance of her servants; it is her own extravagance, or, more properly speaking, her want of management which causes all; but this I really think, that if everybody were more cautious in receiving and giving characters to servants other than what they are, we should not hear the continual complaint we do, when often assembled in the drawing-room after dinner, when, perhaps, some dear old lady complains of the education given to young people of the present day, and that, in time, there will be no such thing as servants. To some extent I am of her opinion, and consider that the education given by all classes to their children, is a great deal more ornamental than useful. I would rather see the child taught some of the accomplishments of housekeeping, than that she should be considered as the mere ornament of the drawing-room. I think it is the bounden duty of every mother, where the income of the husband may be dependent on trade or profession, to give her children that education which even the most adverse of circumstances may call upon them to assume. Look at the advertisements which appear in the public press every day!—Young girls offering themselves as governesses, to be remunerated by their board; whereas, if they had been educated with a knowledge of some useful employment, they would have made good ladies' maids or housekeepers, or useful wives to tradesmen.

BILLS OF FARE.

WHEN I was first married and commencing business, and our means were limited, the following was our system of living:

Sunday's Dinner.—Roast-Beef, Potatoes, Greens, and Yorkshire Pudding.

Monday.—Hashed Beef and Potatoes.

Tuesday.—Broiled Beef and Bones, Vegetables, and Spotted Dick Pudding.

Wednesday.—Fish if cheap, Chops and Vegetables.

Thursday.—Boiled Pork, Peas Pudding, and Greens.

Friday.—Peas Soup, Remains of Pork.

Saturday.—Stewed Steak with Suet Dumpling.

The Sunday's dinner I used to vary, one time Beef, another Mutton, another Pork or Veal, and sometimes a Baked Sucking Pig; our living then, including a good Breakfast and Tea, cost us about 32s. per week.

In case we had a few friends, we used to make an addition by having one Fish, Leg of Mutton, Roast Fowls, Pickled Pork, and Peas Pudding, with a Mould Pudding and Fruit Tart, and a little dessert.

This was for the first two years; our means and business then increasing, and having the three young men to dine with us, we were of course obliged to increase our expenditure and to alter our mode of living, besides which I had accompanied Mr. B. to France, where my culinary ideas received a great improvement.

The following is the plan we then adopted:

Sunday. — Pot-au-Feu, Fish—Haunch of Mutton or a Quarter of Lamb, or other good joint—Two Vegetables—Pastry and a Fruit Pudding—A little Dessert.

Monday. — Vermicelli Soup made from the Pot-au-Feu of the day previous—The Bouilli of the Pot-au-Feu—Remains of the Mutton—Two Vegetables—Fruit Tart.

Tuesday. — Fish—Shoulder of Veal stuffed—Roast Pigeons, or Leveret, or Curry—Two Vegetables—Apples with Rice, and light Pastry.

Wednesday. — Spring Soup—Roast Fowls, Remains of Veal minced, and Poached Eggs—Two Vegetables—Rowley Powley Pudding.

Thursday. — Roast-Beef—Remains of Fowl—Two Vegetables—Sweet Omelette.

Friday.   — Fish — Shoulder of Lamb — Miroton of Beef — Two Vegetables — Baked Pudding.

Saturday.   — Mutton Broth — Boiled Neck Mutton — Liver and Bacon — Two Vegetables — Currant Pudding.

Our parties then, when we had them, never consisted of more than ten.

We had: Julienne Soup — Fish — a quarter of Lamb — Vegetables, Cutlets — Vegetables, Bacon and Beans — Boiled Turkey — Pheasant — Jelly or Cream — Pastry — Lobster Salad — Omelette or Soufflé — Dessert, &c.

At present, though the number of our establishment is not greater, yet the style and manner of our living have changed. We dine alone, except when Mr. B. invites somebody to dine with him, which is most generally the case; our daily bill of fare consists of something like the following: —

One Soup or Fish, generally alternate — One Remove, either Joint or Poultry — One Entrée — Two Vegetables — Pudding or Tart — A little Dessert.

This may seem a great deal for two persons; but when you remember that we almost invariably have one or two to dine with us, and the remains are required for the breakfast, lunch, nursery and servants' dinners, you will perceive that the dinner is the principal expense of the establishment, by which means you are enabled to display more liberality to your guests, and live in greater comfort without waste. Our parties at present, to many of which you have constantly been, and therefore know, vary according to the season; here are a few bills of fare of them; the following is one for two persons: —

One Soup, say Purée of Artichokes — One Fish, Cod Slices in Oyster Sauce — Remove with Smelts or White Bait.

Removes. — Saddle of Mutton — Turkey in Celery Sauce.

Two Entrées. — Cutlets a la Provençale — Sweetbreads larded in any White Sauce.

Two Vegetables. — Greens — Kale — Potatoes on the Sideboard.

SECOND COURSE.

Two Roasts. — Partridges — Wild Ducks. Jelly of Fruit — Cheesecakes — Meringue à la Crême — Vegetable — French Salad on the Sideboard.

Removes.   — Ice Pudding — Beignet Soufflé. *Dessert* of eleven dishes.

The following is one for a birthday party, which generally consists of twenty persons: —

FIRST COURSE.

Two Soups — Two Fish.

Removes.   — Haunch of Mutton — Broiled Capons à l'Ecarlate.

Flancs.   — Fricandeau of Veal—Currie of Fowl.

Entrées.   — Fillets of Beef, sauce Tomate—Cutlets Soubise—Oyster Patties, or Little Vol-au-Vent; Croquettes of Veal or Fowl.[10]

SECOND COURSE.

Wild Ducks—Guinea Fowl larded—Charlotte Russe—Punch Jelly, Crusts of Fruit—Flanc Meringue—Apple with Rice—Scolloped Oysters—Mayonnaise of Fowl—Sea Kale or Asparagus.

Removes.   — Turban of Condé Glacée—Cheese Soufflé à la Vanille. *Dessert* of nineteen dishes.

The bills of fare for our small evening parties, say thirty persons, are as follows; everything is cold, although I know that the fashion has been progressing towards having hot removes.

Our table on those occasions is, as you know, in the form of a horseshoe, which, in my opinion, is the most sociable after that of a round one, and upon the sociability of the supper depends in a great measure the success of the party. In the centre, and at the head of the table, I place a large Grouse-pie, the same as Nos. 249, 285, of which, by my recommendation, everybody partakes; I then on each of the wings have Fowls, Lobster Salads, Mayonnaises of Fowl, Ham, Tongue, cut in slices, and dished over parsley, ornamented with Aspic Jelly; and on the sideboard I have a fine piece of Sirloin of Beef, plain roasted, or an Aitch-Bone of Beef, or Fillet of Veal. Should there be no game, I have a Turkey or Fowls en Galantine, instead of the Grouse-pie, or if game is plentiful, I have less poultry, and add roast Pheasants—mind, not fowls with black legs larded, and a pheasant's tail put to them, but real ones,—or Partridges or Grouse, or a fine Salad of Game.

With the Sweets I generally place about twelve—four on each table, that is 4 Jellies, 2 Creams, 2 Bavaroises, 4 Iced Cabinet Puddings, and 4 Raised Dishes of small Pastry, all of which are artistically disposed upon the table.

The fruits are likewise placed on the table: they consist of simple Compotes, 6 of various kinds and 6 of Dried Fruit, Biscuits, Wafers and Cossacks, which last are getting much out of fashion, but are very amusing.

The following is the Bill of Fare for Mr. B.'s Birthday Party, for which he allows me £15, with which I find everything in the shape of refreshments, with the exception of wine; it is—

One Raised Pie—Two Mayonnaises of Fowl—Two Lobster Salads—One Piece of Roast Beef—Four Dishes of Fowl—Two Dishes of Pheasant—Four Dishes of Tongue—Four Dishes of Ham—Four Jellies with Fruit—Two Creams with Noyeau—Two Flancs with Apple Meringue—Two Iced Cabinet Puddings—Two Puddings à la Eloise—Six Various Pastry—Eight Various Compotes—Four Pièces Montées in China with Bonbons, Cossacks, &c.—Four of Fruit, as Pears, Grapes, &c.—Four of Dried Fruit, &c.—Four of Biscuits, &c.

---

[10]   These should be served on dishes with a napkin.

This perhaps may appear extravagant, but we always have them, some country friends stopping a few days with us, so that I manage to make the best of everything, and make my week's account look very well. We sometimes have as many as sixty on an evening.

Our Children's Parties are as follows, there are generally about fifty present:

16 Dishes of Sandwiches. 4 Dishes of Lamb. 4 Dishes of Ham. 4 do. of Slices of Beef. 4 do. of Tongue. 6 do. of Fowls. 10 Dishes of Slices of Galantine of Veal. 1 Dish of Dressed Beef. 24 Dishes of Various Pastry, Custards, Jellies, Bonbons, &c.

But I remember when in business, on those occasions we only used to have a large quantity of Sandwiches and Patties, and used to amuse the children by labelling the Dishes as Sandwiches of Peacock's Tongues, Patties of Partridge's Eyes, &c., and also a large quantity of plain Sweets; and at that period Mr. B.'s birthday party was not so extensive or *recherché* as at present. It consisted of something like the following:

A Roast Turkey—2 Dishes of Fowls—1 Ham—2 Pigeon Pies—1 Piece of Boiled Beef—4 Lobsters—4 Salads—4 Jellies—4 Tarts—4 of Preserved Fruit, &c.—4 of Pastry; with about twelve of various kinds of Fruit, &c.

You will have seen by the previous Bills of Fare that I have not at all encroached upon the high-class cookery, they being selected from the receipts I have given you; in order that you may see the difference, I inclose the Bill of Fare, of a dinner given by—Bass, Esq., M. P., at the Reform Club, the other day, and a copy of yesterday's *Post*, containing one given in the country. You will find that the dishes mentioned in these Bills of Fare are not to be found in our receipts.

REFORM CLUB.

7 *Juillet*, 1849. *Diner pour 18 Personnes.*

Deux Potages.
One Thick Turtle.
One Clear Ditto.

Deux Poissons.

Crimped Salmon,
en Matelote Normande.

Turbot,
à la Richelieu.

Deux Relevés.
La Hanche de Venaison aux haricots verts.
Les Poulardes en Diadème.

Six Entrées.
Vol-au-Vent de Foies gras à la Talleyrand.
Côtelettes d'Agneau demi Provençale.
Petits Canetons Canaris aux jeunes légumes glacées.
Noix de Veau demi grasse à la purée de concombres.
Ortolans à la Vicomtesse.
Aiguillettes de petits Poussins à la Banquière.

Deux Rôtis.
Les *Turkey Poults* piqués et bardés,
garnis de Cailles aux feuilles de vignes.
Les Jeunes Levrauts au jus de groseilles.

Huit Entremets.

Gelée à l'eau de vie
de Dantzick.
Aspic de Homard
à la Gelée.
Petits Pois
à l'Anglaise.
Pain de Pêches
au Noyau.

Flanc d'Abricôts
aux Liqueurs.
Quartiers d'Artichaux
à la Vénitienne.
Gâteau Milanais
au Parmesan.
Bombe glacée
au Café Moka.

Jambon en surprise glacé
à la Vanille.
Pudding à la Méphistophiles.

A. SOYER.

FESTIVITIES AT GRENDON HALL.

A series of festivities are taking place at the seat of Sir George Chetwynd, Bart., Grendon Hall, Atherstone, Warwickshire, to celebrate the christening of Sir George's infant grandson. The christening took place on Tuesday, at Grendon church, and in the evening a grand dinner was given in celebration of the event, under the able superintendence of M. Alexis Soyer. As the dinner, which was provided for twenty persons, was of a very *recherché* description, we subjoin the bill of fare.

Deux Potages.
One of Clear Turtle.
Ditto à la Nivernaise.

———

Deux Poissons.
Crimped Severn Salmon — Turbot
à la Régence. — à la Cardinal.

———

Deux Relevés.
La Hanche de Venaison. ——— Deux Poulardes à la Nelson.

Six Entrées.
Les Ortolans à la Vicomtesse.
Epigramme d'Agneau à la purée de concombres.
Grenadins de Veau aux petits pois.
Filets de Caneton au jus d'orange.
Côtelettes de Mouton à la Provençale.
Turban de Volaille à la Périgord.

———

Deux Rôtis.
Cailles bardées aux feuilles de vignes.
Gelinottes des Ardennes.

———

Huit Entremets.

Turban de Meringues — Pain de Fruit
aux Pistaches. — aux Pêches.
Galantine — Croûtades d'Artichaux
à la Volière. — à l'Indienne.
Vegetable Marrow — Miroton de Homard
à la Béchamel. — à la Gelée.
Bavaroise Mousseuse — Blanche Crême
à l'Ananas. ——— au Marasquin.

Ices. — Deux Relevés — St. James's
Pine Apple — Hure de Sanglier en surprise glacé — Cake,
and — à la Vanille. — the first
Strawberry. — Petits Biscuits soufflés à la Crême. — ever made.

Rissolettes de Foie gras à la Pompadour. (left and right margins)

After dinner M. Soyer had the honor of presenting the youthful heir the proof copy of his new work on Cookery.

Morning Post, July 26, 1849.

LETTER XX
A NEW ALIMENT.

Bifrons Villa.

Here, dear Eloise, is an entirely new aliment, which has never yet been introduced into this country. A semi-epicure of our acquaintance, on returning from his visit to the National Guard of France, presented me with a pound of it, which he had purchased in Paris; but even there, said he, it is almost in its infancy; you may fancy, if I were not anxious of making an immediate trial of it; but before I give you the receipt how to use it, let me tell you I have found it most delicious. Mr. B. has not yet tasted it, being for a week in the country, but I am confident he will like it, especially for breakfast: but the puzzle is, after my pound is used, how we are to get more? Time, I suppose, will teach us. It appears that we are indebted for it to a celebrated French gentleman, M. le Docteur Lamolte, the inventor of the electric light, who ingeniously, though oddly, named it Cho-ca, being a scientific composition of *chocolat* and *café*, the alliance of which balancing admirably their excellence and virtue, and partly correcting their evils, the first being rather irritable, the second heavy. But I think, if my recollection serves me rightly, the idea of this compound must have originated from that great French philosopher, M. de Voltaire, who constantly, for his breakfast, partook of half café-au-lait and half chocolate, which were served at the same time in separate vessels in a boiling state, and poured from each slowly, about eighteen inches in elevation from his cup, which, he said, made it extremely light and digestible.

Years after, that still more extraordinary man, Napoleon Bonaparte, became so partial to it, that he made a constant use of it, and it has often been remarked by those who surrounded his person, that after the great excitement and fatigue of a battle he has often partaken of two or three cups, which seemed to restore all the strength and energy which used to characterize that great man; on ordinary occasions one cup would suffice him, but served more *à la militaire*, not being poured so scientifically as did the Fernaise philosopher.

The approval of this mixed beverage by two such eminent characters speaks volumes in favor of the Cho-ca, which ought to be immediately introduced in England. It will also, no doubt, interest you to learn that the first cup of coffee ever introduced in Europe was made and presented to Louis XIV, at his magnificent palace of Versailles, by the Ambassador from the Sublime Porte in the year 1664, when the noble potentate, whose palate was as delicate as he was himself great, pronounced it excellent; and immediately perceived the immense advantage it would be to introduce such a delicacy into France as food, which a short time after took place, and was very successfully received there; also the chocolate, which is made from cacao, was first introduced to the Cardinal Mazarin, who, having partook of the first cup like Louis XIV. did of the coffee, and not a worse judge than his illustrious master, remunerated with a handsome reward its inventor. It is much to be regretted that such interesting and useful subjects have never yet attracted the attention of our great Painters, instead of continually tracing on innumerable yards of canvass the horrors of war, the destruction of a fleet by fire and water, the plague, the storm, the earthquake, or an eruption and destruction of a city by an avalanche or an inundation; if we cannot do without those painful historical reminiscences, why not add to those mournful collections a group of Louis XIV. and his court at Versailles, where he, magnificently dressed, was receiving from the hands of the said Pacha, not a cup of coffee, but a branch of that plant covered with its precious berries; and why not also, as a pendant, Mazarin surrounded by his satellites, taking the first cup of chocolate; or the characteristic Voltaire pouring a cup of Cho-ca to Frederic the Great in his tent on the field of Potsdam? These subjects seem to have been entirely neglected in being immortalized on canvass, why? because they have never done harm or evil to any one; but, on the contrary, have, are, and ever will prove to be, among the greatest boons ever conferred upon humanity: it would also engrave in our minds, as well as in our history, to what mortals we are indebted for the importation and introduction of such important productions, which daily constitute a part of our comforts, and have conferred an everlasting benefit on mankind; but, as usual, dear Eloise, you will no doubt reproach me for having so much enthusiasm; however, as on this subject you have been tolerably quiet lately, I not only here inclose you the receipt, but also two of the thin round cakes of this new aliment, the Cho-ca, which will produce two cups by making it as follows:—

880. *Cho-ca.*—Scrape or grate it; put a pint of milk in a stewpan or chocolate-pot, and place it on the fire, with two ounces of sugar, boil it, put the Cho-ca in it, and stir it well for two minutes, and serve.

ON CARVING.

YOU reproach me for not having said a word about carving; I have not done so, as I think that is an accomplishment which our sex need not study, but at the same time it is well to know a little of it. It is rather difficult to give you a correct description without drawings, but a few general remarks may be useful.

Cut Beef, Veal, Ham, Tongue, and Breasts of Poultry, with a sharp knife, very thin; Mutton, Lamb, and Pork rather thicker.

Never rise from your seat to carve; never cut across the grain of the meat, that is, not across the ribs of beef, as I have seen some persons do, and Mr. B. tells me is often done at clubs, but it is only those do so who do not know how to carve or appreciate the true flavor of the meat.

Never place a fork through the back of a fowl, in order to carve the leg and wings, but run the knife gently down each side the breast, detaching the leg and wing at the same time, which is greatly facilitated by the use of the Tendon Separator—one of which I purchased at Bramah's, in Piccadilly; it is the greatest boon ever conferred on a bad carver: the directions for using it are given with it. If it was more generally used, there would be no more birds flying across the table in the faces of guests; no more turkeys deposited in a lady's or gentleman's lap; no more splashing of gravy to spoil satin dresses; but all would be divided with the greatest facility, and in the most elegant manner, and the poultry would look much better at table.

Never cut up the body of poultry at table, that should always be left; but game should be cut up, as many epicures prefer the backbone. For a sirloin of beef the under part of the loin should always be cut when hot, and the upper part cut straight from the backbone towards the outside of the ribs, by this plan you will not spoil the appearance of the joint.

Ribs of Beef should be carved in the same way, cutting thin and slanting.

Round of Beef: cut a slice half an inch thick from the outside, and then carve thin slices, with a little fat.

Aitch-bone, the same.

Fillet of Veal, the same.

Loin of Veal, carve as the Sirloin of Beef, serving some of the kidney, and fat to each person.

Shoulder of Veal, begin from the knuckle, cut thin and slanting.

Saddle of Mutton will, if properly carved, serve a great many persons; instead of cutting a long slice the whole length, put your knife under the meat and cut it away from the bone, then cut it like thin chops, serving lean and fat together; according to the usual plan, a saddle of mutton will serve but few people, and the flavor of the meat is not so good as when served this way.

Necks and Loins: the bones should be severed by a small meat-saw, and not a chopper, and the bone cut through when serving, and carve slanting.

Haunches are usually carved by making a cut near the knuckle and cutting a slice from that through the loin; but by a plan I have adopted, I find that the meat eats better, and the joint goes farther. I carve it like the leg and saddle, that is, I cut a slice out of the leg part and a slice from the loin, and serve together. This is more economical, but would not do for venison.

Lamb.—For Leg and Shoulders, proceed as for Mutton. The Ribs, when well prepared and the bones properly separated, carve into cutlets, and serve with a piece of the brisket.

Quarter of Lamb: the ribs should be sawed through, and the bones disjointed previous to cooking. The shoulder should be then nicely removed, the seasoning added; then divide the ribs and serve one part of the brisket to each person.

Pork: proceed like the Mutton.

In carving a Ham, remove a thick slice, of about one inch, flat cut slantways from the knuckle-end—a Tongue, begin three inches from the tip, and cut thin slanting slices.

LETTER NO. XXII.

THE SEPTUAGENARIAN EPICURE.

MY DEAR ELOISE,—Having now arrived at the conclusion of our labors, during which you have in many instances thought me rather severe, and perhaps too *exigeant* in my remarks, especially about the selection, preparation, and cooking of food in general, which even to the last I must maintain, that for want of judgment and a little care, the greatest part of the nutrition of our aliments is often destroyed, which constitutes a considerable waste, being of no good to any one, but an evil to everybody; and when you consider the monstrous quantity of food our fragile bodies consume in this sublunary sphere during the course of our life, the truth of my observation will be more apparent, and make you agree with me that in every instance people ought really to devote more time, care, and personal attention to their daily subsistence, it being the most expensive department through life of human luxury. I shall, for example, give you a slight and correct idea of it, which I am confident you never before conceived. For this I shall propose to take seventy years of the life of an epicure, beyond which age many of that class of "bon vivants" arrive, and even above eighty, still in the full enjoyment of degustation, &c., (for example, Talleyrand, Cambacérès, Lord Sefton, &c.;) if the first of the said epicures when entering on the tenth spring of his extraordinary career, had been placed on an eminence, say, the top of Primrose hill, and had had exhibited before his infantine eyes the enormous quantity of food his then insignificant person would destroy before he attained his seventy-first year,—first, he would believe it must be a delusion; then, secondly, he would inquire, where the money could come from to purchase so much luxurious extravagance? But here I shall leave the pecuniary expenses on one side, which a man of wealth can easily surmount when required. So now, dearest, for the extraordinary fact: imagine on the top of the above-mentioned hill a rushlight of a boy just entering his tenth year, surrounded with the recherché provision and delicacies claimed by his rank and wealth, taking merely the medium consumption of his daily meals. By closely calculating he would be surrounded and gazed at by the following number of quadrupeds, birds, fishes, &c.:—By no less than 30 oxen, 200 sheep, 100 calves, 200 lambs, 50 pigs; in poultry, 1200 fowls, 300 turkeys, 150 geese, 400 ducklings, 263 pigeons; 1400 partridges, pheasants, and grouse; 600 woodcocks and snipes; 600 wild ducks, widgeon, and teal; 450 plovers, ruffes, and reeves; 800 quails, ortolans, and dotterels, and a few guillemôts and other foreign birds; also 500 hares and rabbits, 40 deer, 120 Guinea fowl, 10 peacocks, and 360 wild fowl. In the way of fish, 120 turbot, 140 salmon, 120 cod, 260 trout, 400 mackerel, 300 whitings, 800 soles and slips, 400 flounders, 400 red mullet, 200 eels, 150 haddocks, 400 herrings, 5000 smelts, and some hundred thousand of those delicious silvery whitebait, besides a few hundred species of fresh-water fishes. In shell-fish, 20 turtle, 30,000 oysters, 1500 lobsters or crabs, 300,000 prawns, shrimps, sardines and anchovies. In the way of fruit, about 500 lbs. of grapes, 360 lbs. of pine-apples, 600 peaches, 1400 apricots, 240 melons, and some hundred thousand plums, greengages, apples, pears, and some millions of cherries, strawberries, raspberries, currants, mulberries, and an abundance of other small fruit, viz., walnuts, chestnuts, dry figs and plums. In vegetables of all kinds, 5475 pounds weight, and about 2434¾ pounds of butter, 684 pounds of cheese, 21,000 eggs, 800 do. plovers'. Of bread, 4½ tons, half a ton of salt and pepper, near 2½ tons of sugar; and, if he had happened to be a covetous boy, he could have formed a fortification or moat round the said hill with the liquids he would have to partake of to facilitate the digestion of the above-named provisions, which would amount to no less than 11,673¾ gallons, which may be taken as below:—49 hogsheads of wine, 1368¾ gallons of beer, 584 gallons of spirits, 342 liqueur, 2394¾ gallons of coffee, cocoa, tea, &c., and 304 gallons of milk, 2736 gallons of water, all of which would actually protect him and his anticipated property from any young thief or fellow schoolboy, like Alexandre Dumas had protected Dante and his immense treasure from the pirates in his island of Monte Christo. You now, dearest, fancy that I am exaggerating in every way; but to convince you, and to prevent your puzzling your brain to no purpose, I also enclose you a medium scale of the regular meals of the day, from which I have taken my basis, and in sixty years it amounts to no less than 33¾ tons weight of meat, farinaceous food and vegetables, &c.; out of which I have named in detail the probable delicacies that would be selected by an epicure through life. But observe that I did not count the first ten years of his life, at the beginning of which he lived upon pap, bread and milk, &c., also a little meat, the expense of which I add to the age from then to twenty, as no one can really be called an epicure before that age; it will thus make the expenses more equal as regards the calculation. The following is the list of what I consider his daily meals:—

Breakfast.—Three quarters of a pint of coffee, four ounces of bread, one ounce of butter, two eggs, or four ounces of meat, or four ounces of fish.

Lunch.—Two ounces of bread, two ounces of meat, or poultry, or game, two ounces of vegetables, and half a pint of beer or a glass of wine.

Dinner.—Half a pint of soup, a quarter of a pound of fish, half a pound of meat, a quarter of a pound of poultry, a quarter of a pound of savory dishes or game, two ounces of vegetables, two ounces of bread, two ounces of pastry or roasts, half an ounce of cheese, a quarter of a pound of fruit, one pint of wine, one glass of liqueur, one cup of coffee or tea; at night one glass of spirits and water.

Now that I have given you these important details, perhaps you will give me some little credit for my exaction and severity respecting the attention which ought to be daily paid to the indispensable and useful art of cookery by our middle classes. I shall also observe to you, that those masses of provisions above described in the exposé of sixty years, have been selected, dressed, and served, by scientific hands, every real epicure choosing through life the best cook, and consequently the best of provisions, which, had they have fallen into the hands of inexperienced persons, would very likely have wasted one third, thereby increasing the expenses, and never giving any real satisfaction to the consumer; therefore let us act in a small way as becomes us, as it is for the wealthy according to their incomes; let every housekeeper devote more time to the study of domestic and practical economy; in many instances it will increase their incomes as well as their daily comforts, as I remarked to you that the pleasures of the table being not only the most expensive part of human luxury, but also the soul of sociability, require more attention bestowed upon it than is done at the present day.

Fare you well,
HORTENSE.

THE END.

C

I

J

P

S

Y

Lector House believes that a society develops through a two-fold approach of continuous learning and adaptation, which is derived from the study of classic literary works spread across the historic timeline of literature records. Therefore, we aim at reviving, repairing and redeveloping all those inaccessible or damaged but historically as well as culturally important literature across subjects so that the future generations may have an opportunity to study and learn from past works to embark upon a journey of creating a better future.

This book is a result of an effort made by Lector House towards making a contribution to the preservation and repair of original ancient works which might hold historical significance to the approach of continuous learning across subjects.

HAPPY READING & LEARNING!

LECTOR HOUSE LLP
E-MAIL: lectorpublishing@gmail.com